Studies in Natural Language Processing
Sponsored by the Association for Computational Linguistics

Natural language parsing

Studies in Natural Language Processing

This new series will publish monographs, texts, and edited volumes within the interdisciplinary field of computational linguistics. Sponsored by the Association for Computational Linguistics, the series will represent the range of topics of concern to the scholars working in this increasingly important field, whether their background is in formal linguistics, psycholinguistics, cognitive psychology, or artificial intelligence. *Natural language parsing* is the first volume to appear.

Natural language parsing

Psychological, computational, and theoretical perspectives

Edited by

DAVID R. DOWTY
Department of Linguistics, Ohio State University

LAURI KARTTUNEN
Artificial Intelligence Center,
SRI International, Menlo Park

ARNOLD M. ZWICKY
Department of Linguistics, Ohio State University

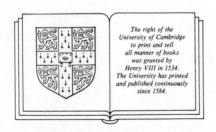

The right of the
University of Cambridge
to print and sell
all manner of books
was granted by
Henry VIII in 1534.
The University has printed
and published continuously
since 1584.

CAMBRIDGE UNIVERSITY PRESS

CAMBRIDGE

LONDON   NEW YORK   NEW ROCHELLE

MELBOURNE   SYDNEY

Published by the Press Syndicate of the University of Cambridge
The Pitt Building, Trumpington Street, Cambridge CB2 1RP
32 East 57th Street, New York, NY 10022, USA
10 Stamford Road, Oakleigh, Melbourne 3166, Australia

First published 1985
Reprinted 1985

Printed in the United States of America

Library of Congress Cataloguing in Publication Data
Main entry under title:
Natural language parsing.
  (Studies in natural language processing)
  Includes index.
  1. Parsing (Computer grammar) I. Dowty, David R.
II. Karttunen, Lauri. II. Zwicky, Arnold M. IV. Series.
P98.N3 1985 415 84-4360
ISBN 0 521 26203 8

Contents

v

Contributors

Greg N. Carlson, Department of English, Wayne State University

Stephen Crain, Department of Linguistics, University of Connecticut

Alice Davison, Department of Linguistics, University of Illinois, Urbana-Champaign

David R. Dowty, Department of Linguistics, Ohio State University

Elisabet Engdahl, Department of Linguistics and Phonetics, Lund University

Janet Dean Fodor, Department of Linguistics, University of Connecticut

Lyn Frazier, Department of Linguistics, University of Massachusetts

Aravind K. Joshi, Department of Computer and Information Science, University of Pennsylvania

Lauri Karttunen, Artificial Intelligence Center, SRI International, Menlo Park

Martin Kay, Xerox Palo Alto Research Center

Richard Lutz, Department of Linguistics, University of Illinois, Urbana-Champaign

Fernando C. N. Pereira, Artificial Intelligence Center, SRI International, Menlo Park

Mark S. Seidenberg, Department of Psychology, McGill University

Mark Steedman, School of Epistemics, University of Edinburgh

Michael K. Tanenhaus, Department of Psychology, University of Rochester

Arnold M. Zwicky, Department of Linguistics, Ohio State University

Acknowledgments

Earlier versions of the papers by Davison and Lutz, Engdahl, Crain and Fodor, Frazier, Joshi ("Tree Adjoining Grammars"), Karttunen and Kay, Crain and Steedman, and by Tanenhaus, Carlson, and Seidenberg were originally presented at a conference, *Syntactic Theory and How People Parse Sentences,* held at the Ohio State University on May 14–16, 1982. This conference was supported by the Linguistics Department of that university with assistance from the Ohio State University Graduate School.

Two papers, by Joshi ("Processing of Sentences with Intrasentential Code Switching") and by Kay, were originally presented at a conference on parsing held at the Cognitive Science Center of the University of Texas in 1981, supported by a grant from the Alfred P. Sloan Foundation.

The editors would like to thank the following referees for their advice regarding revisions of these papers for publication: Janet Fodor, Stephen Isard, William Marsh, Ellen Prince, Geoffrey Pullum, Jane Robinson, Kenneth Ross, Richmond Thomason, and Ellen Woolford. Others who provided suggestions directly to the authors are acknowledged by the authors in their individual papers.

The final preparation of the manuscript was supported by a grant from Ohio State University College of Humanities.

Introduction

LAURI KARTTUNEN and ARNOLD M. ZWICKY

1. Parsing in traditional grammar

Like so many aspects of modern intellectual frameworks, the idea of parsing has its roots in the Classical tradition; (*grammatical*) *analysis* is the Greek-derived term, *parsing* (from *pars orationis* 'part of speech') the Latin-derived one. In this tradition, which extends through medieval to modern times,

(1) parsing is an operation that human beings perform,

(2) on bits of natural language (usually sentences, and usually in written form),

(3) resulting in a description of those bits, this description being itself a linguistic discourse (composed of sentences in some natural language, its ordinary vocabulary augmented by technical terms);

(4) moreover, the ability to perform this operation is a skill,

(5) acquired through specific training or explicit practice, and not possessed by everyone in a society or to equal degrees by those who do possess it,

(6) and this skill is used with conscious awareness that it is being used.

Parsing, in the traditional sense, is what happens when a student takes the words of a Latin sentence one by one, assigns each to a part of speech, specifies its grammatical categories, and lists the grammatical relations between words (identifying subject and various types of object for a verb, specifying the word with which some other word agrees, and so on). Parsing has a very practical function:

It is not generally realized, even in the schools, how difficult it is for anyone to control the expression and interpretation of language, and that control is as difficult to teach as it is to achieve. The traditional means of teaching control, to pupils at all levels, in their own language as well as in foreign languages, is the set of analytical procedures called grammar.

(Michael 1970:1)

In other words,

(7) the reason for a discipline of parsing is to increase one's mastery over expression in language.

1

Another important part of the tradition is a separation between grammar and logic. Parsing is analysis for the purposes of grammar; quite a different sort of analysis is appropriate in the study of argument. Although the distinction between grammatical form and logical form has been drawn in a number of ways, not always clearly, it plays a role in linguistic discussions from Aristotle through Port Royal to Chomsky. Here we must stress the fact that, in its traditional sense, parsing is in no way an extraction of properties and relations that are of direct *semantic* relevance. In rather modern phrasing,

(8)   the descriptions in (3) are grammatical in nature; that is to say, they describe facts relevant to the co-occurrence of and alternation between units in a particular language.

Note that (8) does not specify any particular theory of grammar; one can parse sentences with respect to any given theory. Indeed, much of the history of parsing until a few decades ago can be understood as the direct consequence of the history of (partial) theories of grammar. Changes in the list of parts of speech, in the list of grammatical categories, or in the list of grammatical relations carry with them changes in what has to be said in parsing a sentence.

We now summarize these eight characteristics of parsing in the Western grammatical tradition. Characteristic (1) says that parsing is done by human beings, rather than by physical machines or abstract machines. Characteristic (2) specifies that what is parsed is a bit of natural language, rather than a bit of some languagelike symbolic system. Characteristic (3) specifies that the analysis itself is a bit of natural language, rather than a bit of some languagelike system, and characteristic (8) that the analysis concerns grammatical rather than logical properties. Characteristic (4) tells us that parsing is heuristic rather than algorithmic, characteristic (5) that it is learned by certain people and not "given" within a society. According to characteristic (6), parsing is overt rather than covert. Characteristic (7), finally, says that the function of parsing is pedagogical.

2. New notions of parsing

In this century the word *parsing* has come to be extended to a large collection of operations that are analogous in some ways to the traditional one just described, but differ from it in one – or usually more – of the eight characteristics. These changes result from a series of new conceptualizations, partially independent of and partially interconnected with one another, in theoretical linguistics, formal language theory, computer science, artificial intelligence, and psycholinguistics. Although the historical roots of these ideas are in some cases fairly deep, they flower together only about the middle of this century, in the 1950s and early 1960s.

3. Parsing in formal linguistics

In linguistics the first of these changes was to view the rationale for parsing not as pedagogical, but rather as scientific – in other words, to emphasize the descriptive, rather than the prescriptive, side of characteristic (7). This shift in emphasis was largely the work of structuralist linguistics, and in its train came a significant change in characteristic (3), as a concern for precision in grammatical descriptions led increasingly to their formalization. The end of this movement away from the informal and discursive descriptions of traditional grammar was a view of these descriptions as completely formal objects – in particular, as *constituent structures* (assigning words to parts of speech and describing which adjacent constituents can combine with one another, in what order they combine, and what phrase category the combination belongs to).

This particular formalization of grammatical descriptions is bought at some cost, for the information coded in constituent structures is considerably less than that supplied in traditional parsing. For example, in such structures heads and modifiers are not systematically marked, discontinuous constituents are not recognized, the relationship between the determined and determining constituents in government and agreement is not generally indicated, and only some of the applicable relations between NPs and Vs are noted. It is striking in this regard to compare the "coverage" of an elaborated traditional approach to parsing, such as Reed and Kellogg diagrams (see Gleason, 1965:142–51 for a succinct presentation), with that of formalized constituent structures (for instance, Harris, 1946 and Chomsky, 1956). Succeeding developments in grammatical theory can, in fact, be seen as attempts to devise fully formalized types of grammatical descriptions with something approaching the coverage of traditional grammars.

Before turning to these developments, however, we must comment on a further conceptual change set off by the move to formalized grammatical descriptions (in particular, constituent structures) as the output of the parsing operation. It is now possible to view parsing as algorithmic rather than heuristic. That is, it is now possible to see the parsing operation as the application of a series of language-particular principles, *phrase structure rules* like NP + VP = S and V + NP (+NP) = VP, to (a representation of) a sentence, in such a way that all the appropriate grammatical descriptions for that sentence, and no others, will be obtained.

Once such a change in characteristic (4) of parsing has been made, the way is open to view principles like NP + VP = S either analytically, as instructions for assigning structures to given sentences in a language, or synthetically, as instructions for composing the sentences of a language. That is, the full set of such principles constitutes a *formal grammar* for the language, which can be seen, indifferently, as having an analytic or *parsing function*, or a synthetic or *generative function*. (Both interpretations appeared early in the history of formal grammatical theory – the generative interpretation most prominently in Chomsky's early work, the parsing interpretation in Hockett's "grammar for the hearer" [1961] and in "dependency grammar" [Hays, 1964; Robinson, 1970; àmong others].) Indeed, phrase structure rules can also be viewed neutrally, as having a *checking function*, an idea first mentioned in the linguistic literature by McCawley (1968) and developed recently in such work on generalized phrase structure grammar as Gazdar, 1982.

On its analytic or parsing interpretation, the phrase structure rule NP + VP = S licenses the grouping of a constituent known to be (or suspected of being) an NP along with an immediately following constituent known to be (or suspected of being) a VP, into a single constituent of type S; an acceptable constituent structure is then one that is headed by S and can be constructed from entirely by a sequence of such groupings. On its synthetic or generative interpretation, the rule is a *rewrite rule*, customarily formalized as S → NP VP, licensing the replacement of the symbol S in a line of a derivation by the string NP VP, or, equivalently, licensing the branching of a node labeled S in a constituent structure tree into two ordered nodes, labeled NP and VP, respectively; an acceptable constituent structure is then one that can be constructed from the symbol S by such rewriting, or from a node labeled S by such branching. On its neutral or checking interpretation, the rule is a *node admissibility condition*, stipulating that the subtree

is well formed; an acceptable constituent structure is then one that is headed by S and contains only admissible branchings.

When it is recognized that there is more than one way to view the function of phrase structure rules, then it is no longer necessary (though it is not barred) to think of parsing, or for that matter generation or checking, as something human beings do. Instead, these operations can be viewed abstractly, as performed by an idealized device – a change in characteristic (1) of parsing, one that makes characteristics (5) and (6) simply irrelevant.

The consequence of all these reconceptualizations is a distinct second notion of parsing, associated with formal theories of grammar. In this notion

(9)   parsing is an operation performed by an abstract device,

(10)   on (representations of) sentences in a natural language,

(11)   resulting in a formal representation of sentence structure;

(12)   this operation is algorithmic.

The next development is for the parsing, generative, and checking functions of a formal grammar for a natural language to be separated. It is a consequence of the particularly simple form of principles like NP + VP = S that they can be interpreted as steps in parsing, as rules for generation, or as node admissibility conditions. But if the steps, the rules, or the conditions are not of this simple, technically *context-free*, form, there is no guarantee that parsing operations, generative operations, and checking operations can be matched in a one-to-one-to-one fashion, and we must contemplate the possibility that the *parser*, the *generator* (sometimes referred to simply as the *grammar*), and the checking device or *acceptor* are three separate devices.

Historically, just such a separation, of parser and generator, followed on the development of transformational grammar as a particular generative framework. And more recently the development of generalized phrase structure grammar has required that generator/parser and acceptor be distinguished. In the first case, the perceived limitations of context-free generative grammar motivated a syntactic theory with at least two distinct components. What is relevant here is that in the new theory constituent structures are not generated directly by rewrite rules, so that a parser cannot be merely a generator run backward. In the second case, the intention was to rehabilitate context-free grammar as a plausible theory of syntactic structure. Part of this program depends on the fact that an acceptor making reference to local context accepts a set of constituent structures generable by a context-free generator (or parsable by a context-free parser); context-sensitive acceptors are thus not simply context-sensitive generators or parsers viewed in a different light.

In general, then, changes in the shape of syntactic theory carry with them consequences, often profound, with respect to the role and nature of a parser. In *monostratal theories* there is only one sort of syntactic representation, and it is the parser's business to assign just the right representations to any given sentence. The representations themselves will of course vary from one theoretical framework to another; the representations of arc pair grammar (Johnson and Postal, 1980) are graphs of a type quite different from the tree structures of classical constituent structure grammar, while the graphs of generalized phrase structure grammar are trees, but trees with node labels decomposed into sets of features (including a slash feature indicating a missing constituent). In *polystratal theories*, with two or more distinct levels of syntactic representation posited, the parser must either construct one level of representation (a *surface*, or *final, structure*) and then translate that into another (a *deep, basic*, or *initial structure*), or it must reconstruct the appropriate initial structures directly, thus operating in a fashion that bears no visible relationship to the operation of the generator.

4. Parsing in formal language theory

Abstracting away from the numerous, undeniably significant, differences in theories of formal grammar and in the parsers associated with them, we observe that the branch of discrete mathematics called *formal language theory*, especially as developed by theoretical computer scientists, has provided most of the conceptual apparatus now current in discussions of parsing, including such fundamental distinctions as those between *top-down* analysis (which begins by examining rules for the top level of structure and attempts to work down to the string of words) and *bottom-up* analysis (which begins by attempting to combine words into larger units and then works "up" to still larger units), between *deterministic* analysis (in which there is only one next step for any particular configuration) and *nondeterministic* analysis (in which a configuration can lead to more than one subsequent step), between *parallel* analysis of alternatives and *sequential* analysis with *backtracking* to alternatives not pursued at earlier stages in analysis, and so on.

Parsing in formal language theory has the same characteristics as parsing in formal linguistics, with the exception of characteristic (10). In formal language theory, the objects of analysis are not (representations of) sentences in a natural language but are instead strings in a symbolic system.

Context-free languages (those with context-free generative grammars) have gotten special attention in formal language theory, and a considerable body of mathematical results on the parsing of them – including upper bounds on the number of steps and amount of storage space for symbols – has been accumulated. In part because there is this body of knowledge in formal language theory, and in part because linguists strive for syntactic theories that are as restricted as possible, the literature on parsing in formal linguistics has been heavily preoccupied with parsing context-free languages.

5. Parsing computer languages

The notion of parsing in formal linguistics and formal language theory closely resembles notions developed in several other contexts. Consider, as a first example, the task confronting the designer of a computer "language." If an actual machine is to do anything with the strings of symbols that serve as its input, it must group them into particular types of "words" and "phrases" that can then serve as signals for specific alterations in the machine's internal states. This is a task quite analogous to the grouping of phonemes or letters into words and phrases, and the assignment of these units to categories, in a linguistic analysis – except that the designer of a computer language is free to *stipulate* the principles of grouping and interpretation (in particular, the designer is free to legislate that all "sentences" and "discourses" are unambiguous in structure and interpretation), whereas the linguist is obliged to *discover* the principles that happen to hold in the (natural) language in question. The closer the designer would like the computer language to approximate the appearance of some existing natural language, the more the designer is engaged in something like linguistic analysis, but even if a particularly simple sort of context-free grammar is stipulated for a computer language, the machine has to do something akin to parsing. That is, for the designer,

(13) parsing is an operation performed by a computer (including both software and hardware),

(14) on symbolic input in a constructed (more or less) languagelike system,

(15) resulting in successive (partial) groupings of symbols into larger units of particular types, and the interpretation of these groups as changes in machine states;

(16) this operation is algorithmic.

Note that in (15) we have left open the possibility that changes in machine states might begin to be effected before a complete parse of the input is constructed. In parsing for computational purposes, as opposed to parsing for the purposes of formal language theory, there are two rather different types of operations: parsing proper, the task of grouping and labeling; and the transformation of symbol groups into real-world effects. Nothing says that the first sort of operation must be completed before the second engages. The two processes might be interleaved.

6. Natural language parsing in artificial intelligence

A second example of an operation analogous to parsing in formal linguistics and formal language theory comes from artificial intelligence (AI), in particular from studies of "natural language understanding" by computer. The machine's task in this case is essentially the same as in the previous section – except that the input is a symbol string in a natural language rather than a (designed) computer language, and also that the so-called understanding might proceed in a strategic rather than algorithmic fashion (hence, might fail for some inputs). Here,

(17) parsing is an operation performed by a computer (including both software and hardware),

(18) on (representations of) sentences in a natural language,

(19) resulting in successive (partial) groupings of symbols into larger units of particular types, and the interpretation of these groups as changes in machine states;

(20) this operation may be either algorithmic or heuristic.

The third characteristic here, in (15) and (19), appears to be the same for parsing computer languages as for parsing in a natural language understanding system, yet it is obvious from reviews of AI approaches (Barr and Feigenbaum, 1981:256–72; Winograd, 1983:chs. 3, 7) that these latter are typically much more complex than the parsing schemes that have been advanced for computer languages. Computer languages have usually been designed as especially simple (and unambiguous) context-free languages, so as to permit rapid interpretation; the historical exemplar is Backus Naur Form in the syntactic definition of ALGOL 60 (Naur, 1963). Natural language understanding programs, even those restricted to small conceptual worlds and reduced means of expression, have to cope with some of the messiness of ordinary language.

In AI parsing, as in parsing computer languages, many options exist for apportioning work between parsing proper and the interpretation of symbol groups, and also for coordinating these two types of operations. Existing AI parsing systems range from those in which parsing proper gives a complete structure of the sort provided in formal grammatical analysis, to those in which parsing proper is reduced to a minimum – in the extreme case, to the recognition of a few key words. AI parsing schemes can also be devised on principles quite different from those of formal grammars, for instance on the basis of pattern-matching routines. And as before, interpretation might follow parsing proper, or (as is very common these days) take place in tandem with in and interacting with it.

Note that AI parsing shares with computer-language parsing, but not with formal-language parsing, the central role given to interpretation. Formal language theory assumes a clear separation between syntax on the one hand and semantics and pragmatics on the other, and it concerns itself only with the former. In computer language design a clear separation is usually assumed, but interpretation is the dominant concern. In approaches to natural language understanding by computer, it is not axiomatic that a clear separation be made, and interpretation is unquestionably the dominant concern.

Note finally that approaches to parsing based on formal language theory are extraordinarily restricted in scope.

a.   They do not embrace an explicit semantics.
b.   They do not specify, even informally, the relationship between syntactic rules/representations and principles of semantic interpretation.
c.   The sentences analyzed exist outside any social context, having no identifiable source or audience, so that there is no body of mutually assumed knowledge with respect to which interpretation can proceed, nor is there any basis for calculating the intentions of a source or effects upon an audience.
d.   The sentences analyzed are not anchored in any spatial or temporal context, so that deictic elements cannot be interpreted.

e.   The sentence is the largest unit of analysis, so that formal or semantic organization in larger discourse units is not recognized.

f.   The word is the smallest unit of analysis, so that meaningful structuring below the word level is not recognized.

g.   It is assumed that the chunks listed in a lexicon are word-sized, so that no allowance is made for multiword idioms and formulas.

Undoubtedly this list could be extended, but it will do for now. Computer-language parsing must remedy at least the first two defects, and AI parsing schemes must remedy all seven (or explicitly recognize that they are significantly idealizing away from natural language).

7. Parsing in psycholinguistics

Psycholinguistics provides a third situation in which an operation analogous to parsing in formal theories of grammar might arise. Psycholinguistics proposes to supply an account of mental processes involving language, in particular the processes at work in the perception and comprehension of language, the production of language, and memory for language. It is natural to think of perception and comprehension as including analogues of the parsing operations of formal grammars, and so to view AI parsing schemes as potential models of (portions of) some mental processes. In this view (compare characteristics (1)–(7) listed at the beginning of our discussion of parsing),

(21)   parsing is an operation that human beings perform,

(22)   on bits of natural language (sentences and discourses, sometimes in spoken form, sometimes in written form),

(23)   resulting in mental representations of (aspects of) the syntactic structure associated with these bits, and their interpretation as alterations in other mental representations;

(24)   this operation is heuristic (on occasion, it can fail to assign structures or interpretations, or assign the wrong ones),

(25)   acquired without specific training or explicit practice, and possessed in some form by everyone in a society,

(26)   and used tacitly, rather than with conscious awareness.

As in AI parsing, the defects a–g of formal-language approaches to parsing must be remedied in any extended model of perception and comprehension. Also as in AI parsing, there is a serious question as to how syntax-driven the processes of interpretation are. Does interpretation temporally follow parsing proper, or do they operate interactively and in tandem? Is parsing even necessary at all? In AI work the answers to these questions are in a sense a matter of taste; an AI system has only(!) to mimic aspects of human behavior, not (necessarily) to mirror actual mental organization and functioning, so that a wide variety of approaches are a priori available. In psycholinguistics these are empirical questions, with answers that are, in principle, discoverable. Consequently, psycholinguistic research on parsing has been preoccupied with issues of mental representation: For which hypothesized units is there evidence that they are accessed or constructed during comprehension? For which hypothesized processes is there evidence that they take place (hence, take time) in comprehension?

While there are no universally accepted answers to this last set of questions, it is clear that a model in which parsing proper is completed before interpretation is undertaken has little to recommend it. At the very least, we must assume that as the (surface) constituents of a sentence are identified they are, at least partially, interpreted. There is abundant evidence both that some (surface) constituents are identified during comprehension and that some interpretive processes take place before a sentence is completed (see the survey in Clark and Clark, 1977:45–57). Beyond this, psycholinguists disagree as to whether comprehension is primarily syntax-driven, with the dominant strategies those of parsing proper, or primarily meaning-driven, with the dominant strategies those of interpretation (semantics and pragmatics taken together); and of course they differ on details (for a survey, again see Clark and Clark, 1977:57–79).

The phenomenon of *ambiguity* has come to play a special role in these discussions, because it appears to offer a testing ground on which to compare alternative accounts of language comprehension. If account A predicts that two distinct (partial) representations are constructed during the comprehension of an ambiguous sentence, while account B predicts that only one corresponding representation is constructed, then it ought to be possible to detect the extra time required for the construction of representations in account A as against account B. It ought also to be possible to detect (traces of) the presence of the extra material accessed during the construction of representations in account A as against account B. Ambiguity might then provide a small window into the workings of the parsers we all use.

8. Summaries of the papers

8.1. Alice Davison and Richard Lutz, "Measuring syntactic complexity relative to discourse context"

This paper discusses results from an experiment in which different versions of the same sentence were presented in alternating discourse contexts. Each context was designed to introduce a bias for interpreting some constituent in the test sentence as *topic*, as the element that the rest of the sentence is about. As expected, the authors found that the processing of the sentence is facilitated when the primed constituent is the one that is also syntactically marked for that role.

Davison and Lutz consider two competing hypotheses about how topics are syntactically marked: position versus surface grammatical function. They conclude that the latter is closer to being correct. The facilitating effect of appropriate context shows up only when the favored constituent is syntactically the surface subject. Subjects tend to be perceived as topics even if some other constituent, such as a sentence-initial adverbial, precedes them.

The authors also find a bias toward structures that transparently encode the underlying grammatical relations. All other things being equal, simple active sentences are faster to process than their passive counterparts; existential sentences with *there* take more time than ordinary locatives. However, because surface subjects should always be topics, in certain contexts these marked constructions are in fact easier to process.

8.2. Elisabet Engdahl, "Interpreting questions"

Scandinavian languages have recently acquired a certain notoriety for permitting many types of "filler-gap" dependencies that are disallowed in English and most other European languages. A filler is a "dislocated" interrogative, relative, or topicalized phrase; the gap is the location where its filler would be placed on the basis of its syntactic role. Examples like the following are bad English, but they translate word-for-word to good Norwegian: *Which speaker did everyone forget that ___ had been invited?* (the "*that*-trace filter"); *Who would you never vote for who supports ___?* (the "Complex NP Constraint"). Engdahl argues that the attempts to account for such restrictions on extraction, in particular the *that*-trace filter, in government binding theory (Chomsky, 1981) have not been successful.

The central topic of the paper is the linkage that appears to hold in many constructions between extraction possibilities and the possibility of interpreting a constituent with wide scope. Judgments about sentences like *Who forgot that which speaker had been invited?* seem to correlate with the status of sentences like *Which speaker did everyone forget that ___ had been invited?*. In English both are ungrammatical; in Norwegian both are grammatical. The same correlation seems to hold in other similar cases and in other languages, although there are some exceptions.

Engdahl suggests that the correlation between the two phenomena may indicate something about how interpretations are assembled in the course of parsing. What is common in the two cases is that the interpretation of an element has to be postponed for a while. This would involve some storage mechanism of the sort proposed by Cooper (1983). One observation that Engdahl makes about Swedish is very interesting in this context. In Swedish, the third-person possessive determiner has a special reflexive form. In a sentence like *John asked Peter to invite one of his* (*own*) *friends*, the possessive can refer to either John or Peter. In the Swedish counterpart of *Which of his* (*own*) *friends did John ask Peter to invite* ____? only *John* is possible as the antecedent. This phenomenon suggests that the interpretation of a filler element can nevertheless be modified while it is being held in store.

8.3. Stephen Crain and Janet Dean Fodor, "How can grammars help parsers?"

The central issue of the paper is the relationship between grammar and human sentence processing. Since transformational rules in general cannot be used efficiently to recover deep structures from surface strings, it has traditionally been assumed that grammar rules need not correspond in any direct way to principles that human beings unconsciously use when they parse sentences. In a theoretical framework in which there are no transformations, such as generalized phrase structure grammar (GPSG), the relation between parsers and grammars need not be so opaque. One would expect to find a very close correlation between some features of the grammar and some aspects of human parsing performance.

This is what Crain and Fodor want to show. They start by discussing critically some experimental results that seem problematic for their thesis. The last section of the paper presents supporting data from their own experiment.

Freedman (1982) found that sentences that violate constraints on extraction (e.g., *What did you buy Picasso's painting of* ____?) were processed in a sentence-matching task just as easily as grammatical sentences. Violations of syntactic rules (e.g., *Mary were writing a letter to her husband*) took longer to process. This suggests that phrase structure rules and constraints on filler-gap dependencies reside in different modules for the human parser, contrary to the assumptions of the GPSG model that Crain and Fodor are arguing for. They suggest an alternative explanation for the data. They point out that rule violations, unlike constraint violations, are generally easy for the subject to correct. For constraint violations there typically is no grammatical alternative. If subjects have to leave such violations uncorrected, it could account for the fact that these sentences are matched more quickly than correctable violations. If their explanation is correct, the Freedman study does not indicate that rules and constraints on gaps and fillers come into play at different points in the course of parsing.

The second critical section reviews a study by Frazier, Clifton, and Randall (1983) on gap-filler pairings. The experiment involves two types of sentences:

> Recent Filler:
> Everyone liked the woman who [the little child] started __ to sing NP for __ PP.

> Distant Filler:
> Everyone liked the woman [who] the little child forced __ __ to sing NP PP.

Examples of the former type are called *Recent Filler* sentences because the gap after *started* is bound by *the little child*, which is the most recent potential filler NP. In the latter example the gap after *forced* is bound to a *Distant Filler*, the relative pronoun *who*. Frazier, Clifton, and Randall found that Recent Filler sentences were comprehended faster than sentences with distant fillers. They explained the result by suggesting that the subjects were using a processing strategy that has no counterpart in the grammar: Always associate gaps with the most recent filler. This proposal would account for the fact that there was a delay in cases where the initial gap-filler assignment had to be undone.

Crain and Fodor conducted their own study using the same test materials. Unlike the original study, which measured only the total comprehension time for each sentence, Crain and Fodor timed the processing of the sentence word by word. In this manner they obtained a measure of relative processing load at each position. If the subjects were really using the strategy the earlier study attributes to them, at the location of the gap there should be no difference in complexity between Distant and Recent Filler sentences. This is contrary to what Crain and Fodor found. The processing of Distant Filler sentences was slowed down when the gap was encountered. This suggests that the subjects were in fact making the correct gap-filler assignments as soon as the gap was encountered. Crain and Fodor argue that the strategy of assigning the most recent filler is used only as a default in cases where there is a local ambiguity.

The central conclusion of the Crain and Fodor paper is that all the evidence supports the view that constraints on filler-gap dependencies are available for the human parser at the same time as the information about constituent structure. This is important for the GPSG theory, which expresses them in a single, uniform system of rules. If it were found that the human parsing mechanism separates phrase structure assignment and filler-gap constraints into different modules, it would undermine the claim that there is a simple direct connection between grammar rules and parsing strategies – at least from the GPSG point of view.

8.4. *Lyn Frazier, "Syntactic complexity"*

Proposals for a metric to measure syntactic complexity tend to be viewed by many researchers with skepticism, especially after the demise of the "derivational theory of complexity," which was based on transformational grammar. There is a feeling that even a correct metric would not in itself have been of much theoretical interest; rather, it is something that should follow as a consequence from a correct theory of sentence comprehension. Nevertheless, Frazier points out that a successful metric could have a heuristic value in helping to pinpoint correlations between properties of grammars and those of the language processing mechanism. The new complexity metric that she proposes is compatible with experimental results that have been obtained so far.

Frazier first surveys a number of cases where it has been argued that certain syntactic constraints are motivated by the need to facilitate parsing by avoiding ambiguity. The examples tend to be unconvincing. She argues, however, that there are such constraints, designed to limit word order variation. Two constraints are proposed. They are designed to guarantee that major constituents retain their structural integrity, so that they will be easier to identify.

Frazier's new complexity metric is similar to an earlier proposal by Miller and Chomsky (1963), which was a reaction to Yngve's "depth hypothesis" (1960). It is based on the idea that syntactic complexity involves the number of nonterminal nodes that the parser must construct when it processes new words. What counts is not the number of nodes in the yet unfinished structure, but rather the number of new nodes that have to be hypothesized to get the current chunk of words properly attached to the existing structure. The amount of syntactic complexity thus varies across the sentence. By comparing the peak of local nonterminal counts, one can arrive at a complexity ranking for complete sentences. They seem to be in agreement with empirical observations of complexity, although Frazier admits that there is no independent justification for some of the parameter settings in her metric. For example, complexity is measured within a three-word window, and S and $\bar{S}$ nodes count more than other nonterminal nodes.

The last part of the paper makes a number of interesting conjectures about semantic processing. Along with many other researchers, Frazier assumes that constituents may be interpreted semantically as soon as they are syntactically complete, even though the rest of the sentence may still be unfinished. It may also be the case that the original syntactic structure is discarded as soon as it has been interpreted. Frazier suggests that this process of semantic replacement affects "complete minimal governing categories," that is, minimal NPs or Ss containing no unassigned pronouns or gaps. If semantic replacement reduces the number of things that have to be retained in memory during processing, the phenomenon may be seen as a functional explanation for the fact that languages tend not to allow extractions from sentential subjects, complex noun phrases, and adverbial clauses. Structures that are extraction islands can always be interpreted immediately without waiting for the rest of the sentence to be completed.

8.5. Aravind K. Joshi, *"Processing of sentences with intrasentential code switching"*

The title refers to cases where a bilingual speaker switches from one language to another, perhaps several times, in the course of an utterance. This phenomenon has received much attention among sociolinguists, but very few studies so far have addressed computational issues. From a formal point of view, the phenomenon is interesting because there seem to be constraints on the kind of switches that can be made. People who participate in code switching tend to have fairly consistent acceptability judgments about mixed sentences. The two languages are interacting in some systematic way.

Joshi's paper is based on data and judgments collected informally from a small number of bilingual speakers of English and Marathi, an Indic language. The basic assumption is that the grammars for the two languages are separate, not mixed, as far as the participants are concerned. There is a "switching rule" that transfers the control of the production (or parsing) of the sentence from the "matrix grammar" to the "embedded grammar." The acceptability data can be accounted for in terms of two constraints on the switching rule. The main constraint says that switching is asymmetric; a phrase generated by an embedded grammar cannot contain elements of the matrix language. Second, switching is not allowed for nodes that dominate a closed class of items. Thus adjectives and nouns can be switched but not determiners or prepositions.

One important question that remains open in the paper is whether these constraints on switching have to be postulated separately or whether they follow naturally somehow from the way sentences are processed. (This issue is also addressed in a related paper by Doron, 1983.) With respect to parsing, it apparently would entail that top-down strategies are dominant.

8.6. Aravind K. Joshi, *"Tree adjoining grammars"*

The subtitle of the paper is "How much context sensitivity is required to provide reasonable structural descriptions?" It presents in very accessible form a number of linguistically significant mathematical results about tree adjoining grammars (TAGs) and tree adjoining languages (TALs). The last part of the paper outlines a TAG for English.

There is a large body of literature on the question of how much formal power is required to give adequate descriptions of all human languages. If we knew the answer we would know where natural languages belong on the well-known Chomsky hierarchy for formal languages (regular expressions < context-free languages < context-sensitive languages < recursively enumerable sets). It would also tell us something about processing issues. For example, it would determine an upper bound on the time required to parse a sentence of a given length. Transformational grammars, in their classical form, are too powerful. Context-free grammars (CFGs) appear to be too weak, but it is widely believed that some small extension of their capabilities would be sufficient.

Tree adjoining grammars are in a class of mildly context sensitive grammars that are close relatives of CFGs. The first part of Joshi's paper discusses a number of textbook cases from formal language theory. It demonstrates that TAGs are indeed more powerful than CFGs but less powerful than some other known systems that fall between context-free and context-sensitive grammars. For example, TAGs are less powerful than indexed grammars. This result places TAGs between the generalized phrase structure grammars (GPSGs) of Gazdar, Pullum, Klein, and Sag and the lexical functional grammars (LFGs) of Bresnan and Kaplan, because LFG is known to have at least the power of indexed grammars.

The characteristic property of TAGs is an operation that under certain conditions allows trees to be adjoined. The adjunction operation does not destroy any part of the host tree; displaced material is attached to the bottom of the adjoined tree. For example, substituting the auxiliary tree corresponding to *did Mary say* for the S node dominating *John saw* in the structure for *who John saw* results in the tree for *who* (*did Mary say*) *John saw*. The part corresponding to the adjoined auxiliary tree is marked with parentheses. Another example of tree adjunction is *the boy* (*who met Mary*) *left*, where an NP with a relative clause has been adjoined to the middle of *the boy left*.

The point of these examples in the last part of the paper is simply to illustrate TAGs. They are not intended as definitive analyses of English. Nevertheless, there are some interesting details. For example, the difference between the so-called equi-verbs and raising verbs can be seen in the structures corresponding to (*John tries*) *to please Mary* and *John* (*seems*) *to please Mary*. Auxiliary trees containing equi-verbs like *try* are sentential; auxiliary trees for raising verbs like *seem* are verbal.

For the treatment of dependencies between fillers and gaps, TAGs are allowed to contain links of the same sort as in Peters and Ritchie (1982).

As trees are adjoined, these links "stretch" accordingly. Since the basic relationship between a filler and a gap is stated on simple trees, no special machinery is required for long-distance dependencies. Since TAGs can handle crossing as well as nested dependencies, it appears that they have the necessary formal power for describing the syntax of relative and interrogative constructions in Scandinavian languages, where crossing dependencies are allowed. Joshi also suggests an analysis for a celebrated case of crossing serial dependency in Dutch. One interesting point in the last section of the paper is the observation that, in TAGs, there is no need to stipulate any island constraints to prevent ungrammatical questions like *To whom what did John do?*. They are a corollary of how TAGs are defined.

Because they are so close to context-free grammars, TAGs should not be any less efficient so far as parsing is concerned. It is not known yet whether this in fact is so. The only existing paper on this issue is by Joshi and Yokomori (1983), which presents an $O(n^4)$ algorithm. For context-free grammars the time bound is $O(n^3)$, where n is the length of the input.

8.7. Martin Kay, "Parsing in functional unification grammar"

This paper discusses the theory and the descriptive formalism used in the joint paper by Karttunen and Kay. (An earlier version was presented at a conference on parsing at the University of Texas in 1981 under the title "An algorithm for compiling parsing tables from a grammar.")

One characteristic feature of Kay's unification grammar is that rules are formulated as functional descriptions, as collections of attribute-value pairs. Rules differ from descriptions of individual sentences only because they are less detailed and may contain disjunctions. They do not describe particular phrases but sets of them. There is a deliberate blurring of the distinction between constituent structure and features. This is one major difference between Kay's unification grammar and lexical functional grammar (Kaplan and Bresnan, 1982). The formalism is otherwise very similar as far as functional descriptions are concerned.

The term *unification* refers to an operation that merges several functional descriptions (FDs) into a single one. It is similar to forming a union of sets, but there are two important differences: (1) unification fails if the FDs have different values for the same attribute, and (2) the operation is *destructive* (if it succeeds, the original FDs have literally become identical). Unification is the basic operation both for generation and for parsing in Kay's system. The generation of a sentence may begin with a skeleton description containing, perhaps, only its semantic description. The complete structure for the sentence is produced by unifying the initial description with the rules of the grammar.

Given Kay's formalism, it is easy to see how a grammar can be used to produce sentences. It is much harder to see how to apply it for recognition. This is not a matter of concern for Kay, because he thinks of unification grammar as a "competence grammar" and sees no reason to expect that its rules are directly involved in parsing. It is sufficient that a mapping can be provided to some other equivalent representation that is specifically designed for the benefit of a particular parsing algorithm. The last part of the paper outlines such a procedure. It derives from a unification grammar an ATN (augmented transition network)-like parsing system. The method involves a great deal of computation, and the resulting parsing grammar may well be much larger than the original.

Most of the papers in this book assume without any question that the human mind parses sentences using rules that are similar (if not identical) to the rules that linguists write down. Kay's paper is a notable exception. His position, which he calls "conservative" in the paper, is that there are separate grammars for generation and recognition.

8.8. Lauri Karttunen and Martin Kay, "Parsing in a free word order language"

The question raised by the Davison and Lutz paper of how sentence topics are syntactically marked is discussed here with data from Finnish, a language in which other things besides subjects can be sentence topics. Another discourse function discussed in the paper is *contrast*. This is similar to the role that the preposed constituent has in English sentences like *The book he read.* Because the two discourse roles in Finnish are assigned on the basis of structural configuration and prosodic pattern, Finnish is not really a free word order language except in the sense that word order does not determine the assignment of syntactic functions like subject and object.

The focus of the paper is on developing an outline of Finnish syntax in the framework of functional unification grammar. (The theory itself is discussed in more detail in the preceding paper by Kay.) One feature of the theory, important for the description of Finnish, is that constituent order is specified by means of patterns rather than by standard phrase structure rules.

Although it is simple to generate sentences from a unification grammar, no efficient technique has been developed so far for using the rules in their original form for parsing. It is possible, however, to convert a unification grammar to an equivalent set of rules of a more standard type for which efficient parsing algorithms have already been developed. As the authors point out, it would even be possible, although certainly impractical, to expand their unification grammar for Finnish to a standard phrase structure grammar. The solution that they consider most efficient for the case at hand is to compile it to a set of constituent structure rules with unordered right-hand sides. For each such rule, a set of possible orderings can then be derived from the grammar with further constraints on the constituents. In this way standard parsing techniques can be used and one can avoid the combinatorial explosion that would result from turning the grammar to a set of ordinary phrase structure rules.

From a descriptive point of view, the main result of the paper is the demonstration that the complexity of surface ordering in Finnish arises from the interplay of a small number of relative simple ordering principles that involve both syntactic functions (subject, object) and discourse functions (topic, contrast).

8.9. *Fernando C. N. Pereira, "A new characterization of attachment preferences"*

The author of this paper was invited to contribute it to this volume because it opens a new perspective on data that has been discussed in a number of well-known works on human parsing strategies (Kimball, 1973; Frazier and Fodor, 1978; Wanner, 1980; Fodor and Frazier, 1980; Marcus, 1980). It is an interesting postscript to the controversy between the "sausage machine" model proposed by Frazier and Fodor and the ATN model championed by Wanner.

One of the issues in these works concerns the preference that speakers of English tend to have for associating the adverbial *yesterday* in sentences like *Bill said that John left yesterday* with the embedded rather than the main clause. The favored interpretation is *Bill said that [John left yesterday]*, not *Bill said that [John left] yesterday*. This tendency, which of course could be overcome by contextual or semantic factors, led Kimball to propose a principle of Right Association (RA). This principle says that phrases are added to the same partially completed phrase as long as possible.

A second principle, due to Frazier and Fodor (1978), is Minimal Attachment (MA). It was introduced to account for the preference for structures like *John bought [the book] for Susan* over structures like *John bought [the book for Susan]*. This principle says that, whenever possible, new phrases should be attached without creating additional structure.

Pereira notes that the subsequent debate over the formulation and interaction of these principles was in part caused by lack of precision in stating them; the problem was the absence of a suitable general framework. The point of the paper is to show that the two principles can be reformulated and sharpened by adopting a simple general parsing model, namely shift-reduce parsing. This well-known technique employs a push-down stack and an input buffer. There are only two operations: moving the next word from the buffer to the stack (shifting) and replacing the topmost symbols of the stack, if they constitute the right-hand side of a grammar rule, by the corresponding left-hand symbol (reducing).

The basic shift-reduce parser can be made more sophisticated by adding a control mechanism an ("oracle") that determines the parser's behavior in cases where it could either shift or reduce. Such an oracle can be mechanically derived for each particular grammar. The parser in effect can thus make use of top-down information although it seemingly operates in a bottom-up manner. In this context the two principles can be interpreted as maxims that are invoked when the oracle cannot select among available alternatives because of structural ambiguity in the language. The RA principle corresponds to solving shift-reduce conflicts in favor of shifting; the MA principle corresponds to choosing the largest possible reduction in cases where more than one rule could be applied.

It is not the intent of the paper to advocate shift-reducing as a model of human parsing, but rather to point out that it offers a very simple account of the data discussed in the early papers by Frazier and Fodor and by Wanner. For more recent work on the same topic, see Shieber, 1983.

8.10. Stephen Crain and Mark Steedman, "On not being led up the garden path"

This extended version of a paper presented at a conference in Austin, Texas, in spring 1981 consists of three relatively independent sections. The first two are mainly theoretical; the last one discusses experimental results. The paper begins with a discussion of the concept of syntactic autonomy. Although the authors believe that there exists an independent syntax module in sentence processing, for them this belief does not entail that the syntax module builds syntactic representations that are subsequently interpreted semantically. Crain and Steedman conjecture that semantic interpretations are constructed directly. They assume that there is a "weak" interaction between syntactic and semantic processing. From time to time the semantic component is called upon to decide which syntactic alternative the processor should pursue. The range of available choices, however, is determined by the grammar, not by the mental model that the hearer may have about the state of world.

The main thesis of the paper is that local conflicts between competing syntactic analyses are resolved by semantic interaction, not by some built-in biases that favor particular constructions or types of structural attachment. In this respect Crain and Steedman differ radically from many other researchers in the field, including several of the contributors to this book

(Fodor, Frazier, Pereira). For Crain and Steedman there are no structural biases or intrinsic "garden path" sentences. In their view the alleged experimental evidence for such notions is inconclusive, because possible interactions between syntactic processing and semantic interpretation have not been controlled adequately. In particular, there are no null or neutral contexts, because the interpretation of a sentence typically leads the subject to make assumptions about the very context in which the sentence is presented. The plausibility of these inferences and the cost of making them can have a significant effect on processing time.

A case in point, which Crain and Steedman discuss in detail, concerns presuppositions that go with definite noun phrases. The noun phrase *the horse which was raced past the barn* presupposes that in some particular situation known to the speaker there was known to be a unique horse of the aforementioned sort. Furthermore, it implies that there were other horses there as well. This noun phrase is structurally identical to *horses which were raced past the barn*, but from the semantic point of view the two are different. In a context that satisfies none of the presuppositions, the first sentence requires the hearer to make more extensive modifications in this mental model than the second. Consequently, Crain and Steedman predict that the following variants of Bever's famous garden path sentence should differ from each other with respect to ease of processing: *The horse raced past the barn fell; Horses raced past the barn fell.*

This prediction was verified in an experiment where the subjects had to make a quick judgment about the grammaticality of the test sentence. The same experiment also showed that the plausibility of the required addition to the context can have an effect on processing. *The teachers taught by the Berlitz method passed the test* was perceived as ungrammatical more often than *The children taught by the Berlitz method passed the test.* In a second experiment Crain showed that the context can induce garden path effects as well as overcome them. A sentence that begins *The psychologist told the wife that he was having trouble with . . .* is ambiguous because the word *that* can be interpreted either as a relative pronoun or as a complementizer. The ambiguity is resolved by the two alternative endings: *. . . to leave her husband* versus *her husband.* When the context strongly favors one reading, the subjects in Crain's experiment often perceived the other sentence as ungrammatical. The fact that the complement reading is favored in a null context need not be the result of any structural bias but could merely be a reflection of the fact that it involves fewer presuppositions. In the third experiment the same test sentences were presented in a context that was designed to make both interpretations seem equally plausible. No evidence for a purely structural bias was found.

8.11. Michael K. Tanenhaus, Greg N. Carlson, and Mark S. Seidenberg, "Do listeners compute linguistic representations?"

The paper begins with a critical review of recent psychological studies by Bransford (1979), Marslen-Wilson (1975), Marslen-Wilson and Tyler (1981), and others that seem to cast doubt on the psychological reality of linguistic representations. The authors argue that the data are fully compatible with a model of language comprehension such as the one found in Forster (1979), which consists of a set of autonomous processing modules operating under the guidance of a general cognitive system (GCS). The outputs from these modules, they assume, are linguistic representations, and the modules themselves may correspond to *levels* in linguistic theory (phonetics, phonology, lexicon, syntax, semantics).

The best evidence for the modularity hypothesis comes from the studies of lexical processing. Swinney (1979) and others have demonstrated that multiple readings of an ambiguous word are all present when a word is recognized, regardless of context and syntactic environment. The effects of lexical ambiguity can be experimentally demonstrated even though the subjects themselves may not realize that any ambiguity exists. Word recognition appears to be a very fast automatic process, independent of conscious or unconscious control. The output is available to the GCS for ambiguity resolution and further processing, but the inner workings of the module are sealed off.

Studies of word recognition have important implications for parsing research. They show that experimental tasks that are based on conscious awareness of some process or output may be very inconclusive. In the case of syntactic ambiguity, for example, it is unclear whether the choice among alternative syntactic structures is made in the course of the parsing process itself or afterward. The question cannot be answered on introspective judgments about ambiguity and preferred readings. In order to resolve the matter, new experimental techniques must be developed that are sensitive to the presence of multiple syntactic structures. The authors warn against accepting too uncritically the prevailing view that the assignment of syntactic structure is done by the GCS just because the GCS determines the final outcome. There are many ways in which the same result can arise from an interaction between the GCS and one or more independent syntactic modules.

The experiments reported in the paper focus on the interpretation of gaps and anaphors. Gaps and anaphors are similar in that they need to be linked to something in order for the sentence to be understood. The central question addressed by the experiments in the paper is whether the linking is to the literal form of the filler/antecedent, to its semantic interpretation (logical form), or to the referent of that expression in a discourse model that the hearer constructs. In the case of gaps, the results are surprising. The data from a rhyme priming experiment suggest that the literal form of the filler is preserved in store until the corresponding gap occurs. More detailed follow-up studies on the finding are under way.

The results from one of the experiments on anaphora support the distinction between surface and deep anaphora (Hankamer and Sag, 1976). The former type (VP-deletion, for example) involves the literal form of the antecedent phrase. Pronouns, on the other hand, appear to be linked either to some semantic representation of the antecedent or to its referent. Words that are related to the antecedent of the pronoun are processed faster than unrelated words when they are presented right after the pronoun. The authors point out that the same experimental method can give answers to more detailed questions about the process of anaphoric linkage. For example, in a discourse such as the following, the pronoun *it* is in an anaphoric relation to *the more expensive meat*, which in turn has the same referent as *steak*.

> Mary couldn't decide whether to buy steak or hamburger. She finally chose the more expensive meat when she heard that it was on sale.

A new experiment, now in progress, in which *steak* and *meat* are presented at varying delays after the pronoun, should bring interesting results about the speed of anaphoric linkage and inferencing.

References

Aho, Alfred V., and Jeffrey D. Ullman. 1972. *The theory of parsing, translation, and compiling. Vol. 1: Parsing.* Englewood Cliffs, N.J.: Prentice-Hall.

Barr, Avron, and Edward A. Feigenbaum, eds. 1981. *The handbook of artificial intelligence. Vol. 1.* Stanford and Los Altos, Calif.: HeurisTech Press and William Kaufmann.

Bransford, John D. 1979. *Human cognition: Learning, understanding and remembering.* Belmont, Calif.: Wadsworth.

Chomsky, Noam. 1956. Three models for the description of language. *IRE Transactions PGIT* 2:113–24.

Chomsky, Noam. 1981. *Lectures on government and binding.* Dordrecht, Holland: Foris.

Clark, Herbert H., and Eve V. Clark. 1977. *Psychology and language: An introduction to psycholinguistics.* New York: Harcourt Brace Jovanovich.

Cooper, Robin. 1983. *Quantification and syntactic theory.* Dordrecht, Holland: D. Reidel.

Doron, Edit. 1983. On formal models of code-switching. *Texas Linguistic Forum* 23.

Fodor, Janet D., and Lyn Frazier. 1980. Is the human parsing mechanism an ATN? *Cognition* 8:417–59.

Forster, Kenneth I. 1979. Levels of processing and the structure of the language processor. In: William E. Cooper and Edward C. T. Walker (eds.), *Sentence processing: Psycholinguistic studies presented to Merrill Garrett.* Hillsdale, N.J.: Lawrence Erlbaum.

Frazier, Lyn, and Janet D. Fodor. 1978. The Sausage Machine: A new two-stage parsing model. *Cognition* 6:291–325.

Frazier, Lyn, Charles Clifton, and Janet Randall. 1983. Filling gaps: decision principles and structure in sentence comprehension. *Cognition* 11:187–222.

Freedman, S. A. 1982. Behavioral reflexes of constraints on transformations. Unpublished Ph.D. dissertation, University of Texas, Austin.

Gazdar, Gerald. 1982. Phrase structure grammar. In: Pauline Jacobson and Geoffrey K. Pullum (eds.), *The nature of syntactic representation*. Dordrecht, Holland: D. Reidel, pp. 131–86.

Gleason, Henry A., Jr. 1965. *Linguistics and English grammar*. New York: Holt, Rinehart and Winston.

Hankamer, Jorge, and Ivan Sag. 1976. Deep and surface anaphora. *Linguistic Inquiry* 7:391–426.

Harris, Zellig S. 1946. From morpheme to utterance. *Language* 22:161–83.

Hays, David G. 1964. Dependency theory: A formalism and some observations. *Language* 40, 4:511–25.

Hockett, Charles F. 1961. Grammar for the hearer. In: Structure of language and its mathematical aspects. *Proceedings of the Symposium on Applied Mathematics* 12:220–37.

Johnson, David E., and Paul M. Postal. 1980. *Arc pair grammar*. Princeton, N.J.: Princeton University Press.

Joshi, Aravind K., and Takashi Yokomori. 1983. Some characterization theorems for tree adjoining grammars and recognizable sets. Technical report, Department of Computer and Information Science, University of Pennsylvania.

Kaplan, Ronald M., and Joan Bresnan. 1982. Lexical-functional grammar: A formal system for grammatical representation. In: Joan Bresnan (ed.), *The mental representation of grammatical relations*. Cambridge, Mass.: MIT Press, pp. 173–281.

Kimball, John. 1973. Seven principles of surface structure parsing in natural language. *Cognition* 2:15–48.

Marcus, Mitchell. 1980. A theory of syntactic recognition for natural language. Cambridge, Mass.: MIT Press.

Marslen-Wilson, William. 1975. The limited compatibility of linguistic and perceptual explanations. In: Robin E. Grossman, L. James San, and Timothy J. Vance (eds.), *Papers from the parasession on functionalism*. Chicago: Chicago Linguistic Society, pp. 409–20.

Marslen-Wilson, William D., and Lorraine K. Tyler. 1981. Modeling human parsing strategies? Paper presented at University of Texas Conference on Modeling Human Parsing Strategies.

McCawley, James D. 1968. Concerning the base component of a transformational grammar. *Foundations of Language* 4:243–69.

Michael, Ian. 1970. *English grammatical categories and the tradition to 1800*. Cambridge, England: Cambridge University Press.

Miller, George A., and Noam Chomsky. 1963. Finitary models of language users. In: R. Duncan Luce, Robert R. Bush, and Eugene Galanter (eds.), *Handbook of mathematical psychology*, vol. 2. New York: Wiley, pp. 419–91.

Naur, P. (ed.). 1963. Revised report on the algorithmic language ALGOL 60. *Communications of the ACM* 6, 1:1–17.

Peters, Stanley, and Robert W. Ritchie. 1982. Phrase linking grammars. Technical report, Department of Linguistics, University of Texas at Austin.

Robinson, Jane J. 1970. Dependency grammar and transformational rules. *Language* 46, 2:259–85.

Shieber, Stuart M. 1983. Sentence disambiguation by a shift-reduce parsing technique. *Proceedings of the 21st Annual Meeting of the ACL*, pp. 113–18.

Swinney, David A. 1979. Lexical access during sentence comprehension. (Re) consideration of context effects. *Journal of Verbal Learning and Verbal Behavior* 18:645–60.

Wanner, Eric. 1980. The ATN and the Sausage Machine: Which one is baloney? *Cognition* 8:209–25.

Winograd, Terry. 1983. *Language as a cognitive process. Vol. 1: Syntax.* Reading, Mass.: Addison-Wesley.

Yngve, Victor H. A. 1960. A model and a hypothesis for language structure. *Proceedings of the American Philosophical Society* 104:444–66.

1   Measuring syntactic complexity relative to discourse context

ALICE DAVISON and RICHARD LUTZ

In this paper we describe an experiment in sentence processing which was intended to relate two properties of syntactic structures that have received much discussion in linguistics and psychology (see references cited in the next section). First, some syntactic structures, such as the passive construction, require more processing effort than corresponding structures which express the same grammatical relations. Passive sentences in particular have been the subject of much experimental work. Second, it is clear, as was observed by Jespersen (1924), that the difference between active and passive sentences has something to do with focus of attention on a particular constituent, the grammatical subject. And the consequences of the difference of focus of attention is in some way related to the context formed by the discourse in which the sentence occurs. In this experiment we wanted to study syntactic structures which might have similar properties to the passive/active construction, so as to define exactly what features of passive sentences are responsible for their observed greater processing demands and definition of focus of attention, or sentence topic. One of the bases of the experiment, underlying the hypotheses we wanted to test, is that processing load and definition of sentence topic are related in some way.

We combined sentences exemplifying five different syntactic constructions with context sentences having different relations to the target sentences, and measured reaction time for reading and understanding the second or target sentence. The results show that there is a fairly consistent relationship of processing load for the other constructions as well as passive, and that overall processing time is sensitive to both syntactic structure and contextual information. The results allow us to distinguish between two characterizations of sentence topic.

One of the main motivations of the study was to see how closely actual processing could be predicted by using the descriptive devices of a theory of syntax, that is, transformations or their equivalents, in combination with pragmatic information, that is, contextual, referential information.

26

As this kind of information is usually available in natural discourse, the discussion of the psychological reality of syntactic structures is not very realistic if linguistic contextual information is either absent or poorly defined in the experimental items. So we were concerned with isolating the crucial factors of sentence structure which could define a sentence topic, and its specific role in sentence processing, which we believe is primarily to link one salient referring expression with previously known information. In this way we hoped to explain some of the observed properties of sentences while exploring the ways in which syntactic theories model linguistic competence.

1.1. Previous experimental studies of passive sentences, sentence topic, and context

Some of the earlier experimental studies of passive sentences form a good starting place for defining the main points about sentence structures at issue in this experiment. Experimental results of various kinds have shown consistently that passive sentences are harder to process than the corresponding active sentences. They take longer for a subject to verify on the basis of a picture (Olson and Filby, 1972; Glucksberg, Trabasso, and Wald, 1973); they take a subject longer to produce when cued by a picture and verbal preamble (Tannenbaum and Williams, 1968); and they take children longer to recall when cued by pictures (Turner and Rommetveit, 1968). The difficulty of passive sentences is even greater if the sentence is semantically "reversible" (Slobin, 1966), requiring actual processing of syntax and morphology rather than a successful guess based on the inherent nonagency of the grammatical object.

It is still legitimate to ask why passive sentences are more difficult to process than the corresponding active sentences. In the terms of Chomsky (1965), passive sentences are the outcome of applying an "optional" transformation. This view derives active and passive sentences from the same deep structure, and expresses the generalization that they will have different surface form but express the same grammatical relations. This is true of (1a) and (1b), and other similar active-passive pairs which are synonymous when quantifiers and negation are not involved.

(1)   a.   The lion chased the unicorn all around the town.
       b.   The unicorn was chased by the lion all around the town.

Both versions have *the lion* in the role of agent and *the unicorn* in the role of patient, even though the surface subjects and objects differ. Non-derivational theories of grammar express the same equivalence of grammatical roles with different descriptive devices which do not make the claim that a sentence structure actually undergoes changes of word order and constituent structure provided by a theory of syntax. Fodor and Garrett (1967) demonstrated that it cannot be true that the processing complexity of syntactic structures exactly matches the transformational operations which have applied in the derivation of the surface structure. They propose that a far more accurate prediction of complexity can be gotten from the amount of surface structure information about semantic/grammatical relations. If surface word order and morphological distinctions match more than one interpretation of well-formed structures in the language, then the structure is likely to be more complex to process. A correct interpretation involves integrating information from different parts of the sentence, taking note of special features of lexical items, and so on.

On this view, passive sentences would be difficult to process in English because the noun phrase associated with a verb – preceding it, agreeing with it – is the subject of the verb in surface structure, but semantically it is the object. But this is not the usual pattern in English. If the verb has no special morphology, its subject is not a semantic object. Some of the "normal" unmarked or canonical patterns in English matching surface relations with grammatical functions often yield the "right" answer on the first guess with the least computational effort. These have been expressed as processing strategies, based on observed behavior (Bever, 1970), and in augmented transition network (ATN) grammars (Wanner and Maratsos, 1978), as the first-ranked path taken.[1]

In both transformational grammars without a passive transformation (e.g., Freidin, 1975) and nontransformational grammar such as the dependency grammar of Hudson (1976), the equivalence of grammatical functions in the different active and passive surface structures is expressed by rules of semantic interpretation, which apply to the independently specified surface syntactic structures. For Freidin, the equivalence of grammatical functions of the NPs associated with the active or passive verb forms is stated in the lexicon, and this method of relating the different surface expressions of the grammatical functions relevant to semantic interpretation is further developed in lexical functional grammar of Bresnan (1978), replacing most other transformations except for unbounded movement rules. In the version of Montague grammar in Bach (1980), the rule of semantic translation for passive sentences is matched by a syntactic rule specifying a passive verb phrase (PVP), a special subtype of intransitive verb phrase. The semantic translation of a PVP ultimately makes the sentence it is part of equivalent semantically to an active sentence.

We want to emphasize that in speaking of the Passive "transformation," we are referring to a statement that two distinct surface structures express the same grammatical roles, such as *object*, which are relevant to the semantic interpretation of the relation between verbs and NPs (e.g., "patient"). Exactly what form this statement may take, whether it includes syntactic operations such as movement, or information specified by the lexical entry of a verb, is not relevant to the issues discussed here. We will use terms like *Passive transformation* as a convenient way of referring to a specific combination of syntactic and morphological features of a class of sentences.

A major goal of syntactic theories which make some claim for psychological realism is to be able to show that the perceptual complexity of passive sentences is matched in some way by its description. Wanner and Maratsos (1978) represent this feature of passive sentences with a device allowing reanalysis of NP–V as object–verb when later information shows that the first assignment of a grammatical function is wrong. If passive sentences are harder to process than active sentences, it is legitimate to ask why there is a passive construction at all, why there is such surface variation of syntactic constructions, variation which serves to obscure the expression of grammatical roles. The answer lies in another aspect of sentences: their use in a discourse. From Jespersen (1924) onward, it has been recognized that there is a different focus of attention or viewpoint associated with active and passive sentences like (1). Further, this difference is important with respect to prior context, which may contain elements matching the focus of attention defined by the syntactic surface form of a sentence.

In this paper, we will be concerned with the contribution of *syntactic* properties of a sentence toward defining a focus of attention or *sentence topic*, and the role of syntactically induced salience in the integration of a sentence with prior context. Some well-known studies have shown that the comprehension and retention of a sentence is hindered if it cannot easily be integrated with information available from prior context. Since the main focus of this study is on the syntactic properties of the sentences whose processing is being described, this experiment is somewhat different from others. Bransford and Johnson (1972) asked subjects to understand and recall short paragraphs containing vague descriptions of things and actions. Without explicit contextual information given from a heading (*Washing clothes*) or other means, the paragraphs were less easily recalled than when the organizing contextual information was present. The linguistic features of text that were varied were more semantic and pragmatic (drawing on knowledge of the world) than syntactic.

Haviland and Clark (1974) asked subjects to read and comprehend sentences with definite NPs in them, such as *the alligator*. It took subjects longer to read and comprehend sentences if they contained NPs implying knowledge of a referent and also were preceded by contexts containing no explicit referent, such as *an alligator*. Again, the syntactic form of the sentences in question was not a variable, and syntax was not related to questions of integration with context material.

The syntactic properties of passive sentences have been investigated in connection with context. Four studies of passive sentences are particularly interesting for the similar results obtained for different tasks and age-groups of subjects. Turner and Rommetveit (1968) asked very young children, preschool age to third grade, to learn and recall active or passive sentences when cued with pictures. The pictures represented the agent, the patient, or the entire proposition, and thus served to focus attention on some *part* of the sentence. The responses were counted as correct if both the semantic contents and surface form were given correctly. Although more active forms than passive forms were given overall, it was found that recall of passive sentences was facilitated by a picture of the patient, while recall of the active form was facilitated by pictures representing the agent or the whole proposition. It would seem in a broad sense that the active form has something more in common with an encoded representation of an event than the passive form does, additional evidence that the active form is less "marked" than the passive.

In the study by Tannenbaum and Williams (1968), junior high school students were asked to produce sentences describing a picture, responding to instructions specifying whether the sentence was to be active or passive. The picture was preceded by a short paragraph, which was written either consistently in active sentences or consistently in passive sentences. The content of the preamble focused attention on the agent, the patient, or the whole event represented in the picture. The latter formed a "neutral" context, and in this context passive sentences took longer to produce (from onset of the picture to end of the response). In the context focusing on the agent, response time for active sentences went down, and response time for passive sentences went up. The difference is nearly erased in the context in which the focus of the preceding context is on the patient (see Figure 1.1). The contents of the preamble influenced reaction time, but responses were not significantly affected by whether the preamble had active or passive form.

A much discussed study by Olson and Filby (1972) suggests that responses to sentences are facilitated by a match between a prior context (verbal or nonverbal) and what comes first in a sentence, which of course differs in active and passive sentences. College students were asked to verify a sentence as true or false as a description of what is represented in a picture. The prior content focused attention on the agent or the patient, in various ways. There were several tasks: a picture of the agent preceded the overall picture, and subjects were instructed to focus on one or the other, and verify the sentence, or they were required to answer a *wh*-question about the agent or the patient. Quite consistently in all of

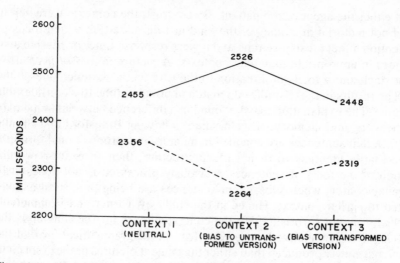

Figure 1.1.   Mean response times (msec) for the Passive transformation._____ = transformed version of target sentences; – – – – = untransformed version of target sentences.

these situations, responses were faster when the surface subject of the sentence being verified (or responded to as a question) matched what the prior context defined as focus of attention.

In response to this study, Glucksberg, Trabasso, and Wald (1973) investigated the encoding of pictures as well as sentences. They varied the order of presentation of the picture and the sentence to be verified, and introduced a number of false cases, in which the sentence and picture did not match in verb, agent, or patient. For true sentences, response times for reversible passive sentences were significantly higher than for active sentences, strongly so for sentences following pictures, less strongly so for sentences preceding pictures. For false sentences, response times for both kinds of passive, and for active sentences, was fastest when the verb did not match the picture. They propose that this fact suggests Verb–Subject–Object order in the mental representation of both active and passive sentences. (This question will be discussed in more detail in section 1.9.) For active sentences being verified after the presentation of the picture, response times for nonmatching subject and objects was the same, and slower than for verbs, while nonmatching objects for passive sentences took longer than subjects to detect. These results are somewhat puzzling and in any case do not offer an immediate explanation for the difficulty of passive sentences. But the results do show a difference of active and passive sentences that is consistent with other studies of responses to sentences in a neutral context, a difference that does not single out either the agent or the patient. By contrast, the contexts were verbal and not pictorial in studies of the kind just discussed, in which focus of attention affects response time and lowers response time for passive sentences in appropriate matching contexts. A picture *in and of itself* does not single out a focus of attention in the way that a sentence does.

The results in these studies do match in broad outline to a considerable degree. The explanation may be found in a difference between immediate processing and memory. If we assume, following Bransford and Franks (1972), that sentences are encoded in memory in a propositional form not necessarily identical to their surface structure, then an exact representation of the form of sentences previously processed is not necessarily available later, when subsequent sentences are being processed and related to earlier context. Hence in the study by Turner and Rommetveit (1968), it is not surprising that the contextual cues for recalling and *producing* a sentence have far greater effect on the grammatical form of the sentence newly produced than either the context pictures or the associated sentence when it was originally presented. In the study by Tannenbaum and Williams (1968), the grammatical form of the preamble did not significantly affect response time for producing an active or passive sentence, while the immediate cues did. The reason seems to be that cues defined focus of attention when the response sentence was being produced. The distinctive form of the preamble, however, would presumably not be available after processing, later in the sequence of tasks. At the time when the response was elicited the material in the preamble had been processed and stored in memory. So it is not surprising that there was no significant effect of the active or passive form of the preamble on the time needed to produce an active or passive description of the picture.

There are several important themes in these studies. One is that passive sentences are somewhat more difficult to process than active sentences, for young children as well as adults. Another is that passive sentences express a different focus of attention from the active, and this difference can be shown to match properties of a context, in cases where it introduces a referent for the subject noun phrase, either verbally or nonverbally. The match of contextual information and sentence form facilitates processing of a sentence, while a mismatch adds to the difficulty of the task. Finally, this match is relevant more for immediate processing than for retrieval of information from memory. If this is true for passive sentences, we would want to know if it is also true for other sentence types.

Gourlay and Catlin (1978) wanted to generalize from the case of actives and passives to other syntactic constructions, and they were only partially successful. Their general approach was to test sentence structure interpretation assuming that people use a processing strategy which interprets the earlier parts of a clause as given information, and later parts as new information (Firbas, 1963, and Halliday, 1967). By this rule, a prepositional indirect object as in (2a) should express new information to a greater degree than an indirect object which comes before the direct object in (2b).

(2) a. Stein gave a gold watch *to his Chinese interpreter.*
     b. Stein gave *his Chinese interpreter* a gold watch.

Active and passive sentences should also conform to the same strategy, which interprets what is in initial or subject position as *given* information. The four constructions (1) and (2) were contrasted with cleft sentences with clefted agent and clefted patient, which violate the strategy because asserted, new information is in the first part of the sentence. These sentences were read to preschool and young primary school children. The target sentence was read in three conditions: (1) isolation; (2) in an appropriate context, which introduced an antecedent for the given information; or (3) in an inappropriate context, which did not introduce an antecedent. The task was to match the sentence correctly with one of two pictures. The results showed, as expected, that sentences such as passive sentences, whose structure does not express grammatical relations in a canonical way, are harder to process in isolation and in an inappropriate context than those which do (Bever, 1970). But the interpretation of "marked" sentence structures is *facilitated* by an appropriate context. This was the case for passives and clefted patients, but there were no significant results for indirect objects, showing that, at least for young children, indirect objects do not participate in the pattern whereby certain constituents are processed as old information.

So the question remains, what properties of passive sentences make them hard to process in isolation and are sensitive to contextual information? And are these properties particular to passive sentences, or more general? The difference between active and passive sentences can be expressed in several different ways. The order of constituents is different; in the active form the NP with the verb is associated refers to the agent of a transitive verb, while in the passive the corresponding NP refers to the patient. The difference of word order is really a difference of expression of the underlying grammatical relations in terms of surface syntactic marking, word order, and case marking. Whatever the difference, it is also associated with a difference of *sentence topic* (the term will be discussed in more detail in section 1.5). Two competing definitions of sentence topic apply equally well to simple active-passive pairs; definition 1 says that sentence topics are initial elements (Firbas, 1963), while definition 2 says that sentence topics are subjects (Halliday, 1967; Chafe, 1974; Li and Thompson, 1976).

Both definitions make reference to general properties that can be found in other constructions, and can be tested for similar effects of match and mismatch with contextual information. Further, definition 1 is distinct from definition 2 in that subject properties are less variable than position. That is, there are various degrees of initial position: a constituent may be absolutely initial, or *more* initial than some other constituent. But subject properties are less variable. Given a certain configuration of elements in a clause, only one of those elements counts as a subject syntactically. The justification for this assertion will be given in more detail as specific syntactic configurations are discussed in the examples below.

The experiment reported here uses sentences in which five optional transformations applied. As passive sentences constitute the construction against which other constructions have been compared, there are active-passive pairs included in this study. Besides Passive, the other transformations are Adverb Preposing, *There* Insertion, Raising to Subject, and Raising to Object. Examples of all five will be given below, along with a description in each case of what is marked or unmarked about the way that grammatical relations are expressed, in terms of the matching of surface syntactic and morphological information with grammatical functions relevant to semantic interpretation. These patterns will be related to the different predictions made by the two definitions of topic about which constituents will be perceived as sentence topic.

What is at issue in this study is whether *syntactic properties* alone are able to define sentence topic. The syntactic effects of this type depend on the *differences* in surface structure of related sentences such as active-passive pairs. In describing the repertory of five constructions represented in the experimental materials, we will be concerned not only with what word order differences there are, and how grammatical relations are expressed in surface structure, but also with what structures are marked and differ from normal patterns.

I will assume that processing may be directed by the strategies in Bever (1970), and that syntactic and semantic processing are done simultaneously (Bever, 1970; Marslen-Wilson, 1973; Wanner and Maratsos, 1978). In most of what follows, the expression of clause-internal relations is relevant, though the assignment of clause boundaries for subordinate clauses also is at issue for Raising to Subject and Raising to Object.[2] I will return in the later sections to a discussion of why markedness and the definition of sentence topic are related, and note how the latter follows from the former.

1.2. Syntactic structures represented in the target sentences

Besides passive and corresponding active sentences, the sentences used as target sentences in the experiment represented four other constructions: *There* Insertion, Adverb Preposing, Raising to Subject, and Raising to Object.[3] Within each construction type, there are pairs of sentences which differ syntactically in specific ways, so that one member of the pair represents the underlying grammatical relations less directly, or less canonically, than the other. Each construction type is described below, with an example and discussion of the ways in which the related sentences differ in word order and morphology.

1.2.1. Passive

In pairs of sentences such as (3a) and (3b), the sentences differ in the marking of both the agent and direct object/patient of the verb.

(3) a. (untransformed or active)

$$\begin{bmatrix} A\ man\ in\ California \\ NP_1 \\ (nom) \end{bmatrix} \begin{bmatrix} abducted \\ \\ V \end{bmatrix} \begin{bmatrix} a\ six\text{-}year\text{-}old\ girl. \\ NP_2 \\ (acc) \end{bmatrix}$$

   b. (passive)

$$\begin{bmatrix} A\ six\text{-}year\text{-}old\ girl \\ NP_2 \\ (nom) \end{bmatrix} \begin{bmatrix} was\ abducted \\ \\ BE \quad V\text{-}ed \end{bmatrix} \begin{bmatrix} by \\ \\ PREP \end{bmatrix} \begin{bmatrix} a\ man\ in\ California \\ NP_1 \\ (obl) \end{bmatrix}$$

In the active form (3a), the noun phrase directly following the verb represents the grammatical direct object, with accusative marking if it is a pronoun, and also the semantic object (patient or other grammatical role assigned by the particular lexical item under the verb node). The NP preceding the verb is both the grammatical subject, with nominative marking if it is a pronoun, and also the logical subject (agent or other role such as experiencer or recipient, etc., assigned by verbs like *feel*, or *receive*, etc.). In the passive the agent is expressed with a *by* NP prepositional phrase following the verb, if the agent is expressed at all. The NP with nominative marking preceding and agreeing with the verb expresses the patient.

In English, the subjects and agents of both intransitive and transitive verbs have nominative marking, and precede and agree with the verb. For this reason, a reasonable expectation in processing a sentence containing the sequence NP–V is that it expresses the syntactic configuration of subject and verb, and the corresponding semantic interpretation. But this expectation, or first approximation, in processing would not yield the correct semantic interpretation.[4] As a processing strategy it would give an interpretation which must later be revised, first on the basis of the verbal morphology and second on the basis of the presence of a prepositional phrase which expresses an agent NP, though the latter is not essential for interpretation. The logical object of (3a), *a six-year-old girl,* is not in the canonical position for objects (3b), and in fact it has *some* of the syntactic properties of a subject. This NP, and not the prepositional agent, is inverted with the auxiliary verb in a question or similar construction (4a,b). This NP would also undergo Raising as in (5a,b).

(4) a. Did a man in California abduct a six-year-old girl?
      b. Was a six-year-old girl abducted by a man in California?

(5) a. A man in California seems to have abducted a six-year-old girl.
      b. A six-year-old girl seems to have been abducted by a man in California.

1.2.2. There *Insertion*

Sentences in which *There* Insertion has applied present a different though comparable problem.

(6) a. (untransformed)

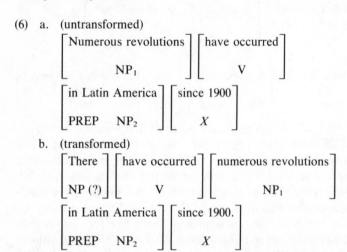

     b. (transformed)

The NP–V sequence in (6a) does correspond to the interpretation Subject–Verb, and corresponding semantic role assigned by the verb – that is, agent, experiencer, etc. But interpretation of the NP–V combination in (6b) falls afoul of the expletive NP *there*. *There* has grammatical subject properties; it precedes and inverts with the auxiliary verb, though verbal agreement is with the postverbal NP. The "real" subject is the NP *numerous revolutions*, which determines the plural form of the verb. The word order and morphology of constituents of (6a) give consistent information about a subject and also unambiguously indicate the underlying role of the NP. Word order and morphology in (6b) give conflicting and therefore ambiguous information about what the real subject is. In one sense, the NP *numerous revolutions* ceases to have subject function in (6b), so that, as in the case of the passive construction, both word order *and* grammatical roles are different from the untransformed syntactic structure.

1.2.3. Adverb Preposing

The application of Adverb Preposing reorders a constituent, but without changing any grammatical relations. There is a difference of the position of an NP or prepositional phrase, such as *on state highways*, but the expression of major constituents as arguments of the verb (subject, object) is not affected. In particular, the subject of the sentence is the same, *whether or not* an adverb has been reordered.

(7) a. (untransformed)

$$\begin{bmatrix} \text{Littering} \\ \text{NP}_1 \end{bmatrix} \text{is} \begin{bmatrix} \text{a legal offense} \\ \text{NP}_2 \end{bmatrix} \begin{bmatrix} on\ state\ highways. \\ \text{PREP} \quad \text{NP}_3 \end{bmatrix}$$

b. (transformed)

$$\begin{bmatrix} On\ state\ highways, \\ \text{PREP} \quad \text{NP}_3 \end{bmatrix} \begin{bmatrix} \text{littering} \\ \text{NP}_1 \end{bmatrix} \text{is} \begin{bmatrix} \text{a legal offense.} \\ \text{NP}_2 \end{bmatrix}$$

In the processing of the structures of the type shown in (7a), assignment of grammatical roles to constituents proceeds normally, assigning subject role to the NP in the combination NP–V. But in (7b), the first constituent is a preposition, signaling unambiguously the beginning of a prepositional phrase, which the grammar of English does not allow to have subject interpretation (except for *by* agent phrases in passive sentences, regardless of their position in linear order). Some adverbials are not explicitly marked with prepositions or adverbial suffixes (*at 6:00, slowly*), but even adverbials such as *tonight, last Wednesday*, and *somewhere* will generally not be misleading because another NP will usually appear before or inverted with the verb. The sequences will be of the type Prep NP NP V or NP NP V, and so the first constituent will generally not be adjacent to a verb. It will not receive a grammatical role subcategorized by the verb by virtue of its position in the sentence. Exactly how the adverbial is processed is not crucial here; it might remain in temporary memory until the major constituents of the sentence have been identified, and then be assigned an adjunct role (Townshend and Bever, 1978).

1.2.4. Raising to Subject

The last two sentence types are similar in that the sentences exemplifying them necessarily consist of two clauses, and the subject of the lower clause is marked in surface structure in a misleading and grammatically ambiguous way. Although Raising to Subject and Raising to Object are different in some respects, they are both linked to the presence of a member of specific classes verbs in the higher clause: *seem, happen, turn out*, in the case of Raising to Subject and *believe, report, reveal*, in the case of Raising to Object (see discussion of verb classes associated with Raising rules in Postal, 1974).

In sentences in which Raising to Subject has applied, the subject of the lower clause occupies subject position in the higher clause, and functions as its grammatical subject (8b). In (8a), in which the rule has not applied, the lower clause subject is associated with the finite lower clause verb.

(8) a. (untransformed)

$$\begin{bmatrix} \text{It} \\ \text{NP}_1 \end{bmatrix} \begin{matrix} \text{seems} \\ \text{V}_1 \end{matrix} \begin{bmatrix} \text{that} \\ \text{COMP} \end{bmatrix}_{S_2} \Biggl[$$

$$\begin{bmatrix} \text{many American Indians} \\ \text{NP}_2 \end{bmatrix} \begin{matrix} \text{died in epidemics.} \\ \text{V}_2 \quad\quad\text{X} \end{matrix} \Biggr]\Biggr]$$

b. (transformed)

$$\begin{bmatrix} \text{Many American Indians} \\ \text{NP}_2 \end{bmatrix} \begin{matrix} \text{seem} \\ \text{V}_1 \end{matrix} \begin{bmatrix} \begin{bmatrix} \text{——} \\ \text{NP}_2 \end{bmatrix} \end{bmatrix}_{S_2}$$

$$\begin{bmatrix} \text{to have died in epidemics} \\ \text{V}_2 \quad\quad\quad\quad X \end{bmatrix}$$

The NP moved from S_2 into S_1 affects the agreement properties of V_1, which are plural in (8b), in contrast with the singular (8a). Processing of these sentences must assign syntactic and semantic interpretations to NP–V sequences, as in the previous cases, and also assign clause boundaries to the two clauses making up the complex sentences in (8a,b). The sentence structure (8a) is fairly straightforward: The first NP–V sequence is interpreted as subject–verb. The complementizer *that*, which is optional in sentences like these, signals the beginning of a new, subordinate clause. The following NP–V sequence is also assigned the subject–verb interpretation, within the new clause. In (8b), however, the first NP–V sequence is syntactically interpreted as subject, correctly for the purposes of rules of morphological agreement, inversion, and so on. But semantically the NP is the subject of the lower clause verb, though the subject of V_2 is represented syntactically only by a gap between *seem* and *to* (compare *want Ø to go* with *want Susan to go*). Raising to Subject changes word order: a NP in the lower clause corresponds to a NP in subject position in the higher clause. The rule also changes the morphological marking of the NP if it is a pronoun.

1.2.5. Raising to Object

Raising to Object involves no difference of word order between the transformationally related surface structures, but clause membership and grammatical marking are ambiguous in the transformed version.

(9) a. (untransformed)

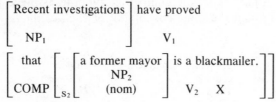

     b. (transformed)

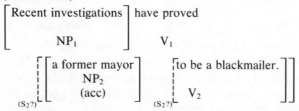

The subject of the subordinate clause has nominative marking in (9a), and verbal agreement matches it in the usual features. Processing of the untransformed version proceeds normally as in the preceding case, to yield the correct association and interpretation of elements. The same strategies, if applied to the transformed version (9b), will go wrong because of the ambiguity of the role of NP_2. It has accusative marking (if it is a pronoun) and follows V_1 without an apparent clause boundary. Hence normal expectations should give the sequence V_1–NP_2 the interpretation verb–object. But then V_2 is without a subject, and NP_2 must be reinterpreted as its subject, entailing that a clause boundary is placed to mark the beginning of a new clause.

1.2.6. Summary

Let us summarize the marked properties of the preceding constructions and the predictions of the two hypotheses: the word-order definition of topic (1) and the grammatical role definition of topic (2). The *marked* structures according to the preceding discussions of specific cases are

a.   The patient marked as subject in Passive sentences
b.   The logical subject displaced by *there* in *There* Insertion sentences

c.   The lower clause subject that appears as higher clause subject in Raising to Subject sentences

d.   The lower clause subject marked as an object of the higher clause in Raising to Object sentences

And possibly:

e.   The preposed adverbial, which is placed in temporary memory storage until the major constituents of the sentence have been identified

Hypothesis I defines the initial element as topic, while hypothesis II defines a subject as topic. Thus, the competing hypotheses make the following predictions about the topic constituent of each of the five transformed sentences:

		I	II
a.	Passive	Subject (if nothing precedes)	Subject
b.	*There* Insertion	*There* (" ")	*There*
c.	Adverb Preposing	Adverbial	Subject
d.	Raising to Subject	Higher clause subject (if nothing precedes)	Subject of S_1 or S_2
e.	Raising to Object	Subject of S_1 (" ")	Subject of S_1 or S_2

In three cases, but not for the Passive and *There* Insertion, the two hypotheses yield different predictions about what will or can be perceived as topic. The present study is intended to separate these hypotheses, combining examples of these five transformations will be combined with contexts of different types, which will be related to what is perceived as sentence topic. Differences in responses to these combinations should be able to disconfirm one of these hypotheses, leaving results consistent with the other. Note that markedness predictions correspond more closely to hypothesis II than hypothesis I.

1.3. The experimental materials: context and target sentences

The experimental items were created by combining two versions of a sentence, the transformed and untransformed versions, with one of three contexts: a neutral one, one favoring the untransformed version of the target sentence, and one favoring the transformed version. Before describing the relation between the context and parts of the target sentence, we want to note some general restrictions placed on the experimental sentences, to guarantee that effects of topic perception in the target sentences were due to syntactic structure alone, and to the particular syntactic structure associated with a given transformation.

As Haviland and Clark (1974) showed, definite NPs convey that there is previous mention of its referent, or that the referent of the NP is known to both speaker and hearer. Sentences with definite NPs are harder to process if there is no antecedent given explicitly in the context. Since grammatical properties *within* an NP, the definite article *the*, have the effect of requiring relation to prior context, the use of definite NPs would independently introduce context-target links, regardless of syntactic structure. The experimental materials (with a small number of exceptions) therefore contained *only* indefinite NPs, bare plurals, or ones marked with *a, some*, etc. These are NPs of a type which Haviland and Clark say are *not* likely to suggest prior mention. Each target sentence also contained at least two NPs, so that a given NP would not be perceived as topic by default of any other competing NPs. Finally, the target sentences were exemplars of one and only one transformation, even though, for example, *There* Insertion can apply in Passive sentences.

1.3.1. Passive

The contexts used for the active and passive sentences are illustrated in (10), paired with the targets in (11).

(10) a. (neutral)
          Police reported the details of *a recent kidnapping.*
     b. (Favors active)
          Strange men have been on the prowl recently.
     c. (Favors passive)
          Children should never be allowed to walk alone.

Target sentences:

(11) a. (active)
          A man in California abducted a six-year-old girl.
     b. (passive)
          A six-year-old girl was abducted by a man in California.

In the neutral context, the phrase *a recent kidnapping* indirectly suggests antecedents for both *a man . . .* and *a six-year-old girl*, but does not make one more salient than the other. The context favoring the active form mentions *strange men* but not children, so that it contains an explicit antecedent for *A man in California*. An exact repetition of the same NP would have required a pronoun in the target sentence, to which the same objection can be made as to definite NPs. Hence the antecedent and target sentence mentioned were related in one of several ways. In the sequence (10b) followed by (11a), as well as in the sequence (10c) followed by (11b), the context mentions a general class, of which a specific instance or subset is mentioned in the target sentence. Other relations between content and target NPs include equivalent descriptions, specific/general relations, and inferred connections, as in the neutral context.

1.3.2. There *Insertion*

In the active-passive pair above, the two NPs appearing in subject position in one or the other version are NPs which refer to actual entities in the world, and so are able to have antecedents. In the case of *There* Insertion, the original subject is a referential NP, but the expletive *there* which displaces the subject has no reference. Hence if it is perceived as a topic, it is not a topic with an antecedent, and it lacks connection with anything in the context. For this reason, *there* cannot facilitate processing by introducing a link with the context. The postverbal, displaced NP lacks subject qualities, and is noninitial, and so should be hard to perceive as topic *even if* it has an antecedent in the context.

(12) *Contexts*
    a. (neutral)
        Political instability is a common feature of Third World countries.
    b. (Favors untransformed version)
        Revolutions are typically glossed over in American textbooks.
    c. (Favors transformed version)
        Latin America is a difficult region to study.

(13) *Targets*
    a. (untransformed version)
        Numerous revolutions have occurred in Latin America since 1900.
    b. (transformed version)
        There have occurred numerous revolutions in Latin America since 1900.

In the neutral context, *political instability* can be taken either as a general case of which *numerous revolutions* is a specific instance, or it can be regarded as an equivalent under a different description. Hence neither the untransformed version nor the transformed version is especially favored. The second context allows the nearly equivalent expressions *revolutions* (class) and *numerous revolutions* (set of instances) to match. The empirical question here is whether the transformed version *allows* the match: Is the postposed phrase *numerous revolutions* accessible for matching with an antecedent? Finally, the third context provides an antecedent for a phrase *not* in subject role or subject position – that is, *Latin America*, which also occurs in the target sentence in an adverbial prepositional phrase. Hence the transformed version is favored, because it introduces mention of something that typically has not occurred before and is *not* represented in the context (cf. Milsark, 1977).

1.3.3. Adverb Preposing

The contexts used for Adverb Preposing were of the following type:

(14) *Contexts*
    a. (neutral)
        Discarding trash properly is important while driving.
    b. (Favors untransformed version)
        People can be fined for not properly disposing of trash.
    c. (Favors transformed version)
        You must obey state laws when traveling in Illinois.

(15) *Targets*
  a. (untransformed)
      Littering is a legal offense on state highways.
  b. (transformed)
      On state highways, littering is a legal offense.

The neutral context here has inferable antecedents for both the subject of the target sentence (*Littering – discarding trash properly*) and the object of the preposition (*state highways – while driving*), so that neither is favored. The context in (14b) provides no antecedent for *on state highways*, but there is at least an implicit connection between *people* of the context and the expressed subject of *littering* for other cases. Finally, context (14c) has an antecedent for *on state highways* in *traveling in Illinois*, connected by real world knowledge. If this connection is the same antecedent-topic connection made in cases like the Passive, then combinations of the type (14c) followed by (14b) should show a drop in processing time, and the results will support hypothesis I, the linear order hypothesis, over hypothesis II, based on grammatical relations.

1.3.4. Raising to Subject

The contexts in the Raising cases have been defined so as to vary the presence of an antecedent for the subject of the lower clause. There are several reasons for this: the higher clause verbs like *seem* and *believe* are perceived more as epistemic modifiers of the lower clause than as real main clauses (Davison, 1979); the lower clause subject is actually the topic of the whole sentence. And since the higher clause subject of *seem* is *it*, which has no independent referent, it would not be possible in any case to construct an antecedent for it in the context. Contexts for Raising to Object sentences were constructed the same way, to make the context parallel with Raising to Subject sentences, and to see also if a noninitial, nonnominative NP in a marked syntactic structure *could* participate in context-topic links.

The contexts for Raising to Subject were as follows:

(16) *Contexts*
  a. (neutral)
      Research often produces a clearer picture of our past.
  b. (Favors untransformed version)
      Typhoid and cholera may once have been widespread in the New World.
  c. (Favors transformed version)
      The Indian population has almost vanished in some areas.

(17) *Targets*
  a. (untransformed version)
      It seems that many American Indians died as a result of epidemics.
  b. (transformed)
      Many American Indians seem to have died as a result of epidemics.

The context in (16a) is a vague and general statement of which the target sentence is a specific instance, but no specific antecedents occur. The context in (16b) provides a specific antecedent for a general term *not* in subject position, so that the transformed version, which focuses on a topic *without* an antecedent, is strange. The context in (16c) provides an equivalent antecedent for the lower clause subject, whatever its surface position.

1.3.5. Raising to Object

The contexts for Raising to Object were very similar to the previous case.

(18) *Contexts*
    a. (neutral)
        You can't trust anyone anymore.
    b. (Favors untransformed version)
        Blackmail is a fairly common type of white collar crime.
    c. (Favors transformed version)
        City officials can be very corrupt.

(19) *Targets*
    a. (untransformed version)
        Recent investigations have proved that a former mayor is a blackmailer.
    b. (transformed version)
        Recent investigations have proved a former mayor to be a blackmailer.

The neutral context is again a very vague general statement, with the target sentence as a whole a specific instance. The second context provides no antecedent for *a former mayor*, so that *if* the syntax of the transformed version defines it as a topic, the sequence (18b)–(19b) should be odd, at least by comparison with (18b)–(19a) or (18c)–(19b). The sequence of the third context and the transformed version should be well-formed (18c)–(19b) because of the general–specific relation of *city officials* and *a former mayor*; the other sequence of (18c)–(19a) is also possible if the upper clause material is also pragmatically interpreted as an epistemic modifier, a source of the asserted proposition, rather than a part of the asserted proposition as its syntactic structure suggests (Davison, 1979).

1.3.6. Summary: features of context and target sentences

In general, context I is a plausible introduction to either form of the target sentence, but nothing in it matches one target form more than the other form. In the strongest case, context II provides a match with one target form, the untransformed version, but not with the other. Context III should provide a clear match for the transformed version of the target sentence, but not the untransformed version. Because of particular features of certain transformations, and the syntactic conditions and semantic elements governing the rules, *all* of these contrasts are not always found. The relations between context and target vary somewhat over the five transformations. The sequences used for Raising to Subject were based on inferences from real-world knowledge somewhat more than for other transformations; but this fact could be ascribed to the nature of the verbs, *seem, appear, happen*, and the like, which govern Raising to Subject.

A primary consideration in composing the context-target sequences was to produce natural sounding texts, which might be excerpts from a paragraph in a newspaper or magazine story. The context-target combinations were judged by two or three people other than the person who wrote them, and judgments were based on (1) whether one or the other target version would be a preferred continuation from the context, and (2) whether there was in the mismatched cases an "abrupt shift" from the context to target sentence, or something "disconnected" or "illogical."

The constraints on the target sentences have been mentioned. These include the avoidance of pronouns and define NPs in most cases and the application of at most one of the five transformations described in the previous sections. The constraints on the contexts included (1) presence or absence of a referent for an NP in the following sentence and (2) a relation to the target sentence as described above. One constraint that could have been imposed, but was not, was a matching (or mismatch) of the sentence topics of both the context and target sentences. As the items were constructed, the NP antecedent in the context sentence is either in a grammatical subject NP, or it is part of the predicate, interpreted as *focus* of the sentence, with sentence stress as the last major constituent, and interpreted as new information. Strict parallelism of grammatical role of the coreferent NPs in the context and the target was not imposed. There were several reasons for this.

One major reason has to do with experimental evidence for memory for the exact syntactic form in which previously processed sentences are encoded. The results of Jarvella (1971) show that sentence processing proceeds clause by clause, and that material in a clause already processed is less accessible than material in the clause being processed. Various experiments have shown that memory for the exact syntactic form of a sentence is not very exact, and that therefore sentences are not necessarily encoded in memory, after processing, in verbatim form. Properties of surface form not encoded include the various ways in which clauses can be connected (Bransford and Franks, 1971); verbs, deleted subjects, and active versus passive structure (Wanner, 1974); and active versus passive structure (Olsen and Filby, 1972; J. R. Anderson, 1974; Glucksberg, Trabasso, and Wald, 1973). If the sentence topic is defined as a subject or initial element of a sentence, and subject role and initial position in surface structures can vary, then this syntactic information is just the kind of sentence property which is generally not encoded in long-term memory after processing. This information in the context sentence is therefore not certain to be available when the following target sentence is processed. What *is* certain to be available is mention of an NP in the preceding context, which is stored in long-term memory as a referential index. The results of Haviland and Clark's study (1974) shows that explicit previous mention of an antecedent NP facilitates processing a sentence containing the definite NP. But the facilitation is not dependent on the surface syntactic role of the antecedent.

A study of a somewhat different kind, by Kantor (1977), supports the notion that the match of an NP and a previous mention is not necessarily related to the syntactic role of the antecedent. Kantor noted that it is sometimes quite easy to find the antecedent of a pronoun in a text, and sometimes difficult. He defined three degrees of accessibility of antecedents, called "activation": (1) *inactivated*, because of intervening NPs that could serve as antecedents; (2) *activated*, with no deceptive intervening competitors; and (3) *highly activated*, highlighted by lexical factors such as demonstratives *this, that*, or other semantic means. He found no purely syntactic factors, such as subject versus nonsubject role, or occurrence in main versus subordinate clauses.

Meanwhile we have become aware of studies showing that *some* residual memory for surface structure may remain. This seems to be especially the case when the task makes the subject concentrate on retrieving the semantic role of a definite NP and the surface form of the sentence in which it occurred (J. R. Anderson, 1974) or to retrieve the referent of a pronoun (J. Fredericksen, 1982). But in our experiment, the task was to read and integrate two sentences, so that the subjects' attention was not specially directed to individual NPs or to sentence form. In the experimental materials, the role of the antecedent was approximately evenly distributed between topic and focus position, and when the experimenters reexamined the items, no bias attributable to the role of an NP in a context sentence was detected. We do not have any evidence that the results were distorted by this factor.

1.4. Predictions

We may summarize the predictions in the following way. The transformed versions of all the sentence types will be harder to process than the untransformed versions, all other things being equal. Processing time will not be affected by the neutral context, which is equally compatible with either version. But in contexts establishing a discourse referent for some item in the following sentence, it will be the grammatical structure of the target sentence which determines a salient constituent for linking to previous context and so reduces or increases processing time. Since the transformed and untransformed versions differ in grammatical relations and also in word order, in most cases, the sentence structure will define different salient elements to link to previous context.

There are two possible hypotheses about *which* sentence constituents will be perceived as salient, as linkable to previous context, or as sentence topic. Hypothesis I defines topic purely by position. Hence any initial item will be topic, and perhaps the closer it is to the beginning of the sentence, the more salient it will be. Thus preposed adverbs ought to be more salient and topiclike than subjects if they occur together. Hypothesis II defines sentence topic in terms of *subject*, including both preverbal position and grammatical marking. Subjects are often initial in the sentence, if nothing else precedes, but if they retain their grammatical role and preverbal position, they should remain salient.

Adverb Preposing is a crucial case which distinguishes hypothesis I from hypothesis II, since adverbials are moved to initial position but do not acquire subject marking. If hypothesis I is correct, there should be a difference in processing time between transformed and untransformed version in biased contexts, just like what is predicted for active and passive sentences. There should be no difference under hypothesis II. The Raising to Object case is also an interesting test of whether initial position and grammatical subject marking are *always* required for topic status. In the transformed version, the lower clause subject remains in preverbal position, but is not initial in the whole sentence and has object marking. If grammatical subject marking is *invariably* and hence linguistically associated with topic, then the lower clause object should not be perceived as topic in the transformed version, and there should be a difference in processing time in biased contexts. If it remains topic, then this fact would suggest that the association of grammatical marking with topic is pragmatic and essentially not the direct effect of the operation of rules of grammar in English.

1.5. Defining sentence topic and discourse topic

These notions are exceedingly difficult to define exhaustively, the most probable reason for the difficulty being that they are pragmatic and not grammatical categories. Yet topic, particularly sentence topic, is closely linked to linguistic structures, both semantic and syntactic. Differences of syntactic structure often convey differences of sentence topic, and features of syntax or morphology are often used, in many languages, to mark a sentence topic to be related to the topic of the discourse as a whole (Li, 1976). One of the most common regularities is the identification of grammatical subject with sentence topic (Li and Thompson, 1976). All other things being equal, it is generally the case that subject equals sentence topic in English.

Reinhart (1981) makes the useful distinction between *sentence topic* and *discourse topic*. The latter is defined by features of discourse outside the sentence, including knowledge of the immediate context, and does not necessarily correspond to any constituent of a particular sentence. It need not even be a property of a linguistic entity; pictures and films may have (discourse) topics. A *sentence topic* is an overt linguistic constituent of a sentence, marked by grammatical properties of the sentence, including word order, choice of lexical items, and various morphological features. It is what is perceived as what the sentence is *about* (Reinhart, 1981), to which other information in the sentence is related. Hence topic in our view has more to do with salience of some sort, often marked by grammatical features, and less with the pragmatic condition that the content of the expression is old information at that point in the discourse. Of course communication is sometimes less effective if the speaker does *not* have prior and detailed knowledge of what is being talked about, but the status of "old information" is not enough to define a topic. The role of grammatical salience is shown by the fact that a sentence *in isolation*, with no prior context, may differ in what is perceived as sentence topic. Clear examples of this are found in the active-passive pairs in (1a,b) and (3a,b).

Finally, we are assuming that every sentence has at most one sentence topic. There would appear to be a functional basis for this restriction, since communication at a specific point in discourse may be facilitated if it is clear that new information is to be related to a single entity, and hindered if there are several possible individuals or things that the information could be predicated of.[6] The following example shows that, for whatever reason, English does not permit a sentence to have two distinct explicit topics. Compare (20a) with (20b).

(20) a. That guy, we believe him/ Ø to be the mastermind behind those crimes.
      b. ??Those crimes, we believe that guy to be the mastermind behind them/ Ø.

If a topicalized or dislocated phrase such as *that guy* or *those crimes* may be perceived as a topic, and the lower clause subject is a topic when Raising to Object occurs, then a sentence may have both these syntactic properties if they match in defining the *same* topic, as in (20a). But a sentence like (20b) is pragmatically very strange in comparison to (20a), because it defines two NPs as the sentence topics.

1.6. The task

The subjects were 59 undergraduates at the University of Illinois, who volunteered to participate in the experiment as part of a requirement for the introductory course in educational psychology. The items were presented in randomized order on the screen of a PLATO 4.5 terminal, and response times were recorded for the target sentences. Each subject was instructed to read the paired items in each sequence as though they were excerpts from ordinary texts, such as newspaper or magazine feature articles or news items. They performed the task individually, because the computer program did not allow simultaneous presentations. The features of the experimental items have been described in sections 1.2 and 1.3. After a subject had read and comprehended (as in the study by Haviland and Clark, 1974) the first sentence in a pair, he or she was to press the space bar. This action would erase the context sentence and cause the target sentence to appear on the terminal screen. Time was measured in milliseconds from the onset of the second sentence (which appeared as a whole) to the time that the subject pressed the space bar. The next item was presented in the same fashion after a short interval. The full set of instructions is included in Appendix 1. Note that the subjects were instructed to read at whatever rate was normal for them for the kind of material in the task (e.g., newspapers or magazines). After all the experiment items were presented, subjects were asked to fill out a questionnaire about how they approached the task, and what they felt about the items (interesting or not, natural sounding or unnatural). Data from one subject was discarded, of the original 60 subjects, because this subject reported that she read the items as though studying for a test.

For a given target sentence, there were six combinations of context and target version (see examples in section 1.3). To guarantee that each subject would not see the same target sentence twice, there were six sets of the six combinations, in a Latin square design. Thus each subject saw an exemplar in each of the six possible combinations (e.g., context 1 – with untransformed target version), but not two from the same paradigmatic set. There were 3 complete arrays of these paradigms for each of the 5 transformation types, so that there were 540 sentence pairs in all. Of these, each subject saw 90, representing 3 comparable pairs for each of 30 combinations (6 paradigms × 5 transformation types). The sentence pairs of the correct type were chosen and presented in randomized order by the PLATO program used.

1.7. Results

The 59 subjects responded to 90 items each, generating a total of 5,310 items. A very small number of these (about 18) were discarded because they were deviant, below 1,000 milliseconds (msec) or above 8,000 msec, and probably represent errors of response or recording. The 90 responses represent three responses to the same *type* of context-target combination, and these were averaged for each subject. Mean response times for all

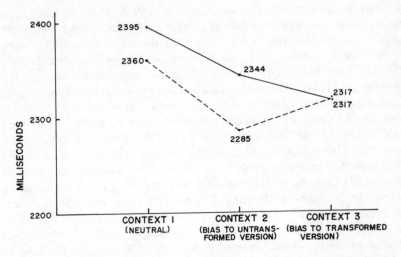

Figure 1.2.   Comparison of mean response times (five transformations) for transformed and untransformed versions of target sentences, in three contexts. ——— = transformed version of target sentences; − − − − = untransformed version of target sentences.

transformation classes, transformed version and untransformed version, in three contexts, are given in Figure 1.2. The results were analyzed using an analysis of variables (ANOVA) with transformation type (passive, etc.), target version (transformed and untransformed) and context properties (neutral, biased to untransformed, biased to transformed version) as factors. Initially, the ANOVA included all five transformation types. The analysis revealed a significant effect for transformation type, $F(4,232)$ = 14.82, $p < .001$, and a significant interaction of transformation type by target version, $F(4,232) = 4.63$, $p < .01$. The effect of context was significant, $F(2,116) = 3.85$, $p < .05$, but in this analysis the difference of target versions alone was not significant. Other interactions were not significant.

The means for the individual transformation types, which will be discussed in detail in the next section, revealed one transformation type where the results did not conform to the overall pattern found elsewhere. This transformation type, Raising to Subject, was dropped from the subsequent statistical analyses (see also section 1.8). An ANOVA similar to the first one was done, but without the means for this transformation, and the results were the same except that the difference between transformed and untransformed versions was significant, $F(1,58) = 6.70$, $p < .05$. Another ANOVA was performed using as a covariate the average word length and the transformed and untransformed versions for each transformation type (e.g., passive sentences average 13.5 words, although

Table 1.1 *Statistical Analyses*

Variables	Analysis 1		Analysis 2		Analysis 3	
Transformation	$F = 14.82$	$p < .00$	$F = 21.95$	$p < .00$	$F = 10.99$	$p < .00$
Context	3.85	.05	3.37	.05	1.78	n.s.
Target version	2.02	n.s.	6.70	.02	6.70	.02
Transformation × target	4.63	.01	4.15	.01	1.35	n.s.

Analysis 1: five transformations, analysis of variance.
Analysis 2: four transformations (excluding Raising to Subject transformation), analysis of variance.
Analysis 3: four transformations (excluding Raising to Subject), average sentence length a covariate.

active sentences are 2 words shorter; and these in turn are both longer than Adverb Preposing sentences, both versions having 11.6 words on average). The effect for transformation and for target version were of the same degree of significance as before (respectively, $F(3,173) = 10.99$, $p < .001$, and $F(1,57) = 6.70, p < .05$). The difference of number of words is therefore not sufficient to account for the characteristic response times for transformation types, or for the difference of transformed and untransformed versions. Other effects were not significant in the covariate analysis. The results are summarized in Table 1.1. Overall, the difficulty in parsing created by the sentence structure of the transformed version is offset, or more than offset, by the facilitating effect of the "right" kind of context. This is true for the means over all five transformation types (Figure 1.2) and even more so over four transformation types, excluding Raising to Subject (Figure 1.3).

The "right" kind of context was defined in terms of the *topic* of the target sentence. As we have seen, there are several ways that *sentence topic* could be viewed. It could be regarded as the initial element in the sentence, including main clause preverbal subjects in general, and also preposed elements (hypothesis I). Alternatively, topic might include just preverbal subjects, regardless of what is initial in the sentence (hypothesis II). If hypothesis I is correct, we would expect complete uniformity in the results for each transformation type, that is, some gap between higher values for transformed versions in contexts 1 and 2, and lower values for the untransformed version, with the gap widest in context 2 and narrowest in context 3. In fact, what we find is some variation in the transformation types, sufficient to show that hypothesis I is incorrect, and that *sentence topic*, which does seem to serve as the facilitating link between context and target, should be regarded as a preverbal *subject*. Position alone does

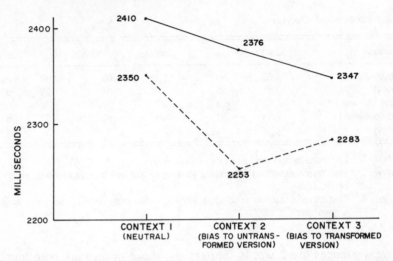

Figure 1.3.   Comparison of mean response times (msec) (four transformations, excluding Raising to Subject). ____ = transformed version of target sentences; - - - - = untransformed version of target sentences.

not define topic; the grammatical role of subject is also a critical factor, as is the composition of the whole sentence (that is, what elements must be present for the transformation to apply). In some cases, subordinate clause subjects may also be topic of the whole structure. The results for individual types, which will be discussed in detail in the following section, point toward hypothesis II as the correct view.

1.8. Discussion

Figure 1.2 shows the overall effects of context and target sentence. Note that in the neutral context there is some difference between means for transformed and untransformed versions of the target sentence. The difference is in the direction that was predicted, according to the parsing difficulty hypothesis mentioned earlier. The context biased for the untransformed version does lower response time for the untransformed version, much more than for the transformed version. Any difference between the two versions disappears in context 3, biased toward the transformed version. Response time for the transformed version is lowered still more in context 3, while not being increased overall for the untransformed version. Figure 1.4 gives means for contexts.

The results for four of the types fall into natural pairs. Passive and *There* Insertion follow approximately the same pattern, Figures 1.1 and 1.5. Note that context 2 and the untransformed version are highly con-

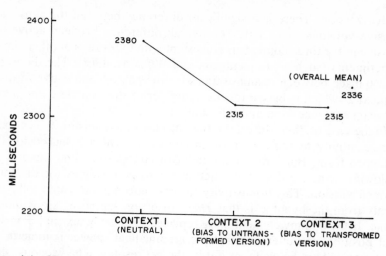

Figure 1.4.   Mean response times (msec) to both versions of target sentences, in three contexts. _____ = transformed version of target sentences.

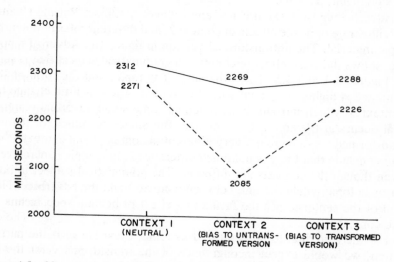

Figure 1.5.   Mean response times (msec) for *There* Insertion transformation. _____ = transformed version of target sentences; - - - - = untransformed version of target sentences.

gruent, as shown by the sharp drop in reaction time. The context leads the reader to expect the topic of the following sentence in subject position, and this expectation is borne out by the form of the untransformed version. The transformed Passive sentence is incongruent with context 2, as shown by an increase in reaction time. There is little change in context 3 from the neutral case, even with the incongruence of context 3 and the active version. There is a significant difference between the active and passive versions, $p < .001$. The overall difference between active and passive in the three contexts is consistent with the results of other similar experiments (such as Tannenbaum and Williams, 1968). The difference of 260 msec between response times for the passive and active forms in context 2 (which is biased for the active form) shows a clear interaction between sentence form and this context.

In the case of *There* Insertion, the untransformed version shows a similar sensitivity to sentence form in context 2, which is biased for that sentence form. But information about discourse topic and topic of the following sentence does not much affect response times for the transformed version. This insensitivity to topic information would follow directly from the hypothesis that *There* Insertion sentences are without a topic. If the dummy element *there* replaces a referring lexical NP in subject position, the inference that the grammatical subject is topic of the sentence will not be made, or if it is, the net result will be vacuous, since *there* expresses nothing for the sentence to be *about*. The effect of context is significant, $p < .05$.

Adverb Preposing (Figure 1.6) and Subject to Object Raising (Figure 1.7) illustrate opposite effects of context 2, and different roles of potential topic material. The untransformed version in figure 1.6, Adverb Preposing, shows the same effect of context on grammatical subject that is seen in Figures 1.1 and 1.5. Thus, the subject is topic, and the form of the sentence is highly congruent with the context. There is little change for context 3, which introduces as potential topic some adverbial material that occurs at the end of the sentence. But since the values for the untransformed version are not very different in context 2 and context 3, we can conclude that there is not much difference in how topic is perceived, even though the contexts are different. The grammatical subject in both cases is topic, while the link between context 3 and the adverbial at the end of the sentence has the facilitating effect of being a specific link to the context.

For the adverbial to be perceived as topic, by virtue of its initial position, we would expect incongruence of the transformed version with context 2, which is biased toward the grammatical subject as topic, as in the case of Passive. Further, we would expect congruence of the transformed version with context 3, but instead reaction time is increased in context 3. Moreover, the general trend is for reaction times to *both* versions of the sentence to go in the same direction. This case is decisive against hypothesis I, initial elements as topic, and for hypothesis II, preverbal grammatical subjects as topic. Preposed adverbial material is usually felt to express old information, taken for granted, and thus similar to some definitions of topic, as given information or information previously men-

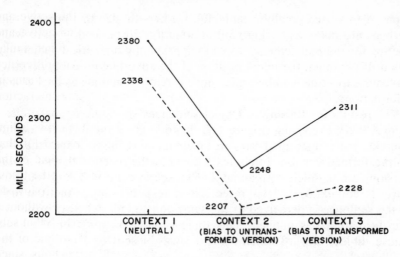

Figure 1.6.   Mean response times (msec) for the Adverb Preposing transformation. ____ = transformed version of target sentences; ____ = untransformed version of target sentences.

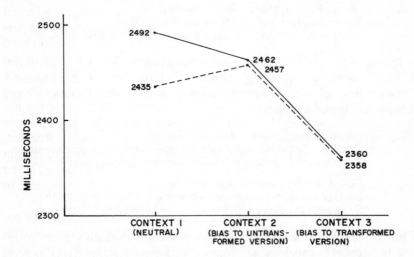

Figure 1.7.   Mean response times (msec) for the Raising to Object transformation. ____ = transformed version of target sentences; ____ = untransformed version of target sentences.

tioned. But we see that the preposed material is apparently not taken as *salient* enough in contexts which bias the reader toward the grammatical subject as topic. The response times simply parallel the times for the untransformed version. Note also that there is a slight rise for the transformed version in context 3, biasing the reader toward the adverbial as topic. If this rise is really meaningful, we hypothesize that preposed adverbials are taken as background information, to be held in store while waiting for the real sentence topic to appear, in grammatical subject position. If anything, the initial position of the adverbial probably confuses a reader expecting it to be topic, since it really functions as background information.

The results for Raising to Object sentences show the opposite effect from Adverb Preposing (Figure 1.7), in contexts 2 and 3. In the neutral context, the transformed version takes about 60 msec longer than the untransformed version. In contexts 2 and 3, the reaction times for *both* versions are parallel, both about 2,460 msec in context 2, and 100 msec *lower* in context 3, or 2,360 msec. These responses argue that the topic of the sentence is perceived as the same constituent, whether or not the transformation has applied. This topic constituent must be the lower clause subject, toward which context 3 was biased:

(21) − Object Raising, context favors Raising
         There are reports of UFOs on the West Coast.
         Some people believe that a flying saucer is heading toward L.A.

(22) + Object Raising, context favors Raising
         There are reports of UFOs on the West Coast.
         Some people believe a flying saucer to be heading toward L.A.

In this example, the NP *a flying saucer* has an antecedent *UFOs* in context 3, which establishes it as an existent thing and part of the discourse. Contrast this pair above with the corresponding pairs of context 2 and Raising to Object sentences:

(23) − Object Raising, context disfavors Raising
         Southern California might soon become a dangerous place to live.
         Some people believe that a flying saucer is heading toward L.A.

(24) + Object Raising, context disfavors Raising
         Southern California might soon become a dangerous place to live.
         Some people believe a flying saucer to be heading toward L.A.

There is clearly an incongruence between the transformed version in (24) and the context that does *not* contain an antecedent for *flying saucer*. Apparently the combination in (24) was treated the same way, in that *flying saucer* was perceived as topic without a discourse antecedent, and thus not clearly compatible with the context that preceded.

The Raising rules which operate on two-clause structures and affect the lower clause subjects are somewhat different from other cases such as Passive and Adverb Preposing. For one thing, the Raising rules depend crucially on the presence of a particular type of verb in the matrix clause. Various syntactic factors are associated with the presence of a verb like *seem* or *believe*, and in both cases the lower clause subject is affected: it is extracted into the higher clause (Raising to Subject), or marked as an object (Raising to Object). In Raising rules, both semantic and syntactic conditions of a special nature are involved, while Adverb Preposing simply applies to an adverbial, with minor nonlexical exceptions.

It can be argued that the Raising rules create marked combinations of syntactic constituents, and that they serve (or *can* serve) to make a particular NP salient and topiclike as a result of the marked syntactic properties of the NP. A subject displaced out of its clause and a subject with inappropriate accusative marking are not found in any other construction in English and so are not the run of the mill subjects. They fail to conform to normal expectations, which yield correct interpretations elsewhere. We hypothesize that these NPs will be perceived as sentence topics because of salience based on the markedness of their properties. There is some evidence that this is so for Raising to Object based on the restrictions on the NP types which occur in Raising to Object sentences. The restrictions are illustrated by the contrast of raised and unraised sentences in (25) and (26).

(25) a. ??They believed *the slightest noise* to be irritating to him.
       b. ??We supposed *any doctor* to know the answer.
       c. ??They declared *tabs* to have been kept on all the suspects.

(26) a. They believed that the slightest noise was irritating to him.
       b. We supposed that any doctor would know the answer.
       c. They declared that tabs had been kept on all the suspects.

Borkin (1974) found, in a study of speakers' preferences, that NPs such as superlatives, generic *any* phrases, and parts of idioms (such as *tabs*) made poor NPs in subordinate clause subject position when Raising applies. Davison (1979) proposes that the explanation lies in properties of the NPs as possible topics: they do not have clear referents, and it is hard to pick out directly the objects which such NPs refer to – if there is such a thing at all. Yet to be communicating something *about* a given entity, referred to by a sentence topic phrase, suggests that the speaker has some knowledge of the thing in question. Hence a pragmatic conflict arises in sentences of the kind in (25), where the markedness of the syntax defines an NP as a salient element but the internal content of the NP suggests that it is something the speaker cannot know much about, and so it is not a good topic phrase. This conflict internal to the sentence is also paralleled in the combination of Raising sentences with contexts that provide no antecedent for the NP made salient and defined as topic. Response time is longer in this case than when the context does provide an antecedent (Figure 1.7).

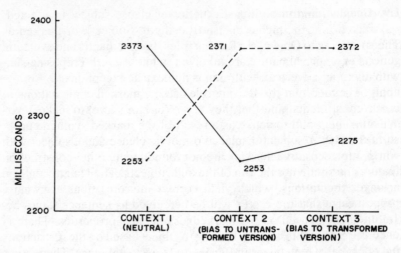

Figure 1.8.   Mean response times (msec) for the Raising to Subject transformation. ___ = transformed version of target sentences; – – – – = untransformed version of target sentences.

The results for Raising to Subject appear anomalous by comparison. Response times are much faster than for Raising to Object, and the untransformed version has longer response times than the transformed version in both facilitating and nonfacilitating contexts. Overall, it may be that the surface structure produced by Raising to Subject is simply less marked, or unusual, than for the other Raising case. Raising to Subject produces a surface structure very similar to the structure in which Equi-NP Deletion applies:

(27)   a.   Miss Garbo$_i$ wants (___$_i$ to be alone).
       b.   Miss Garbo$_i$ seems (___$_i$ to be here).

The raised case does seem to match facilitating contexts, with resulting decrease of processing time (Figure 1.8).

The puzzle is to explain the increase of processing for the untransformed case. The answer may lie in the meaning of the verbs governing the rule. These are verbs indicating doubt, lack of definite knowledge, or accidental truth (*seem, appear, happen, turn out, likely,* etc.). Sentences with these as main verbs convey hedged assertions and may be pragmatically strange if they follow unhedged or categorical assertions. Something of this kind is involved in many of the context-target pairs, and if so it was not noted beforehand in norming the experimental items. Work still remains to be done to explain exactly why Raising to Subject cases differ from the other Raising rule both in markedness and in how topic NPs are perceived.

1.9. Concluding discussion and summary

The overall results (Figures 1.3 and 1.4) suggest that processing time in general is greater for the transformed version of a sentence as compared with the corresponding sentence in which the transformation does not apply. These results are consistent with the view that syntactic processing is automatic and simultaneous with other kinds of processing (Marslen-Wilson, 1973). These results support the *markedness hypothesis*: If the surface structure contains *marked* syntactic and morphological features, which represent underlying grammatical relations less directly than the features of another corresponding surface structure, then there should be a longer processing time for the first type of sentence compared with processing necessary for the latter kind of sentence. The results in Figures 1.3 and 1.4 also indicate that the preceding linguistic context may influence the *amount* of processing difference, in some cases the difference between transformed and untransformed versions, in other cases where there is a meaningful difference and where there is not.

In the preceding discussion we have noted that in each subcase, or set of sentences in which a particular transformation could apply, the pattern of responses is different from the other cases. Some of these idiosyncratic differences can readily be explained in terms of certain features of the constructions in question; others are not. Inevitably, there will be differences in the overall patterns of responses to sentence representing different transformations. As we noted in section 1.7, one of the largest effects was in the responses by transformation type. This sort of effect is a consequence of the fact that the syntactic constructions of English are not uniform. The Passive transformation (or construction) requires a main verb of a certain kind, generally one describing a volitional act, and a subject NP and object NP. There is no other construction in English *exactly* comparable to the Passive – that is, having exactly the same features as Passive. The reason is that constructions are defined and distinguished from others by syntactic, morphological, and lexical traits. Some transformations do not apply to single clauses, only to combinations of one clause within another (e.g., the Raising rules). Some, like the Raising rules and Passive, require a main verb belonging to a specific lexical class, others, such as *There* Insertion, require a verb belonging to a much more loosely defined semantic class, and still others, such as Adverb Preposing, impose no lexical conditions at all. In order to generalize across transformations in choosing the sentence constructions to be included in the experiment, it was necessary to compare transformations in more abstract terms, noting common properties such as movement to or from subject position, case marking, and subject-defining properties such as verb agreement. Because of the variation inherent in the sentences representing different transformations, there may be some degree of variation in the results. We have tried, however, to make the sentences within each transformation as uniform as possible in the general traits we believe are relevant to the variable in the experiment.

It is inevitable also that there will be some reservations about data produced in the kind of task used in this experiment. Reaction times obtained in this experiment are fairly long (the overall mean was 2,336 msec), so that differences of a certain value among them are less striking than if the times being compared were shorter. The task itself introduces some uncertainty. If the results are meaningful as measures of the amount of processing being done, it must be assumed that the subjects were attending closely to reading and understanding the sentences, and that there was no lag between the time they decided that they had understood the sentence and when they pressed the key. Sharper results might be obtained by using a different task, such as asking the subjects to decide if the relations between the context and target sentences was a good, bad, or indifferent match. With somewhat greater complications for the construction of the items for the PLATO program and the procedures, we might have used monitoring for rhymes or semantically related words (Seidenberg and Tanenhaus, 1981) to indicate where high processing loads occurred. A task of this sort was initially discussed in planning the experiment but rejected because of the additional complexities it would place on an already rather complex design.

We would predict that the high load of processing would occur in subject position of the target sentence, particularly in the transformed version of the constructions in which the position or marking of the subject is affected. The syntactic element in this position is what matches or fails to match with information in the context sentence. We are assuming that the processing time for a given sentence includes identification of syntactic constituents, semantic interpretation of their grammatical roles (and other interrelations), and finally, matching of referential expression with the context. In particular, the information derived from processing the context sentence contains referential indices for each individual (or class) mentioned. The context information probably does not always affect the processing time for syntactic identification and assignment of grammatical roles relative to the verb.

But it clearly does affect the time needed to match referential indices already available with NPs and the referents in the sentence being processed. Concerning the importance of syntactic markedness in context-target matches, we hypothesize that marked syntactic features, associated with subject properties, define a salient constituent, the *sentence topic*. This salient element is immediately matched with the array of referential indices derived from context information. Success in matching indices reduces processing time in the amounts shown; if we had used definite NPs and proper names exclusively, the NPs would have been even more salient and the results might have been more striking. But we were interested in seeing the degree to which syntactic structure *alone* could define a NP as salient and therefore a topic.

If we had been able to perform this experiment with equipment which measured eye-movements, we would have had a more accurate measure of actual reading time for the sentences as wholes. We would also have had information about the specific locations in which the subject's eyes paused for longer times, or where regressions occurred. We would predict that where the context matched the salient NP in the target sentence, there would be short fixations on the subject NP. In the case of the mismatch of context and target, there would be longer fixations and some regressions at or shortly after the subject NP (Frazier and Rayner, 1982). There is some indication from studies of eye movement that the subject NP does not receive long fixations in normal cases. Rayner (1978) replicated several earlier studies that indicated that fixations on the major constituents of active, declarative sentences are longer for the verb than for the subject or object. Compare this fact with the fact that verbs are verified faster than other constituents (Glucksberg, Trabasso, and Wald, 1973).

Even though the subject is normally encountered before the verb in English sentences, the subject does not undergo as much processing as the verb, assuming that fixation time is an approximate measure of cognitive processing (see the caveats in McConkie, 1982). In normal English discourse, subjects are likely to refer to elements represented in the context (Prince, 1980). That is, speakers use sentence structures in which the syntactic constituent expressing the subject tends to refer to an element in the discourse context, or *evoked* in Prince's term. Hearers try to interpret elements having syntactic subject properties as referring to entities present in the discourse context. Our model of sentence processing is consistent with the results reported in Rayner (1978), and does not postulate an underlying constituent order placing the verb before the subject as in Glucksberg, Trabasso, and Wald (1973). An NP given the interpretation of subject is immediately matched with context, especially if it has "marked" syntactic and morphological properties. Thus this constituent is likely to be processed rapidly, if the discourse is not abnormal, as in our context-target mismatch cases. The verb, and in particular the lexical item that instantiates the verb, encodes a great deal of information, such as the exact semantic role assigned to its subject, and the role of the object, as well as whether there must be or may be objects, and other constituents. The verb carries a high information load about sentence structure and the relations of its constituents (Bresnan, 1978; Chomsky,

1981) so that it is not at all surprising that it receives greater attention than other major constituents which in fact will tend to be longer and more elaborated than the verb. There is no need to postulate a verb-initial semantic encoding, as in Glucksberg et al. (1973), nor to assume that active and passive sentences have different semantic encodings. The differences between active and passive, untransformed and transformed sentences can be explained without assuming an otherwise unmotivated semantic difference of this kind.

In this experiment, reaction time for reading and comprehending the second of two sentences in sequence was used as a measure of the processing load required by the syntactic structure of the target sentence in relation to the information provided by the preceding context sentence. By making the NPs in the target sentences indefinite, and therefore *semantically* nonsalient (at least in terms of prior reference), we were able to define the contribution of the syntactic surface structure of the target sentence in defining a salient constituent or sentence topic. The particular features of syntactic structure word order and morphology, which make an NP salient, were arrived at by comparing five different syntactic constructions, which were related in the same way to preceding contexts.

The pattern of responses to each syntactic construction was different, but there were overall similarities. These common features of different constructions showed that the transformed version of a sentence does place a higher processing load on a hearer/reader than the corresponding untransformed structure, at least in a neutral context. The higher processing load can be attributed not to semantic differences, but to marked features of surface structure, which make recovery of grammatical relations less straightforward than in the unmarked case. The marked features of syntax also serve to define as sentence topic a salient NP constituent in the sentence, generally a subject. In at least four of the syntactic constructions studied, the responses showed that processing time is affected by contextual information related to the sentence topic. Further, the results allow us to distinguish between two definitions of sentence topic; the definition based on subject properties including word order matches the results better than the definition based on initial order in the sentence. For four constructions out of the five, we were able to isolate to some degree the relative contributions of syntactic surface structure, meaning and pragmatic information, which all enter into the interpretation of a sentence in actual uses of language. Variations of word order and morphology as in the English passive–active correspondence and other English constructions also are found widely in other natural languages. While we can only speculate about why this kind of syntactic variation is a property of human language, we have shown how this variation in English can be adapted functionally for efficient processing of sentences in discourse.

APPENDIX 1. INSTRUCTIONS TO SUBJECTS

1. You will see pairs of sentences written out on the screen – these will be part of the same paragraph, so that they will be connected in some way.

   The first sentence will be written out by itself. Read it and when you have finished reading it and feel you have comprehended it, press the spacebar. This will bring on the next sentence. Do the same thing – read and comprehend the second sentence, and as soon as you have done this, press the space bar.

2. There will be a practice session to show you how the sentence pairs work, and what you are supposed to do. You can go through all the items in the practice, or go on at any time to the experiment.

3. You can pause at any time between items. You can tell when this is because it is when the middle of the screen says

   Press the space bar to continue.

   Please don't pause between sentences, or when the second sentence is still on the screen.

4. The texts in the experiment are about a lot of different things. The information in the sentences is not necessarily true, though most of it is true.

5. You should rest your hand near the space bar, so that you don't have to reach each time you press it. (But don't keep your finger right *on* the space bar all the time.) Have you ever used a PLATO terminal before? If so, you can use another key if it is more comfortable for you; all of them will work to activate the program.

6. When you read the sentence pairs, read at your normal rate. Don't try to speed up and hurry, or go slower than normal. Read as though you would read something from a feature article or news story in the newspaper. There are no right or wrong answers, and there are no tricks in the task you are asked to do.

7. There may be some short delays between items while the machine is choosing the next sentences.

   When the experiment is over, there will be a sentence on the screen telling you this. After you have finished, you will be told more about what the experiment was about.

(Administer debriefing questionnaire.)

Notes

The research reported in this paper was supported by the National Institute of Education under Contract US-NIE-C-400-76-0116. We received extremely helpful information and much useful advice in planning the experiment from Mark Seidenberg, and we are also indebted to George McConkie for valuable discussion of the experimental items and our interpretation of the results. We thank Jean Hannah for her collaboration in constructing, norming, and revising the experimental items. We are indebted to various people for comments and discussion at various stages of the writing of this paper. These include Robert Kantor, Georgia Green, Carlota Smith, and David Dowty. The PLATO program was written by Bob Yeager of Intercom, whom we thank for his care, patience, and generous assistance. We thank Bill May and Gail Nottenburg for their participation in the statistical analysis of the data.

1. The possibility allowed in ATNs of backtracking or revising the analysis of a string allows access to other but less highly ranked network paths, such as the one accepting passive sentences. The computational cost of backtracking or retrospectively revising an interpretation models the greater complexity or markedness of the passive (Wanner and Maratsos, 1978). The first-ranked or less marked active sentence network corresponds roughly to the structures NP V NP and grammatical interpretations AGENT–ACTION–OBJECT of the clause-level strategy of Bever (1970).

2. We could have included other transformations or constructions, including one moving an object in a lower clause to higher clause subject position (*This story is difficult to believe ∅*) or one leaving behind a pronoun instead of a gap (*That building; looks like it's; going to collapse*). We decided to restrict the items to a fairly small manageable number of transformations, including the ones like Passive and *There* Insertion, which have long been associated with topic perception, the two Raising rules, which might involve topics in the same or in different ways, and Adverb Preposing, which reorders within a clause but does not change grammatical relations.

3. As in the previous section, the names of transformations are used to specify classes of sentences, namely the ones to which the syntactic transformation could apply because its conditions are met. But we are using the names of transformations metaphorically and for convenience without implying a particular derivational model of grammar. The points we make in the text are independent of whether there is some number of transformations that relate syntactic structures in a derivation, or whether rules specifying grammatical relations are lexical, configurationally defined, or are primitives.

4. For example, *The prisoner was released (by the governor)*. In left-to-right sentence processing, there is inevitably some degree of ambiguity of the information available in a passive sentence, even if the auxiliaries *be* or *get* are identified as specific elements and not just representatives of the category V. The distinctive morphology of the passive verb is not available until the main verb has been located, at a point in the sentence beyond the tense, auxiliaries and *be* or *got*. Nonpassive sentences may contain subjects followed by these auxiliaries, and the nonpassive interpretation is therefore a perfectly likely one.

5. Most verbs are subcategorized for the number of objects they may take, or must take, and whether they take nominal, prepositional or sentential complements. A few verbs may be analyzed as being subcategorized for taking adverbial complements, such as *place* (Bresnan, 1978).

6. The restriction of at most one topic to a sentence as having a functional basis was suggested by Adrienne Lehrer (private communication). The range of referring properties of different types of NPs is discussed in Davison (to appear) in relation to a range of syntactic constructions.

References

Anderson, John R. 1974. Verbatim and propositional representation of sentences in immediate and long-term memory. *Journal of Verbal Learning and Verbal Behavior* 13:149–62.

Bach, Emmon. 1980. In defense of passive. *Linguistics and Philosophy* 3:297–341.

Bever, Thomas. 1970. The cognitive basis for linguistic structures. In: John R. Hayes (ed.), *Cognition and the development of language.* New York: Wiley.

Borkin, Ann. 1974. Raising to Object Position: a study of the syntax and semantics of clause merging. Unpublished Ph.D. dissertation, University of Michigan.

Bransford, John, and Jeffrey Franks. 1971. The abstraction of linguistic ideas: a review. *Cognition* 1:211–49.

Bransford, John, and M. K. Johnson. 1972. Contextual prerequisites for understanding: some investigations of comprehension and recall. *Journal of Verbal Learning and Verbal Behavior* 11:717–26.

Bresnan, Joan. 1978. A realistic transformational grammar. In: Morris Halle, Joan Bresnan, and George A. Miller (eds.). *Linguistic theory and psychological reality.* Cambridge, Mass.: MIT Press.

Chafe, Wallace. 1974. Language and consciousness. *Language* 50:111–53.

Chomsky, Noam. 1965. *Aspects of the theory of syntax.* Cambridge, Mass.: MIT Press.
   1981. *Lectures on government and binding.* Dordrecht, Holland: Foris.

Davison, Alice. 1979. Linguistics and the measurement of readability: the case of Raising. In: *Metatheory III, application of linguistic theory in the human sciences.* East Lansing: Michigan State University.
   1984. Syntactic markedness and the definition of sentence topic. *Language.*

Firbas, Jan. 1966. Non-thematic subjects in contemporary English. *Travaux linguistiques de Prague* 2:239–56.

Fodor, Jerry A., and Merrill Garrett. 1967. Some syntactic determinants of sentential complexity. *Perception and Psychophysics* 2:289–96.

Frazier, Lyn, and K. Rayner. 1982. Making and correcting errors during sentence comprehension: eye movements in the analysis of structurally ambiguous sentences. *Cognitive Psychology* 14:178–210.

Frederiksen, John. 1982. Understanding anaphora: rules used by readers in assigning pronominal referents. Technical Report 239. Center for the Study of Reading, Champaign, Ill.

Freidin, Robert. 1975. The analysis of passives. *Language* 51:384–405.

Glucksberg, Samuel, Tom Trabasso, and Jan Wald. 1973. Linguistic structures and mental operations. *Cognitive Psychology* 5:338–70.

Gourlay, J. W., and Jack E. Catlin. 1978. Children's comprehension of grammatical structures in context. *Journal of Psycholinguistic Research* 7:419–34.

Halliday, Michael A. K. 1967. Notes on transitivity and theme in English, II. *Journal of Linguistics* 3:199–244.

Haviland, Susan E., and Herbert H. Clark. 1974. What's new? Acquiring new information as a process in comprehension. *Journal of Verbal Learning and Verbal Behavior* 13:512–21.

Hudson, Rodney. 1976. *Arguments for a non-transformational grammar.* Chicago: University of Chicago Press.

Jarvella, Robert. 1971. Syntactic processing of connected speech. *Journal of Verbal Learning and Verbal Behavior* 10:409–16.

Jespersen, Otto. 1924. *Philosophy of grammar.* (Reprinted 1966, New York: W. W. Norton.)

Kantor, Robert. 1977. The management and comprehension of discourse connection by pronouns. Unpublished Ph.D. dissertation, Ohio State University, Columbus.

Li, Charles (ed.). 1976. *Subject and topic.* New York: Academic Press.

Li, Charles, and Sandra A. Thompson. 1976. Subject and topic: a new typology of language. In: Charles Li (ed.), *Subject and topic.* New York: Academic Press.

Marslen-Wilson, William R. 1973. Linguistic structure and speech shadowing at very short latencies. *Nature* 244:522–23.

McConkie, George. 1982. Eye movements and perception during reading. Technical Report 264. Center for the Study of Reading, Champaign, Ill.

Milsark, Gary. 1977. Towards an explanation of certain peculiarities of the existential construction in English. *Linguistic Analysis* 3:1–30.

Olson, David R., and Nikola Filby. 1972. On the comprehension of active and passive sentences. *Cognitive Psychology* 3:361–81.

Postal, Paul. 1974. *On Raising.* Cambridge, Mass.: MIT Press.

Prince, Ellen. 1980. Towards a taxonomy of given-new information. In: Peter Cole (ed.), *Radical pragmatics.* New York: Academic Press.

Rayner, K. 1978. Eye movements in reading and information processing. *Psychological Bulletin* 85, 3:618–60.

Reinhart, Tanya. 1981. Pragmatics and linguistics: an analysis of sentence topics. *Philosophica* 27:53–94.

Seidenberg, Mark, and Tanenhaus, Michael. 1981. Discourse context and sentence perception. *Discourse Processes* 26:197–220.

Slobin, Dan I. 1966. Grammatical transformations and sentence comprehension in childhood and adulthood. *Journal of Verbal Learning and Verbal Behavior* 5:219–27.

Tannenbaum, P. H., and F. Williams. 1968. Generation of active and passive sentences as a function of subject and object focus. *Journal of Verbal Learning and Verbal Behavior* 7:246–50.

Townshend, D. J., and Thomas Bever. 1977. *Main and subordinate clause: a study in figure and ground.* Bloomington: Indiana University Linguistics Club.

Turner, E. A., and Rommetveit, Ragnar. 1968. Focus of attention in recall of active and passive sentences. *Journal of Verbal Learning and Verbal Behavior* 7:543–48.

Wanner, Eric. 1974. *On remembering, forgetting and understanding sentences: a study of the deep structure hypothesis.* Janua Linguarum, series minor, no. 1970. The Hague: Mouton.

Wanner, Eric, and Michael Maratsos. 1978. An ATN approach to comprehension. In: Morris Halle, Joan Bresnan, and George Miller (eds.), *Linguistic theory and psychological reality.* Cambridge, Mass.: MIT Press.

2 Interpreting questions

ELISABET ENGDAHL

In this paper I want to draw together a number of observations bearing on how people interpret constituent questions. The observations concern the interpretation possibilities for "moved" and "unmoved" *wh*-phrases, as well as wide scope interpretation of quantifiers in embedded sentences. I will argue that languages typically display a correlation between positions that do not allow extractions and positions where a constituent cannot be interpreted with wide scope. Given this correlation, it seems natural to investigate the processes of extraction and wide-scope interpretation from the perspective of sentence processing, in the hope of explaining correlations between the two. I have singled out constituent questions because they illustrate the parsing problem for sentences with nonlocal filler-gap dependencies[1]; they are a particularly interesting case to consider because of interactions between scope determining factors and general interpretive strategies for filler-gap association.

2.1. Gap-filling

To what extent is the process of gap-filling sensitive to formal, as opposed to semantic, properties of the linguistic input? One type of evidence that is relevant here is the existence of a morphological dependency between the filler and the environment of the gap, as illustrated in (1).

(1) a. Which people did Mary say __ were invited to dinner?
    b. *Which people did Mary say __ was invited to dinner?

In languages with productive case marking, a similar type of dependency will hold between the case of the filler and the local environment of the gap. This kind of morphological agreement is typically determined by properties having to do with the surface form of the items in question, or with inherent formal properties, such as which noun class a given noun belongs to. Normally such formal properties have very little to do with the meanings of the words and will presumably not be reflected in the listener's representation of the content of the sentence. It is thus conceivable that the parser would disregard such information as soon as possible. This is actually what one would expect if Frazier (this volume) is

67

correct in assuming that remembering nonsemantic information is an active process that contributes to the processing complexity of the sentence. The fact that people recognize (1b) as ungrammatical seems to show that this cannot be the whole story. The contrast between (1a) and (1b) suggests that a linguistic representation of the filler is maintained during the processing of the sentence and that filler-gap association takes place at a level at which morphological information is available.[2]

It could be argued that the type of dependency illustrated in (1), number agreement, is really a semantic phenomenon. The reason people detect the illformedness is that *was coming* is not the right kind of VP to predicate of an inherently plural NP like *which people*. Nevertheless, people detect morphological mismatches also in cases that involve grammatical gender. In Swedish, nouns are either neuter or nonneuter, a property that is mostly lexically determined. Adjectives agree with nouns, both in attributive and predicative position. We can thus construct minimal pairs as in (2).

(2) a. *Vilken elev påstod alla* ___ *hade ofta blivit förbigången?*
             [−NEUT]   [−NEUT]
         Which pupil did all claim ___ had often been bypassed?
     b. * *Vilken elev påstod alla* ___ *hade ofta blivit förbigånget?*
             [−NEUT]   [+NEUT]

Failure to make the predicative adjective agree with the subject is noticed right away by any speaker of Swedish. There are also very few speech errors of this type in the corpora I have seen. It is worth noting that the morphological dependency need not be immediately adjacent to the gap but that several words can intervene, as is the case in (2). This indicates that some formal representation of the filler is maintained even beyond the point at which the gap is recognized.[3] Further evidence that the actual form of the filler is maintained during the processing of the sentence comes from the rhyme-prompt experiments reported by Tanenhaus, Carlson, and Seidenberg in paper 11 of this volume. In these experiments, subjects were quicker to respond correctly to a word that rhymed with the filler than to a nonrhyme, when the cue was flashed at the position of the gap.

It is tempting to speculate on why gap-filling routines should be sensitive to purely formal properties of the filler and the gap. One rather straightforward reason would be that gap detection is facilitated if the formal specifications of the gap context are readily accessible. Furthermore, this might enable the parser to disregard certain potential gaps quicker and thus reduce ambiguity on-line. This would fit in with the agreement facts illustrated by the example in (2) from Swedish, a language that allows multiple filler-gap dependencies into the same clause. It is less obvious why phonological properties of fillers should be maintained, as shown in the rhyme prompt experiments reported by Tanenhaus, Carlson, and Seidenberg. Still, it seems to me that sentences with morphological dependencies of this kind provide good materials to test both the hypothesis that morphological information is used actively as an ambiguity-reducing device and the assumption that remembering nonsemantic information increases the processing complexity of the sentence, as well as the possible trade-off between these two factors.

2.2. Questions with bound anaphors

The next issue I want to address is to what extent the interpretation of the initial interrogative phrase is affected by the position of the gap. In a simple constituent question like (3),

(3) Which girl did John invite __ to the party?

it seems that listeners can use the information in *which girl* to begin to construct a situation involving a girl as soon as they hear the initial constituent, although they have to wait until the gap is located to determine which role this unknown girl plays in the question, which properties she should have. There are other questions where it seems that the initial constituent cannot be interpreted independently of the rest of the question. These are questions where the interpretation of the *which* phrase crucially depends on the interpretation of some other NP in the sentence. One case is when the interrogative quantifier contains an anaphor, as in (4).

(4) Which of *his* friends did *John* invite __ to the party?

We are here interested primarily in the reading on which *his friends* is referring to the group denoted by *John's friends*. This reading may be emphasized by using *his own friends* instead. Following common practice in linguistics, we will refer to *John* as the *antecedent* for *his*. Languages with a special reflexive form of the possessive pronouns typically express this reading by using the reflexive, as in the Swedish version of (4).

(5) *Vilken av <u>sina</u> vänner bjöd <u>Johan</u> __ på festen?*
    Which of POSS friends did Johan invite to the party?
        REFL

sina in Swedish can never be interpreted deictically. Like all reflexives in this language, it must have an antecedent within the sentence.

Examples (4) and (5) illustrate that there are questions where the listener cannot assign a complete interpretation to the interrogative constituent without finding an antecedent for *his* and *sina*. How does the listener go about finding an antecedent? One way would be to keep the interpretation of the initial constituent incomplete until the parser has come across an antecedent matching the anaphor in number and gender. At this point, the interpretation of the interrogative phrase can be assembled. Another strategy would be first to locate the gap and then to choose among the NPs that are possible and/or plausible antecedents for the anaphor with respect to this position according to the rules or strategies for bound anaphora resolution in the language.[4] The examples we have looked at so far only have one possible antecedent, so the two strategies would give the same results. In sentences with several NPs intervening between the filler and the gap, the two strategies make different predictions. According to the first strategy, speakers should always associate an anaphor in an initial constituent with the first matching antecedent. The second strategy predicts that the listener will disregard an intervening NP if this NP could not be the antecedent of an anaphor in the gap position, according to the anaphora rules of the language in question. To my knowledge, no experiments on the resolution of anaphors in preposed constituents have been done yet that could tell these strategies apart. A preliminary investigation with Swedish-speaking subjects shows that they have a tendency to choose the first compatible NP as antecedent in questions like (6), where both intervening NPs are possible antecedents.

(6) *Vilken av sina vänner bad Sven Johan bjuda ___ på festen?*
     Which of his-own friends did Sven ask Johan to invite to the party?

The results from sentences like (6) differ systematically from the results on the corresponding declaratives as in (7).

(7) *Sven bad Johan bjuda en av sina vänner på festen.*
     Sven asked Johan to invite one of his-own friends to the party.

In the declarative sentence, most speakers understand *Johan*, the closest NP, to be the antecedent for *sina*, although the matrix subject NP, *Sven*, also is a possible antecedent. If the closest NP is not of the right person to serve as the antecedent for the third-person reflexive *sina*, the matrix subject is understood to be the antecedent, as in (8).

(8) *Sven bad mig bjuda en av sina vänner på festen.*
     Sven asked me to invite one of his-own friends to the party.

We get a different result, however, if the first NP that intervenes between the initial interrogative phrase and the gap is not a possible antecedent for a reflexive in the gap position. A possessive NP cannot act as the antecedent for a reflexive in Swedish, as shown in (9).

(9) [*Johans$_j$ äldste bror*]$_i$ *ville bjuda en av sina$_{i,*j}$ vänner på festen.*
     Johan's oldest brother wanted to invite one of his-own friends to the party.

When asked about the corresponding question,

(10) *Vilken av sina vänner ville Johans äldste bror bjuda på festen?*
     Which of his-own friends did Johan's oldest brother want to invite to the party?

none of the Swedish speakers who participated in this test understood *Johan* to be the antecedent of *sina*, although, in terms of linear order, *Johan* is the first matching NP the listener encounters.

These are just preliminary results from one questionnaire and it is impossible to draw any conclusions about when the resolution of anaphors in dislocated initial constituents takes place. It seems to me that we can formulate three hypotheses, which are all compatible with the present evidence.

(11) a. When the parser has recognized an explicit or potential anaphor in a filler position, it entertains as many hypotheses as there are possible antecedents and chooses between them on the basis of pragmatic plausibility.
      b. The parser tries the first compatible antecedent. If this assignment turns out to be incorrect due to syntactic or semantic information later in the sentence, the parser makes an "intelligent reanalysis."[5]
      c. The parser waits until the gap is detected to resolve the anaphor.

In the absence of any on-line experiments, it is impossible to argue conclusively that any one of these hypotheses is the correct one. I think it would be extremely interesting to try to apply the on-line techniques for demonstrating availability of referents that Tanenhaus, Carlson, and Seidenberg (this volume) have used to sentences with anaphors in filler positions to see if this would enable us to choose among (11a)–(11c). Another aspect that clearly needs investigation is to what extent the resolution of such anaphors is sensitive to the contextual effects which are shown in the experiments discussed in Crain and Steedman (this volume).

2.3. Relational interpretations of questions

In the preceding section we looked at questions with overt anaphoric dependencies between the initial interrogative phrase and some other NP in the question. This is not the only type of question where the interpretation of the initial interrogative phrase may be affected by the interpretation of some other constituent. Take a question like (12), which can be answered in two ways, as illustrated here.

(12) Q: Who did everyone want to invite __ to the party?
      A: a. John
          b. his or her best friend

The (a) answer is approprate in a situation when there is one particular person that everyone agrees to invite, e.g., John. We can also think of a situation where different people have different prospective guests in mind. In this case an answer like (b) would be appropriate. The (b) response indicates what I will call a *relational* reading of the question. On the relational reading of (12), the initial interrogative phrase, *who*, does not denote any one individual directly. Rather, the denotation of *who* varies with the interpretation of *everyone*. For each person x in some contextually determined set of people, *who* will denote a different individual, for example the individual that is x's best friend.

In the literature on the semantics of questions, relational readings of questions have not been much discussed (but see Groenendijk and Stokhof, 1982 and Hintikka, 1982). To the extent that people have dealt with the type of answer shown in (12b), they have considered them as abbreviations for lists of pairs of individuals. In a situation where Bill, Sam, and Nancy constitute the domain that *everyone* ranges over, (12b) would be just another way of expressing the answer in (12c).

(12) c.   Bill (wanted to invite) Mary,
            Sam (wanted to invite) Joe,
            and Nancy (wanted to invite) Lucy.

On this reading, asking the question in (12) would amount to asking a whole set of questions, which for each person x contains the question who x wanted to invite to the party. In order to get this reading, we would have to pull out the universal quantifier *everyone* and give it wider scope than *who*. There is a semantic problem with quantifying into questions, which makes it a nontrivial matter to generate these readings,[6] but I will leave this technical problem aside here and instead take issue with one of the consequences of the claim that (12b) readings are merely convenient abbreviations for (12c) readings. The consequence is that relational readings should be possible only when the antecedent quantifier phrase is given wider scope than the interrogative phrase, as illustrated by the paraphrase of the (c) reading above. However, I do not think that a relational reading of (12) requires that *everyone* be given wider scope than *who*. One way to illustrate this is to replace *everyone* by a quantifier that rarely takes wide scope, like *no one*.

(13) Q: Who did no one want to invite to the party?
      A: a. John
            b. His or her parents
          *c.   Bill (didn't want to invite) Mary,
                Sam (didn't want to invite) Joe,
                and Nancy (didn't want to invite) Lucy.

We find that the relational answer in (13b) is possible but the answer in terms of a list of pairs, (13c), does not seem to express a possible interpretation of (13). Instead of trying to account for relational readings by giving the antecedents wide scope, I want to propose that the availability of relational readings reflect a flexibility in the way interrogative expressions are interpreted. Relational answers are quite common. Indeed, as soon as a question contains one or more quantifier NPs a relational answer is possible and sometimes the most natural. Some further examples of relational questions are given in (14)–(16).

(14) Q: Where do *most people* want to settle?
      A: Close to where *they* grew up.

(15) Q: How can I find *a book* in this library?
      A: By looking up *its* author's name in this catalogue.

(16) Q: What does *every father* tell **his children** never to forget?
      A: How *he* has sacrificed himself for **them**.

On the most natural reading of (15), *a book* has narrow scope. The person is not asking about how to find a particular book; rather, what he wants is a general strategy for book finding. The relational answer provides just this. Example (16) illustrates that any number of intervening NPs may affect the way the interrogative phrase is interpreted.

I have argued elsewhere (Engdahl, forthcoming) that these kinds of question-answer pairs show that interrogative quantifiers cannot always be reduced to quantification over individuals, but require quantification over relations. In this context, I will just point out that if we take people's intuitions about possible answers to be indicative of the interpretations they construct for questions, then people often seem to interpret initial interrogative phrases with respect to any quantifier that has scope over the gap position. The range of interpretation possibilities for the interrogative filler is thus crucially affected by the position of the associated gap. Relational answers typically make use of systematic and/or conventionalized ways of relating individuals to each other. This is presumably why it is so easy for people to integrate and evaluate the information given in the form of a relational answer.

2.4. Correlations between extraction and interpretation

So far we have looked at examples involving the interpretation of sentence-initial interrogative constituents that are associated with a gap somewhere in the question. (Within transformational grammar it has become customary to refer to such phrases as "moved" constituents and I will continue to do so, without thereby committing myself to the view that these constituents actually have moved.) We will now turn to sentences with so-called unmoved *wh*-phrases and regular quantifiers and look at their interpretation possibilities. These sentences do not involve any overt syntactic movement, but interpreting them might require that these phrases be given wider scope than the positions where they occur. This will enable us to address the central issue of this paper: In what respect are the processes of interpreting an initial constituent that must in some sense be fitted into the sentence and the processes involved in giving wide scope to some constituent similar and susceptible to being influenced by the same factors? Before going into this issue, we will briefly look at how the type of dependencies we are interested in here are captured in two current grammatical frameworks.

Within the government-binding (GB) framework, the dependencies are seen as the result of a syntactic transformation, as instances of "move α" (Chomsky, 1981, 1982).[7] In the nontransformational framework generalized phrase structure grammar (GPSG), an initial interrogative constituent is accepted by a special type of phrase structure rule, a linking rule, which causes the relevant information about the interrogative phrase to be passed down the tree as a feature on syntactic nodes. (See Gazdar, 1982 and Gazdar and Pullum, 1982 for details.) Not surprisingly, these theories differ not only in the way they account for the dependencies but also in the way they express restrictions on them. In the GB framework, applications of "move α" are constrainted by subjacency, a structurally defined constraint that prevents syntactic dependencies across more than one bounding node except under special circumstances (so-called Comp-to-Comp movement). Within the GPSG framework, constraints can and have been formulated in various ways: as conditions on derived rules (Gazdar, 1981), as conditions on tree paths (Maling and Zaenen, 1982) and as conditions on the generation of rules by metarules (J. D. Fodor, 1983). Fodor argues explicitly that the restricted format of a GPSG actually provides an explanation for the constraints on gap distribution one finds in natural languages. (See also the discussion in Crain and Fodor, this volume.) We will take up the role of the constraints in the two theories after we have looked at some specific examples.

2.4.1. Types of constraints

In order to facilitate the discussion of what restrictions apply to the interpretation of interrogative phrases, both moved and unmoved, I will introduce some terminology. I am going to distinguish two types of restrictions, *local constraints*, illustrated in (17), and *complexity constraints*, illustrated in (18)–(19).

(17)   *Who$_i$ did you reget [$_S$ that [$_S$ ___$_i$ had been invited?]]

(18)   *Which girl$_j$ didn't you know [$_S$ who$_i$ [$_S$ ___$_i$ had invited ___$_j$?]]

(19)   *Which girl$_j$ did you know [$_{NP}$ the man [$_S$ who$_i$ [$_S$ I introduced ___$_i$ to ___$_j$?]

Local constraints cover in principle the same type of phenomena that Chomsky and Lasnik (1977) suggested should be handled by surface filters – that is, restrictions on locally specifiable contexts that characteristically involve complementizers. Under complexity constraints I want to subsume phenomena like extractions out of embedded questions and relative clauses. Complexity constraints can be seen as resulting from the interaction of several filler-gap dependencies, as shown in (18) and (19). A particularly interesting illustration of how a complexity constraint might work is provided by the fact that a sentence like (20) in English has only one reading (see also the discussion in Crain and Fodor, this volume).

(20)
a.
Which student is this professor suitable to introduce __ to __ ?
*b.

Sentence (20) involves two filler-gap dependencies. Hence there are two logically possible ways of associating the fillers with the gaps. But speakers of English reportedly only get the readings where the dependencies are nested, as shown in (20a). In her article "Parsing strategies and constraints on transformations," Janet Dean Fodor (1978) discusses a number of cases where extraction processes interact. She concludes that there exists in English a non-ambiguity constraint, the Nested Dependency Constraint, which systematically excludes intersecting interpretations, as in (20b). This constraint cannot be universal, however, since intersecting readings are possible in Swedish and the other Scandinavian languages. In order to find out what the interpretation possibilities for Swedish sentences with multiple filler-gap dependencies were, as well as what factors determine whether an intersecting assignment is possible, I carried out an experiment (Engdahl, 1982b). The experiment consisted of a controlled paraphrase task. Subjects read sentences with two filler-gap dependencies and were asked to paraphrase the sentences by completing the cue given immediately beneath each test sentence. An example of a test item is given in (21).

(21) *Mina föräldrar är det få personer jag vill presentera för.*
Det är få personer . . . .
My parents, there are few people I'd like to introduce to.
There are few people . . . .

The results show that the intersecting readings are available, especially in cases where semantic or pragmatic factors make the nested reading implausible. Intersecting readings are reported also in unbiased cases like (21), where both assignments result in readings that are equally plausible. However, this does not necessarily mean that both readings were equally easy to get. On the basis of this experiment, it is impossible to draw any conclusions about the relative time it took to get the various readings since subjects just wrote down their responses without timing. This issue should be investigated using some on-line technique. It would also be valuable to investigate, possibly using eye movement recordings, whether people are subconsciously aware of both assignments even in cases where they only report one reading. Another interesting question in this context is of course why English and Swedish speakers get different interpretations for the comparable sentences (20) and (21). By looking at eye movement trackings, I hope to be able to determine whether we can document any systematic differences in the ways English and Swedish speakers process sentences with multiple filler-gap dependencies. If we find systematic differences in the eye movement behavior, then a presumably higher level constraint on the interpretation of complex structures can apparently influence the saccadic movements of the eyes, which have been assumed to be highly automatic. If we find no differences in reading patterns, then the question becomes why one reading is filtered out in English and when this filtering takes place. Presumably, looking at the differences between English and Swedish here might shed more light on the process by which constraints are grammaticalized.[8]

After these preliminaries we turn to the correlation between extraction and interpretation processes. We mentioned earlier that unmoved *wh*-phrases are sometimes interpreted in a way that requires giving them wide scope. This may be the case in multiple questions when the unmoved *wh*-phrase occurs in an embedded question as in (22) (see Baker, 1970).

(22) Q: Who remembers where Mary bought which book?
      A: a.   John does.
          b.   John (remembers where she bought) *Syntactic Structures*,
               Bill (remembers where she bought) *Aspects*, and . . .
          c. *John remembers that she bought *Syntactic Structures* in
               Cambridge,
               Bill remembers that she bought *Aspects* in Oxford, and . . .

If the unmoved *wh*-phrase *which book* is interpreted as part of the embedded question, the (a) type answer will be appropriate. The (b) type answer requires that *which book* is interpreted at the matrix question level – that is, with scope outside the embedded question where it occurs. In this case we typically get an answer in the form of a list of pairs. The moved *wh*-phrase *where*, however, must be interpreted with scope only over the embedded question. It may not be interpreted at the matrix level, as shown by the fact that (c) is not a possible answer. Multiple questions on the readings where type (b) answers are appropriate thus provide us with cases where the interpretation process involves giving a constituent wider scope than its surface position, however this is done.

2.4.2. The "that-*trace*" effect

Similarities between extraction facts and wide scope facts have recently received attention within the framework of the government-binding theory (Chomsky, 1981), especially in the work by Kayne (e.g., Kayne, 1981). Consider the examples in (23)–(25). We are here only interested in the multiple question readings and are ignoring the echo-question reading, which is irrelevant.

(23)   *Who did you think that __ was going out with Mary?

(24)   ??Who thought that which boy was going out with Mary?

(25)   ?Who thought that Mary was going out with which boy?

The issue concerns the contrast between (24) and (25). Apparently, for some speakers, (24) patterns together with (23) in acceptability rather than with (25), which is a more similar sentence from the point of view of the syntactic processes involved. Kayne discusses the contrast with respect to embedded questions rather than direct questions. His examples are given here in (26) and (27).

(26)   ?I know perfectly well who thinks that he is in love with who.
(27)   *I know perfectly well who thinks that who is in love with him.

(Kayne, 1981: [14], [16])

Kayne argues that the greater badness of (27) should be linked to the *that*-trace phenomenon. Kayne has previously argued that the *that*-trace filter introduced in Chomsky and Lasnik (1977) follows from the Nominative Island Constraint (NIC) together with the prohibition against doubly filled Comps. Briefly, the NIC says that a nominative anaphor, e.g., a trace in subject position, must be bound (c-commanded by a coindexed element) within $\bar{S}$. Kayne's argument is best illustrated by an example:

(28)   who$_i$ did you say [$_{\bar{S} \; \text{Comp}}$ [t$'_i$ that] [$_S$ t$_i$ left]]

Example (28) contains two elements in Comp. Hence Comp is branching and t$'_i$ does not c-command t$_i$. If we delete *that*, we get an acceptable sentence, *Who did you say left?*, with trace in Comp binding the trace in subject position. However, if we delete t$'_i$ in Comp, the NIC is violated. Kayne now argues that we can account for (24) and (27) if we assume that NIC constrains Logical Form (LF). We get the LF representations for these sentences by letting the *wh*-interpretation rule (an instance of "move α" in the LF component) raise the unmoved *wh*-phrase *which boy* and Chomsky-adjoin it to $\bar{S}$. The LF representation of (24) will be as in (24'), omitting irrelevant details.

(24')   [for which *x*, *x* a person] [for which *y*, *y* a boy] [*x* thought
         [$_{\bar{S} \; \text{Comp}}$ [that][$_S$ *y* was going out with Mary]]]

By letting the NIC act on representations at LF, where (24) and (28) will have in principle equivalent structures, Kayne can subsume the two cases under one condition.

Kayne also discusses cases of quantifier raising from the position adjacent to *that*. He claims that the same asymmetry between subject and object extractions is found in these cases. Just like most of my informants, I find it very hard to judge the availability of wide scope readings of a quantifier that has been raised out of a tensed sentence. It seems to me that it is equally hard to give *everyone* wider scope than *someone* in (29a) as in (29b).

(29) a.   Someone thought that everyone should be invited.
      b.   Someone thought that we had invited everyone.

David Dowty has pointed out to me that Kayne would predict that *everyone* could take wide scope in (29a) if the complementizer *that* was deleted. However, no one seems to find a contrast between (29a) and (29a′) with respect to wide-scope possibilities for *everyone*.

(29) a.′ Someone thought everyone should be invited.

However, in French, the discontinuous negative quantifier *ne . . . personne* seems to allow sharper judgments, presumably because there is a syntactic reflex of scope. The particle *ne* signals the scope of the quantifier. For instance, (30) only has the reading where *no one* is interpreted inside the embedded clause.

(30) *J'ai exigé que personne ne soit arrêté.* (Kayne, 1981: [5])
      I have required that no one be arrested.

But (31) permits, at least for some speakers, a reading where *no one* takes wide scope.

(31) ?*Je n'ai exigé qu'ils arrêtent personne.*
      (For no *x*, I have required that they arrest *x*.)

The crucial sentence is (32), where the quantifier occurs in subject position, adjacent to the complementizer *que*. According to Kayne, there is a clear contrast in acceptability between (31) and (32).

(32) **Je n'ai exigé que personne soit arrêté.*
      For no *x*, I have required that *x* be arrested.

Kayne takes these three facts, the prohibition against extracting from the position following *that* (23), the impossibility of interpreting an unmoved *wh*-phrase in that position (24) with wide scope, and the unavailability of a wide-scope reading for a quantifier in that position (32), to provide evidence that the *that*-trace filter should really be a constraint on LF, a constraint on interpretation. Chomsky discusses Kayne's argument in the fourth chapter of *Lectures on Government and Binding* and comes to the same conclusion, namely that this cluster of properties shows that here we are dealing with a condition on LF. Chomsky proposes that these effects, which he refers to as RES(NIC) (residue of the NIC), should be

subsumed under the requirement that empty categories must be governed
– that is, the *Empty Category Principle* (ECP):

(33) ECP: [*e*] must be governed.

The notion of government is defined as in (34).

(34) α governs γ in a structure $[_\beta \cdots \gamma \cdots \alpha \cdots \gamma \cdots]$ where
      a. $\alpha = X^0$ or is coindexed with γ.
      b.   where φ is a maximal projection, if φ dominates γ, then ϕ dom-
             inates α.
[and] c. α c-commands γ.   (Chomsky, 1981:250)

The joint effect of (33) and (34) is that an empty category, e_i, must be c-
commanded by a governor (V or P) within the smallest maximal projection
or be c-commanded by an element that is coindexed with e_i. If we assume
the base expansion for S to be as in (35),

(35)

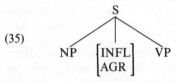

then there are two ways an empty category in the subject position can
be governed, given the definition of government in (34). Either it is governed by a coindexed element in Comp, or it is governed by Agreement
(AGR). Several people (e.g., Taraldsen, 1978) have noticed a correlation
between the possibility of having an empty subject be governed by AGR
and a rich inflectional verb morphology, as in for instance Italian and
Spanish. This correlation is often referred to as the *pro-drop parameter*
within GB theory. It is included in the definition of *proper* government.

(36) α properly governs γ if α governs γ [and $\alpha \neq$ AGR].
      ECP: [*e*] must be properly governed.

The clause within brackets constitutes the pro-drop parameter, which
must be included for non-pro-drop languages such as English and French.
For languages which have the pro-drop option, it is immaterial whether
there is a governor in Comp or not, since AGR will always govern an
empty subject position. These languages will then follow for violations
of the *that*-trace filter, but only superficially so.

One interesting prediction can be made on the basis of these definitions.
If extraction and quantifier raising are instances of the same phenomenon,
then we would expect the counterparts to Kayne's quantifier raising example in French to be good in a pro-drop language like Italian, given the
possibility of government by agreement in this language. The Italian counterpart to (32) would be as in (37), where *e* is properly governed.

(37)

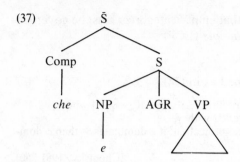

However, as Rizzi (1981) shows, this prediction is wrong. The Italian facts are exactly parallel to the French facts.

(38) *Voglio che nessuno venga.*   (Rizzi, 1981)
       I want that for no *x*, *x* come.

(39) **Non voglio che nessuno venga.*
       For no *x*, I want that *x* come.

No wide-scope interpretation for *nessuno* is possible in (39). But, Rizzi points out, there is a good version with the wide-scope interpretation, namely (40), where the subject and the verb have inverted.

(40) *Non voglio che venga nessuno.*
       For no *x*, I want that *x* come.

In this case, the extraction site would not be immediately adjacent to the complementizer *che*; rather, it would be to the right of the verb, a position that is presumably governed. Consequently, it is possible to conclude that the "*that*-trace" filter (or the NIC) holds in Italian and that apparent violations are really instances of extraction or raising out of a postverbal position, given the existence of free inversion in simple clauses.

The conclusion we can draw from these French and Italian examples is that a language will superficially allow "*that* trace" violations if it has subject pro-drop and free inversion. We will now turn to a language family that shows that neither of these properties is necessary for a language to allow "*that* trace" violations. Consequently, the cluster of properties that Chomsky, Kayne, and Rizzi refer to does not seem to provide a universally valid characterization of languages with "*that* trace" violations. In the modern Scandinavian languages, Danish, Icelandic, Norwegian, and Swedish, there is no evidence for subject pro-drop, nor for free inversion of subject and tensed verb in simple sentences. Nevertheless, the majority of these languages permit extractions from the position immediately adjacent to a filled complementizer. Some relevant examples are given below.[9]

(41) Icel. *Hvað a bragð sagð i hann að __ vaeri gagnslaust?*
which deed   did he say   that __ was useless?
(Maling and Zaenen ([1978:221])

(42) Dan. *Det ved jeg ikke om __ gaar an.*
That know I not if __ goes ('is allowed').

(43) Norw. *Desse konstruksjonar trur eg at __ er meir naturlege uttrykksmåtar.*
These constructions think I that __ are more natural expressions.

(44) Swed. *Det finns mycket man önskar att det skulle vara annorlunda.*
There is a lot   one wishes that it should be different.

As we see, Swedish is exceptional among the Scandinavian languages in not allowing a gap after the complementizer. Instead, a resumption pronoun is used. Note that this use of resumptive pronouns is not associated with substandard speech, as is apparently the case in English, but is considered quite normal. Such resumptive subject pronouns are indeed prescribed in grammar books.[10]

In the light of the Scandinavian data it cannot be correct to link *that*-trace violations exclusively to properties like free subject pro-drop and free inversion. It appears furthermore that the ECP, at least as currently formulated, cannot be universally valid. Kayne's observation that extraction and interpretation phenomena pattern together is probably correct. But for this, we need not draw the conclusion that all languages must behave in the same way with respect to the *that*-trace phenomenon. Rather, we would expect languages either to allow both extractions and wide-scope interpretation in these contexts or disallow both.

We now turn to some more specific evidence for the assumed covariance. To what extent do the extraction facts and the interpretation possibilities in the Scandinavian languages pattern together? We have already seen examples of extractions violating the *that*-trace filter in (41)–(43). Do speakers of Scandinavian languages also allow wide-scope interpretations of quantifiers in these positions? Since it is often hard to determine whether a quantifier in an embedded sentence can take wide scope, I have concentrated on multiple questions, structures where unmoved *wh*-phrases in the relevant position are given a wide-scope interpretation. Such sentences appear by and large to be acceptable, although there is some variation. The acceptability is notably higher than for English speakers judging comparable sentences. We thus get the following pairs in Norwegian.

(45) a. *Hvilken foreleser syntes alle at __ burde innbys?*
Which speaker did all think that __ ought to be invited?
b. *Hvem syntes at hvilken foreleser burde innbys?*
Who thought that which speaker ought to be invited?

Similarly, whereas extraction and interpretation of a constituent adjacent to *if* appears excluded in English, the corresponding Norwegian sentences are fine.

(46) a. *Which speaker were you supposed to find out if __ was coming?
     b. *Hvilken foreleser var det du skulle finne ut om __ ville komme?*

(47) a. ??Who was supposed to find out if which speaker was coming?
     b. *Hvem skulle finne ut om hvilken foreleser ville komme?*

It is interesting to note that Swedish patterns with Norwegian in terms of the interpretation possibilities in this context. As we saw earlier, Swedish does not allow a gap in this position, but sentences with resumptive pronouns are fine. These sentences get the same interpretation as the Norwegian versions. Just as in Norwegian, sentences with unmoved *wh*-phrases next to the complementizer are acceptable.

(48) a. *Vilken föreläsare glömde alla att __ hade inbjudits?*
        Which speaker did all forget that __ had been invited?
     b. *Vilken föreläsare glömde alla att han hade inbjudits?*
     c. *Vem ansåg att vilken föreläsare borde inbjudas?*
        Who thought that which speaker ought to be invited?

We get exactly the same acceptability pattern in *if*-questions:

(49) a. *Vilken föreläsare var det du skulle ta reda på om __ kunde komma?*
        Which speaker was it you were supposed to find out if __ could come?
     b. *Vilken föreläsare var det du skulle ta reda på om han kunde komma?*
     c. *Vem skulle ta reda på om vilken föreläsare kunde komma eller inte?*
        Who was supposed to find out if which speaker could come or not?

It is not clear if the English sentences (46a) and (47a) are ungrammatical because they violate the ECP or because they are violations of the more general *wh*-Island Constraint. However, it appears that many speakers get a contrast between (47a) and (50).

(50) ?Who was supposed to find out if we could afford which speaker?

Here the unmoved *wh*-phrase *which speaker* occurs inside an *if*-clause, but not adjacent to the complementizer. Sentence (50) is generally considered more acceptable, or easier to interpret, than (47a). If this contrast is reliable, it would indicate that the ECP is a stronger barrier against wide-scope interpretations than the *wh*-Island Constraint in English.

2.4.3. Complexity constraints

As far as the *that*-trace constraint goes, we have found a strong correlation between extractability and wide-scope interpretability in both English and Scandinavian languages. Now let us look at some cases in which complexity constraints are at work. For most speakers of English, extractions that violate the Complex NP Constraint lead to sentences that are clearly ungrammatical, as in (51).

(51)   *Who did he come up with the idea that you should talk to __?

Most people also do not accept an unmoved *wh*-phrase in this context, as illustrated in (52).[11]

(52)   *Who came up with the idea that you should talk to who(m)?

The same holds for extraction and wide scope interpretation of a constituent in a relative clause.

(53)   *The Conservatives, I would never vote for someone who supports __.

(54)   *Who will vote for someone who supports which candidate?

In Scandinavian languages, extractions out of complex NPs are much more acceptable than in English. (See the articles in Engdahl and Ejerhed, 1982 for illustrations.) Not surprisingly, we find that the Swedish counterparts to (53) and (54) are good.

(55)   *Högerpartiet skulle jag aldrig föreslå någon som sympatiserar med __.*
        The rightist party I would never suggest someone who has sympathies for __.

(56)   *Vem skulle aldrig föreslå någon som sympatiserar med vilket parti?*
        Who would never suggest someone who has sympathies for which party?

The systematic difference in the reaction to multiple questions like (54) and (56) between English speakers and speakers of Swedish or Norwegian lends further support to the claim that languages correlate structures that permit extraction and those that allow wide scope interpretation. This correlation has been noted in the literature, for example by McCawley (quoted in Seuren, 1972) and Rodman (1976), but these authors do not discuss the variation between languages as to which constraints are relevant.

There is one case where the correlation clearly fails in English: this has to do with embedded constituent questions. It is generally assumed that you cannot extract out of tensed subordinate questions in English, but multiple questions are perfectly grammatical also on the reading that involves giving the unmoved *wh*-phrase wide scope, as we saw before.

(57)   Q: Who remembers which guest brought which wine?
        A: a.   John does.
             b.   John remembers which guest brought the Zinfandel and
                  Mary remembers which guest brought the Cabernet, . . .

There is, however, a restriction on multiple questions in English that is interesting from the perspective we are applying here. I have in mind the so-called *wh*-superiority phenomenon. In a multiple question, you have to front the leftmost *wh*-phrase; that is, there cannot be any unmoved *wh*-phrases between the initial *wh*-phrase and the gap. Judgments about the *wh*-superiority facts vary greatly, but it is common in the literature to see minimal pairs like those in (58) (from Chomsky, 1981:255).

(58) a. *it is unclear [$_S$[what$_j$][$_S$ who said t$_j$]]
      b. it is unclear [$_S$[who$_i$][$_S$ t$_i$ said what]]

The superiority facts bear upon the present discussion of constraints in two ways. First, one could maintain that the superiority restriction is just one instance of the Nested Dependency Constraint, which, as we have seen, is applicable to extractions in English. Hence it would not be surprising if it also applied to the interaction of extraction and wide-scope interpretation that is exemplified in multiple questions. Structures that obey the superiority restriction will automatically obey the NDC.[12] Second, we could bring the *that*-trace effect to bear on this matter. It appears that the most blatant violations of *wh*-superiority involve unmoved subjects, as for instance in (58a). Applying *wh*-interpretation to the unmoved *who* would give rise to an ECP violation in the same way as (24′). We thus have two ways to explain the *wh*-superiority facts in English. Whether or not one would like to subsume the instances of ECP violations under the NDC depends on whether or not there is a clear contrast between violations of superiority that involve unmoved subjects and those that do not. At least some speakers find the contrast between (58a) and (58b) more flagrant than the contrast between (59a) and (59b), which again illustrates that the *that*-trace effect is very strong in English and distinguishable from other constraints.[13]

(59) a. ?Who knows which library Mary donated which manuscripts to __?
      b. Who knows which manuscripts Mary donated to which library?

2.4.4. Overview of correlations

In order to illustrate the discussion about the correlation between extraction and wide scope interpretation, I have summarized the results for four languages in Table 2.1. I include the German data with some hesitation, since I have consulted only three speakers.

If we take one language at a time and do a pairwise comparison of the judgments for extraction and wide-scope interpretation, we find a rather strong correlation. For English, the correlation holds in all cases except indirect constituent questions. We noted earlier that there is a clear difference between wide-scope interpretation out of an embedded question and cases where the extracted or unmoved *wh*-phrase occurs immediately adjacent to a complementizer as in (46a) and (47a). We have suggested that this difference reflects the strong effect of the "*that*-trace" constraint,

Table 2.1 *Extraction and interpretation possibilities*

	Norwegian	Swedish	English	German
that __	ok	* (*pro* ok)	*	*(?)
that wh	ok	ok	*/?	ok
if __	ok	* (*pro* ok)	*	*
if wh	ok/?	ok/?	*/?	*
Ind Q __	ok	ok	*	*
Ind Q *wh*	ok	ok	ok	ok
CNPC __	ok	ok	*	*
CNPC *wh*	ok/?	ok/?	*	ok/??

Note: "/" in a column indicates dialect split, where some speakers give one judgment and others the other.

or more generally, the ECP in English grammar. There is also a semantic difference between the interpretation possibilities for an unmoved *wh*-phrase in an embedded *if*-question (or an embedded *that*-clause) compared with an unmoved *wh*-phrase in an embedded constituent question. The latter questions always permit the unmoved *wh*-phrase to be interpreted either as part of the embedded question or at the matrix level, as was shown in (57). An unmoved *wh*-phrase inside an embedded *if*-question or *that*-clause, on the other hand, must take wider scope than the embedded clause.[14]

If we now turn to German, we find the same lack of correlation between extractability and interpretability for indirect constituent questions. There also appears to be a lack of correlation in the German counterpart to *that*-clauses. Whereas all speakers I consulted had nothing against interpreting unmoved *wh*-phrases adjacent to *dass*, as shown in (60), they in general did not accept extractions out of this position.

(60) *Welcher Ornithologe hat gemeldet, dass welcher Vogel gesehen worden ist?*
      Which ornithologist has announced that which bird has been seen?

It is generally claimed that tensed sentences are extraction islands in German, but there is some indication that this restriction is not absolute (Andersson, 1980 and Kawashima, 1980). Sentences like the following are apparently not infrequent.[15]

(61) *Es ist unsicher, welche Regeln man glaubt, dass __ gelernt werden müssen.*
      It is unclear which rules one believes must be learned.

We find no counterpart to the English *wh*-superiority constraint in multiple *wh*-questions in German. This is probably due to the fact that the word order in German subordinate clauses is quite free, which makes it implausible that there would be a constraint making reference to the order of constituents.[16] Similarly, in Norwegian and Swedish, there is no trace of the superiority effect, but then we would not expect there to be any, since the NDC does not constrain extractions in these languages.

Let us return once more to the contrast between Norwegian and Swedish with respect to the *that*-trace effect. As we have seen, Norwegian overtly violates the ECP but Swedish requires a resumptive pronoun in these positions. The Swedish sentences with resumptive pronouns are considered fully grammatical. Consequently the same range of interpretations is available in both languages for sentences with extractions and unmoved *wh*-phrases. Apparently, what we are dealing with here is a rather superficial variation between two closely related languages with respect to a local constraint. (See also the difference between standard Swedish and the dialect of Swedish spoken in Finland that was mentioned in note 10.) The direct cause for this variation has not yet been satisfactorily determined, as far as I know. It would be implausible, however, to appeal to processing complexity to explain this difference. For the complexity constraints, on the other hand, where it seems intuitively more plausible that there is a processing correlate, Norwegian and Swedish speakers show equivalent response patterns. Sentences of this complexity are less frequent in the language, and as can be seen from Table 2.1, multiple questions with unmoved *wh*-phrases in such structures are considered less acceptable by some speakers of Norwegian and Swedish.

After having seen that there is a rather large covariance with respect to the constraints in the four languages we have considered, we will return to the role of the grammatical constraints. As we mentioned earlier, similarities between extraction facts and wide-scope interpretations in complex constructions have been noted before, but the question of what mechanisms in the grammar are responsible for the correlation has not received much attention until recently. The issue is taken up in recent work by Cooper (1983). In Cooper's framework, both syntactic extraction processes and wide-scope interpretation processes are handled by a "storage" mechanism that so to speak puts the interpretation of some constituent in "store" at some point in the derivation of a sentence. At some later stage, the element in store is retrieved and combined with the rest of the sentence. In this framework, restrictions on both extractions and wide-scope interpretation are expressed as conditions on the elements in store and on the retrieval procedures. The restrictions are expressed as co-occurrence restrictions and ordering constraints. The correlation thus is a consequence of the fact that the same restrictions apply to both processes. Cooper points out that we should expect it to be harder to violate a constraint in case there is a syntactic reflex of the storage operation.

This seems to be true in English and German where wide-scope interpretations are sometimes judged more acceptable than a syntactic extraction, whereas the inverse case is not attested. The way Cooper states the constraints makes it easy to relate them to properties of a parser such as the size of the working memory and sensitivity to left-to-right order of presentation. Cooper does not discuss the *that*-trace phenomenon and consequently says nothing about whether this type of constraint also can be taken to reflect some property of the parser.

Within the government-binding framework, Chomsky and Kayne among others have argued that the correlation between syntactic extraction and wide-scope interpretation shows that the relevant level for stating the constraint must be Logical Form (LF). This argument has been made specifically with respect to the *that*-trace phenomenon. The suggestion is that all *that*-trace effects can be explained if the relevant constraint, the ECP, is taken to be a constraint on LF – i.e., a constraint on well-formed interpretations. Constraints of this form are presumably universal and the ECP has indeed been suggested as a linguistic universal. However, we have seen that there are languages where the ECP constrains neither extractions nor wide-scope interpretations. This casts doubt on the status of the ECP as a universal and shows that any account for the *that*-trace effect which derives it solely from the ECP is lacking in explanatory status. Subsuming the *that*-trace facts under the ECP without any further conditions obviously begs the question how can there be languages without the *that*-trace effect. As for the correlation between extraction and wide-scope interpretation with respect to complexity constraints, this is generally taken as evidence that "Quantifier Raising" shares certain properties with "move α"; in particular, it obeys subjacency. However, this assumption runs into problems with wide-scope interpretations of unmoved *wh*-phrases in embedded questions. Discussing such cases, Chomsky (1982:235) concludes that the *wh*-interpretation rule is ". . . a 'one-step' movement rule . . . which doesn't observe the standard island conditions that follow from subjacency." If this is the case, it is unclear whether the observed correlation should be explained by reference to grammatical rules at all, or whether one should look for the explanation outside the grammar, for instance in language processing.

So far most of the published work within GPSG has been devoted to syntax. Several suggestions for expressing syntactic constraints have been made. Before integrating them with a semantic component, it is impossible to tell which of these ways of expressing syntactic constraints would tie in most naturally with restrictions on wide-scope interpretations and permit an economic and non–ad hoc way of exploiting the correlations. At the workshop on Syntactic Theory and How People Parse Sentences in May 1982, I. Sag demonstrated an implementation of GPSG made at the Hewlett-Packard laboratory in Palo Alto, California. This implementation made use of Cooper's storage technique in the semantic component. Presumably Cooper's suggestions for expressing constraints as restrictions on storage and retrieval operations would be available within this version of GPSG.

2.4.5. There *Insertion contexts*

David Dowty has pointed out to me that there is one context where extractions are possible but wide scope interpretations apparently are not. This is in *There* Insertion sentences. An NP following the verb in such sentences cannot have wide scope, e.g., over negation.

(62) a.   A dozen students weren't at the lecture.
      b.   There weren't a dozen students at the lecture ($\neq$ (62a))

But you can extract out of this position, as pointed out by Richmond Thomason (private communication).

(63)   What is there in the refrigerator?

Not all questions out of this context are well formed, though. Compare (63) with (64) and (65).

(64)   *Which students weren't there at the lecture?

(65)   *Who is there in the kitchen?

The relevant factor seems to be that only a special type of NPs can occur in *There* Insertion contexts, namely indefinite or nonspecific NPs. (See Barwise and Cooper, 1981 for a semantic characterization of this type of NP.) The same restriction is reflected in questions out of this context. Only the nonspecific interrogative *what* is felicitous when linked to a gap in a *there* context. The fact that (64) and (65) with specific *wh*-phrases are infelicitous thus provides another indication that the interpretation of the preposed interrogative is affected by the context of the gap. The same effect may be illustrated by relativizations out of *there* contexts.

(66)   Mary likes the flowers that there were in the garden (when she grew up).

(67)   (*)John is going to take a picture of the flowers that there are in the garden.

Although relativization always involves a certain amount of specificity in the head NP, it is possible to relativize out of a *there* context, but only if the head NP gets a "kind" interpretation, as in (66). Sentence (67) is ungrammatical on the reading where John is going to take a photograph of the actual flowers in the garden. The sentence can presumably be interpreted as saying that he is going to take a picture of the kinds of flowers that can also be found in the garden. Here again it seems that the interpretation possibilities for the filler are influenced by the context of the gap.

2.5. Conclusion

In this paper we have looked at similarities between restrictions on extraction processes and restrictions on wide-scope interpretation processes in four languages. I have suggested that restrictions on extractions fall into two types, local constraints and complexity constraints.[17] The rather surprising finding is that both types of constraints can be relevant not only to extractions but also to wide-scope interpretation. This finding is reflected in Table 2.1, where we find a tendency toward covariation between the positions or contexts that prohibit extractions and those that exclude wide-scope interpretations. The result is surprising in two ways. First, it is not at all obvious why there should be a correlation between syntactic extraction processes and semantic wide-scope interpretation since in some sense they involve inverse processes as indicated by the metaphoric terms often used. A preposed filler is "fitted back in," whereas a quantifier is "raised" in order to take wide scope.[18] What is similar in the two processes seems to be the need to distinguish the actual recognition of a constituent in the surface string from the point when its interpretation can be integrated with the rest of the sentence. Presumably this involves keeping some representation of the constituent and information about its surface position in working memory until the interpretation of the "raised" or "preposed" constituent can interact with the rest of the processed sentence. The correlation in terms of restrictions that we have found may be taken as an indication that the same type of delayed interpretation process is involved in both cases. This makes it important to design processing experiments that would aim at pinning down exactly in what respect interpreting a preposed constituent and giving an unmoved constituent wide scope constitute the same type of process, or are sensitive to the same factors. It would be interesting to extend this type of experimentation to a language like Japanese, in which *wh*-phrases do not move.[19]

Second, it is surprising that a local constraint like the *that*-trace phenomenon can influence the interpretation possibilities of a quantifier in that position. The strong correlation found in English and several other languages suggests that the existence of a constraint in a language, whether or not it can ultimately be explained by reference to processing demands, apparently influences the interpretation strategies of the speakers of that language, so that we find covariation between extractability and interpretability. Whether or not this is common among languages can be answered only by looking at a larger and more representative sample of languages.

Notes

This paper is based on a presentation that was prepared for the conference on Syntactic Theory and How People Parse Sentences, held at the Ohio State University, May 14–15, 1982, while I was Research Associate at the Faculty of Humanities at the University of Umeå. I want to thank the following people for helpful discussions and for providing judgments on sometimes rather strange questions: Robin Cooper, Eva Ejerhed, Lyn Frazier, Irene Heim, Lars Hellan, Christina Rohrer, Swanni Rusch, Tarald Taraldsen, and Arnold Zwicky. I am also grateful to David Dowty and Richmond Thomason for very helpful comments on a draft of the paper.

1.   The terminology "filler" and "gap" is taken from Fodor (1978).

2.   See Tanenhaus, Carlson, and Seidenberg (paper 11, this volume) for an argument that distinct levels may be simultaneously present.

3.   Another indication that the filler remains available after the gap has been recognized is in the case of across-the-board extraction and in the case of "parasitic gaps" (Engdahl, 1983).

4.   It would take me too far from the present topic to go into the complex issue of how generalizations about possible and impossible bound anaphora are represented in the grammar, or how this kind of information is utilized by the parser. See Reinhart (1983) for some suggestions.

5.   For the notion "intelligent reanalysis," see Frazier and Rayner (1982).

6.   Cf. Karttunen (1977), Bennett (1979), and Belnap (1982). For an extensive discussion why relational readings cannot be handled by a quantifying-in approach, see Engdahl (forthcoming: ch. 4).

7.   This does not necessarily mean that actual movement of a syntactic constituent is involved. Cf. Chomsky (1982) where "move α" is seen as a cluster of properties that define the mapping between D-structure and S-structure.

8.   For a discussion of filler-gap dependencies in Norwegian, see Christensen (1982).

9.   See Engdahl (1982a) for additional examples and discussion.

10.   In the dialect of Swedish spoken in Finland, *finlandssvenska*, *that*-trace violations are allowed without resumptive pronouns, as shown by the following example brought to my attention by Per Linell.

(i)   *Det är en omständighet, som Bengt Loman anser att __ ytterligare ökar.*
    That is a circumstance that Bengt Loman thinks that __ further increases.

In Danish, extractions following *at* ('that') apparently require the dummy *der* to be inserted.

(ii)   *Hvem tror du, at der __ har gjort det?*
    Who do you think that there __ has done it?

For a discussion of Danish *der*, see Jacobsen and Jensen (forthcoming).

11.   Judgments on extractions out of Noun Complement structures vary greatly. There are conflicting reports in the literature: e.g., Baker (1970) and Chomsky (1981).

12. There are certain exceptions to the *wh*-superiority constraint. Kuno and Robinson (1972) and Kuno (1982) note that adverbial *wh*-phrases may be fronted across interrogative NPs as in (i).

(i)   In which subjects did they give A's to what students? (Kuno, 1982: (5b))

Since distinct syntactic categories are involved here, the NDC is not applicable, as shown also by (ii), where intersecting assignments are permitted.

(ii)   Which crimes$_i$ did the FBI not know how$_j$ to solve [$_{NP\_i}$] [$_{ADVP\_j}$]?

13. Chomsky (1981:255) mentions another prediction, namely that the superiority constraint should be voided in languages with free subject-verb inversion. The prediction cannot be tested in Italian, which for some reason does not have multiple questions, but is borne out in Spanish, according to Jaeggli (1980). See also the discussion in Chomsky (1981:255). However, I have been unable to verify Jaeggli's claim with speakers of Castilian Spanish. They all obey the superiority condition.

14. If the unmoved *wh*-phrase were to be interpreted as part of the embedded clause, it would not be possible to determine which proposition or which unit set of propositions the *that*-clause of the *if*-clause denotes. It is interesting to note that this type of multiple question does not display the intermediate scope reading discussed, for example, in Karttunen and Peters (1980) and in Groenendijk and Stokhof (1982).

15. The example in (62) was brought to my attention by Sven-Gunnar Andersson, University of Umeå, who together with S. Kvam has made a systematic investigation of extractions (*Satzverschränkungen*) in modern German (cf. Andersson, 1980). Andersson documents that extractions out of tensed clauses were more common in older German. Grammarians like Paul and Behaghel, for instance, cite several examples. Extractions are still common in certain German dialects, such as Bayerisch. I am grateful to John Nerbonne for the reference to Kawashima.

16. See Uszkoreit (1982) for a discussion of German word order possibilities.

17. In this paper I have not made any precise proposal for how complexity constraints should be defined. One type of constraint that is not immediately covered by the categorization suggested here is the Sentential Subject Constraint and the constraint against extractions out of adverbial clauses. I find Lyn Frazier's proposal (this volume) very appealing. She suggests that all minimal governing categories off the main projection path of a sentence constitute natural interpretation islands because they are the categories that can serve as semantic replacement units during the processing of a sentence. Consequently, extraction out of such a domain would increase the complexity of the interpretation procedure.

18. In this paper I have talked about wide-scope interpretation as if this were a well-known process. Actually, very little is known about how people arrive at interpretations that involve giving a constituent wide scope. I suspect that the process of giving an unmoved *wh*-phrase wide scope is crucially different from interpeting a regular NP with wide scope. Compare the following examples.

(i)   Someone thought that Mary was in love with each boy.
(ii)   Who thought that Mary was in love with which boy?

English speakers hearing (i) might construct a situation with a person who thinks something about Mary. In order to give *each boy* wide scope, there is no easy way listeners can revise the constructed situation. Instead they must presumably begin again with the interpretation of *each boy*, however universal quantifiers are interpreted, and then integrate the interpretation of *someone thought*. . . . An unmoved *wh*-phrase, on the other hand, will always occur in the context of a previous *wh*-phrase (except in echo-questions, which we are leaving aside here). Understanding a multiple question as in (ii) presumably involves constructing a situation with two unidentified individuals. The recognition of the unmoved *wh*-phrase *which boy* does not affect the interpretation of the previous *wh*-phrase, *who*, nor does it force listeners to revise the situation they have constructed so far. This could be the explanation why multiple questions are not perceived as particularly difficult to understand whereas constructing interpretations that involve deviating from the linear order of quantifiers is notoriously hard.

19. Sige-Yuki Kuroda (private communication) has pointed out to me that in order to facilitate certain wide-scope interpretations in Japanese, a kind of topicalization procedure is often used.

References

Andersson, Sven-Gunnar. 1980. Zum Problem der Satzverschränkung und damit funktional verwandter Konstruktionen im heutigen Deutsch. *Akten des VI. Internationalen Germanisten-Kongress*. Basel: Peter Lanz.

Baker, C. LeRoy. 1970. Notes on the description of English questions: the role of an abstract question morpheme. *Foundations of Language* 6:197–219.

Barwise, Jon, and Robin Cooper. 1981. Generalized quantifiers and natural language. *Linguistics and Philosophy* 4:159–219.

Belletti, A., et al. (eds.). 1981. *Theory of markedness in generative grammar*. Scuola Normale Superiore di Pisa.

Belnap, Nuel. 1982. Questions and answers in Montague grammar. In: Stanley Peters and Esa Saarinen (eds.), *Processes, beliefs, and questions*. Dordrecht, Holland: D. Reidel.

Bennett, Michael. 1979. Questions in Montague grammar. Bloomington: Indiana University Linguistics Club.

Chomsky, Noam. 1981. *Lectures on government and binding*. Dordrecht, Holland: Foris.
    1982. *Some concepts and consequences of the theory of government and binding*. Cambridge, Mass.: MIT Press.

Chomsky, Noam, and Howard Lasnik. 1977. Filters and control. *Linguistic Inquiry* 8.

Christensen, Kirst. 1982. On multiple filler gap constructions in Norwegian. In: Engdahl and Ejerhed (eds.).

Cooper, Robin. 1983. *Quantification and syntactic theory*. Dordrecht, Holland: D. Reidel.

Engdahl, Elisabet. 1982a. Restrictions on unbounded dependencies in Swedish. In Engdahl and Ejerhed (eds.).
    1982b. Interpreting sentences with multiple filler gap dependencies. *Working Papers in Linguistics* 24, Lund University, Lund, Sweden.
    1983. Parasitic gaps. *Linguistics and Philosophy* 6(1).
    Forthcoming. *The syntax and semantics of constituent questions with special reference to Swedish*. Dordrecht, Holland: D. Reidel.

Engdahl, Elisabet, and Eva Ejerhed (eds.). 1982. *Readings on unbounded dependencies in Scandinavian languages*. Stockholm: Almquist and Wiksell International.

Fodor, Janet. 1978. Parsing strategies and constraints on transformations. *Linguistic Inquiry* 9.
    1983. Phrase structure parsing and the island constraints. *Linguistics and Philosophy* 6.

Frazier, Lyn, and K. Rayner. 1982. Making and correcting errors during sentence comprehension: eye movements in the analysis of structurally ambiguous sentences. *Cognitive Psychology* 14(2):178–210.

Gazdar, Gerald. 1981. Unbounded dependencies and coordinate structure. *Linguistic Inquiry* 12:155–184.

　　1982. Phrase structure grammar. In Pauline Jacobson and Geoffrey Pullum (eds.), *The nature of syntactic representation*. Dordrecht, Holland: D. Reidel.

Gazdar, Gerald, and Geoffrey Pullum. 1982. Generalized phrase structure grammar: a theoretical synopsis. Bloomington: Indiana University Linguistics Club.

Groenendijk, Jergen, and Martin Stokhof. 1982a. Semantic analysis of *wh*-complements. *Linguistics and Philosophy* 5(2):175–233.

　　1982b. Interrogative quantifiers and Skolem-functions. Unpublished manuscript, Department of Philosophy, University of Amsterdam.

Hintikka, Jaakko. 1982. Questions with outside quantifiers. In: *CLS parasession on nondeclaratives*. Chicago: Chicago Linguistics Society.

Jacobsen, Bent, and P. Anker Jensen. Forthcoming. Some remarks on Danish weakly stressed *der*. To appear in *Nydanske studier*.

Jaeggli, Oswaldo. 1980. On some phonologically-null elements in syntax. Ph.D. dissertation, Massachusetts Institute of Technology, Cambridge, Mass.

Karttunen, Lauri. 1977. Syntax and semantics of questions. *Linguistics and Philosophy* 1(1):3–44.

Karttunen, Lauri, and Stanley Peters. 1980. Interrogative quantifiers. In: Christian Rohrer (ed.), *Time, tense, and quantifiers*. Tübingen: Niemeyer.

Kawashima, Atsuo. 1980. Zur Frageform des Glaubenssatzes: Wohin glauben Sie, dass er fährt? In: Gunter Brettschneider and Christian Lehmann (eds.), *Wege zur Universalienforschung*. Tübingen: Gunter Narr.

Kayne, Richard. 1981. Two notes on the NIC. In Belletti et al. (eds.).

Kuno, Susumu. 1982. The focus of the question and the focus of the answer. In: *CLS parasession on nondeclaratives*. Chicago: Chicago Linguistics Society.

Kuno, Susumu, and Jane Robinson. 1972. Multiple Wh questions. *Linguistic Inquiry* 3(4):463–87.

Maling, Joan, and Annie Zaenen. 1978. The nonuniversality of a surface filter. *Linguistic Inquiry* 9:475–97.

Reinhart, Tanya. 1983. Coreference and bound anaphora. *Linguistics and Philosophy* 6(1).

Rizzi, Luigi. 1981. Remarks on variables, negation and wh-movement. In: Belletti et al. (eds.).

Rodman, Robert. 1976. Scope phenomena, "movement transformations," and relative clauses. In: Barbara Partee (ed.), *Montague grammar*. New York: Academic Press.

Seuren, Pieter A. M. 1972. Autonomous versus semantic syntax. *Foundations of Language* 8(2):237–65.

Taraldsen, Tarald. 1978. On the NIC, vacuous application and the *that trace* filter. Mimeo, MIT. Bloomington: Indiana University Linguistics Club, 1980.

Uszkoreit, Hans. 1982. German word order in GPSG. In: Dan Flickinger, Marlys Macken, and Nancy Wiegand (eds.), *Proceedings from the First West Coast Conference on Formal Linguistics*. Stanford University.

3 How can grammars help parsers?

STEPHEN CRAIN and JANET DEAN FODOR

There has been some interest in recent years in finding functional explanations for various properties of human languages. The general form of these explanations is

(1) Languages have property *P* because if they did not
   a. we couldn't learn them; or
   b. we couldn't plan and produce sentences efficiently; or
   c. we couldn't understand sentences reliably and efficiently; or
   d. we wouldn't be able to express the sorts of messages we typically want to express.

Some linguists are dubious about the legitimacy of such investigations, and they are indeed a notoriously risky undertaking. It is all too easy to be seduced by what *looks* like a plausible explanation for some linguistic phenomenon, but there is really no way of proving that it is the correct explanation, or even that functional considerations are relevant at all. What, then, can be said in favor of this line of research?

Setting aside the sheer fascination of finding answers to *why*-questions, we can point to some more practical benefits that may result. First, we may find out something about the learning mechanism, or the sentence processing mechanism, or whichever component of the language faculty provides a likely functional explanation for the linguistic facts. In this paper we will concentrate on the sentence parsing mechanism. (See Fodor and Crain, in preparation, for discussion of language learning.) It is clear that one can derive at least some interesting hypotheses about how the parser is structured, by considering how it would have to be structured in order to explain why certain sentences are ungrammatical, why there are constraints excluding certain kinds of ambiguity, and so forth. These will be no more than hypotheses, of course, which must then be tested against other data, such as the results of sentence processing experiments, but there is no point to ignoring this source of ideas just because the functional considerations are not by themselves conclusive.

Second, and closer to the hearts of linguists, is the possibility of finding out something about the form of grammars. If we adopt the working as-

94

sumption that the parser and the grammar are well matched, we may be able to appeal to the way in which they interrelate in order to help us decide between various alternative grammars, all of which appear to be compatible with the linguistic facts. This is what we will attempt to do in this paper. Note that this is a more demanding project than merely showing that some constructions that are excluded from the language would have been difficult to parse if they had been part of the language. What we have to consider is not merely which constructions the language contains, but how they are properly to be described.

Rather little of the functional explanation literature has addressed itself to this goal. The obvious exception is Bresnan (1978), where it is argued that to trade certain transformations for lexical rules would make the parsing process more efficient, and also comport better with experimental data on sentence processing. Our project is comparable to Bresnan's, but focuses on the "long-distance" transformations and the constraints that limit the positions of their "fillers" and "gaps."

3.1. Possible relations between grammars and parsers

We want to know how the grammar and the parser for a natural language are related to each other, and we are hoping to gain some insight into this by considering how they might *optimally* be related – in particular, by considering what sort of grammar would facilitate sentence parsing. To get some perspective on this, let us consider first how a grammar could make life *difficult* for a parser.

One obvious problem for any parsing system is ambiguity, including temporary ambiguity for a system that operates "from left to right." The avoidance of ambiguity has been held to motivate a number of grammatical constraints. For example, Bever (1970) and Chomsky and Lasnik (1977) have suggested, with slight differences of detail, that a construction like (2), in which a sentence-initial subordinate clause has no complementizer, is excluded from English because the parser would temporarily misanalyze the first clause as the main clause.

(2) *He is here is obvious.

Kaplan (1973), Fodor (1978), and others have proposed that the prohibition against intersecting filler-gap associations in a construction like (3) serves to eliminate an ambiguity that would otherwise be troublesome to the parser.

(3) What would boxes be easy to store - in - ?
*

Another problem the parser might face if the grammar were unconstrained is the concentration of structural complexity at certain points in a word string. A likely example of this is multiply center-embedded sentences, in which (along with a variety of other potential problems) there is characteristically a high density of nonterminal nodes relative to words, calling for very rapid structure-building operations during parsing. (See Frazier, paper 4 in this volume, for a metric that predicts the severity of various kinds of local concentration of complexity.) It turns out to be difficult to find examples of grammatical constraints that might be motivated by this consideration, because in most cases it can be argued that complex constructions that appear to be ungrammatical are in fact well-formed and merely unprocessable. This, for example, was the proposal of Miller and Chomsky (1963) for center-embedded constructions.

A very different kind of problem that a grammar could create for a parser has to do with the format in which information about the language is presented. One grammar might make the parsing process very cumbersome, because it provides information about legitimate sentence structures in a form that is inconvenient for a parser to apply; a different grammar might package the linguistic facts in a way that is more suited to the nature and sequence of the computations a parser has to perform.

It should be noted that ambiguity and structural complexity are facts about the *language*; they are independent of how we describe it. They would afflict a parser with limited resources regardless of the format of the grammatical information it has access to. Therefore, although these phenomena may be sources of interesting hypotheses about the resources and operating characteristics of the parser, they are unlikely to be very informative about the optimal grammar format for parsers. To resolve the format question it is necessary to consider how, in detail, the human sentence parsing mechanism goes about its task of determining the structure of sentences, and what kinds of information it needs to draw on at various stages. We think some general points about optimal grammar format can sensibly be made just on the basis of what it is that a parser has to be able to do. But empirical data are undoubtedly going to be needed, for it is also obvious that what kind of grammar does or does not suit a parser depends, at least in part, on the particular design and resources of that parser. (As just one example: the optimal balance between lexical entries and syntactic rules may relate, as Bresnan suggested, to the optimal balance between reliance on long-term memory and reliance on on-line computation; and this in turn can be expected to depend on such matters as how the memory is organized and how efficient the access system is.)

Later in this paper we will report some experimental findings about how the human sentence parsing mechanism identifies and associates the fillers and gaps of transformed sentences. But to give some shape to the detailed discussion that follows, it will be helpful to dwell a little longer on the difference we have pointed to between parsing problems inherent in the language, and parsing problems relating to how information about the language is organized within the grammar. Given this classification of potential problems, we can distinguish two different ways in which a grammar might be designed to facilitate sentence parsing. We will exaggerate the contrast here for expository purposes, but the pictures that we will present are not much more extreme than many that can be found in the literature.

The first picture of the grammar/parser relationship is characteristic of the era of *Aspects* grammars, and the associated parsing models of the early 1970s (see Fodor, Bever, and Garrett, 1974, for the most comprehensive statement). We will argue for a move toward the second picture, which is associated with the more recent attempts to eliminate some or all transformational rules from grammars, and with the more algorithmic approach to parsing that is characteristic of computer models.

Model A: *Rich grammar plus special assistance*

Certain theories of grammars, as we have suggested, render the grammar/ parser relationship quite opaque. Given the way that information about the language is presented by the grammar, it is unclear how the parser could make efficient use of this information in its task of computing the structures on which sentence meanings depend. As an illustration of this we can consider transformational grammars of "standard theory" vintage, which never recommended themselves as a basis for efficient sentence parsing.

The transformational component of a standard theory grammar was always particularly troublesome. The parser had to be thought of as computing the deep structure associated with a surface word string, since the semantic rules needed deep structures as their input. But the transformations could be efficiently applied only in the opposite direction, to specify the surface string associated with a given deep structure. Attempts to design a parser based on such a grammar typically involved some sort of prior reshuffling of the information encoded in its rules. Apart from analysis-by-synthesis models, which were empirically implausible, there seemed to be no way in which a parsing mechanism could make *direct* use of the grammatical rules in assigning a structure to a word string. For example, Fodor, Bever, and Garrett (1974) suggested that the parser operates with heuristic procedures whose form does not mirror the form of the rules in the competence grammar. It was suggested that the grammar would be directly employed (by analysis-by-synthesis routines) only in special cases where the heuristics had broken down.

Fodor et al. were apparently prepared to accept the possibility that the parsing heuristics are acquired quite independently of acquisition of the grammar. The closest relation between the grammar and the parsing routines that they considered at all plausible was that the language learner has an algorithm that he can apply to the rules of the grammar to derive parsing procedures of a quite different form. At the very least, then, this model implied that learning to parse sentences imposes significant demands on children over and above learning the rules of the language. And, if we can judge from the nonexistence of a comprehensive specification of the parsing heuristics and how they would interact with each other, we may guess that the parsing process itself would be quite a complicated matter even for a competent adult speaker.

It is this picture of sentence processing as inherently complex that suggests that some or all of the constraints on grammatical phenomena might serve to exclude difficult-to-parse constructions from the language. For a parser that is juggling hypotheses about sentence structure based on unreliable heuristics, there might very well be a danger of overload if sentences contained many ambiguities and local concentrations of complexity. Thus the grammar could assist the hard-pressed parser by removing these sources of difficulty. The familiar successes in the search for functional explanations of grammatical constraints (such as the ambiguity-reducing constraints discussed earlier) obviously lend support to this view.

Model B: *Simple grammar format, no special help*

By contrast, we can picture parsing as in general a quite straightforward business, based on a grammar containing rules of a type that can be applied directly to word strings by fairly efficient algorithms. This appears to be the case for lexical-functional grammars (see Bresnan, 1982) and for generalized phrase structure grammars (see Gazdar, 1981, and Gazdar, Klein, Pullum, and Sag, in press). We will concentrate here on the latter.

The syntactic component of a generalized phrase structure grammar (GPSG) contains a set of basic context-free phrase structure (CFPS) rules, and a set of metarules that apply to these basic rules to generate further CFPS rules. (But see Fodor and Crain, in preparation, for an alternative theory that admits no metarules.) We can suppose that the parser operates with the full derived grammar. Its rules employ "slash categories," which relate filler constituents to their associated gaps, and hence do the work of movement and deletion transformations. For example, in the phrase marker (4) the topicalized noun phrase *John* is associated with an S whose /NP annotation indicates that it must somewhere contain an NP gap. A similar slash annotation appears on nodes beneath the S node; thus the gap information is in effect passed down through the tree to the lexical level, where it is cashed out as a trace. The "moved" noun phrase (which in fact was generated in place and not moved at all) is thus linked to its "underlying" position by the trail of slash annotations, rather than by a transformational operation.

(4)

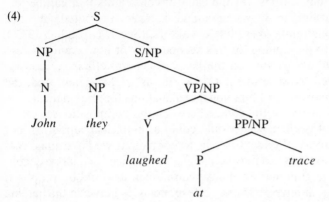

It is argued in J. D. Fodor (1983) that all syntactic constraints in a GPSG grammar apply to the metarules, so that the derived syntactic component does not itself contain any constraints or filters. Thus the syntactic component that the parser refers to is completely uniform; it consists solely of CFPS rules.

Many different procedures for applying such rules to word strings have been proposed. (They differ with respect to whether they operate top-down or bottom-up, with or without look-ahead, and so on.) It is known that an effective procedure exists (see Earley, 1970), and various heuristic strategies for rule sequencing and decision making can improve the efficiency of such a system (at least for the majority of constructions, even if at the expense of a few). Furthermore, since the rules of the grammar are the parser's source of information about the language, a child in the process of acquiring the grammar can immediately make use of the rules he has induced, to parse sentences. (Since linguistic competence can make no contribution to survival without performance routines for applying it, this would seem to be a sensible way for children to be designed.)

Once we see sentence parsing as a rather simple and routine process, we can reasonably consider the possibility that the parsing routines are sufficiently robust to be able to cope with the ambiguity and complexity problems posed by certain sentences. Some (such as center-embedding) may still exceed the capacity of the device; but on this view we would have no reason for expecting grammars to exhibit a host of special constraints designed to solve specific parsing problems. And this is probably just as well, because the very restricted format for the rules of such a grammar would presumably preclude the formulation of all sorts of special constraints, constraints that the parser would have benefited from were they available. Certainly this would be so if the optimum GPSG theory does turn out to be one prohibiting the statement of any constraints over phrase structure derivations, for the class of constraints that can be formulated as constraints in the metagrammar is a very restricted subset of all imaginable constraints over phrase markers. (See J. D. Fodor, 1983.)

We are going to be arguing for this second view of how grammars are designed to facilitate parsing, on the basis of general efficiency considerations supported by experimental data. But as we have indicated, the existence or nonexistence of functional explanations for grammatical constraints is also relevant to the choice between the two positions.

For model A, it is clear what would count as empirical support (if not demonstrative proof). We identify constructions that we have some reason to believe should confound the parsing mechanism; we identify constructions that the grammar excludes even though it would be simpler if it permitted them; and we establish correspondences between the parsing problems and the grammatical restrictions. The closer the match between them, the more confident we can be that the parsing process is indeed the source of the grammatical constraints.

By contrast, it would be more in keeping with model B if grammatical constraints were *not* intimately tied to local parsing complexities, but could be seen instead as consequences of heavy restrictions on the format for grammatical rules, where these format restrictions ensure that linguistic information is packaged appropriately for use by the parser.

Since model B does not predict that languages should contain distinctive superficial clues to the parser's influence on the grammar, it will not be so easy to evaluate as model A. Nevertheless, there are reasons for thinking that it may be on the right track. We have already touched on the fact that a GPSG is constrained to generate a derived syntactic component consisting of CFPS rules, and on the possibility that the derived syntactic component will contain no filters or constraints or any other devices besides CF rules. And it has been argued, by Gazdar (1981) and by J. D. Fodor (1983), that these restrictions on grammar format do entail at least some of the familiar constraints on "transformational" phenomena. Furthermore, the correlation between specific constraints and specific parsing problems is not as strong as one might be tempted to conclude from the handful of well-known examples.

As the search for parsing explanations for syntactic phenomena proceeds, it is becoming more and more obvious that grammars do *not* exclude all, or even most, of the constructions that create difficulty for the parser. Attention in linguistics has naturally tended to center on those cases in which a linguistic restriction *can* be related to a parsing problem. But the parsing literature is full of examples where there is a parsing problem but no associated grammatical restriction. To cite just a few examples, there is the familiar misanalysis of the reduced relative clause in (5), the tendency to misassociate the particle *out* in (6), and the common failure to detect the gap after the verb in (7).

(5) The horse raced past the barn fell.

(6) John threw the apple that Mary had been eating out.

(7) [Which of the children] did you walk - to the bus stop?

Looking at it from the other side, we may also note the failure to identify any special parsing problems that would motivate the most central and most nearly universal syntactic constraints, such as the island constraints of Ross (1967) or any of their more recent formulations. It's not that nobody has tried. A rightly celebrated attempt is found in Marcus (1980), where a severe limit on the size of a memory buffer is argued to limit the analyses the parser is capable of to those obeying Subjacency and the Specified Subject Constraint. However, these constraints do not hold, at least superficially, for long-distance dependencies such as in *wh*-Movement constructions, and Marcus's model therefore has to include more powerful devices for finessing the limits of the buffer for these constructions. But if such devices are compatible with the basic design of the proposed parser, there is no obvious reason why they couldn't be called on for the analysis of Passive and Raising constructions as well. Hence the grammatical constraints on the latter constructions are *not* an automatic consequence of the limited resources of this parsing mechanism.

The inability to explain the major grammatical constraints by appeal to resource limitations or computational problems in sentence parsing doesn't of course entail that they have *no* functional explanation, for they may perhaps be motivated by learning considerations, as proposed by Wexler and Culicover (1980). Nevertheless, the lack of any plausible connection with sentence processing certainly indicates that problems of ambiguity and structural complexity in sentence comprehension have not been a dominating force in the design of human languages.

Thus, without denying that there exist a few striking examples of constraints motivated by specific parsing problems, we might nevertheless judge that the weight of the current evidence falls on the side of alternative B – i.e., that the parser operates quickly and efficiently because the grammar is fundamentally, rather than only superficially, well suited for parsing applications.

Before leaving these general issues, we should indicate where more recent transformational theories fit into our classification. Along with a great many more specific changes, there has been a major reorganization of the components of a transformational grammar. We reproduce here the schema given in Chomsky (1980).

(8) 1. Base rules
     2. Transformational rules
     3a. Deletion rules   3b. Construal rules
     4a. Filters   4b. Interpretive rules
     5a. Phonology and stylistic rules   5b. Conditions on binding

Parsing models based on such grammars can sidestep some of the problems of "undoing" the transformational derivation of a sentence, for it can be assumed that the parser computes a (trace-augmented) S-structure to send to the semantic interpretation routines. It is still true, however, that the rules of the competence grammar cannot be applied to word strings exactly as they stand. The transformational rules, we are supposing, would play no role in sentence parsing at all. The phrase structure rules, which characterize deep phrase markers, could not be used without modification to compute S-structures. And the deletion rules (and stylistic rules?) would presumably still need to be "reversed" in some fashion. Thus the grammar/parser relationship for current transformational grammars still seems to resemble our model A more closely than model B.

Another characteristic of these grammars which threatens to complicate the parsing process (though it might be claimed to facilitate acquisition or other language functions) is their modularity, i.e., the separation of grammatical principles into a number of distinct components. It seems reasonable to suppose that there is extra work involved in accessing and integrating information from many different components, as opposed to having all the relevant facts available in a single body of rules.

In this respect, current transformational grammars contrast strongly with GPSGs. We have already emphasized the uniformity of the (derived) syntactic component of a GPSG, and we will argue in the next section that this makes for very efficient processing of filler-gap constructions. However, we are well aware that uniformity may not strike linguists as a virtue. It may perhaps be reminiscent of Postal's (1972) celebration of homogeneity, which was not well received. The major objection that was raised (see Chomsky, 1974, especially p. 48) was that, in order to allow for the full range of natural language phenomena, Postal's homogeneous definition of "possible rule" had to be extremely permissive in comparison with the narrow definitions permitted by a more modular, nonhomogeneous conception of grammars. It might be thought that the same objection could be raised against nontransformational grammars. However, the format for rules in a GPSG is not only homogeneous but also very restricted, and, as we have noted, the restrictions can be shown to entail some of the peculiarities of natural languages. So there seems to be cause for optimism that, as we approach more closely to the *correct* characterization of "possible rule," homogeneity will re-emerge. And homogeneity of the grammar promises to reduce the number of basic operations that the parser has to be capable of performing and integrating.

To summarize: we have contrasted two different kinds of functional explanation for the structural properties of human languages. The first emphasizes the responsiveness of the grammar to particular cruxes in sentence processing. But it thereby implies, in a backhanded sort of way, that sentence processing is a tricky business that constantly threatens to exceed the capacities of the system. The second approach assumes a deeper fit between the structure of a language and how it is processed. It sees the overall shape of human languages as the consequence of a very restricted format for their rules, and it sees this restricted format as a means for ensuring that the rules can be put to use quite straightforwardly in sentence processing.

These alternatives are not utterly incompatible. Some middle position could well turn out to be the correct one. But model A has been given a good run for its money, and it may be time to see what can be said in favor of model B. We will do our best here to make a case for it, with particular reference to how filler-gap dependencies in sentences are established during sentence comprehension.

3.2. Filler-gap dependencies

In J. D. Fodor (1983) a GPSG parser is compared with an augmented transition network (ATN) parser incorporating a HOLD store for filler constituents that have to be associated with gaps (as described by Wanner and Maratsos, 1978). The ATN model is of interest because it is a precisely formulated, and only minimally indirect, implementation of a transformational grammar. (Each leftward movement transformation, for example, corresponds to an instruction to put the moved constituent into HOLD as soon as it is encountered in the word string, and an instruction to retrieve it from storage at a point in the string corresponding to its deep structure position.)

The Fodor paper argues that, when the constraints on filler-gap associations are taken into account, the operation of this ATN parser is considerably less economical than that of a GPSG parser. The constraints are typically concerned with where a gap may occur in relation to its filler. So in ATN terms, they determine when a filler may legitimately be retrieved from storage, in relation to when it entered the store. Since these constraints refer to structural configurations in phrase markers, building them into the system calls for a HOLD store with internal structure closely matching that of the sentence being parsed, and a variety of traffic rules governing the accessibility and inaccessibility of fillers at various points in the processing of the word string (e.g., they must become inaccessible during the processing of islands).

By contrast, the slashed node labels of a GPSG phrase marker function as memory traces of fillers, so that no separate storage capacity is needed; the HOLD store is in effect incorporated into the memory representation of the structure of the sentence. And the constraints on filler retrieval are implicit in the phrase structure rules of the derived grammar, which specify how the slash annotations on nodes can be passed down through phrase markers from filler positions to gap positions. These rules permit a slash annotation to pass down into a constituent that is not an island, but there will be no rules that permit a slash annotation to pass down into a constituent that does constitute an island. (Such rules will have been screened out in the metagrammar.) A parser employing the derived grammar can thus implicitly keep track of island conditions on how fillers may be paired up with gaps, just by consulting the rules. The option of postulating illegitimate filler-gap associations will simply never arise. Thus no special accessibility conditions are needed in addition to the CF rules that the parser must in any case employ to compute the phrasal structure of the word string; "transformational" phenomena, and the constraints that limit them, are incorporated into these rules determining phrasal configurations. (Of course, these rules do not dictate a unique filler-gap association in cases of genuine ambiguity, where more than one association pattern is acceptable for a sentence. Nor do they provide a semantic interpretation for a filler-gap association. Our claim is only that, since it does not need special mechanisms to exclude the illegitimate association of fillers and gaps across island boundaries, the derived grammar of a GPSG constitutes an efficient basis for establishing the syntactically legitimate correlations between fillers and gaps that are needed to guide semantic rule application, and ambiguity resolution where necessary.)

It should be noted, however, that this argument for the relative superiority of a GPSG-based parser presupposes that the parser detects and fills gaps on-line – that is, at the same time as it is computing phrasal relations among words. Both the GPSG system and the ATN system are designed to do both these jobs simultaneously, and the argument is simply that the GSPG system combines them more efficiently, since they are already combined in the grammar with which the system operates. But it might be suggested that an even more efficient parsing system would not even *try* to do both jobs together, but would establish phrasal structure before attempting to link fillers and gaps.

This is what is proposed in a recent paper by Frazier, Clifton, and Randall (1983), who observe: "The claim that there are distinct components in our linguistic knowledge permits (though it does not dictate) the claim that there are corresponding components in our language comprehension mechanism, and that these components operate at different points in time in the comprehension of a sentence" (p. 31). The suggestion, then, is that the grammar is modular, that the parsing mechanism is correspondingly modular, and (though this is not explicit in the passage quoted above) that the divide-and-conquer approach of a modular system will be as beneficial in the case of sentence parsing as it is in the case of language description.

Why should it be beneficial? In particular, why should we expect greater efficiency from a parser that applies information about fillers and gaps separately from, and later than, information about phrase structure? The reason that Frazier et al. cite is "the uncertainty and complexity of determining the type of filler-gap dependency" a sentence contains (1983, p. 30). There are many temporary ambiguities in filler-gap constructions, and it is suggested that for the parser to appeal to linguistic constraints in order to resolve them might be just a waste of time, since these constraints often decide between competing analyses only in conjunction with facts about much later portions of the input word string. If so, it might be more efficient for the parser simply to ignore the linguistic constraints until a later stage of processing, when they could be applied to greater effect. (Note that ignoring the constraints will save effort only if applying the constraints costs effort. This is so for a modular parser that distinguishes between phrase structure rules and constraints on gap-filling, though not for a GPSG-based parser.)

However, Frazier et al. do not in fact propose that the parser makes no assignments at all on its first pass through the sentence. Rather, they maintain that it does assign fillers to gaps on-line, but on the basis of a simple guessing strategy: *assign the most recent potential filler*. Only later will the parser consult the grammar module containing control and binding principles, to determine whether this initial assignment is acceptable. But then why, as Frazier et al. themselves ask, should the parser bother to make *any* filler-gap assignments at the earlier stage, if it does not take advantage of the grammatical information that defines *correct* assignments?

The answer that is proposed is that the parser needs to know at least which positions in the sentence are gaps and which are not, and that it can distinguish a true gap from a spurious gap by determining that the sentence contains a phrase that could function as its filler. This is not a very convincing argument, however, precisely because of the assumption that the parser is ignoring, at this stage, the control and binding principles that specify which phrases *could* be the filler for a given gap. Without reference to these principles, *any* phrase of the same category as the gap would appear to be a potential filler for it. Thus, in any sentence that contains, for example, a subject noun phrase, any position that *might* be a noun phrase gap will pass the test and will be judged to *be* a noun phrase gap. Hence very little is achieved, in the way of weeding out spurious gaps, by the early assignment of fillers if this assignment ignores the relevant grammatical information. And so we would expect, contrary to the Frazier et al. suggestion, that the parser *either* takes the trouble to make the correct assignments from the outset, *or else* doesn't trouble to make any assignments at all until a later stage of processing.

It is not clear to us that there is any other special advantage to be gained by the separation of these particular syntactic processing operations into distinct modules; in fact we are inclined to suspect the opposite. This is not because we doubt the merits of modularity in general. The modularity idea, very roughly, is that there are many separate little brain mechanisms, each performing its own characteristic computations on the input, and sharing their results with each other only as and when necessary. This contrasts with the idea of there being one large, complex general-purpose computing device that establishes and interrelates all the significant properties of the input. A great deal of work remains to be done on the relative advantages of these two approaches to brain design and on the empirical evidence for either as a model of the human language processing mechanisms (but see J. A. Fodor, 1983; and Crain and Steedman, paper 10 in this volume). Our argument must therefore be tentative.

It seems to us that the potential merits of a modular design are greatest when the various subcomponents are concerned with *distinct* properties of the stimulus. Separate syntactic and phonological modules, for example, would seem reasonable enough, because only a limited amount of cross-talk will be needed between them. But the principles determining legitimate filler-gap associations in sentences make reference to phrase structure configurations (e.g., c-command relations, and the various island conditions). So it is not at all clear that to divide the corresponding processing operations into separate modules would be such a good idea. It would presumably entail some duplication, as the gap-filling module has to retrack over the phrase marker, looking for properties already established by the phrase structure module. Our own hunch, then, is that while modularity *of* the syntactic component seems plausible, modularity *within* it may not be a virtue.

What has to be set against this very general speculation is the experimental evidence that has been adduced in favor of separation of the phrase structure and gap-filling computations in the human sentence parsing routines. We will argue that there is in fact *no* evidence for this position. But there are two important recent studies that appear to support it, and we must give our reasons for thinking that they do not.

3.3. Experimental evidence

Frazier, Clifton, and Randall offer data in support of their claim that the constraints on gap-filling are applied late in the sentence parsing process, and we will discuss their findings in some detail shortly. First we will consider a series of experiments by Freedman (1982), which can also be interpreted as providing evidence of a separation between the phrase structure rules and the constraints on fillers and gaps in the grammar that the parser employs.

3.3.1. The Freedman study

Freedman hit upon a curious phenomenon. She was originally looking for a subtler way of identifying ungrammaticality of word strings than simply asking people for grammaticality judgments. The interesting cases, of course, are strings like *What did you buy Picasso's painting of?*, which are crucial for distinguishing between alternative grammars and yet which often give rise to uncertain or conflicting judgments from native speakers. If naïve informants say that this string is a grammatical sentence, despite linguists' claims to the contrary, this might indicate that it *is* a grammatical sentence, but it might suggest only that naïve informants are not very good at tapping their internally represented grammars and articulating the results. Freedman reasoned that a sentence that conflicts with the mental grammar might nevertheless be understood by some sort of analogical extension of the rules, but the need for this special interpretation process should show up in a performance decrement in various psycholinguistic tasks. So she constructed a variety of sentences that violated constraints on transformations, and tested them in a sentence matching task that had previously been shown to be sensitive at least to gross instances of ungrammaticality (i.e., scrambled word strings, as compared with clearly well-formed sentences). What Freedman found was absolutely nothing – no reduction at all in performance on the matching task for constraint-violating sentences.

The absence of any effect could not be attributed to the insensitivity of the task, or to the subtlety of the ungrammaticality of the constraint-violating sentences, for the expected decrement was found for other sentences which were judged by the subjects to be comparable in their degree of ungrammaticality, but which violated the *rules* of the grammar rather than the constraints. For example, sentence-matching times for number agreement violations, as in (9a), were significantly longer than for their grammatical counterparts, such as (9b).

(9) a. *Mary were writing a letter to her husband.
     b. Mary was writing a letter to her husband.

Yet the supposedly ungrammatical sentence (10a) was no slower than its grammatical control (10b).

(10) a. *What did you buy Picasso's painting of?
      b. What did you buy a painting of?

More precisely, Freedman compared the difference in matching times between (10a) and (10b) with the difference in matching times between the declaratives (11a) and (11b).

(11) a. We bought Picasso's painting of a bullfight.
      b. We bought a painting of a bullfight.

The (a) and (b) sentences differ, in both (10) and (11), by the substitution of *a* for *Picasso's*. By subtracting the difference between the times for the declarative examples from the difference between the times for the interrogative examples, Freedman controlled for the lexical variation between the interrogative examples and isolated the effect of the constraint violation. It was on this four-way comparison that she drew a blank. The *Picasso* question was harder to match than the *a* question, but only to the extent that the *Picasso* declarative was harder than the *a* declarative; the violation of the constraint had no detectable effect.

Freedman concluded that the differential effects of rule-violations and constraint-violations must have something to do with how rules and constraints are mentally represented and applied by the sentence-processing routines. There is more than one way of accounting for the difference, but they all seem to imply, as one might have guessed, a rather sharp distinction between rules and constraints in the grammar that the parser works with.

Perhaps the simplest story is that the rules and the constraints reside in different modules of the system, and that the parser has the ability to switch out the constraints module at will. In the Freedman experiments, many of the sentences that were presented violated constraints. If these violations threatened to interfere with performance on the matching task, the parser would do well to turn off the constraints if it could, and parse the offending sentences just as if they were grammatical. It could not, presumably, take this easy way out for rule violations, since to switch out the rules would leave the parser with nothing to parse with at all. The trouble with this story is that it attributes to the parser an ability which has no obvious value except in certain psycholinguistic experiments. We surely do, in ordinary conversation, come across sentences which are ungrammatical in one way or another but which we would like to be able to understand, and it is not absurd to suppose that the comprehension mechanisms have routines for coping with such cases. But it is hard to imagine that constraint violations have any special status in this respect.

A more interesting idea, suggested by Freedman, takes seriously the notion of *overgeneration*. Let us suppose that in the normal case, the parser somehow reconstructs the full transformational derivation of an input sentence. For a word string that violates a rule of the base, there will be no derivation at all for the parser to compute, since the grammar does not provide even an initial phrase marker for such a word string. But for a word string that violates a constraint on a transformation, there *will* be at least a partial derivation, even though it terminates with the assignment of * at the point at which it offends the relevant constraint. Thus we might conclude that what the constraint-violating sentences have in common with grammatical sentences, which allows them to be handled efficiently in the sentence-matching task, is the fact that the parser can assign them *some* well-formed syntactic representation.

From the point of view of our hypothesis that the human sentence-parsing mechanism employs a GPSG, it hardly matters which of these two stories we tell. The first implies that phrase structure rules and constraints on transformational dependencies are separately represented, because they can be switched in and out separately. The second implies that they are separately represented because they apply at different stages in a syntactic derivation. But in the derived grammar of a GPSG, which is what we are assuming that the parser refers to, the phrase structure rules and the constraints on filler-gap dependencies are inextricably entwined and *must* apply simultaneously. The only way to selectively turn off the constraints would be to turn them off at the metarule level and thus allow the metarules to generate a whole new derived grammar for the parser to work with, but this certainly seems a high price for the system to pay for the privilege of being able to process a limited selection of ungrammatical sentences.

Our only defense against the Freedman argument, it seems, is to challenge the experimental findings – not the actual matching times, or the statistical analysis of them, but the description of the crucially distinguishing property of the sentences whose ungrammaticality had no deleterious effect on performance in the matching task. *One* way of characterizing the difference between examples (9) and (10) above is as a contrast between rule violations and constraint violations. But there might be other ways, which have nothing to do with how ungrammaticality is formally treated in the mental grammar.

A careful look at just what is involved in the sentence matching task suggests a hypothesis about what might be going on. In Freedman's study, a sentence was presented visually to a subject and it stayed on the screen while, two seconds later, another sentence appeared immediately beneath it. In all the critical cases, the second sentence was identical to the first, and the correct response was therefore "yes." (An equal number of mismatched sentence pairs was also presented, to keep the subjects on their toes.) Previous studies with this paradigm have made it clear that subjects do not wait for the second sentence to appear and then compare the two letter by letter; instead they apparently process the first sentence, hold it in memory, and then process the second.

Our suggestion is that the number agreement examples, and others included in Freedman's rule-violation category, were difficult for subjects to match because they were easy for subjects to correct – that in fact the subjects couldn't resist correcting them (e.g., mentally converting *Mary were writing* to *Mary was writing*). If so, a subject would presumably be torn, when the second sentence appeared on the screen, between matching what he had actually seen, and matching what he had mentally converted it into.

The constraint-violating sentences, by contrast, have the interesting property that there is really *no* obvious grammatical way of expressing what they are supposed to express. One could try paraphrasing the meaning indirectly. For example, one might convert *What did you buy Picasso's painting of?* into *What painting of Picasso's did you buy?*. Or one could settle for losing part of the meaning, by reducing a sentence such as *Who did the police believe the claim that Bill had shot?* to *Who did the police believe that Bill had shot?*. However, in none of these constraint-violation cases is there a unique and straightforward strategy that immediately springs to mind for patching up the problem. Since there is such a short interval before the second sentence appears, we might therefore expect subjects to remember the first sentence just as it is, ungrammaticality and all. And their failure to correct it (which is not, after all, what they were asked to do) would have the advantage of not getting them into a tangle about what to match against the second sentence. (Of course, remembering an ungrammatical sentence might be harder than remembering a grammatical one, and this might push up the matching times for the constraint-violating sentences. But memorability is typically highly correlated with the degree of structure that can be imposed on an item, and the constraint-violating sentences do hang together nicely in phrasal chunks; unlike mere word scrambles, they can be assigned phrase markers, even if their phrase markers contain illegalities.)

These observations suggest that what determined the matching times in Freedman's experiments may have been how easy to correct an ungrammaticality was, rather than whether it constituted a rule violation or a constraint violation. We have had subjects make corrections to sentences similar to Freedman's, and rate how difficult they found it to do so. There was a highly significant difference between the ratings for the rule violations and the ratings for the constraint violations; in fact, every rule-violating sentence was judged to be easier to correct than any constraint-violating sentence. It is therefore possible that correctability was the significant factor in the matching experiments. We propose to replicate the matching study with these and additional materials, to see how close the correlation is between the correctability ratings for sentences and their matching times.

If our reinterpretation of Freedman's results is correct, it should follow that correctability determines matching times even when it runs counter to the rule versus constraint distinction. That is, easily correctable constraint-violating sentences should be difficult to match, and difficult-to-correct rule-violating sentences should be easy to match. We have preliminary results for this prediction also. Sentences (12) and (13) violate, respectively, the Fixed Subject Constraint, and the constraint that requires a complementizer for a sentence-initial subordinate clause. Sentences like these were judged by our subjects to be easy to correct, and their matching times were significantly longer ($p < .05$) than those for other constraint-violating sentences such as (10a).

(12) *Which dog did the man think that had bitten him?

(13) *There was no-one there to meet us was disappointing.

By contrast, sentences such as (14) and (15), which violate rules of the base rather than constraints on transformations, were judged to be almost as difficult to correct as Freedman's constraint-violating examples, and they were as easy to match as those examples.

(14) *Part of when the screen went blank.

(15) *John and there was a fly in the soup.

Further studies using a wider range of sentence types are necessary before we can resolve this issue with confidence, but our tentative conclusion at present is that the sentence-matching task does *not* speak to the question of whether constraints on fillers and gaps are represented and applied separately from the phrase structure rules. The notion of correctability that we have appealed to is of no theoretical interest in itself, but its effects need to be recognized in order to keep them from masquerading as evidence for modularity within the syntactic processing system.

3.3.2. The Frazier, Clifton, and Randall study

We turn now to the experimental evidence presented by Frazier, Clifton, and Randall (1983), in support of their hypothesis that the grammatical constraints on legitimate filler-gap pairings are initially ignored in favor of a most-recent-filler assignment strategy. This predicts that sentences for which the most recent filler is the correct filler will be easy to process, relative to comparable sentences for which the most-recent-filler strategy conflicts with the relevant grammatical principles. And this is exactly what their experimental results seem to show.

They presented sentences one word at a time to subjects who were required to indicate, as quickly as possible after the sentence was complete, whether or not they had "got it." (Frazier et al. "They were instructed to indicate 'missed it' (failure to understand) if they would normally be inclined to go back and re-read a sentence, and 'got it' (understand) otherwise" [p. 14].) The sentences included Recent Filler sentences such as (16), in which the filler for the first gap is the subject of the relative clause, and Distant Filler sentences such as (17), in which the filler for the first gap is the relative pronoun, which precedes the subject.

(16)   Everyone liked the woman who [the little child] started – to sing NP for – PP.

(17)   Everyone liked the woman who the little child forced – – to sing NP PP.

(In both examples, NP = *those stupid French songs*, and PP = *last Christmas*; we abbreviate them here to ease the display of filler-gap pairings.)

The same sentences were also presented with ambiguous main verbs which, unlike *start* and *force*, are compatible with both a Recent Filler and a Distant Filler analysis. The verb *begged*, for example, is compatible with both filler-gap patterns, as shown in (18) and (19) (comparable to (16) and (17), respectively).

(18)   Everyone liked the woman who [the little child] begged – to sing NP for – PP.

(19)   Everyone like the woman who the little child begged – – to sing NP PP.

Sentences (18) and (19) are identical except for their last few words, so grammatical information cannot even in principle specify the correct filler for the first gap position, until these last words have been encountered. These temporarily ambiguous sentences provide a standard against which to compare the unambiguous sentences (16) and (17). For the unambiguous sentences, the grammar does locally determine the filler-gap pattern, but the Frazier et al. hypothesis is that this grammatical information is initially ignored, so that these sentences are processed in the same way as the temporarily ambiguous ones.

All sentences (unambiguous and temporarily ambiguous) were also presented with the relative pronoun deleted, in order to test the assumption that a null *wh*-filler, being less salient than an overt *wh*-phrase, would be even more likely to be overlooked in favor of a filler close to the gap.

Over all sentences, the mean response time for the Distant Filler examples (1,165 msec) was significantly ($p < .05$) longer than that for the Recent Filler examples (1,071 msec); and the percentage of "got it" responses for the Distant Filler examples (66%) was significantly ($p < .01$) lower than that for the Recent Filler examples (78%). Thus the results appear to confirm the hypothesis that the Distant Filler sentences are harder to process than the Recent Filler sentences, and Frazier et al. attribute the difficulty of the Distant Filler sentences to the need to revise the initial incorrect filler-gap assignment based on the simple guessing strategy, when it is found to be incompatible with the remainder of the sentence.

Of particular interest is the fact that the difference in response time between the Recent Filler and Distant Filler sentences with unambiguous verbs, such as (16) and (17), was not significantly different from that for the sentences with ambiguous verbs, such as (18) and (19). Over all sentences, these differences were 87 and 101 msec respectively. (For sentences with overt *wh*-fillers, which we will focus on below, the differences were 47 and 51 msec, respectively.) Frazier et al. argue that this similarity in the results for the ambiguous and unambiguous examples strongly suggests that they are processed in a similar fashion. Since the parser can get no useful information from the grammar about how to fill the early gap in the ambiguous sentences, the implication is that it also gets none in the case of the unambiguous sentences, that even where it *could* usefully consult the grammar it does not do so – or at least, it does not do so until a later stage of processing.

If this conclusion is correct, it implies that phrase structure information and information about filler-gap pairings are accessed and used at different times by the parser. This is obviously feasible if the two kinds of information are stored separately, but it constitutes an argument against a GPSG parsing system, in which the two kinds of information would be more or less inextricably combined.

However, there are reasons for doubting that this experiment does provide clear evidence for modularity within the syntactic parsing mechanism. First, the Distant Filler examples contain two gaps after the main verb of the relative clause, where the Recent Filler examples contain only one. Thus in (17) there is a gap in direct object position after *forced*, whose filler is the relative pronoun, and also a gap in subject position in the complement clause, whose filler is the direct object of *forced*. In other words, the relative pronoun has to fill two gaps in close succession. Frazier et al. give reasons for rejecting the possibility that this double gap-filling task might overload the parser and thus make the Distant Filler sentences harder to process than the Recent Filler sentences, but we will argue below that the double gap configuration does impose significant demands on the parser.

Quite apart from this concern, the presence of two adjacent gaps in the Distant Filler examples means that a Recent Filler misanalysis of these sentences would require a greater disregard of grammatical information than even Frazier et al. suggests. *Either* the parser ignores subcategorization information as well as control principles, and thus overlooks the direct object gap entirely, so that the phrase structure as well as the filler-gap structure of (17) is taken to be exactly comparable to that of (16); *or else*, having recognized the direct object gap in (17), the parser makes the extreme mistake of treating this gap as the result of deletion under identity with the subject of the same clause, even though such deletions are never allowed.

A very different problem is that there is a completely independent ambiguity whose presence or absence in these examples is confounded with the Distant Filler versus Recent Filler contrast. The verb *forced* in (17) could be either a past tense main verb (which is the correct reading in this context), or a passive participle in a reduced relative clause modifying *the little child*. The latter reading is almost certainly the less preferred of the two, but it might nevertheless be adopted by the subjects sufficiently often to increase the mean processing time for the Distant Filler sentence. Many of the Distant Filler verbs that were used permit this garden path (e.g., *allowed*, *permitted*, *persuaded*, *urged*, *invited*, etc.), but few of the Recent Filler verbs do. Admittedly, *started* can occur in *the child (who was) started on his way by the teacher*, and *agreed* can occur in *the boy (who was) agreed to be in need of help*, but *hesitated*, *attempted*, *swore*, *seemed*, and other Recent Filler verbs that were used cannot initiate a reduced relative clause. Hence there is less opportunity for the parser to be garden pathed by the Recent Filler examples.

For Distant Filler sentences with no overt relative pronoun, this reduced relative garden path interacts with another tempting misanalysis. The sequence *the woman the little child* in the version of (17) with no relative pronoun is the beginning of a relative clause construction, but locally it could be construed instead as the beginning of a conjoined noun phrase structure. Blumenthal (1966) showed that subjects prefer the conjunction analysis over the relative clause analysis, at least in doubly center-embedded examples. The conjunction garden path is equally likely in both the Recent Filler and the Distant Filler sentences, but it still introduces an important asymmetry into the materials, for once a subject makes the mistake of adopting the conjunction analysis for *Everyone liked the woman the little child*, the reduced relative analysis of *forced* becomes the *only* legitimate analysis. Hence, even if the reduced relative garden path is relatively uncommon in most contexts, we would expect it to be very common in the Distant Filler sentences with no relative pronoun. There is reason to believe that this contributed significantly to the obtained differences between the Recent Filler and Distant Filler examples. The response time difference for the unambiguous examples was 128 msec when the relative pronoun was absent, but was only 47 msec when it was present, and the difference in "got it" responses was reduced from 15 percentage points with the relative pronoun absent, to 5 with the relative pronoun present. (As we have noted, however, Frazier et al. offer an alternative explanation for these differences, which appeals to differences in the salience of the *wh*-filler.)

Finally, if the response time difference was due to a Recent Filler garden path analysis of the Distant Filler sentences, as Frazier et al. propose, then it should follow that subjects would be slow to detect the ungrammaticality of examples like (20), in which there is no legitimate filler for the direct object gap after *forced* (and hence also no filler for the subject gap in the complement).

(20) *The little child had forced ⌐¬ to sing NP PP.

(Observe that in [20] we have eliminated the confounding reduced relative garden path by introducing an auxiliary verb.) The reasoning behind this prediction is that, according to the Frazier et al. interpretation, the presence of a *wh*-filler in (17) is completely irrelevant to the subjects' construal of the first gap. They fill this gap with *the little child* because it is the closest possible filler, regardless of the fact that the gap occurs in a relative clause and thus also has a potential *wh*-filler (overt or null). Hence these subjects should do exactly the same in (20), even though (20) is not a relative clause construction. They should be quite content to fill the first gap in (20) with *the little child*, and not notice until later, when the relevant grammatical principles are eventually consulted, that this is not a valid assignment – and that, since there is no other possible filler, the sentence is ungrammatical. We have not yet run the experiment that would test this prediction, but we have little doubt about its outcome; the ungrammaticality of (20) seems to be readily detectable as soon as the sequence *forced to* is encountered. (Incidentally, the Frazier et al. strategy predicts all sorts of other misparses which could be tested experimentally. For instance, the second gap in a Recent Filler sentence such as [16] should also be incorrectly filled at first.)

Because of these problems, we decided to repeat the Frazier et al. experiment with a number of changes in method and materials.

3.3.3. Our own experiment

So that we could determine the locus of any complication in the parsing of the Distant Filler sentences, we required our subjects to respond to each word of a sentence in turn. They were instructed to read the first word presented, and as soon as they had done so to push a button that would trigger presentation of the next word, and so on throughout the sentence. The reading time for each word was recorded. (There is an obvious danger in this paradigm that subjects will ignore the instructions and call for the whole string of words before attending to any of them, thus obscuring local differences in processing difficulty. We required our subjects to make rapid grammaticality judgments on a proportion of the sentences presented, and although this was a postsentence task it seems to have been sufficient to encourage them to process the word string as it was received, for we did obtain significant word reading time differences.)

In place of relative clause constructions we used *wh*-questions such as (21) and (22), each of which could be compared with its corresponding declarative ((23) and (24) respectively), to control for word frequency effects, plausibility, and any other variables that might affect processing time, independently of the difficulty of filler-gap assignments.

(21) Who could [the little child] have started – to sing NP for – PP?

(22) Who could the little child have forced – – to sing NP for Cheryl PP?

(23) [The little child] could have started – to sing NP for Cheryl PP.

(24) The little child could have forced us – to sing NP for Cheryl PP.

Like Frazier et al., we also used ambiguous verbs in both the Recent Filler and Distant Filler constructions, as illustrated in (25) and (26), with (27) and (28) as declarative controls.

(25) Who could [the little child] have begged – to sing NP for – PP?

(26) Who could the little child have begged – – to sing NP for Cheryl PP?

(27) [The little child] could have begged – to sing NP for Cheryl PP.

(28) The little child could have begged us – to sing NP for Cheryl PP.

We also included two further versions of each sentence, using the verbs of the unambiguous and ambiguous Distant Filler versions but a filler-gap pattern resembling that of the Recent Filler versions. Sentences (29) and (30) illustrate these constructions, which we will call Late *wh*-Gap versions. (Their declarative controls are [24] and [28], respectively.)

(29) Who could the little child have forced us – to sing NP for – PP?

(30) Who could the little child have begged us – to sing NP for – PP?

The verbs *forced* and *begged* are followed here by a lexical direct object rather than by a direct object gap for the *wh*-filler. The *wh*-filler has its gap later in the sentence, in just the same position as in the corresponding Recent Filler sentence. Thus there is only one gap at the early position in these sentences, rather than two adjacent gaps, and its filler is the most recent potential filler. If the Frazier et al. strategy is correct, these sentences should therefore be easier to parse than the Distant Filler sentences (22) and (26).

To eliminate the reduced relative clause garden path analysis, we introduced auxiliary verbs before the main verb in all versions, as shown in (21)–(30).

In order to increase the chance of detecting a "surprise" effect when the putative Recent Filler garden path analysis of the Distant Filler sentences is discovered to be incompatible with the continuation of the sentence, we introduced a lexical noun phrase in the Distant Filler sentences in a position corresponding to the second gap in the Recent Filler sentences. Thus we included the prepositional phrase *for Cheryl* in (22) and (26), for comparison with the *for* plus gap in (21) and (25). Subjects who were analyzing (22) along the lines of (21) would be expected to exhibit some distress at the presence of the noun phrase *Cheryl*, given that they would still need to locate a gap for the unassigned *wh*-filler, and the opportunities for finding a gap after this noun phrase would be minimal (as shown by the difficulty of finding a well-formed completion for the initial fragment *Who could the little child have started to sing those stupid French songs for Cheryl*).

Our materials were otherwise identical to those of Frazier et al. except that we eliminated examples that were arguably not instances of subject-controlled Equi (for Recent Filler examples) or object-controlled Equi (for Distant Filler examples); for example, we eliminated sentences containing the verb *seemed*, and substituted other sentences with verbs of the appropriate type.

Eighteen sentence sets were tested, each set consisting of ten versions that differed with respect to their main verbs and filler-gap patterns but were otherwise identical. One complete set has already been presented, and it is summarized in (31), (where RF = Recent Filler and DF = Distant Filler).

(31) a. Unambiguous RF question, e.g. (19).
      b. Unambiguous DF question, e.g. (20).
      c. Declarative control for (a), e.g. (21).
      d. Declarative control for (b) and (i), e.g. (22).
      e. Temporarily ambiguous RF question, e.g. (23).
      f. Temporarily ambiguous DF question, e.g. (24).
      g. Declarative control for (e), e.g. (25).
      h. Declarative control for (f) and (j), e.g. (26).

i. Unambiguous Late *wh*-Gap question, e.g. (27).
j. Temporarily ambiguous Late *wh*-Gap question, e.g. (28).

All the sentence sets exhibited the same general syntactic pattern, though the number of words between gap positions varied from one set to another. To facilitate comparison of the results across sentences and versions, we aligned and numbered corresponding words as shown in (32), with examples drawn from the sentence set presented in (31).

(32)	Position	Description	Examples
	I	Initial words, not identical across versions	*who could the little child have/the little child could have*
	II	Main verb	*started/forced/begged*
	III	Gap, or single-word object noun phrase	*– / us*
	IV	Complementizer	*to*
	V	Verb of complement clause	*sing*
	VI	All words between V and VII	*those stupid French songs*
	VII	Preposition	*for*
	VIII	Gap, or single-word noun phrase	*– / Cheryl*
	IX	First word of abverbial phrase	*last*
	X	All other words in adverbial phrase	*Christmas*
	XI	Sentence-final punctuation	*. / ?*

Where a sequence of words was assigned to a single numbered position, the reading time for the position was taken to be the average of the reading times for the words in the sequence.

In order to minimize the effects of different overall reading speeds for different subjects, all word reading times were converted to z-scores prior to any further analysis (that is, the reading time for each word for each subject was expressed in terms of the standard deviation from that subject's overall mean word reading time).

For each sentence position of interest, we computed what we will call an *increase score*, as a measure of the processing complexity at that position. For the early gap at position III, the increase score was computed as the mean of the z-scores for positions IV and V, minus the z-score for position II. (*Note*: We included two word positions after the gap on the grounds that a parsing problem could be expected to interfere with the processing of more than just the immediate word that created the problem; we subtracted out the score for the word preceding the gap in order to control for any already accumulated differences in difficulty between sentence versions due, for example, to subject auxiliary inversion or the frequency of the main verb.) For sentence versions with a lexical noun phrase rather than a gap at position III, the increase score was taken (by the same reasoning) to be the mean of the z-scores for positions III and IV, minus the z-score for position II. For the late gap at position VIII, the increase score was calculated in a similar fashion on the basis of the z-scores for positions VII, IX, and X. For a lexical noun phrase at position VIII, the relevant scores were those for positions VII, VIII, and IX. For the sentence-final punctuation at position XI, the increase score was taken to be the z-score for position XI minus the z-score for position X. In all cases, we construe a high increase score as an indication of a heavy processing load at that position in the sentence.

Now we can consider the results. These involve comparisons of increase scores across different sentence versions. The significance levels for the differences we report were calculated using matched-pair t tests, one-tailed. For all of the differences that we cite as significant, $p < .025$; for all differences reported as nonsignificant, $p > .1$.

Let us briefly review the hypotheses to be evaluated. The Frazier et al. hypothesis is that grammatical information about legitimate fillers is not referred to while the phrase structure at a gap position is being established, and that the parser adopts a Recent Filler analysis in all cases, regardless of whether this analysis is compatible with the grammar. This predicts that the unambiguous DF question should be processed in exactly the same way as the ambiguous DF question, at least at the early gap position, and both should be processed as easily as the RF questions at that position. If the parser does not consult the relevant grammatical principles at all, except in cases where its current anaylsis has broken down, then the unambiguous DF question should be processed in exactly the same way as the ambiguous DF question at the late gap position also, and both should be more difficult to process at that position than the RF questions, since the late gap position in a DF sentence actually contains a lexical noun phrase that will force the parser to go back and revise its analysis. If, on the other hand, there is simply a temporal delay in the parser's application of the gap-filling principles, then the garden path in the unambiguous DF question (though not in the ambiguous one) might be noted and corrected prior to the late gap position. Hence the unambiguous question should be more difficult to process than the ambiguous question between the two gap positions, but easier to process at the late gap position. Whichever of these two assumptions is made about the eventual use of linguistic information, it is clearly predicted that the unambiguous DF question should be easy to process at the early gap position (where the simple strategy is applied) but difficult to process later on (when this strategy turns out to have been misguided).

By contrast, our own hypothesis that the phrase structure rules incorporate gap-filling information predicts that the parser will correctly analyze the unambiguous DF question on its first pass through the sentence, though it may misanalyze the ambiguous DF question exactly as Frazier et al. propose. Since a DF question contains two successive gaps to be filled at the early position, we might expect the unambiguous DF question to be harder to process at that position than either an RF question or the ambiguous DF question (assuming that this is being treated as if it were an RF question). At the late gap position, there should be no further gap-filling work for the parser to do in the case of the unambiguous DF question, and also no garden path to correct, so we would expect the unambiguous DF question to be easier to process at this position than the ambiguous DF question.

Our results are in accord with these latter predictions. At the early gap position, the increase score for the unambiguous DF question was significantly higher than that for the ambiguous DF question. This comports with our claim that the two successive gaps at this position were correctly identified and filled in the unambiguous question, though not in the ambiguous question. (Contrary to our predictions, the increase score for the unambiguous DF question was not significantly higher than that for the unambiguous RF question, though the difference between the two was at least in the expected direction. Thus the *direct* evidence that the unambiguous DF question is not assigned an RF analysis is weak. But the previous result, which shows that the unambiguous question is not analyzed as if it were ambiguous, indirectly supports the claim that the unambiguous question is correctly analyzed in accord with grammatical principles. Other results presented below confirm this interpretation.)

Before turning to the results for the other sentence positions, there are two comments we should make about the double gap-filling hypothesis. Frazier et al. conducted a second experiment designed to exclude the possibility that the filling of two gaps at the early position was responsible for the greater difficulty of their DF sentences. They compared sentences with the verbs *ask* and *choose*, which have two successive postverbal gaps in DF constructions, with sentences containing the verbs *want* and *expect*, which – according to certain syntactic analyses at least – have only one gap (in subject position in the complement clause) even in a DF construction. The DF sentences were again found to be significantly harder to process than corresponding RF sentences, but no consistent difference was observed between sentences containing verbs of the two types. These results may appear to contradict our explanation of why the unambiguous DF sentences in our own experiment were harder at the early gap position, but in fact they do not. All four of these verbs are ambiguous between RF and DF analyses, and we do not challenge the Frazier et al. account of ambiguous examples; our disagreement concerns only the unambiguous ones. We can therefore accept the conclusion that both the two-gap verbs and the one-gap verbs in the DF sentences of this second experiment were treated by the parser as if they were RF verbs with a single gap, and still hold to our own evidence that it is a strain for the parser to fill two gaps in rapid succession when it does do so.

The second point to be noted is that Equi gaps are not explicitly represented as gaps, marked by slash annotations, in a GPSG analysis. The complement to an Equi verb is categorized not as an S/NP but as a $\overline{\text{VP}}$, as proposed by Brame (1976) and Bresnan (1978), and semantic principles determine the understood subject to this $\overline{\text{VP}}$. Hence, if what we mean by *gap-filling* is an operation performed by the *syntactic* parsing mechanism, we cannot properly talk of gap-filling at all in the case of Equi constructions. In GPSG terms, the difference between RF sentences and DF sentences at the early position is not a difference between one gap in the RF construction and two gaps in the DF construction, but is a difference between *no* gap in the RF construction and *one* gap (the *wh*-gap) in the DF construction. (In both cases there is also one Equi dependency to be handled by the semantic processing routines.)

For purposes of comparison with the Frazier et al. study, which presupposed a transformational rather than a phrase structure grammar, we have been describing our materials as if they contained explicit Equi gaps. But since we believe that the GPSG description of these constructions is the correct one, we would like to emphasize that it does not substantially alter the conclusions that can be drawn from our experimental data. The fact that the unambiguous DF questions had a higher increase score at the early position than the ambiguous DF questions still indicates that the unambiguous ones (1) were not treated as if they were ambiguous, and (2) demanded more processing effort than the ambiguous examples, which we are assuming (in accord with other results to be presented shortly) were assigned an RF analysis. There are various possible explanations within a GPSG model for why the DF analysis should be more demanding than the RF analysis (even though we do not assume that the syntactic operations involved in pairing fillers with gaps are particularly arduous). For example, on the DF analysis the phrase marker is locally more complex, since the matrix VP/NP has three daughter constituents, while in the RF analysis it has only two. Also, if we assume with Marslen-Wilson (1975) that there is little or no delay between syntactic processing and semantic processing, and make the natural assumption that the application of the semantic rules for gap constructions (see Gazdar,

1982) imposes significant demands, then the semantic processing load would be greater at the early position for the DF analysis than for the RF analysis.

We turn now to the late gap position. The increase score at this position for the ambiguous DF question was significantly higher than that for its declarative control, but the increase score for the unambiguous DF question was not significantly higher than that for its declarative control. This is consistent with our claim that there is a garden path in the ambiguous DF question but not in the unambiguous one.

We did not find, as we had expected to, a significant difference at the late gap position between the ambiguous and unambiguous DF questions, independent of their declarative controls (though the difference between them was in the predicted direction). In other words, the contrast between the ambiguous and unambiguous versions at this position was a relatively weak one. However, it seems likely that this is due to the fact that the garden path in the ambiguous version was not always detected at the gap position itself. That is, the adverbial phrase which followed the gap was not entirely successful in its intended role as a disambiguator of the filler-gap pattern; subjects did not always conclude, when they encountered this adverbial phrase, that there could be no subsequent gap in the sentence for the *wh*-filler to fill. Note that if this suggestion is correct, the processing load associated with revision of the garden path analysis should have been distributed between the adverbial phrase and the sentence-final punctuation (which presumably *was* an unmistakable disambiguator). This is exactly what our data reveal. At the punctuation, the increase score for the unambiguous question was not significantly higher than that for its declarative control, but the increase score for the ambiguous question was significantly higher than that for the unambiguous question. It appears, then, that the punctuation was in many cases the effective disambiguator.

We can conclude from these results that, by contrast with the ambiguous question, the analysis of the unambiguous question did *not* involve an RF garden path which the parser had to recover from at the end of the sentence. Earlier, we considered the possibility that there might be a short-lived garden path in the unambiguous question, corrected by reference to grammatical principles *prior* to receipt of the disambiguating words later in the sentence. But there is no sign of this either. That is, the unambiguous DF question was not significantly harder to process than either its declarative control or the ambiguous DF question at position VI, which includes all the words between the early gap region and the later disambiguating words.

Finally, there are the results for the Late *wh*-Gap sentences. Since an RF analysis is correct for the early gap in these sentences, the Frazier et al. hypothesis predicts that they should be easy to process. In fact they were the most difficult of all, both overall and at the early gap position in particular. The increase score at the early gap position for the unambiguous Late *wh*-Gap version was significantly higher than that for its declarative control. That is, subjects found it harder to process the noun phrase *us* in *Who could the little child have forced us to* than in *The little child could have forced us to* (controlling out any accumulated difficulty due to other complications at the beginning of the question). The only explanation we can think of for this is that the subjects were expecting a gap for the *wh*-filler after *forced* in the question, rather than the lexical noun phrase that actually appeared there, but were not expecting a gap in the declarative. And this has important implications. The only difference between the question and the declarative was the presence of the *wh*-filler (and associated subject auxiliary inversion) at the beginning of the question. If the subjects were expecting a gap in the direct object position in the question but not in the declarative, they must have been taking account of this *wh*-filler and recognizing the direct object position as a possible gap for it – even though the *wh*-filler is *not* the most recent potential filler (grammatical principles aside) for a gap in that position. If the grammar were being ignored, the most recent potential filler would have been the subject of the matrix clause (i.e., *the little child*). But since this noun phrase is present in both the question and the declarative, it could not have been the source of the subjects' different expectations. Thus the Late *wh*-Gap sentences provide further evidence that perceivers do consider a more distant filler for a gap, when the grammar dictates that it is the correct filler.

To sum up: compared with the ambiguous DF question, the unambiguous DF question was difficult to process at the early gap position, and easy to process at the late gap and punctuation positions. This strongly suggests that grammatical information was being used to establish the sequence of two adjacent gaps at the early position and to fill them correctly, so that no unassigned fillers remained to complicate the analysis of the remainder of the sentence. The RF strategy proposed by Frazier et al. apparently does exist, but only as an ambiguity resolution strategy for use when the grammar provides no relevant information about the relations between fillers and gaps.

3.3.4. Methodological issues

Some remarks on methodology are probably in order at this point. The on-line response measure used in our experiment is obviously much more informative than a single postsentence measure, such as in the Frazier et al. study, but it does have the disadvantage of making the subjects' task

124   *Crain and Fodor*

even less like normal reading. It might be objected that the word-by-word responses in our study slowed down the presentation of the sentences, giving the subjects time to employ processing strategies that would *not* have been effective under more normal conditions. In particular, one might wonder whether the slow rate gave our subjects extra time to consult grammatical constraints on gap-filling, time not available to people at more normal rates of reading or listening.

In the face of this objection, it is worth pointing out that the situation in our experiment is not vastly worse than for other experimental paradigms. Specifically, for the sentences corresponding to those in the Frazier et al. study, our subjects' mean response time per word (which includes the time for the physical key-press response and a variable mechanical delay of up to 17 milliseconds (msec) between the key press and the presentation of the next word) was 468 msec. The presentation rate was therefore not very much slower than in the Frazier et al. study, in which words appeared successively at intervals of 350 msec (300 msec per word plus an interword interval of 50 msec).

However, one aspect of our results does suggest that the possibility of artifacts due to the slow presentation rate (in both studies) should be considered seriously. Our interpretation of the results for the Late *wh*-Gap examples entails that subjects were anticipating the presence of a gap in the question, before checking the input to see whether a gap actually appeared in that position. This does not violate any grammatical principles, but it does go against the "Try-the-next-constituent" parsing principle of Fodor (1978). Does this imply that our subjects were not employing normal parsing strategies? And if so, does this threaten the conclusions we have drawn about the availability of grammatical information during sentence parsing? We think not.

To start with, there is no need to assume that Try-the-next-constituent is an explicit parsing strategy. The facts it was intended to account for can be handled without assuming that the parser deliberately decides whether to check the word string before or after attempting an analysis. Instead of resulting from a deliberate choice, what the parser does in these circumstances might be merely a consequence of independently given timing relationships (as proposed for other putative parsing strategies by Frazier and Fodor, 1978). Under normal conditions of hearing or reading, the parser will receive the next word of the input very quickly and can make use of the information it carries to decide whether or not a gap is present. On the assumption that it uses all relevant information as it becomes available, the parser will then be behaving *as if* it were employing the Try-the-next-constituent strategy.

In our experiment, the necessity of responding to each word delayed the presentation of the next word, and so the information carried by the next word would have been momentarily lacking. It seems very likely that our subjects were inclined to analyze each fragment of the sentence that they saw as a complete phrase if they could. If so, a verb whose object phrase had not yet been received would have been regarded as a verb followed by a gap, as long as the sentence contained a filler in a suitable position to legitimize this analysis. In this respect, our subjects *were* perhaps behaving differently than under normal reading conditions. But if we are right, the difference is not a principled one, and there is no reason to believe that it undermines the validity of our conclusions. Even if the slow presentation rate led our subjects to anticipate a gap before finding out whether there was one, it is still true that they could not have anticipated it if they had lacked access, at that stage of the parse, to the subcategorization properties of verbs like *force* and to the grammatical constraints on filler-gap pairings.

More generally, experiments such as these, despite their inevitable artificialities, do permit the rejection of some hypotheses about how sentence parsing proceeds under normal conditions. Our results clearly rule out two hypotheses about how and when the grammar is accessed and used in sentence parsing. First, our subjects were referring to the grammatical constraints on filler-gap pairings as they encountered gaps that needed to be filled. It therefore cannot be that the parser is subject to some *inherent* scheduling requirement to apply these constraints only after the application of all phrase structure rules. Second, our subjects were making use of the constraints long before the end of each sentence. We can therefore reject the idea that the parser is designed to postpone consulting the constraints until it has examined the whole of the input word string for any relevant cues.

We are left, then, with the idea that the parser applies the constraints on-line as long as it has time to do so. Under rapid presentation conditions, it might perhaps be unable to access and apply all the information it needs at the point at which it needs it. But this is presumably true for phrase structure analysis also, in cases where complex structure has to be built up rapidly over the word string. And a lag in the use of relevant information in such circumstances would be a purely mechanical phenomenon, not indicative of any fundamental division in the structure of the parser or the grammatical principles it has access to. Specifically, it would be quite compatible with the use of a grammar in which constraints on fillers and gaps are encoded in the phrase structure rules.

One final point. We readily concede that the results of our gap-filling experiment (and our sentence-matching experiment) do not constitute *positive support* for our hypothesis that phrase structure rules and constraints are blended in the grammar available to the parser. Indeed, it is difficult to imagine *any* experimental data that could establish the truth of this hypothesis, for its practical consequences are also compatible with the hypothesis that rules and constraints reside in different modules of the grammar. One tends to think of modularity claims as inherently stronger (and hence more interesting) than nonmodularity claims, but in this instance the modularity hypothesis is the weaker of the two, compatible with a wider range of possible empirical findings. This is not just because it is conceivable that distinct modules of the competence grammar are blended by the parsing routines. Note that even the assumption of modularity within the parser does not by itself dictate the relative timing of the application of rules and constraints during sentence parsing. Frazier et al. have suggested that the constraints are in a different module than the rules, and are applied after the rules. But the constraints might be in a different module than the rules and nevertheless be applied simultaneously with the rules. And if they were, then the relative timing of processing operations would be indistinguishable from their relative timing in a nonmodular system.

In the absence of conclusive evidence, it is generally considered more profitable to adopt a stronger rather than a weaker theory. Other theories of grammar may be compatible with the on-line application of constraints by the parser, but only GPSG predicts it. The GPSG parsing model therefore recommends itself as a basis for current psycholinguistic research. It remains as a challenge for the future to find some empirical method for divining the information base for sentence processing where this is not uniquely inferable from the sequence of mental computations that are performed.

3.4. Conclusion

We have argued that there is after all no clear counterevidence, at least at present, to the claim that the gap-filling routines of the human sentence processing mechanism are designed to use all available grammatical information as and when it becomes relevant to the task. This certainly does not rule out a modular parsing device, as long as the modules are not required to apply sequentially. But it does at least restore the empirical plausibility of a more homogeneous system, in which phrase structure information and filler-gap constraints are blended in a single body of rules. And this in turn allows us to retain the independently more attractive view that the grammar and the parser are fundamentally well designed to operate efficiently together, without a great deal of local patching. This may make it harder to come up with clever examples of functional explanations for this or that odd fact about human languages, but it does promise to simplify our models of how, in detail, people parse sentences.

References

Bever, Thomas G. 1970. The cognitive basis for linguistic structures. In: John R. Hayes (ed.), *Cognition and the Development of Language*. New York: John Wiley and Sons.

Blumenthal, Arthur L. 1966. Observations with self-embedded sentences. *Psychonomic Science* 6:453–54.

Brame, Michael K. 1976. *Conjectures and refutations in syntax and semantics*. New York: Elsevier North-Holland.

Bresnan, Joan. 1978. A realistic transformational grammar. In: Morris Halle, Joan Bresnan, and George A. Miller (eds.), *Linguistic Theory and Psychological Reality*. Cambridge, Mass.: MIT Press.

(ed.). 1982. *The mental representation of grammatical relations*. Cambridge, Mass.: MIT Press.

Chomsky, Noam. 1974. Interview with Herman Parret In: Herman Parret (ed.), *Discussing language*. The Hague: Mouton.

1980. On binding. *Linguistic Inquiry* 12:1–46.

Chomsky, Noam, and Howard Lasnik. 1977. Filters and control. *Linguistic Inquiry* 8:425–504.

Earley, J. 1970. An efficient context-free parsing algorithm. *Communications of the Association for Computing Machinery* 14:453–60.

Fodor, Janet D. 1978. Parsing strategies and constraints on transformations. *Linguistic Inquiry* 9:427–73.

1983. Phrase structure parsing and the island constraints. *Linguistics and Philosophy* 6:163–223.

Fodor, Janet D. and Stephen Crain. In preparation. Towards a restricted theory of innate linguistic knowledge.

Fodor, Jerry A. 1983. *Modularity of mind*. Cambridge, Mass.: Bradford Books, MIT Press.

Fodor, Jerry A., Thomas G. Bever, and Merrill F. Garrett. 1974. *The psychology of language: an introduction to psycholinguistics and generative grammar*. New York: McGraw-Hill.

Frazier, Lyn, Charles Clifton, and Janet Randall. 1983. Filling gaps: decision principles and structure in sentence comprehension. *Cognition* 13:187–222.

Frazier, Lyn, and Janet D. Fodor. 1978. The Sausage Machine: a new two-stage parsing model. *Cognition* 6:291–325.

Freedman, Sandra A. 1982. Behavioral reflexes of constraints on transformations. Unpublished Ph.D. dissertation, Monash University, Australia.

Gazdar, Gerald. 1981. Unbounded dependencies and coordinate structure. *Linguistic Inquiry* 12:155–84.

1982. Phrase structure grammar. In: Pauline Jacobson and Geoffrey K. Pullum (eds.), *The nature of syntactic representation*. Dordrecht, Holland: Reidel.

Gazdar, Gerald, Ewan Klein, Geoffrey K. Pullum, and Ivan A. Sag. In press. *English syntax*. Cambridge, Mass.: Harvard University Press, and Oxford, England: Blackwell.

Kaplan, Ronald. 1973. A multi-processing approach to natural language. In *Proceedings of the First National Computer Conference*.

Marcus, Mitchell P. 1980. *A theory of syntactic recognition for natural language*. Cambridge, Mass.: MIT Press.

Marslen-Wilson, William. 1975. Sentence perception as an interactive parallel process. *Science* 189:226–28.

Miller, George A., and Noam Chomsky. 1963. Finitary models of language users. In: R. Duncan Luce, Robert R. Bush, and Eugene Galanter (eds.), *Handbook of mathematical psychology*. vol. 2. New York: John Wiley and Sons.

128   *Crain and Fodor*

Postal, Paul M. 1972. The best theory. In: Stanley Peters (ed.), *Goals of linguistic theory*. Englewood Cliffs, N.J.: Prentice-Hall.

Ross, John R. 1967. Constraints on variables in syntax. Unpublished Ph.D. dissertation, Massachusetts Institute of Technology, Cambridge, Mass.

Wanner, Eric and Michael Maratsos. 1978. An ATN approach to comprehension. In: Morris M. Halle, Joan Bresnan, and George A. Miller (eds.), *Linguistic theory and psychological reality*. Cambridge, Mass.: MIT Press.

Wexler, Kenneth, and Peter W. Culicover. 1980. *Formal principles of language acquisition*. Cambridge, Mass.: MIT Press.

4   Syntactic complexity

LYN FRAZIER

The ostensive goal of this paper is to construct a general complexity metric for the processing of natural language sentences, focusing on syntactic determinants of complexity in sentence comprehension. The ultimate goal, however, is to determine how the grammars of natural languages respond to different types of syntactic processing complexity.

A complexity metric that accurately predicts the relative complexity of processing different syntactic structures is not, in itself, of much theoretical interest. There does not seem to be any compelling reason for linguistic theory or psycholinguistic theory to incorporate such a metric. Rather, ultimately the correct complexity metric should follow directly as a theorem or consequence of an adequate theory of sentence comprehension.

Different theories of sentence comprehension typically lead to distinct predictions concerning the relative perceptual difficulty of sentences. Hence, one reason for developing a complexity metric is simply to help pinpoint inadequacies of current theories of sentence comprehension and to aid in the evaluation and refinement of those theories. An explicit complexity metric should also help to reveal the relation between the human sentence processor and the grammars of natural languages. In particular, developing a well-motivated complexity metric is a crucial prerequisite for evaluating the hypothesis that the grammars of natural languages are shaped in some respect by the properties of the human sentence processor since the most common form of this hypothesis claims that grammars tend to avoid generating sentences that are extremely difficult to process. Indeed, one of the most intriguing questions in psycholinguistics is whether any of the properties of specific natural languages, or any principles of universal grammar, can be explained by appeal to the basic structure or mode of operation of the human sentence processor that determine what linguistic structures could not be processed by humans in real time.

Jim McCawley has remarked that when a linguist says the word *ex-*

129

planation you had better put your hand on your wallet. Many people think that when a psycholinguist says the word *explanation* you had better keep an eye on your watch, too. Given the rather pervasive skepticism about the very nature of the present endeavor, we will begin with a brief look at what would count as a functional or processing explanation of some grammatical fact. In section 4.1 it is argued that the reason why many functional explanations seem unsatisfying is because they offer only a partial explanation for the grammatical fact in question. It is then suggested that even such partial explanations can be extremely useful in uncovering the fundamental properties of grammars and explaining why grammars of natural languages exhibit certain properties and not others.

4.1. Functional explanations

Chomsky and Lasnik (1977) discuss one problem with functional or processing explanations. They point out that to explain some grammatical property by appeal to language performance systems, the explanation must hold at the level of the evolution of the species. That is, over the course of evolution, processing considerations may favor certain grammatical principles over others and thereby affect the composition of the human language faculty.

Chomsky and Lasnik's remark was probably directed at one particular type of functional explanation that has been offered in the literature, namely, explanations based on establishing that some particular grammatical constraint facilitates sentence processing and then offering this correlation as an explanation for why the grammar of some language contains this constraint. The problem with this type of explanation is that, if offered in a vacuum, a correlation of this sort is at best a partial explanation. The mere existence of a correlation does not explain why the grammar responded to the exigencies of sentence processing in one particular case, given that it does not do so across the board in all cases where a feasible constraint would facilitate sentence processing. Further, a correlation of this sort typically does not explain why the particular constraint that the grammar incorporates takes the specific form that it does. Hence, explanations based on such correlations must be offered in the context of a larger theory of language, including a specification of the relation between grammars and processors and the ways in which they interact.

Another problem with functional explanations concerns the direction of causality. To argue that the grammar has developed a particular constraint because of some property of the sentence processor, and not vice versa, it must be shown that the relevant property of the sentence processor follows from independently explained facts about the basic structure of the human processing mechanism, and not from some particular strategy or processing routine that might itself have been adopted only in response to the language-particular constructions that the processor has to cope with.

Now, let us suppose that we know the reason why different perceivers adopt the same parsing strategies and that the reason is not due to the particular linguistic structures being processed. Under such circumstances, is it true that the only conceivable type of functional explanation is one that holds at the level of the evolution of the human language faculty? In principle, at least, this is not the only possibility. Imagine, as argued by Solan (ms.), that certain grammatical decisions are nondeterministic in the sense that more than one decision about the grammar is consistent both with the principles of universal grammar and with the input data available to a child. Under such circumstances, which of two available hypotheses about the structure of an input sentence a child will postulate might well depend on which structure is easier to process (due, say, to limits on immediate memory capacity). Hence, a processing explanation of some grammatical fact might hold at the level of language acquisition, without being governed by an innate grammatical principle in the language acquisition device per se.

Another possibility is that the probability of innovative constructions being incorporated into a language is influenced by the ease of processing the innovative construction. If so, a functional explanation might hold at the level of language change, without necessarily affecting the evolution of the species or the composition of the human language faculty. In short, as soon as one admits the possibility that the human sentence processing mechanism is not to be identified with the grammar, but that it may have interesting properties of its own that are explained by appeal to independent facts about the human cognitive make-up, it is easy to construct situations in which certain types of processing considerations could affect the acquisition of grammars or the development of languages without a concomitant evolutionary change in whatever principles of universal grammar govern children's hypotheses about their language.

To the extent that some language processing mechanism is particular to a specific language, its effects on the grammar may be expected to be rather limited and of course language specific. To the extent that some processing mechanism is tied to biological limitations on memory and computational capacity that are common to all members of the species, the processing mechanism might exert a pressure on the grammars of all natural languages. But, just as there are a variety of mechanisms by which processing considerations might influence a language, there are a variety of different effects that might result in particular grammars, even given some consistent pressure from universal processing considerations. As

Chomsky and Lasnik (1977) emphasized, one possibility is that, through the course of evolution, processing considerations alter the composition of the language acquisition device by favoring the inclusion of certain grammatical principles over other (possibly contradictory) principles. Alternatively, processing considerations might simply lead to certain grammatically available options being preferred to others and thereby influence the frequency with which some property occurs in natural languages. If there are certain abstract constraints to which the sentences generated by a grammar must conform for the language to be easily parsed, then these constraints might affect the frequency with which various grammatically independent properties co-occur within a particular language. None of these possibilities can be ruled out a priori.

What, then, do these considerations suggest about the attempt to provide functional explanations of grammatical facts? Surely they do not suggest that we should abandon the search for correlations between properties of grammars and properties of the language processing mechanism. Rather, they suggest that mere observation of a correlation between grammars and processing will not suffice to explain the relation between grammars and processors. As usual, what is needed is a theory of grammar, a theory of processing, and a theory of the ways they interact. Observing correlations, and the lack thereof, is an important part of constructing a theory of the interaction between grammars and processors because these correlations will comprise the primary data for this endeavor. But, of course, to construct a theory of this interaction entails performing a systematic analysis, not simply collecting isolated observations. To do this, we must identify each of the sources of complexity in processing sentences, so that we may systematically inspect grammars to see where they have responded to each type of complexity, what type of devices are available for this, and so on.

In short, evaluating the hypothesis that grammars are shaped by the human sentence parsing mechanism does not amount to answering a simple yes/no question. Identifying situations where the grammar seems to have responded to the exigencies of sentence processing, and those where it has not, will not by itself provide much insight into the structure of natural languages or the way grammars change over time.

Surely it would be naïve to expect a complete and transparent fit between grammars and processors. Bever and Langendoen (1971) proposed that grammars can be viewed as a compromise between the needs of language producers, language perceivers, and language learners. Their point, of course, is that there is no reason to focus narrowly on a single performance system (production, comprehension, acquisition) since language, to be useful, must simultaneously satisfy the requirements of all performance systems. Fodor (ms.) has recently emphasized that grammars must also satisfy the expressive needs of humans to communicate a wide range of messages. Further, there are good reasons to believe that even this rather complicated picture is oversimplified, since there may well be innate constraints on the format for mentally representing grammatical information which are not explained by any of the above factors. Thus there is every reason to expect that an accurate theory of the relation between the grammar and the processor will be constructed not on the basis of superficial inspection of grammars and processors but only on the basis of a great deal of analysis directed at developing theories in each of the relevant domains, with an eye to explaining what we can, how we can, in a principled manner. Pretheoretic prejudices about where we will find explanations for particular facts are of little value in this endeavor; they are a poor substitute for developing empirically motivated theories of language.

For at least two decades, mainstream linguistic research has been dominated by two related goals. One is to provide explicit grammars for specific natural languages in a framework embodying plausible universals that might constrain, and thus help to explain, a child's acquisition of his language. The second is to provide a characterization of the notion of possible human language. It is with respect to this second goal that functional explanations of the sort discussed above (mere correlations) fail to be explanations at all, since there is no evidence that a grammar lacking some parsing-motivated constraint would not compose a possible human language.

Though it is natural to focus on the question of why grammars included in the set of grammars characterizing attested natural languages correspond to possible human languages, it is perhaps overly limiting to ignore the larger range of potential grammatical systems that are believed not to characterize human languages. There may be much to be learned from the endeavor to explain why various conceivable grammars are not attested. Formal work on language learnability, for example, can be viewed from this perspective: grammars lacking certain constraints, or grammars with an unruly number of nonterminals, can be shown under reasonable assumptions to increase dramatically the amount and complexity of data required to learn the language (in the limit). This work thus begins to explain why certain grammars do not characterize possible human languages, given the biologically reasonable assumption that all possible human languages must be learnable by all normal (intact) members of the species within some fixed amount of time. Similarly, work on the processing systems available to humans for understanding languages may be expected to restrict further the range of possible human languages by excluding languages that would be unparsable given the normal limits on human memory and processing capacity. If some proper subset of the class of unparsable grammars should happen to also be excluded by a known grammatical universal, a functional explanation for the existence of the grammatical universal might at first blush appear to be trivial. After all, the argument goes, if the grammatical universal cannot be explained in full detail by the processing explanation, what has been gained but a redundant explanation? But this argument misses an important point, namely, that the human language faculty seems to comprise a number of interacting systems, limited in quite distinct ways. It is precisely the mismatch between these different systems that can reveal essential properties within each system. Thus in situations where the exigencies of sentence processing exert a pressure on grammars to avoid certain types of constructions or rule interactions, grammars may consistently incorporate some small subset of constraints in response to this pressure, but *not* incorporate some other set of constraints that would function equally well with respect to avoiding the complex constructions. This surely would tell us something important about the essential properties of some component of the human language system. Such evidence would throw the properties of this system into relief, allowing the properties of the different language subsystems to be pulled apart. Given this, partial explanations of the sort discussed should not be scorned but rather exploited. They may be useful in revealing the truly essential properties of, say, the format for mentally representing grammatical information, indicating that certain grammatical properties cannot be sacrificed or certain grammatical constraints contravened even under considerable pressure.

We turn now to substantive proposals concerning the sources of complexity in sentence parsing. It should be emphasized from the outset that the description of the sources of processing difficulty provided here must be viewed as sufficiency conditions for processing complexity. Hence the descriptions are of the form: A sentence will be relatively difficult to process if. . . (not "if and only if").[1]

A further cautionary note concerns the contribution of several different factors to the complexity of any given sentence. Implicit in the organization of this paper is a taxonomy of the distinct sources of syntactic complexity, which, taken together, are intended to predict the syntactic complexity of a sentence. The sources of complexity to be examined include those due to (full or temporary) ambiguity, complexity due to segmentation and memory burdens imposed by alternative word orders, complexity in the analysis of unambiguous sentences, and complexity that results from the interaction of particular syntactic and semantic processing considerations. To discuss for each example the contribution of each of the proposed complexity principles would give rise to an expositional nightmare. Thus, factors that either contribute, or appear to contribute, to the interpretation of individual examples are often omitted from the text, and discussed in notes appended to the example.

4.2. Ambiguity

One source of processing complexity that has been recognized and studied for a relatively long time is ambiguity. According to the garden path theory of sentence comprehension (see Frazier and Rayner, 1982, and references therein), syntactically ambiguous strings give rise to processing difficulty when the processor's initial decision about the structure of the string turns out to be incorrect. The strategies that characterize the processor's decision preferences at choice points where the grammar permits more than one decision about the structure of the input string have now been studied rather extensively. It appears that most known structural parsing preferences can be explained as a consequence of the extremely general preference for the syntactic processor to take the first analysis available of each word of the input string. This explanation has been offered for the Minimal Attachment strategy (Frazier and Fodor, 1978), the Late Closure strategy (Frazier, 1978) and the Recent Filler and Salience strategies (Frazier, Clifton, and Randall, 1983). Hence, with respect to structural ambiguity, the garden path theory of sentence comprehension itself provides a complexity metric that predicts the relative processing complexity of temporarily ambiguous syntactic structures.

There now exists considerable experimental evidence for the predictions of the strategies above and, as just noted, an explanation for why different perceivers adopt the same strategies (i.e., time pressure). This evidence indicates that the processing pressures exerted on the grammar do not vary radically from person to person; rather, considerable uniformity exists in the way different perceivers process sentences. Hence processing pressures on the grammar may be assumed to be fairly consistent, rather than varying randomly from person to person. In fact, it is this uniformity across different perceivers that makes it reasonable to raise the question of whether the grammars of natural languages respond to processing complexity due to temporary ambiguity, at least in cases where devices available in the grammar could be used to disambiguate the structures that the sentence processor would misanalyze.

The Minimal Attachment strategy specifies that incoming items are attached into a constituent structure representation of the sentence using the fewest nodes consistent with the wellformedness constraints of the language. Hence it predicts that the syntactic processor will initially misanalyze the temporarily ambiguous phrases (underlined) in sentences (1)–(3). In (1) the noun phrase *the answer to the difficult problem* will initially be misanalyzed as the simple direct object of the verb *know*. In (2) the phrase *her sister* will initially be interpreted as one conjunct of a conjoined noun phrase. In (3) the string *the horse raced past the barn* will initially be analyzed as a simple main clause.[2]

(1) Sandra knew *the answer to the difficult problem* was correct.

(2) John kissed Mary and *her sister* laughed.

(3) *The horse* $\left\{ \begin{array}{l} ridden \\ raced \end{array} \right\}$ *past the barn* fell.

In each of these cases there is a clear minimal change in the grammar that in principle could be used to prevent the temporary garden path. The requirement that $\bar{S}$ contain an obligatory complementizer would prevent the garden path in (1). The incorporation of distinct lexical items for noun phrase conjunction and sentential conjunction would prevent the ambiguity in (2). The disambiguation of reduced relatives could be accomplished by maintaining distinct forms for the simple past tense and the passive participle of a verb, or perhaps by prenominal placement of the participial phrase. Yet the grammar of English has not incorporated any of these devices, despite the fact that they would prevent the above misanalyses.

The Late Closure strategy specifies that incoming items are preferentially analyzed as a constituent of the phrase or clause currently being processed. Thus in a sentence like (4) the temporarily ambiguous phrase *in the library* will initially be misanalyzed as a constituent of the lower verb phrase. In (5) the adverb *carefully* will be misinterpreted as a constituent of the lower verb phrase. In (6) the phrase *the sock* will initially be misanalyzed as the direct object of the verb *mend*.

(4) Jill put the book that her son had been reading *in the library*.

(5) The secretary worded the long memo that Jane had been composing *carefully*.

(6) While Mary was mending *the sock* fell off her lap.

(7) What was Mary mending (___) with ___?

Again it is clear that various mechanisms could, in principle, be used to disambiguate these structures. If either Extraposition of Relative Clauses or Complex NP Shift were obligatory, this would disambiguate the structure in (4). Sentence (5) could also be disambiguated by either of these mechanisms. If adverbs were obligatorily placed at the beginning of constituents, this too would serve to disambiguate the analysis of clause-final adverbials in right-branching structures such as (5). A constraint prohibiting optionally transitive verbs would eliminate the ambiguity in (6), and related clause-boundary ambiguities in other multiclausal structures. In addition, the constraint would eliminate many temporary ambiguities involving doubtful gaps, such as that following the verb in (7).

The examples above (and many others) suggest that in general the grammar does not respond to processing complexity due to the presence of temporary ambiguity. Numerous temporary ambiguities do exist in the language. There is clear evidence that they complicate the processing of sentences. Nevertheless, the examples above show that the grammar tolerates such ambiguities, even in cases where there are mechanisms available in the grammar that would allow the grammar to eliminate this type of processing complexity.

One might object to this argument by pointing out that there are possible reasons why the grammar could not adopt the disambiguation mechanisms described. For example, it might turn out that the Fixed Subject Constraint (which prohibits *Who did John say that __ wrecked the garden?*) is a necessary property of a grammar that in other respects is like the grammar of English. If so, then requiring an obligatory complementizer in all S̄'s would restrict the expressive power of the language since it would be impossible under such circumstances to question embedded subjects. Therefore, the argument goes, the grammar could not facilitate the processing of sentences like (1) without sacrificing the expressive power of the language. Similarly, with respect to all of the other examples discussed, we can think of some reason why the disambiguation mechanism proposed would not in fact be accessible to the grammar. For example, the use of different lexical items for noun phrase conjunction and sentential conjunction might complicate the language acquisition process. Hence this might not be an accessible mechanism for disambiguating structures like (2).

While there is nothing incoherent about such counterarguments, they do not affect the basic conclusion. Whatever the reasons may be for the grammar taking the particular shape it does in the examples above, the reason is clearly not an obsessive or predominant concern with maximizing the ease of processing sentences.

Though in general the grammar does not seem to make even minimal changes to disambiguate temporarily ambiguous structures, there is one class of ambiguous structures that grammars do seem to exclude. These structures are characterized in (8), under the rubric of Impermissible Ambiguity.

(8) *Impermissible Ambiguity Constraint.* Languages prohibit constructions containing a clause that is misanalyzed the same way every time it occurs regardless of the particular words contained in the clause.

Bever and Langendoen (1971) pointed out that the obligatory presence of an overt relative pronoun in subject relative clauses in English can be explained by the fact that subject relative clauses would be misanalyzed as simple main clauses if the relative pronoun were not overtly present as in (9). Fodor and Garrett (1967) suggested that the presence of an obligatory complementizer in sentential subjects may be attributed to the fact that such structures would be misanalyzed as main clauses if the complementizer were not present, as in (10).

(9)   *The man entered tripped.

(10) *It is sunny upsets the pessimists.

The main clause misanalysis of such structures follows from the Minimal Attachment strategy, and thus there is evidence that the structures in (9) and (10) would be misanalyzed in the same way every time the construction occurred; the fact that the same co-occurrence restrictions hold in subject relative clauses and simple main clauses (and in sentential subjects and in simple main clauses) entails that the constructions would be open to misanalysis regardless of the particular items occurring in the construction. Hence, the structures in (9) and (10) fall under the Impermissible Ambiguity Constraint formulated in (8).

Looking at the English examples alone, it might appear that the devices available for satisfying the Impermissible Ambiguity Constraint are restricted and always involve the complementizer system. But this is not true in general. When a wider array of languages is considered it is clear that a variety of devices are employed. In German, for example, distinct word orders in subordinate clauses and main clauses preclude the misanalysis of an initial subordinate clause as a main clause, as illustrated in (11).

(11) a.   *Wäre ich menschlicher, würde ich dir helfen.*
      b.   **Ich wäre menschlicher, ich dir helfen.*
           'If I were kinder I would help you.'

Grammatical particles may also be used to indicate the subordinate status of initial clauses (e.g., the use of the genitive marker *-in* in Turkish). Thus, there do not seem to be tight restrictions on the set of devices employed to satisfy the Impermissible Ambiguity Constraint.

The full range of effects of the Impermissible Ambiguity Constraint on the structure of natural languages is difficult to assess at present since we are likely to notice examples of its application only if there is a surprising gap in the grammar or if the constraint leads to some noticeable complication of the grammar. In many cases, looking for the effects of the constraint is comparable to searching for a missing person; one must know whose absence to take note of. Identifying all of the effects of the constraint presupposes not just a more adequate theory of language comprehension (which predicts all systematic misanalyses that occur in processing natural languages) but also a deeper understanding of the principles of grammar so that we know what constructions we would expect to find in natural languages if languages were not constrained by this ambiguity principle.

The status of the Impermissible Ambiguity Constraint has not yet been addressed. Can even this rather limited constraint be defended as an invariant or absolute restriction imposed on the grammars of all languages? Or does the constraint merely characterize the limited class of constructions where the grammar may be expected to respond to processing difficulty due to temporary ambiguity if the grammar should happen to respond at all? In English at least, it is true that most of the ambiguities that are permitted in the language do not fall under the Impermissible Ambiguity Constraint. For example, the ambiguities in sentences (1)–(7) do not fall under the constraint, either because they do not involve the misanalysis of an entire clause, in (1) and (2) and in (4)–(7), or because the misanalysis does not occur regardless of the choice of lexical items, in (3). Other well-known ambiguities in English are also exempt from the constraint either because they do not involve the misanalysis of an entire clause (e.g., the prepositional phrase ambiguity in *hit the girl with a stick*) or because there is no clear evidence that the construction is misanalyzed the same way every time the construction (i.e., preterminal string) occurs (e.g., *eating apples; shooting of the hunters; John told the girl that Bill liked the story;* etc.). Given the numerous ambiguities in English, these considerations do encourage the view that the Impermissible Ambiguity Constraint can be maintained in its strongest form, as an absolute restriction on the grammar.

However, Tony Kroch has pointed out to me that the dialect of Black English discussed in Chomsky and Lasnik (1977) does permit relative pronouns to be deleted in subject relative clauses, which should not be possible if the Impermissible Ambiguity Constraint is an absolute constraint. Similarly, an example like (12a) may be problematic for the strong interpretation of the constraint.

(12) a. Those burritos I will eat __ for dinner.
      b. Those burritos I will eat __ for dinner are extremely hot.

A sentence in which the object has been topicalized is confusable with a relative clause in which the object has been relativized, as illustrated in (12). It is of course possible that the discourse constraints or the intonation patterns of the sentences in (12) are mutually exclusive and that this information is used by the sentence processor to avoid systematic misanalysis of these constructions. However, until it can be shown that these same factors would not serve to disambiguate the structures in (9) and (10), which were taken as support for the Impermissible Ambiguity Constraint, it would not be principled to appeal to these factors to exempt the sentences in (12) (or perhaps subject relative clauses in Black English) from the constraint.

To summarize briefly, it seems that in general the grammar does not respond to the presence of temporary ambiguities which complicate the processing of sentences, even in cases where devices are in principle available to the grammar which could serve this purpose. The Impermissible Ambiguity Constraint provides one rather minor exception to this observation, but it is not clear at present that even this extremely limited constraint can be defended as an invariant constraint on the structure of languages.

A set of constraints proposed in the linguistic literature provide a potential challenge to this conclusion. The so-called No Ambiguity Constraints, which exclude one interpretation of a sentence just in case an alternative interpretation exists, have often been assumed to have a parsing motivation. Fodor's (1979) XX Extraction Principle claims essentially that extraction of the second of two adjacent phrases of like categories will be more acceptable than extraction of the first. The constraint is intended to account for the fact that people tend to report only the (a) reading of a sentence like (13) (where the nurse brings the patient to the doctor).

(13)   Which patient did the nurse bring the doctor?
  a. Which patient did the nurse bring the doctor __?
  b. Which patient did the nurse bring __ the doctor?

Fodor suggests that this constraint follows from the parser's tendency to check the next item in the incoming lexical string before it postulates a gap. This parsing motivation for the XX Extraction Principle is certainly plausible; however, to date there is no clear experimental evidence that supports (or refutes) this gap detection strategy. Further, the constraint can not in any case be maintained in its fully general form as indicated by examples like (14), which clearly may have the interpretation indicated in (14b) in violation of the constraint.

(14)   Who did Kathy tell Lynne was sick yesterday?
  a. Who did Kathy tell Lynne [__ was sick yesterday]?
  b. Who did Kathy tell __ [Lynne was sick yesterday]?

Klima's Constraint on Relational Ambiguity (discussed in Langendoen, Kalish-Landon, and Dore, 1974) essentially specifies that no transformational rule may apply if it creates an ambiguity with respect to the grammatical relations of the sentence. The constraint accounts for the fact that, in German for example, Topicalization of a phrase is not acceptable if it results in the same surface string as some simple sentence in which Topicalization has not applied. Though again examples like (14) would seem to pose a problem, at least for any fully general statement of the constraint.

(15) a. *Die Mädchen sehen die Frauen.*
          'The girls see the women.'
      b. *Die Mädchen sehen die Frauen.*
          'The girls the women see.'

It is not clear that either of these constraints must be contained in the grammar. Rather it appears that perceivers simply compute a preferred reading of sentences like (13) and (15) and do not revise that reading unless they are provided with some evidence that a revision is necessary. Hence, a sentence like (16) seems perfectly acceptable since lexical information from the noun phrases, together with information about the thematic structure of *give*, provides sufficient information for detection of the post-verbal gap.

(16) Which doctor did the nurse give the note?

Similarly, if the Constraint on Relational Ambiguity is to be maintained as a grammatical constraint, it must be shown that perceivers will not accept the Topicalized analysis of sentences like (15) when they are embedded in a discourse that disambiguates the relations in favor of the Topicalized analysis of the sentence.

Hankamer (1970) proposes a No Ambiguity Constraint on Gapping, which specifies that any derivation resulting in a gapped structure that is identical in surface form to a structure derivable by some other derivation is blocked. The Constraint is intended to account for the non-availability of the (b) reading of sentences like (17).

(17)   John gave Fred a nickel and Mary a dime.
      a. John gave Fred a nickel and John gave Mary a dime.
      b. John gave Fred a nickel and Mary gave Fred a dime.

A discussion of alternative formulations of this constraint would take us beyond the scope of this paper. However, it appears in this case that some grammatical constraint is called for; an attempt to account for the data in (17) solely in terms of parsing preferences would not explain why, in sentences like (18) where there are strong pragmatic biases toward the (b) reading of the sentence, perceivers still reject the (b) reading of the sentence.

(18)   John gave the dog a cracker and Mary a bone.
      a. John gave the dog a cracker and John gave Mary a bone.
      b. John gave the dog a cracker and Mary gave the dog a bone.

At present very little psycholinguistic work has been directed at questions concerning the processing of deletions, so it would perhaps be premature to assess the validity of the hypothesis that whatever constraint excludes the (b) reading of sentences like (17) and (18) is motivated by the difficulties associated with processing these structures. Thus, at present, the constraint provides a potential counterexample to the conclusion arrived at above. Whatever turns out to be the correct conclusion to draw about gapped structures, we must evaluate it in light of other constructions involving "deletion," such as VP Deletion in sentences like (19), where ambiguity is permitted.

(19)   Tom thought Edwin went to France and Roger did too.
    a. Tom thought Edwin went to France and Roger thought Edwin went to France.
    b. Tom thought Edwin went to France and Tom thought Roger went to France.

Fodor (1978) argued that the grammar of English must contain a no-ambiguity constraint that prohibits an intersecting assignment of filler-gap dependencies if either a nested or disjoint assignment is licensed by the grammar. This Nested Dependency Constraint accounts for the fact that most speaker-hearers of English reject the pragmatically more sensible reading of (20), shown in (20b), even though they seem to be able to compute this reading. (In other words, just as people can understand what the sentence *The armadillos is coming north* would mean if it were grammatical, people will report the sensible meaning of (20) but nevertheless claim that it is not a well-formed sentence of their language.)

(20)   Which soup is this pot easy to cook in?
    a. Which soup$_i$ is this pot$_j$ easy to cook ___$_j$ in ___$_i$?
    b. Which soup$_i$ is this pot$_j$ easy to cook ___$_i$ in ___$_j$?

Frazier, Clifton, and Randall (1983) do provide experimental evidence for a processing strategy of assigning the most recent potential filler to the first gap encountered, which automatically results in the assignment of nested dependencies in sentences like (20). Hence, it looks as though the Nested Dependency Constraint excludes a perceptually difficult or unpreferred structure; thus it provides a counterexample to the claim that the grammar in general does not respond to processing difficulties due to the presence of ambiguity.

In fact, the Nested Dependency Constraint, if it must be treated as a grammatical constraint, provides a very nasty counterexample indeed. In constructions where the sentence processing mechanism consistently prefers (initially computes) one interpretation of the construction and where it would not complicate the grammar to exclude the alternative interpretation of the construction, it is fairly easy to construct a plausible mechanism by which a no-ambiguity constraint of some sort (not necessarily a transderivational one) could enter the language and be incorporated into the grammar. However, the Nested Dependency Constraint appears to complicate the grammar of English. Further, it is not at all clear that it is stated in a vocabulary that is otherwise needed in the theory of grammar. Thus, while it is a limited counterexample in that it by no means eliminates all of the processing difficulties associated with processing filler-gap dependencies, it is an extremely problematic counterexample with respect to the goal of constructing a theory of the interaction between the grammar and the processor. (In Frazier, 1982, I suggested that the only time the grammar will go outside of its generally available vocabulary to incorporate a constraint that presupposes an expansion of its vocabulary is when (1) there is collusion between the sentence production and sentence comprehension system and (2) the problematic constraint would simultaneously facilitate both performance systems. However, I am not aware of any strong evidence suggesting that the Nested Dependency Constraint actually facilitates the task of the sentence producer.)

Engdahl (this volume) provides evidence that speaker-hearers of Swedish exhibit a preference for nested assignment of dependencies in pragmatically neutral sentences; however, unlike English speakers, Swedish speakers also report the intersecting reading of a sentence, especially when the sentence contains pragmatic information biased toward the intersecting assignment of filler-gap dependencies. Engdahl's study thus suggests that similar processing strategies are operative in Swedish and in English but that the resulting bias toward nested dependencies has not been grammaticized in Swedish (or Norwegian, see Engdahl, 1979). Thus, while the status of the Nested Dependency Constraint as a grammatical constraint in English weighs against the conclusion that grammars do not respond to processing complexity due to ambiguity, the Swedish and Norwegian facts support the conclusion.[3]

An adequate theory of the interaction of grammars and processors must attempt to explain why different languages should vary in their response to what appears to be the same parsing problem. (In section 4.5, one rather speculative explanation for these differences is suggested; it predicts that the "squishiness" of the Nested Dependency Constraint in some language should correlate with "squishiness" of the island constraints in that language.)

The evidence discussed in this section suggests that the limited cases where the grammar does respond to the complexities associated with processing ambiguous structures fall into two classes, one concerned with phrase structure ambiguities (characterized by the Impermissible Ambiguity Constraint) and one concerned with gap-filling ambiguities (characterized by the Nested Dependency Constraint). Presumably the worst phrase structure ambiguities from the perspective of the sentence processors are ambiguities which are systematic and which involve the misanalysis of an entire clause; and the worst filler-gap ambiguities are those involving multiple filler-gap dependencies which defy the processor's recent filler strategy. This suggests that the grammar of a language will respond to processing complexity due to ambiguity only in cases of extreme processing complexity, and even then a grammatical constraint prohibiting the complex construction is not inevitable, as indicated by cross-language variation.

Though only cases of syntactic ambiguity have been examined here, it should perhaps be noted that even a superficial inspection of other grammatical components strongly suggests that the avoidance of ambiguity per se does not tightly constrain any component of the grammar. Phonological rules such as Auxiliary Contraction in English give rise to systematic ambiguities, as indicated by the multiple ambiguity of the contracted form of *is* or *has* in (21)

(21)   The boy[z] . . .
  a. The boys are . . .
  b. The boy's hat . . .
  c. The boy's here.
  d. The boy's been here.

Ambiguity is rampant in the morphological inventory of the language, including the closed class inventory, where functional considerations might have led us to expect the strongest pressure to exist for excluding ambiguities. These ambiguities affect derivational morphemes (e.g., the agentive and comparative suffixes *-er*; the negative and reversative prefixes *un-*); inflectional morphemes (e.g., past tense and participial *-ed*); grammatical markers of case or thematic role assignment (e.g., instrumental and comitative *with*; locative and agentive *by*); and lexical category assignment (e.g., auxiliary and prepositional *to*); to cite just a few examples. In the semantics, where pretheoretically we might at very least have expected a constraint against ambiguities that permit a sentence to be interpreted as meaning either P or NOT P, we find negation operators that permit just this situation to arise, as in (22a), despite the fact that unambiguous scope-marking devices are available to the grammars of natural languages. Consider, for example, the use of *any* to disambiguate (22b).

(22) a. The president didn't resign because of the problems in Central America.
      b. The president didn't resign because of any problems in Central America.

In sum, nonsyntactic components of the grammar also seem to permit ambiguities to exist even in cases where they could be excluded without resorting to transderivational mechanisms (e.g., in the examples just listed simply by excluding the rule of Auxiliary Contraction from the grammar, by excluding homophonous closed class items from the morphological inventory, and by introducing obligatory scope markers).

At least in informal discussions, ambiguity is often attributed some causal role in explanations of language change (e.g., attributing the development of a relatively fixed word order in English to the erosion of the case system). The observations here suggest that the existence of ambiguity per se is unlikely to offer an explanation for either the existence or the direction of linguistic change. In diachronic analyses of a language, one might try to determine, say, whether some unprecedented construction was first observed exclusively in the environment of an "impermissible ambiguity" and thus argue that positing a functional motivation for the change helps to elucidate the precise process by which some innovation entered the language. But in the absence of a detailed examination of the relation between grammars and the human language processor, simply invoking the avoidance of ambiguity as a causal factor in change is to ignore facts such as those discussed in this section.[4] It adds little to our understanding of language and probably serves only to draw attention away from whatever grammatical principles may be at play.

4.3. Word order

In this section we will examine the question of whether there are certain basic word orders that would complicate the processing of sentences. Given a characterization of perceptually complex word orders, we may then determine whether such word orders either do not occur at all in natural languages or perhaps occur only infrequently compared to perceptually simpler word orders.

We will assume a two-stage parsing model, in which the first stage has a limited viewing window of five or six adjacent words. Closed class items are used by the first-stage parser to identify reasonable places to break the incoming lexical string (cf. Frazier and Fodor, 1978). Given this model, two constraints immediately follow. First, closed class items should occur on the peripheries of phrases, rather than occurring somewhere in the middle of a phrase. Further, the placement of closed class items should be consistent throughout a language, as specified by the "In-position" Constraint in (23).

(23) *In-position Constraint.* In the unmarked case, closed class items occur consistently on the left or consistently on the right of the phrase that introduces them.

In parsing a language that abides by the In-position Constraint, the first-stage parser may break the incoming lexical string on the basis of very superficial information and still be assured that the resulting phrasal packages will respect the constituent structure of the sentence. The parser need only identify an incoming item as a member of the closed class vocabulary to identify a reasonable place to terminate a phrasal package:

if the language being parsed is a prepositional language, then the parser may break the lexical string before any closed class item; if the language is a postpositional language, the parser may break the lexical string after any closed class item, regardless of the identity of the particular closed class item contained in the string.

The second constraint that follows from this view of parsing is the Head Adjacency Constraint, formulated in (24).

(24) *Head Adjacency Constraint.* In the unmarked case, major (recursive) phrases must follow the head of a mother phrase in prepositional languages and must precede the head in postpositional languages.

The Head Adjacency Constraint prevents the head of a phrase and the head of its complement from being separated in the lexical string by the occurrence of some phrase in the complement. If the head of a phrase and the head of its complement were separated, then the phrasal packages constructed by the limited-window procedure would not form a coherent semantic unit. The basic word order of the language would thus preclude on-line semantic interpretation. This can be illustrated by considering the difficulties inherent in the processing of a prepositional language that placed relative clauses prenominally, as indicated in (25).

(25) Preposition Relative Clause] Head NP

Given this word order, the first-stage parser would often be forced to package the preposition and the relative clause together; if the relative clause subsumed more than a few words of the lexical string, the limited viewing window of the first-stage parser would force it to terminate the phrasal package before the head of the relative clause. But of course, this phrasal package could not be semantically interpreted until subsequent items were received, because the preposition and the relative clause do not form a coherent semantic unit.

The In-position and Head Adjacency constraints ensure that the parser can easily identify reasonable phrasal packages and that these packages will form coherent semantic units. Together, they explain Greenberg's (1965) universals concerning the placement of pre-/postpositions, objects, genitives, relative clauses and question particles (see Frazier, 1979). In each case, the explanation offered by the correlation in the order of different constituents within a language takes the form illustrated before. Thus in a postpositional language, relative clauses should precede their heads since the alternative postnominal placement would permit the relative clause to separate the head of the relative from a postposition. Likewise in a postpositional language, the object must precede the verb, since otherwise a relative clause (or some other modifier of the object) would separate the head of the verb phrase (the verb) from the head of its complement.

In terms of the 30 languages analyzed by Greenberg, 26 of the languages are unmarked with respect to the In-position and Head Adjacency constraints, at least in terms of the data presented by Greenberg. What this suggests is that the frequency with which different word orders occur in the languages of the world are heavily influenced by parsing considerations. However, these considerations do not favor some absolute or invariant order of constituents (e.g., SVO over SOV), but rather they place certain abstract constraints on the order of constituents, which may be satisfied in a variety of ways. Thus, grammatical options that are in principle distinct (e.g., whether a language exhibits prepositions or postpositions and the relative order of constituents in a complex noun phrase) become linked together because of their effects on the ease of processing the language.

This view of the basic word order of languages helps to explain why there is not one fixed ideal language type that is optimal from the perspective of processing efficiency. If my conclusions are correct, the human sentence processor simply does not care whether, say, a verb precedes or follows its object; rather, what matters is the overall design of the language in terms of the entire set of ordering options that the grammar of the language exhibits. Given a change in one parameter of a grammar, say, a change from a consistent prepositional language (i.e., placement of closed class items on the left peripheries of phrases) to a postpositional language, the pressure on the ordering of other constituents in the language that stems from processing considerations may be reversed entirely and thus potentially lead to a restructuring of the entire grammar over time.

It may be premature to hazard a guess about where processing considerations have had their strongest effects on the grammars of natural languages. However, the contrast between the grammatical effects of processing complexity due to ambiguity and processing complexity due to basic word order seems rather clear. In the case of ambiguity, processing exigencies at most seem to nibble around the edge of the grammar, placing a few boundary constraints on the grammar in limited cases where the grammar generates constructions that are systematically extremely complex to process; but in the case of word order, the constraints stemming from processing exigencies seem to be much more fundamental to the basic design of the language. This suggests that the exigencies of human sentence processing require that grammars conform at least roughly to the requirement that units useful for processing be well demarcated and appropriate for on-line semantic interpretation.

4.4. Unambiguous sentences

Clearly there are differences in the perceptual complexity of different types of unambiguous sentences. However, no existing complexity metric adequately characterizes these differences. In this section, we will explore the problems with the general complexity metrics that have been proposed in the literature and see how those metrics must be revised. We will begin with a depth hypothesis of Yngve (1960) and then turn to the nonterminal to terminal node ratio first proposed by Miller and Chomsky (1963). The derivational theory of complexity will not be discussed since there are numerous discussions of this metric, and its failings, in the psycholinguistic literature.

4.4.1. The depth hypothesis – Yngve's proposal

Yngve (1960) proposed a model of sentence production in which, roughly, the dept of embedding of a phrase was the major predictor of processing complexity. The central idea behind Yngve's depth hypothesis was the observation that speakers take on certain commitments when they utter any word or phrase of a sentence. Keeping track of these commitments imposes a burden on memory. On this view, left-branching structures such as that in (26a) will be more difficult to process than right-branching counterparts, such as (26b) since the speaker will have more commitments or predictions to keep track of.

(26) a.   b.

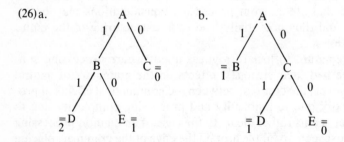

Yngve's measure of depth involves numbering each daughter branch from right to left starting with zero. The depth of any word is the sum of the numbers of all branches leading from the root of the tree to that word. The maximum depth of the sentence is the largest number associated with some terminal. For example, the maximum depth of (26a) is two. We will refer to the overall depth of a sentence, the sum of the depth of each word, as simply the depth of the sentence.

Yngve assumed that the grammar of a language consisted of a finite set of unordered constituent structure rules stored in permanent memory. These rules are applied in a top-down left-to-right fashion, with the leftmost daughter of the topmost node being expanded first, then its left daughter, and so forth. When all sisters to some node have been expanded, then the mechanism moves to the next higher right node. When a node is expanded, the leftmost daughter is placed in a computing register; all other nodes must be stored in the temporary memory register. Crucial to Yngve's system is the assumption that the temporary memory in the production mechanism can store only a finite number of symbols. Yngve hypothesizes that this number coincides with the short-term memory capacity of human beings and thus that humans should not use sentences whose maximum depth exceeds this number. One concern of Yngve's was whether the grammars of natural languages allow this situation to arise or whether grammars of natural languages are well behaved, in the sense that all sentences generated by the grammar are producible.

Implicit in Yngve's discussion is the assumption that grammars try to be well behaved; that is, grammars will tend to incorporate rules and devices that permit the depth of sentences to be reduced, permitting all the sentences generated by the grammar actually to be used. In fact, Yngve offered this hypothesis as an explanation for why natural languages should permit discontinuous constituents. The basic idea is that the depth of a sentence will be reduced if long and complex constituents occur at points of low depth in the sentence.

Though Yngve proposed the depth hypothesis as a model of sentence production, it has often been interpreted as a model of sentence comprehension as well, with varying degrees of success in predicting the complexity of understanding and recalling different constructions. Though Martin and Roberts (1966) found that the depth hypothesis did a better job of predicting complexity than did transformational measures of complexity, Martin and Roberts (1967), Wright (1966), Perfetti (1969a, 1969b), and Perfetti and Goodman (1971) challenged this finding, using tighter controls on the lexical content of the different sentences tested.

Though we will interpret and evaluate this model as a model of language comprehension, we will see that certain objections to the model extend to language production as well.[5] We will now take up various examples to illustrate certain properties of the model.

Perhaps the most basic prediction of Yngve's model is the prediction that left-branching structures will be more difficult than corresponding right-branching structures. This is easily illustrated by considering the alternative structures assigned to the passive sentences in (27) where it is clear that the (odd) left-branching structure in (27a) has a high maximal depth as well as a higher overall depth than the correct right-branching counterpart in (27b).

(27) a. = 10   b. = 8

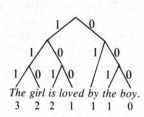

(28) = 13

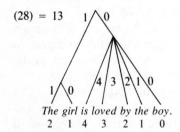

If we consider the depth of a flat conjoined structure for the verb phrase, as in (28), we may illustrate another property of Yngve's system, namely, the preference for binary branching. The preference for right-branching structures and for binary branching constructions conspire to predict the low attachment of an item (to items on its left) will be preferred since in this position it will contribute to the depth of fewer phrases, as illustrated in (29), which should be contrasted with (27b).

(29) = 10

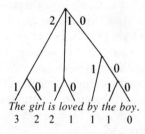

The fact that the complexity of a sentence will be reduced if complex constituents occur at points of low depth can be illustrated with respect to the order of main and subordinate clauses, shown in (30), and with respect to relative clauses occurring in subject versus object position, as illustrated in (31). In both sentence types, it is better for the embedded sentence to occur at or near the end of the sentence, where few or no predictions must be held in memory.

(30) a. Subordinate – Main = 6   b. Main – Subordinate = 5

After Mary left Sam laughed.
  2   2   1   1   0

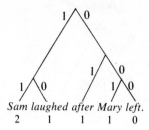

Sam laughed after Mary left.
  2   1   1   1   0

(31) a. Relative in Subject Position = 10

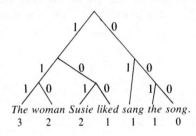

The woman Susie liked sang the song.
  3   2   2   1   1   1   0

  b. Relative in Object Position = 8

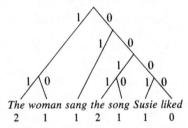

The woman sang the song Susie liked
  2   1   1   2   1   1   0

This observation was the basis of Yngve's explanation for the existence of discontinuous constituents in natural languages; it further predicts that extraposition rules should in general be highly valued in natural languages, especially when movement of a complex constituent is involved. The relative perceptual ease of a discontinuous constituent can be illustrated with respect to the phrase in (32). In (32a), the constituent *good for the job* is deeply embedded, where it adds more to the depth of the sentence than it does in (32b) (taken from Yngve),[6] where a discontinuous constituent has been formed.

(32) a. = 8   b. = 5

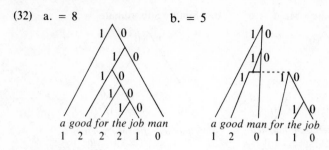

a good for the job man   a good man for the job
1 2   2   2 1   0   1 2   0 1 1 0

Thus the depth of the phrase in (32) has been reduced in (32b) by moving
an embedded constituent to a less embedded position. (Exactly the same
situation obtains in the construction "as ADJ as NP.") Similarly, rules
that extrapose an embedded constituent to the end of the sentence will
reduce depth, as may be seen in the case of extraposition of a sentential
subject in (33).

(33) a. Sentential Subject = 8

That Ernie ate frogs upset me.
  2   2   2   1   1   0

      b. Extraposed Sentential Subject = 7

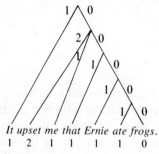

It upset me that Ernie ate frogs.
 1   2   1   1   1   1   0

4.4.2. Problems with the depth hypothesis

We will now take up each aspect of Yngve's proposal from which interesting predictions follow and evaluate each with respect to the currently
available evidence concerning the relative processing complexity of dif-

ferent constructions. We begin with the general prediction that binary branching is preferred over flatter structures with more than two branches. The problem with this prediction is that available evidence, both from language acquisition and from adult language processing, runs exactly counter to this claim. Evidence from language acquisiton is relevant to this claim in so far as one assumes that children should adopt the more highly valued structure for an input when there is an ambiguity of analysis. But we do not find children opting for binary branching structures; rather, consistently they opt for the flattest structure consistent with their grammar. For example, Matthei (1982) examined the acquisition of phrases like *the second green ball* and shows the children exhibit a strong preference for the flatter conjoined analysis of this phrase. Similarly, Tavakolian (1978) shows that children opt for the "Conjoined Sentence Interpretation," or "TOP-S attachment" (cf. Roeper and Tavakolian, 1977) of relative clauses, again the flattest structure available (though see Goodluck and Tavakolian, 1982, for a more recent discussion of these structures). In fact, I am not aware of any claims in the acquisition literature which would support the view that children opt for binary branching structures where this and a conjoined structure are both permitted by their grammars.[7]

With respect to adult language processing, there is considerable evidence for a general principle of minimal structure (the Minimal Attachment strategy) that favors flatter structures over binary branching structures (Frazier, 1978; Frazier and Fodor, 1978; Fodor and Frazier, 1980; Frazier and Rayner, 1982; Rayner, Carlson, and Frazier, 1983). Though not all of the evidence adduced in favor of this strategy is directly relevant to the proposed preference for binary branching, it includes cases that clearly are relevant, such as the preference for a ternary branching verb phrase over a binary branching verb phrase in the analysis of ambiguous prepositional phrases immediately following the direct object in the verb phrase (Rayner, Carlson, and Frazier, 1983).

With respect to the prediction that left-branching constructions are more difficult to process than right-branching constructions, the situation is more difficult to assess. While it is true that some experimental evidence supports the prediction that main-subordinate order is preferred over subordinate followed by main clause (Smith and McMahon, 1970; Bever, 1970; Bever and Townsend, 1979), that relative clauses in subject position are more difficult than relative clauses in object position (Levin et al., 1972; Wanat, 1971), and that sentences with sentential subjects are harder to process than corresponding sentences in which the subject has been extraposed (Frazier, Rayner, and Carlson, in progress), each of these predictions could be attributed to a general preference for complex constituents to occur at points of low complexity, rather than due to their left-branching structures per se. Any complexity metric that predicts that clauses are relatively complex structures and that the end of a sentence is a point of low complexity would thus suffice to account for the experimental evidence that has been marshaled in support of the above generalizations.

Further, the predictions of the depth hypothesis concerning the relative difference between a left-branching sentence and its right-branching counterpart simply do not correspond to either intuitive evidence or experimental evidence. For example, the difference between the two orders of a main and a subordinate clause should be the same as the difference between a sentence with a sentential subject and its right-branching counterpart where the subject is extraposed. This prediction is not borne out by intuition, as can be determined by comparing the difference between the two sentences in (30) with the difference between the two sentences in (33). (Using the eye movement recording technique, these intuitions were confirmed for sentences that do not contain anaphoric relations between items in the two clauses.[8])

Another (potential) problem for the prediction that left-branching constructions are always more difficult than right-branching counterparts is the fact that many, perhaps a majority, of the world's languages are predominantly left-branching. If it is true that left-branching per se leads to considerable perceptual complexity, this fact becomes difficult to explain given that Universal Grammar obviously does permit right-branching languages.

It could be true that there are language-specific factors in left-branching languages which mitigate the complexity associated with a left-branching structure. But even if there are language-specific mitigating factors in left-branching languages which minimize the complexity associated with left-branching structures, we are left with a puzzle concerning why a language would ever develop a left-branching pattern in the first place.

The prediction that low attachment of a phrase is preferred seems to be correct (Kimball, 1974; Frazier and Fodor, 1978; Wanner, 1980), but for the wrong reasons in this system. The problem may be illustrated with respect to the structures in (27a) and (27b). In (27b), the agentive *by*-phrase is attached low, relative to its attachment in (27a), where it contributes to the depth of *preceding* phrases in the sentence. However, note that this will effectively increase the difficulty of processing these earlier phrases (which precede the *by*-phrase) *only* if it can be determined at the beginning of the sentence that the *by*-phrase will eventually arrive. But the preference for low attachment certainly is not restricted to cases where the phrase to be attached is an obligatory or predicted constituent of the sentence. Thus the depth hypothesis seems to predict that low attachment is easier but for the wrong reason, namely, that it reduces the depth of preceding phrases.

In fact, the problem is more serious than this example by itself would suggest. The real problem is that (as Yngve noted) the depth hypothesis makes explicit predictions for sentences only where the number of branches for any node is unambiguous. But of course natural languages have numerous optional constituents and thus this constraint does not hold, even in the general case. Note that this same fundamental problem for the depth hypothesis probably holds in production as well as comprehension, assuming that speakers do not plan entire sentences before they begin to utter them. Indeed, if one interprets hesitation pauses as indicators of sentence planning during the ongoing production of speech, the evidence suggests that speakers plan something like individual clauses or breath groups (Boomer, 1965; Ford and Holmes, 1978; Grosjean, Grosjean, and Lane, 1979; Frazier, 1982), not entire sentences. Hence the number of branches is at most locally determinate or unambiguous even in the case of sentence production.

To summarize briefly, the depth hypothesis incorrectly predicts that flat "conjoined" structures should be perceptually more complex than binary branching structures. The prediction that left-branching structures are more complex than corresponding right-branching structures is too general, both within a language like English and across languages. The correct prediction that low attachment of constituents should be preferred seems to make incorrect claims about the source of the processing difficulty associated with high attachment of constituents. Other correct predictions of the hypothesis are also undermined to some extent by the fact that they are based on the assumption that the processor knows from the outset the number of daughter nodes that each mother node will dominate.

We turn now to the hypothesis that complex constituents optimally occur at points of low depth. This hypothesis offered an explanation for why natural languages permit discontinuous constituents, it predicted that extraposition rules are highly valued, and it correctly predicts the preference for main clauses to precede subordinate clauses (though see note 8), the preference for extraposed sentential subjects, the preference for relative clauses to occur in object, rather than subject, position. The problem, of course, is that this particular explanation is difficult to maintain if the depth hypothesis is not in general correct, as I have been arguing. However, notice that Yngve's basic insight might well be preserved in a quite distinct model of comprehension that offers a more refined or accurate account of the perceptual complexity of sentences. The basic insight is simply that complex constituents should not occur at points of high complexity within a sentence. We will turn now to an alternative complexity metric, the nonterminal-to-terminal node ratio; we will see that certain fundamental problems for this complexity metric are problems for the depth hypothesis as well.

4.4.3. *The nonterminal-to-terminal node metric*

The nonterminal-to-terminal node ratio provides a conceptually simple metric for determining the perceptual complexity of sentences. The basic claim is that the complexity of a sentence correlates with the amount of superstructure that must be assigned to the words of a sentence. Hence, the complexity of a sentence may be determined by simply dividing the number of nonterminals in the sentence by the number of terminals. Obviously this metric will not encounter some of the problems of the depth hypothesis noted above. This metric will favor flat conjoined structures over binary branching structures, as illustrated in (34).

(34) a. Binary branching   b. Ternary branching

                 5/3   4/3

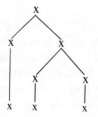 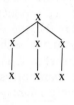

It will also predict that left-branching structures and right-branching structures should be equally complex to process, other things being equal (i.e., the number of nonterminal and terminal nodes) as illustrated in (35).

35. a. Left branching   a. Right branching

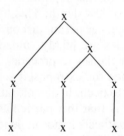

Taken by itself, it will not make any prediction about low versus high attachment of a phrase or about discontinuous constituents, providing that these alternatives do not change the number of nonterminals or terminals in the sentence. Notice that this metric will make differential predictions concerning different types of extraposition: extraposition of a sentential subject is predicted to be preferred because a new terminal (*it*) will be introduced; by contrast, extraposition of a relative clause will not introduce any new terminals though, on the Chomsky-adjunction analysis of extraposed relative clauses, a new nonterminal S-node will be introduced.

4.4.4. The local nonterminal count

The major problem with the nonterminal-to-terminal node ratio stems from the fact that it is not sensitive to the precise distribution of nonterminals over the lexical string. Two sentences with an equal nonterminal-to-terminal ratio may vary radically in their processing complexity. Further, under some circumstances, a sentence with a lower global nonterminal ratio can be more difficult to process than a sentence with a high global ratio due to local concentrations of nonterminals.

To show that the distribution of nonterminals over the string matters and not just the overall ratio of nonterminals to terminals, we may examine phrases like those in (36).

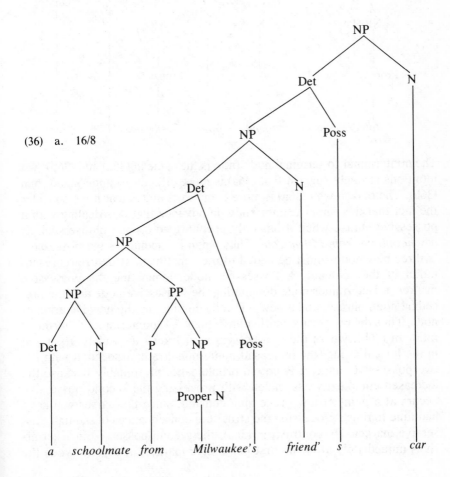

(36) a. 16/8

(36) b. 16/8

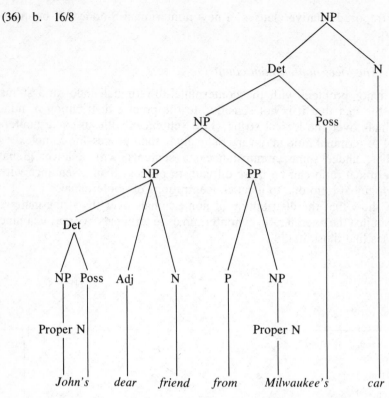

The nonterminal-to-terminal node ratio is the same in (36a) and (36b); yet intuitions strongly suggest that (36a) is more difficult to understand than (36b). The reason why (36a) is more complex is quite clear if we consider the fact that the parser cannot know in advance that it is dealing with a possessive phrase when it has only encountered a noun phrase such as *a schoolmate from Milwaukee*. Thus when it encounters the possessive *'s* three new nodes must be added to the constituent structure representation of the sentence: a Possessive node dominating the possessive marker, a Determiner node dominating the Possessive node and the preceding noun phrase, and a new NP node dominating the new Determiner node. Thus the possessive marker has a high, 3/1, nonterminal-to-terminal ratio. In (36b), where the two possessive markers are widely separated in the lexical string, the increased nonterminal ratio associated with the two possessive markers is not so problematic, presumably because the increased complexity associated with processing the second possessive occurs at a point of low processing demand, since the parser will have had time to finish processing the structural consequences of the first possessive marker. By contrast, in (36a), the second possessive marker arrives immediately after the first possessive marker, at a point when the parser may be assumed to still be engaged in computing the constituent structure implications of the first possessive marker. This example illustrates two points. First, the overall nonterminal ratio in a sentence does not suffice to predict the complexity of the sentence. Second, simply looking at the highest nonterminal count for any word of the sentence will also not suffice, since this does not differ in (36a) and (36b). What seems to matter is the precise distribution of nodes over the lexical string, in particular, clusters of nonterminals that are warranted by adjacent words in the input seem to contribute more to the complexity of a sentence than do the same nonterminals when they are spread out over (nonadjacent) words in the input. This type of local nonterminal count is very much in the spirit of Yngve's observation that complex phrases should occur at points of low complexity (which reduces local complexity) and in the spirit of the nonterminal-to-terminal ratio, which captures the fact that it is not simply the absolute number of nonterminals in a sentence that contributes to the complexity of the sentence, but also the number of lexical items that warrant the postulation of these nonterminals. The example in (36a) suggests that a sentence will be noticeably difficult to parse anytime that the nonterminal-to-terminal ratio is particularly high for more than one of any three adjacent terminals.[9]

Notice that the introduction of an extra word further separating the two possessive markers seems to facilitate processing, as illustrated by the contrast between (37a) and (37b).

(37) a. a friend from Milwaukee's brother's car
      b. a friend from Milwaukee's older brother's car

Thus we will assume that a local nonterminal count should be computed over a three-terminal window subsuming any three adjacent terminals in the lexical string. To formulate the local nonterminal count explicitly, we must determine when nonterminals are postulated during the processing of sentences, what nonterminals contribute to the complexity of the sentence, and how much each node contributes. For the moment we will assume that all nodes contribute equally to the complexity of a sentence, though we will return to this assumption shortly.

Before proceeding, it is necessary to digress briefly to consider precisely what it means to assign, say, a value of 1 to each nonterminal node that must be postulated. The point of assigning numerical values to nodes is to permit the local nonterminal count to be formulated in a sufficiently precise manner to be useful in uncovering unexpected contributions to the complexity of a sentence. Thus the ordinal relations between the numerical values postulated below are to be taken seriously. However, it is abundantly clear that considerable further work is needed before these values can be interpreted in terms of a real time and used to project a complete complexity profile for the on-line processing of a sentence. It will become obvious below, for example, that high numerical values must be weighted, to reflect the fact that the difference between a local non-terminal count of 3 versus 6 does not translate into the same difference (in terms of real time) as the difference between a local nonterminal count of 6 versus 9. (I am fairly sure that the increase in complexity associated with the addition of one node should not increase exponentially as one moves to positions associated with higher local nonterminal counts, however the limited data currently available to me do not suffice to distinguish between several other alternatives.)

Given the evidence for the Minimal Attachment strategy summarized briefly in section 4.3, we will assume that nonterminals are introduced only when warranted by the need to connect the first word of a sentence to the matrix sentence node or any subsequent word into the current (partial) constituent structure representation of the sentence in a manner consistent with the phrase structure rules of the language. This procedure is illustrated in (38), which provides a word-by-word count of the nodes introduced in the parsing of (36a).

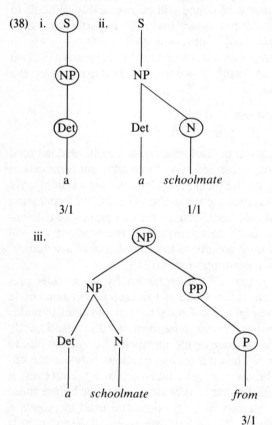

iv.

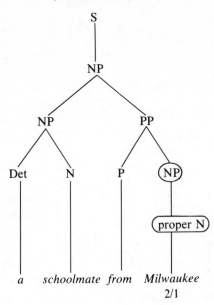

```
                    S
                    |
                    NP
                  /    \
               NP       PP
              /  \      /  \
           Det    N    P   (NP)
            |     |    |     |
            |     |    |  (proper N)
            |     |    |     |
            a  schoolmate from Milwaukee
                              2/1
```

v.

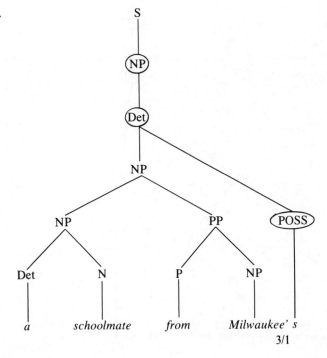

```
                        S
                        |
                      (NP)
                        |
                      (Det)
                     /      \
                    NP       \
                  /    \      \
               NP       PP    (POSS)
              /  \      /  \      |
           Det    N    P    NP    |
            |     |    |    |     |
            a  schoolmate from Milwaukee's
                              3/1
```

vi.

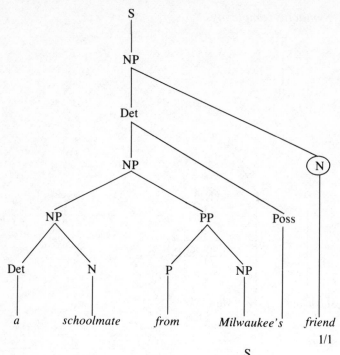

a   schoolmate   from   Milwaukee's   friend
1/1

vii.

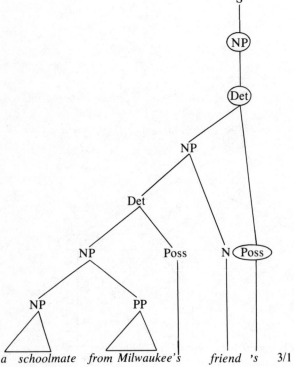

a   schoolmate from Milwaukee's   friend 's   3/1

162

viii.

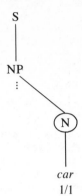

ix. *a   schoolmate   from   Milwaukee's   friend's   car*
   3/1   1/1   3/1   2/1   3/1 1/1 3/1 1/1

In (38) we have followed the assumption that all nodes contribute an equal amount to the complexity of processing a sentence. However, if the syntactic processor does not assign lexical category labels, preterminal symbols should not contribute to the local nonterminal count. We will thus assume that preterminal symbols do not contribute to the nonterminal count. Of course, excluding preterminals from the local nonterminal count will decrease the maximal local nonterminal counts of different sentences an equal amount and thus the major consequence of excluding preterminals is only that differences in the number of nonterminals introduced locally is emphasized.

If all nonterminal nodes contributed equally to the complexity of a sentence, we would expect the maximal local nonterminal count of the sentences in (39) to be equal. But, intuitions suggest that (39a) is more difficult to comprehend than (39b), which in turn is more difficult than (39c) even when we consider only the initial portion of the sentences. If we were to assign an equal value to all node types, this difference in complexity would not be accounted for. These differences in complexity suggest that S and $\bar{\text{S}}$ nodes contribute more to complexity than do other node types.[10] We will thus assign these nodes a value of $1\frac{1}{2}$; all other nonterminals will be assigned a value of 1. Given these assumptions, the local nonterminal count will correctly capture the differences in (39), as illustrated in (40).

(39) a. That that that men were appointed didn't bother the liberals wasn't remarked upon by the press upset many women.
      b. That that men were appointed didn't bother the liberals wasn't remarked upon by the press.
      c. That men who were appointed didn't bother the liberals wasn't remarked upon by the press.

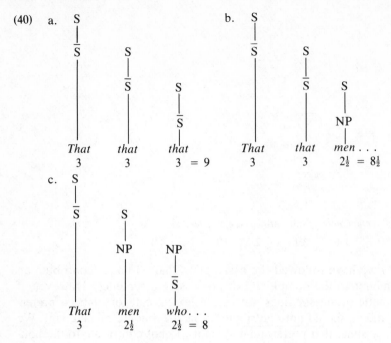

(40)   a. ... That that that / 3 3 3 = 9

b. ... That that men... / 3 3 2½ = 8½

c. ... That men who... / 3 2½ 2½ = 8

To summarize briefly, we are assuming that the local nonterminal count is simply the sum of the value of all nonterminals introduced over any three adjacent terminals and thus the maximal local nonterminal count of a sentence is the largest such sum in a sentence. Minimal Attachment governs the postulation of nonterminal nodes, preterminal nodes are excluded from this count, but all other nonterminals receive a value of 1, except for S and $\bar{S}$, which receive a value of 1½.

The claim to be defended here is simply that given two sentences with an equal overall nonterminal ratio, the sentence with the higher maximal local nonterminal count will be more difficult to process. Ultimately, of course, the local nonterminal count must be further developed to predict the word by word complexity profile of sentences, so that sentences with different global nonterminal counts may be compared as well, but that would take us beyond the scope of this paper.

The local nonterminal count predicts the asymmetry in processing complexity between relative clauses in subject position and relative clauses in object position, as illustrated in (41). As noted above, the relative complexity of relative clauses in subject position as compared to object position has been demonstrated by Wanat (1971), using eye movement recording techniques, and by Levin et al. (1972), using the eye voice span as a measure of processing complexity.

(41) a.

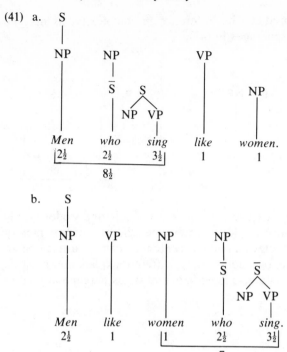

Frazier, Rayner, and Carlson (in progress) show that sentences with extraposed relative clauses take longer to read than their nonextraposed counterparts.[11] This too follows from the local nonterminal count, assuming that extraposed relatives are Chomsky-adjoined to the minimal S containing the head of the relative, as indicated in (42).

(42) a.

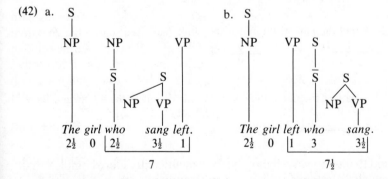

The complexity of sentences with sentential subjects compared to their counterparts in which the subject has been extraposed is also captured by the local nonterminal count, though in this case a global nonterminal-to-terminal ratio also predicts the difference in complexity, as may be seen by examining the sentences in (43).

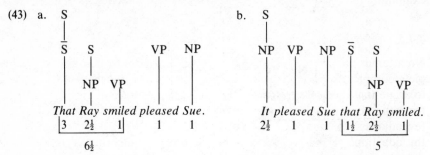

(43) a.

That Ray smiled pleased Sue.
3   2½   1   1   1
6½

b.

It pleased Sue that Ray smiled.
2½   1   1   1½   2½   1
5

Using a reading time measure of complexity, Eady and Fodor (1981) tested sentences like those in (44) to determine whether the complexity often associated with center-embedded sentences can be attributed to center-embedding per se, or whether some different explanation must be invoked to explain why center-embedding is at times perceptually complex.

(44) (Taken from Eady and Fodor; a,b < c < d)

a. Jack met the patient the nurse sent to the doctor the clinic had hired.
2½   1   1   0   5   0   1   2   1   0   5   0   1   1
4½   6   6

b. The patient the nurse sent to the doctor the clinic had hired met Jack.
2½   0   5   0   1   2   1   0   5   0   1   0   2   1
7½   6   6

c. Jack met the patient the nurse the clinic had hired sent to the doctor.
2½   1   1   0   5   0   5   0   1   0   2   2   2   1   0
4½   10

d. The patient the nurse the clinic had hired sent to the doctor met Jack.
2½   0   5   0   5   0   1   0   2   2   1   0   1   1
10
7½

They found that (44b) was slightly but nonsignificantly more complex than (44a). Crucially, sentence (44c) was significantly more complex than (44b) and (44d) was significantly more complex than (44c). A global nonterminal-to-terminal node ratio will not distinguish between any of these sentences types; the depth hypothesis predicts that (44c) should be easier to process than (44b). The local nonterminal count, however, provides the correct ranking of these sentence types as may be seen in (41) by examining the highest local nonterminal counts in each sentence.[12]

4.4.5. Applying the local nonterminal count

No attempt has been made here to develop a metric to predict the complete complexity profile of entire sentences. Rather the attempt has been to argue that the source of complexity in unambiguous sentences derives from the need to postulate several nonterminals all at once, over just a few adjacent words in the incoming lexical string. We will briefly examine the questions raised by the local nonterminal count proposed here and then explore the effects (if any) of high concentrations of nonterminals on the shape of the grammar.

Prince (1982) discusses the various devices available in the phonological systems of natural languages for avoiding stress clashes and establishing a basic alternating stress pattern. He appeals to a principle of minimal structure that is suggestive of the Minimal Attachment principle evidenced in the processing of syntactic structures. He views the rhythm rules found in English and many other languages as a response to a high density of strong beats in a metrical grid; it may be of interest to note that strong or stressed positions receive more attention than weak or unstressed positions during language processing (cf. Cutler, 1976). This seems remarkably similar to the avoidance of a high density of nonterminals in the syntax of natural languages. Prince also emphasizes the importance of the peripheries of domains in characterizing the stress systems found in natural languages. Here too there is a rather striking similarity with the concluding remarks in section 4.3, where it was emphasized that the boundaries of syntactic phrases must be well demarcated for a language to be easily parsed.[13]

These basic similarities between principles of metrical structure and principles of syntactic structure may amount to more than loose or accidental analogies. Fundamental similarities such as these may suggest that certain aspects of a complexity metric for natural language sentences will be common to all components of the grammar and may reflect properties common to the distinct processing systems implicated in language comprehension. A pressure for minimal structure may be shared by all components of the grammar, though the rules defining well-formed structures do obviously differ depending on whether the relevant structures are phonological, syntactic, or semantic. A pressure for some structural unit that provides a reasonable domain for processing to be clearly demarcated may also be common to each of the components of the grammar, though the particular unit may differ from component to component. Likewise, across all components or all levels of structure there may be a pressure for points of high computational complexity to be spread out, permitting demands on attentional and computational resources to be distributed evenly throughout the processing of a structure. Thus the basic phenomenon underlying the local density count may not be tied to characteristics that are unique to the syntactic processor.

In broad outline the local nonterminal count would seem to be explained by the assumption that there is quite general preference for the demands on processing capacity to be approximately constant (thus predictable) and below some threshold level. What is not in any sense explained here is why syntactic complexity seems to be influenced by computational demands of a local window defined by three adjacent terminals. One possibility is that a three-item window just happens to coincide with, say, the size of some perceptual buffer which holds partially structured items and is overburdened if more than three items must be held simultaneously.[14] Alternatively, the speed or duration of syntactic computations may be such that the processing of items typically is completed before more than two subsequent items have been received. When processing lags of more than two items arise, processing resources other than those usually drawn on during the comprehension of sentences might be deployed. (Indeed, the deployment of special resources that are not characteristically tapped during sentence processing might be what gives rise to the intuition of processing complexity experienced in sentences with an extremely high local density count.[15]) To my knowledge, there is no decisive evidence at present to choose between these (or other easily imagined) possibilities.

What is clear, however, is that the local nonterminal count is in general accord with the assumptions of many current theories of sentence processing which claim that the "work" involved in the syntactic processing of unambiguous sentences is to be identified with the postulation of nonterminal nodes. Garden paths aside, these theories lead us to expect the syntactic complexity of a sentence to correlate with the number and complexity of the computations involved in checking the wellformedness constraints of the language to identify the syntactic type of each phrase so that the constituency relations of the items in the sentence may be determined.

Only rather limited evidence has been presented for the hypothesis that S and S̄ contribute more to the complexity of a sentence than do other nonterminal nodes. Thus it is quite possible that the hypothesis will have to be altered or undergo revision as the local nonterminal count is further refined in attempts to predict very precisely the complete complexity profile of entire sentences. There is certainly no a priori reason for expecting S and S̄ to contribute more to perceptual complexity than other nonterminals. However, if S and S̄ are not headed constructions (cf. Williams, 1982) the unexpectedly large contribution of these nodes to the complexity of a sentence may indicate that it takes the processor more time to postulate nonterminals if the nonterminals may not be projected from the head of a phrase.

We return now to the question of whether languages try to avoid generating constructions with a high local nonterminal count. Is it possible, for example, to preserve Yngve's explanation for the existence of discontinuous constituents in natural languages in terms of a pressure for grammars to reduce the processing complexity (local nonterminal count) of sentences?

We have already seen that extraposition rules can either increase or decrease the local nonterminal counts in a sentence depending on the details of the extraposition rule involved. Thus, this explanation of extraposition rules does not really seem to explain any of the details of the particular set of extraposition rules found in English. (A similar point may be made about other discontinuous constituents.)

Extraposition rules do provide an optional device for moving complex phrases from positions in the sentence with a high local nonterminal count. Given that the actual complexity of a sentence will depend on the precise details of the length and complexity of its various constituents (a factor that cannot be referred to by syntactic rules given restrictive theories of syntax), the existence of optional rules that may move constituents to the ends of clauses (which tend to have low local nonterminal counts) may be viewed as an accommodation to the exigencies of sentence processing. In other words, extraposition rules may be viewed as a grammatical device available to speakers to cope with nonsystematic complexities that arise when a particular set of options available in the grammar happen to conspire in the generation of some sentences to produce especially high local concentrations of complexity. (Similarly, such optional devices may be employed by speakers to disambiguate accidental ambiguities of, say, constituent boundaries which arise due to the particular lexical items used in some sentences.)

While parsing considerations do seem to offer an explanation for why the grammar should contain some rules permitting constituents to be moved to the ends of clauses, and an explanation for why these rules should be optional, parsing considerations do not seem to explain why the grammar makes available the particular set of extraposition rules actually found in the grammar. For example, these considerations do not explain why English permits extraposition of a prepositional phrase or relative clause but does not permit the entire subject noun phrase or object noun phrase to move leaving behind some semantically empty placeholder (in a fashion comparable to extraposition of a sentential subject). Nor do they explain why it should be possible to extrapose prepositional phrases and full relative clauses but not "reduced" relatives (e.g., *The horse fell ridden past the barn*). In short, the explanation that parsing considerations offer for the existence of extraposition rules and for the gross form of the rules (why they move constituents to the ends of clauses, why they tend to move complex constituents, why their application is optional) do not go very far in explaining the details of the rules and especially the restrictions on them. (In this respect, the local nonterminal count seems to fare no better and no worse than the depth hypothesis in explaining the existence of discontinuous constituents.)

There is one very basic fact about natural languages that does seem to be explained by the complexity of processing high local densities of nonterminals. In general, the strict subcategorization restrictions associated with particular lexical items are imposed only on sisters of the lexical items, not on the ancestors of the lexical item or on the offspring of their sisters. For example, natural languages do not contain, say, one complementizer (*that*) which may be used only in the case of a single level of embedding, another (*twet*) used only for two levels of embedding, still another (*thret*) for three levels of embedding, as illustrated in (45). Nor do they contain verbs that may co-occur with an $\bar{\text{S}}$-complement just in case that $\bar{\text{S}}$ itself contains an $\bar{\text{S}}$-complement.

(45)   a.   b.   c.

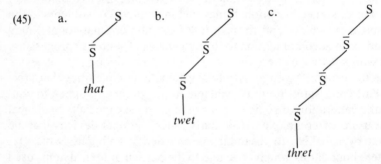

It is surely true (as Janet Fodor has pointed out to me) that restrictions of this sort may correspond to somewhat improbable meanings if we think in terms of the particular lexical items actually found in natural languages. However, in the case of complementizers, for example, different complementizers might simply convey syntactic information without altering the meaning of the sentence (i.e., a class of complementizers might be synonymous). And, in the case of verbs subcategorizing for an $\bar{\text{S}}$ containing a sentential complement, one can easily imagine a natural language being more like the "deep structures" in generative semantics and thus containing, say, predicates expressing a propositional attitude toward some class of causatives which in turn take sentential complements (e.g., [want [s . . . Cause . . . [s]]]). Similarly, one can imagine a natural language in which certain predicates subcategorize for a complement expressing the source of the speaker's information about some proposition or event (e.g., [want [s . . . BE KNOWN FIRST HAND . . . [s]]]). In short, "lexicalization" of concepts or meanings might in principle have occurred in a variety of manners. Indeed, it is rather striking that there is such considerable uniformity across languages in terms of permitting semantic notions of "tense," "causation," or "source of information" to be expressed in the meaning of individual morphemes (-ed) or words (*kill, apparently*, etc.), or expressed by obligatory grammatical distinctions (e.g., the causative marker or *-miş* "source of information" marker in Turkish) but not as predicates associated with highly specific subcategorization restrictions.[16]

A priori, we might have expected languages to contain such lexical items; indeed, items like the hypothetical complementizers in (45) would be extremely helpful in disambiguating recursive structures. But notice that according to the local nonterminal count, such markers would be intolerably complex to process because even though they would disambiguate syntactic structures they would do so only at the expense of forcing the processor to postulate lots of nonterminals all at once. Thus one basic aspect of the grammars of natural languages, the sister constraint on strict subcategorization, does seem to be explained by processing considerations. Alternative conceivable co-occurrence restrictions that might be imposed by individual lexical items would guarantee that the basic design of the language would defy the capacities of the human sentence processing mechanism.

There are, of course, certain constructions in natural languages that may be analyzed as violating the sister principle on strict subcategorization. For example, it is not uncommon for verbs to impose restrictions on the particular complementizer that may occur in a sentential complement to the verb (e.g., *want for* versus **want that*). However, even the violations of the sister principle on strict subcategorization are of a form that the sentence processor may easily cope with since they do not force the processor to postulate more nonterminals than would a corresponding restriction that abided by the sister principle. Thus, when processing a verb that selects for a sentential complement, the processor must postulate the same number of nonterminals regardless of whether the verb selects for a particular complementizer.

In short, a grammar containing an "ancestor constraint" or an "offspring constraint" on strict subcategorization, rather than a sister constraint, would not be a grammar of a possible natural language and thus should be excluded by a theory of possible human languages, i.e., by the theory of universal grammar. In this instance, it is a theory of human sentence processing which explains why universal grammar should prohibit a particular class of conceivable grammars. However, there is no particular reason to believe that the prohibition against ancestor or offspring constraints is, or is not, a property of the initial state of the human language learner. It might turn out that humans are constitutionally predisposed to look only at sisters for co-occurrence restrictions imposed by individual lexical items or it might turn out that there is no biological predisposition of this sort. The evidence we have examined here simply does not bear on the issue. Of course, in principle we should be able to settle this issue by looking at the ease with which children acquire different sorts of restrictions on strict subcategorization, including naturally occurring restrictions that violate the sister constraint and perhaps ancestor restrictions in the acquisition of artificial languages.

4.5. Syntactic complexity and semantic processing

At present, very little is known about the on-line semantic processing of sentences. The proposal to be put forth in this section is thus quite speculative. It does, however, have some interesting consequences and explain some otherwise extremely puzzling facts.

To begin, it should be pointed out that semantic interpretation cannot be a matter of strictly bottom-up semantic composition, where the semantic interpretation of a constituent does not occur until after all daughter constituents have been semantically interpreted. If semantic interpretation did proceed in this manner, right-branching sentences should be more complex than corresponding left-branching sentences because in right-branching constructions interpretation could not begin until the most deeply embedded constituent had been received and interpreted. Further, on this view, the complexity of right-branching sentences should be a function of the length of the sentence because the longer the sentence the more material there will be that must be held uninterpreted in memory.

Here it will be assumed that semantic interpretation occurs on-line and that semantic expressions are combined as soon as possible. Apart from some interesting exceptions (including the determination of the scope of quantifiers, determining the truth conditions of sentences and the drawing of certain inferences), intuitions do in general seem to support the assumption that semantic interpretation of a sentence proceeds as the words of the sentence are encountered. Some experimental evidence exists that supports the view that semantic interpretation of major phrases occurs on-line (e.g., Marslen-Wilson, 1975; Potter and Faulconer, 1979). It will also be assumed that remembering nonsemantic information is an active process that contributes to the processing complexity of a sentence.

Given the assumptions above, we are immediately led to the question of when the sentence processor is licensed to forget nonsemantic information (e.g., information about the phonological or syntactic representation of some portion of a sentence). There are known to be rather severe restrictions on the immediate memory capacity of humans. Presumably the reason why people can manage to understand very long sentences is that they need not retain all information about the sentence throughout the processing of the entire sentence. If we think of this in terms of the units that license the sentence processor to forget nonsemantic information, the question is simply what are the "semantic replacement units" in language comprehension.

Here we will explore the consequences of the assumption that "complete minimal governing categories" are the semantic replacement units in sentence processing. I will provisionally define "minimal governing category" as the minimal NP or S containing both a governor and governed material (where tense governs the subject, verbs and prepositions govern their objects, and nouns govern their complements).

Examples of commonly occurring governing categories in English are presented in (45). Noun phrases and clauses that would not constitute minimal governing categories include noun phrases that consist simply of a pronoun, proper noun, or simple noun phrases without a complement, or clauses that contain a Pro subject and a predicate consisting simply of an intransitive verb, as illustrated in (46a). (Note that an infinitival clause containing a transitive verb or prepositional phrase will constitute a minimal governing category according to the preceding definition, as illustrated in (46b) and (46c).[17])

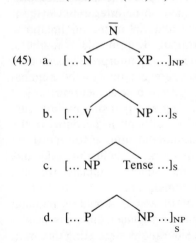

(45) a. [... N   XP ...]$_{NP}$

      b. [... V   NP ...]$_S$

      c. [... NP   Tense ...]$_S$

      d. [... P   NP ...]$_{NP}$
                                  $_S$

(46) a. The students tried [Pro to learn]$_{S \neq MGC}$
      b. The students tried [Pro to learn phonetics]$_{S = MGC}$
      c. The students tried [Pro to learn about each other]$_{S = MCG}$

By *complete minimal governing category* I mean a minimal governing category containing no unassigned pronoun, bound anaphor (reciprocal or reflexive) or gap. The need for this "completeness" restriction may be seen by examining sentences like (47)–(49). In these sentences there is a pronoun or gap that cannot be reliably interpreted until after the end of the minimal governing category containing the pronoun or gap. In (47) this is because the antecedent for the pronoun will not have been encountered by the end of the relative clause. In (48) the verb phrase of the embedded clause in the relative clause has been Right Node Raised and thus will not be available until after the relative clause from which the VP has been raised has been encountered.

(47)   The refugees [he$_i$ had seen] haunted Victor$_i$

(48)   The elephant trainer who John thought ____ and the zookeeper who Peter was sure ____ had appeared on the Tonight Show last week were eating lunch at the next table.

(49)   Here is a man who everyone who meets ____ admires ____.

(50)   *Here is a man who everyone who meets ____ admires Reagan.

In (49) the parasitic gap following *meet* is licensed only by the occurrence of the gap following *admire* (as indicated by the ungrammaticality of (50)). Thus the parasitic gap may not be safely interpreted (in fact, its existence can not be securely determined) until after the true gap following *admire* has been identified. If incomplete minimal governing categories were allowed to serve as semantic replacement units, then the unassigned pronouns or gaps in these sentences would have to be interpreted without the aid of syntactic information about the material in the minimal governing category containing the gap or pronoun. In principle, it might be possible for these pronouns and gaps to be reliably interpreted using only the information contained in a semantic representation of the minimal governing category of the pronoun or gap. But unless the grammatical constraints on pronouns, Right Node Raising and parasitic gaps can be recast in purely semantic terms, it would be difficult to account for the fact that people do seem to notice ungrammaticalities involving these constraints (e.g., the ungrammaticality of (50)). We will thus take this observation as suggestive evidence that incomplete minimal governing categories do not serve as semantic replacement units.

We have not yet addressed the question of why it should be minimal governing categories that define the semantic replacement units in language comprehension. There are two considerations suggesting that minimal governing categories are extremely plausible candidates for defining semantic replacement units. First, these units are semantically complete. Emmon Bach has pointed out to me that Frege recognized that in some sense noun phrases and clauses are the only semantically complete units in natural languages. Second, assuming that the proper formulation of the structural restriction on pronoun-antecedent relations is that pronouns must be free in their minimal governing category, these units will be extremely useful to the processor in its attempt to interpret pronouns on-line. The processor need only consider phrases occurring outside the minimal governing category of the pronoun to insure that any morphologically appropriate antecedent it selects will be a grammatically permissible antecedent for a pronoun. (Similar arguments apply to bound anaphors, assuming that they must be bound in their minimal governing category; cf. Chomsky, 1981.)

If the processor must keep track of minimal governing categories regardless of whether there are any pronouns in a sentence (as it must according to the semantic replacement hypothesis), then the presence of a decoy antecedent (*the girls* in (51a)) occurring within the minimal governing category of the pronoun should not complicate the processing of the sentence. However, if the processor does not in general have to

(51) a. Mary was laughing because *the girls* tickled *them*.
      b. Mary was laughing because *the girls* tickled *him*.

keep track of minimal governing categories, then we might expect the presence of a potential antecedent inside the minimal governing category of the pronoun to complicate the processing of a sentence. In this case, the processor must do something extra to determine that the decoy antecedent is not a legitimate antecedent for the pronoun. Hence, we would expect (51a) to be more difficult than (51b) (assuming that the processor can use morphological information about number and gender to dismiss potential antecedents which do not agree with the pronoun, as argued by Ehrlich (1980)).

Frazier, Rayner, and Carlson, (in progress) examined the processing of sentences like (51a) and (51b) using the eye movement recording technique. They did not find any difference in the complexity of the two sentence types, as we would expect according to the semantic replacement hypothesis. Of course, a null effect of this sort cannot be taken as conclusive evidence. It is always possible that the experimental technique used is simply not sufficiently sensitive to reflect subtle differences in complexity (though it should be pointed out that the eye movement recording technique has been shown to be sensitive to other variables influencing pronoun interpretation; cf. Ehrlich and Rayner, 1982).

The prediction that pronouns that have not yet been assigned an antecedent lead to incomplete minimal governing categories that are not semantically replaced receives some support from the psychological literature. For example, Tanenhaus and Seidenberg (1981) show that clause boundary effects which are present when an antecedent is available to be assigned to a pronoun occurring in a sentence-initial subordinate clause disappear when no antecedent is available (though see also Bever and Townsend [1979] where it is argued that it is necessary to maintain a surface representation of initial subordinate clauses regardless of whether they contain an unassigned pronoun).[18]

Let us define the "main projection path" of a sentence as the maximal unique unbroken chain of $\{V^n, S^n\}$ which includes the matrix VP,[19] as illustrated in (52) where nodes on the main projection path are circled.

(52)

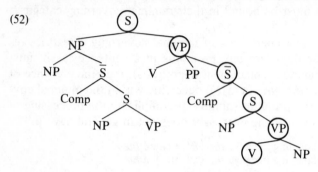

Notice that it is only complete minimal governing categories lying off the main projection path of a sentence that will be able to serve as semantic replacement units *during* the comprehension of a sentence, because the end of minimal governing categories lying on the main projection path will not be reached until the end of the highest S.

Hence, from the assumption that complete minimal governing categories define the semantic replacement units in natural language processing, it immediately follows that all minimal governing categories lying off the main projection path are *natural interpretive islands*. Extraction out of these units will increase the memory burden associated with processing a sentence if the extraction gives rise to an incomplete minimal governing category since this will prevent semantic replacement. Even if the extraction does not give rise to an incomplete minimal governing category (as in the case of leftward extractions) extraction from a potential semantic replacement unit will create a serious problem because of the numerous ambiguities and uncertainties in the identification of gaps and in the left-to-right assignment of filler-gap dependencies. Any incorrect filler-gap assignment in a minimal governing category lying off the main projection path would be extremely difficult to revise once semantic replacement had occurred.

In sum, extraction out of a minimal governing category lying off the main projection path should increase the complexity of a sentence. If the minimal governing category is incomplete, it will not be able to serve as a semantic replacement unit, and this will increase the memory burden associated with processing the sentence. Further, if an incorrect filler-gap assignment is made within a minimal governing category lying off the main projection path, it should be difficult to revise, because the nonsemantic information in that unit may not be available once semantic replacement has occurred.[20] Hence, we expect that across languages there should be a tendency for all minimal governing categories off the main projection path to be extraction islands, including adverbial clauses, sentential subjects, and complex noun phrases. (Note that the *wh*-Island Constraint and the Fixed Subject Constraint are not accounted for by these observations.)

Rightward movement out of a noun phrase should be limited in two respects. First, the moved phrase should not be permitted to move beyond the next higher minimal governing category. Otherwise semantic replacement will occur before the moved material is processed. Second, if a phrase is moved from a noun phrase, the material remaining in the noun phrase must not appear to compose a complete minimal governing category since this would lead to the noun phrase being semantically replaced. The first consideration should lead to a pressure for languages to incorporate a right roof constraint; the second consideration should lead to a constraint restricting rightward movement to movement of the entire complement or modifier of a noun phrase. If only part of the complement to a noun phrase moved, then the remaining noun phrase could contain governed material and appear to be a complete minimal governing category and thus the noun phrase would be semantically replaced before the moved constituent was encountered. Thus movement of the preposition phrase *from the National Gallery* in (53a) should be prohibited; hence (53b) should be unambiguous.

(53) a. The painting by Rembrandt from the National Gallery was stolen.
      b. The painting by Rembrandt was stolen from the National Gallery.

Of course, this explanation of the island constraints does not explain why the constraints are relatively absolute in some languages and relatively squishy or nonexistent in other languages. It only predicts that there should be a pressure across languages for minimal governing categories lying off the main projection path to be interpretive islands. The hypothesis does, however, make several empirical predictions that may be tested. For example, it predicts that in a language without a Complex NP Constraint, the processing complexity of a sentence containing an extraction out of a complex noun phrase (compared to a corresponding sentence lacking the extraction) should be higher than a sentence containing an extraction out of a clause lying on the main projection path of the sentence (compared to a corresponding sentence lacking the extraction). Hence, the difference in the processing complexity of (54a) and (54b) should be greater than the difference between (54c) and (54d) in a language like Swedish.

(54) a. Which test did the students who received ___ not do very well?
      b. The students who received this test did not do very well.
      c. Which test did the teacher claim the students received ___?
      d. The teacher claimed the students received this test.

Elisabet Engdahl has pointed out a further prediction of this account for languages like Swedish which permit extractions out of relative clauses. She observes that extractions out of a relative clause should be easier in such languages when the relative clause appears relatively late in the sentence and notes that her intuitions confirm this prediction (as well as the predictions concerning the relative complexity of the sentences in (54)).

In addition to offering an interesting (though as yet still largely untested) explanation for the island constraints, the assumptions I have been making about the semantic processing of sentences also help to explain some puzzling intuitions about sentence processing. I have been assuming that constituents are semantically interpreted as soon as possible, that complete minimal governing categories serve as semantic replacement units, and that remembering the nonsemantic information in a sentence is an active process that contributes to the processing complexity of a sentence.

The assumption that remembering nonsemantic information is an active process contributing to the processing complexity of a sentence predicts that more "forgetting" should occur at points of high complexity than at points of low complexity, due to competition with other processing operations that contribute to the complexity of processing a sentence. Under circumstances where the language processing system is under duress due to exceptionally high memory and computational demands, we might expect the language processor to concentrate its limited resources on remembering the structure associated with lexical items that have not yet been semantically interpreted. This hypothesis is formulated in (55) as the Disappearing Syntactic Nodes Hypothesis.

(55) At points of high complexity, syntactic nodes will tend to be forgotten if they dominate no lexical material or only dominate material that has already been semantically combined.

One's first intuition about a sentence like (56a) is that the sentence is well formed. Unlike (56b), in (56a) people do not immediately notice the missing verb phrase, providing that it is the "middle" verb phrase that is missing. (This observation is initially due to Janet Fodor.)

(56) a. The patient the nurse the clinic had hired met Jack.
      b. The patient the nurse sent to the doctor the clinic met Jack.

This observation is easily explained given our assumptions; when the processor receives the verb phrase *met Jack*, the material crossed-out in (57) will have been semantically replaced.

(57)   The patient [t̶h̶e̶ ̶n̶u̶r̶s̶e̶ ̶t̶h̶e̶ ̶c̶l̶i̶n̶i̶c̶ ̶h̶a̶d̶ ̶h̶i̶r̶e̶d̶] met Jack.

The Disappearing Syntactic Nodes Hypothesis predicts that the predicted verb phrase node of the highest relative clause is likely to have been forgotten as is the verb phrase node of the matrix clause since neither node dominates semantically uninterpreted lexical items. Thus, given the representation in (57) it is natural for the processor to assume that the verb phrase *met Jack* is the verb phrase of the matrix clause, since there is no semantically uninterpreted material in the relative clause warranting or necessitating the postulation of the verb phrase in the highest relative clause.

Similarly, we might expect people not to notice the missing verb phrase in (58a), for the inner complementizer *that* may semantically combine with the sentential subject (*men were appointed*) to form a proposition. This proposition in turn may combine with the outer complementizer *that* to form a proposition; the fact that this is not a syntactically licensed interpretation should go undetected only when the processor is under duress – that is, at points of high complexity. Under such circumstances, the verb phrase node of the matrix clause will tend to be forgotten; thus, again, there will be no semantically uninterpreted material to necessitate the postulation of the obligatory verb phrase that is missing. Therefore the absence of this obligatory verb phrase will tend not to be detected in (58a). (By contrast, in (58b) the violation occurs at a point of lower complexity and thus the processor should be more likely to notice the syntactic violation.)

(58)   a.   [That [that [m̶e̶n̶ ̶w̶e̶r̶e̶ ̶a̶p̶p̶o̶i̶n̶t̶e̶d̶] didn't bother the liberals.

b.   It didn't bother the liberals that that men were appointed.

Exactly the same reasoning explains why the missing *that* in (59) tends not to be noticed.

(59)   a.   That John went bothered Mary upset her husband.

In fact, sentence (59) seems easier to process than the expected grammatical form in (60), since the additional complementizer in (60) simply increases the complexity of the sentence by introducing a high local density of nonterminals, which do not in any case successfully serve their role of marking the upcoming verb phrase (since the nodes will often have been forgotten before they may serve this function).

(60)   That that John went bothered Mary upset her husband.

We would for the same reasons expect the missing clause in (61a) to go undetected. However, in this sentence, people do seem to immediately notice that a clause is missing.

(61)   a.   The fact that if whoever left had asked Mary to go too bothered her parents.
       b.   The fact that if whoever left had asked Mary to go too she would have gone bothered her parents.

This may be explained, however, by the assumption that semantically *if* is a function which, when combined with a proposition, makes a function from propositions to propositions (i.e., (t/t)/t). Hence, the semantic representation of (61a) will not be well formed and will itself signal that some constituent (semantically a proposition) is missing from the sentence.

To summarize, the hypothesis that complete minimal governing categories license the forgetting of nonsemantic information helps to explain why people can process very long sentences despite limitations on immediate memory capacity. It accounts for the finding that a decoy antecedent occurring within the minimal governing category of a pronoun does not appear to complicate the processing of a sentence. It predicts that minimal governing categories lying off the main projection path of a sentence should tend to be extraction and interpretive islands across languages. The hypothesis also contributes to an explanation of why people initially tend to notice the absence of certain obligatory constituents but not others.

4.6. Conclusion

We have examined a variety of different sources of processing complexity and tried to evaluate the effects of each type of complexity on the grammars of natural languages. It was proposed that the effect on the grammar of complexity due to ambiguity is minimal and that when such effects are observed they tend to fall into a natural class characterized by the Impermissible Ambiguity Constraint and constraints against intersecting dependencies of fillers and gaps. Complexity due to the effects of basic word order on phrasal packaging and on-line semantic interpretation of a sentence were argued to have more fundamental grammatical consequences, strongly influencing the set of grammatically independent options that are likely to co-occur within a particular language. Complexity due to a high local density of nonterminals was argued to underlie the constraint on the co-occurrence restrictions individual lexical items may impose, and thus was offered as an explanation for the absence of "ancestor" or "offspring" constraints on strict subcategorization in the grammars of natural languages. Complexity due to delayed semantic replacement was offered as an explanation for why minimal governing categories lying off the main projection path of a sentence tend to be interpretive islands as we look across languages.

The evidence discussed here suggests that it would be premature to abandon the search for processing explanations of constraints on grammars. In the past, we may simply have been looking in the wrong place for such explanations by focusing narrowly on the avoidance of ambiguity as a pressure for grammatical change. The broad outlines of the human sentence processing system have begun to emerge only in the last few years and even now theories of language comprehension are much too heavily based on investigations of the processing of English. As theories of language comprehension become further refined and more adequate to the task of explaining the processing of radically different types of languages, we will surely be in a better position to construct explanatory theories of the ways grammars are, and are not, shaped by the exigencies of sentence processing.

One question raised by the current investigation that has not received much attention in the literature is whether a single theory of the interaction of grammars and processors will suffice. In evolutionary terms, this approach seems inadequate and likely to lead to serious misconceptions about the evolution of the species and the evolution or development of languages. A more promising approach would involve separating what might be called *homologous* similarities of languages (due to shared parent structure) from *analogous* similarities (due to similar pressures operating on historically different structures), thinking of these terms in their evolutionary sense. Certain processing constraints might act as selective pressures on a language, modulating any changes in a grammatical system and thus accounting for the fact that different grammars converge over time on the same solution to a functional problem of maintaining a language in a form that can be acquired, mentally represented, and easily processed. This seems to be a natural perspective from which to view the effects of complexity due to word order discussed in section 4.3 and perhaps the effects of complexity due to delayed semantic replacement discussed in section 4.5.

It must be emphasized that selective pressure is being used here only to mean a pressure that favors the development or spread of one change over another. Clearly there is no reason to believe that some members of the species that happened to develop a language that was relatively difficult to process died, say, because they could not comprehend warning messages quickly or reliably enough to survive. This strict interpretation of selective pressures as factors that may only exert an influence through survival of the most fit individuals would seem totally inappropriate in terms of ongoing language change as evidenced in modern societies.

In one important sense, natural languages have an existence independent from speaker-hearers of the languages, namely, in the utterances of speakers that form the data for new language learners. Hence, language both is and is not invented anew with each child or generation. Mistakes are regularly made during the language acquisition process and innovations regularly occur even in adult language users; which particular mistakes and innovations have a lasting effects on the language may well be influenced by selective pressures of the sort discussed here. In short, selective pressures may operate directly on the language to determine the success of variations introduced into the language by whatever means. Ultimately these pressures may stem from the structure of the species, but certainly in principle they may change a language without changing the biological structure of the species. Hence there may be convergence in grammars over time, and the appearance of analogous similarities across different languages. Homologous similarities between grammars may superficially resemble analogous similarities but the mechanism responsible for the similarities may be quite different. Some properties of grammars may have been present from the outset or the very origin of natural languages and have been preserved over time because a grammar lacking those properties could not be used by human beings. If, as argued in section 4.3, a grammar with a general ancestor constraint on subcategorization would simply defy the processing abilities of humans, then this is an instance of a true homologous similarity in the grammars of all languages, assuming that the human processing capacity has not diminished over the millennia.

Notes

This work was supported by NIMH Research Grant MH35347 to C. Clifton and L. Frazier and NSF Research Grant BNS79-17600 to K. Rayner and L. Frazier. I want to thank the participants at the Ohio State University workshop on "Syntactic Theory and How People Parse Sentences" for helpful discussion of the paper. I am also grateful to Emmon Bach, Charles Clifton, Stephen Crain, Alice Davison, Elisabet Engdahl, Janet Fodor, and Stephen Isard for providing comments on the written paper.

1. The work discussed here is primarily concerned with the processing of sentences presented in isolation. For discussion of the effects of preceding context on sentence complexity see Davison and Lutz (this volume), Crain and Steedman (this volume), and Frazier, Rayner, and Carlson, (in progress).

2. In section 4.4 it is argued that postulating a large number of nonterminal nodes gives rise to processing complexity in unambiguous sentences and thus it might appear that there is a redundant explanation for the complexity of these garden path sentences. In fact, however, there is considerable evidence that the garden path sentences discussed in the text involve complexities due to a temporary misanalysis of part of the sentence and not due simply to the complexity of the ultimate (correct) syntactic structure of the sentence. This evidence comes from studies in which subjects' eye movements are recorded as they read sentences (cf. Frazier and Rayner, 1982; Rayner, Carlson, and Frazier, 1983). These studies show a significant increase in the duration of the first fixation in the disambiguating region of the sentence, which is not a point of particular complexity in terms of the number of nodes that must be postulated. Also, regressive eye movements follow a pattern that is completely expected given an actual error of analysis of the garden path sentence but that would not be expected simply in terms of subjects encountering a point of high processing complexity (here one typically finds longer fixation durations possibly accompanied by shorter saccades; cf. Ehrlich and Rayner, 1982, for example). Further, a comparison between unambiguous (unreduced) relative clauses and ambiguous (reduced) relatives show that the expected effects of a garden path are present in the latter, but not the former. All of these effects are explained in a transparent manner on the assumption that the reading of the garden path sentences involves an actual error of analysis but are left unexplained on the assumption that the complexity of these sentences is due directly to the number of nodes that must be postulated to arrive at the correct structure of the sentence.

3. Quintero (ms.), following Bordelois (1974), argues that an adequate account of extractions from embedded questions in Spanish also requires appeal to a grammatical constraint prohibiting intersecting unbounded dependencies.

4. Butler (1977) discusses interesting grammatical evidence that also argues against the speculation that ambiguities in the case system played a crucial role in establishing a fixed S–V–O order in English. In particular, he discusses a variety of examples where noun phrases were reanalyzed as subjects despite the presence of unambiguous case marking.

5. See Forster (1966, 1968) for experimental evidence supporting the depth hypothesis as a model of sentence production.

6. Yngve's presentation of the sentence in (32b), his Figure 27, assigns *man* a depth of one. Presumably this was a typographical error since his algorithm would assign *man* a depth of zero as indicated in (32b).

7. Recently Crain and his colleagues have argued that the apparent preference for flatter structures may in fact be due to general cognitive strategies (Crain and Hamburger, 1981) or to the failure of the "null context" to satisfy the presuppositions of possible alternative structures (Crain, 1980; Crain and Steedman, this volume). On this account, the processing of a sentence presented in isolation may still lead to a preference for adopting an analysis of the sentence involving a flatter structure than alternatives, but the reason for this preference is not attributed to structural factors per se. A full discussion of the interesting issues raised by this account would take us beyond the scope of this paper. It should perhaps be noted, however, that this type of nonsyntactic analysis of the processing of, say, restrictive relative clauses seems to presuppose that restrictive relatives are used only in contexts where a simple definite noun phrase would be infelicitous. In my dialect at least, it is perfectly possible to use (i) below in a context where there is only one toy in the domain of discourse (i.e., in a context where (ii) is felicitous).

  (i)   Pick up the toy that's on the floor.
 (ii)   Pick up the toy.

Hence, for speakers who agree with these judgments, a null context would satisfy the presuppositions of at least one use of a restrictive relative clause.

8.   Using the average reading time per character as a measure of processing complexity, Frazier, Rayner and Carlson, (in progress) found that sentences with sentential subjects (e.g., (i)) took significantly longer to process than sentences in which the sentential subject was extraposed (e.g., (ii), 41.6 msec versus 34.3 msec, $p < .01$), in an experiment using the eye movement recording technique. Though reading times were shorter for both sentence types when the sentence were presented as the final sentence of a preceding paragraph (e.g., (iii)) than when presented in isolation, the relative complexity of the two sentence types was preserved when the sentences were presented in context (34.3 msec versus 26.6 msec $p < .002$).

  (i)   That the use of marijuana will be legal before 1985 is unlikely.
 (ii)   It is unlikely that the use of marijuana will be legal before 1985.
(iii)   John and his buddies have been trying to organize a protest against the current statutes outlawing marijuana. John thinks that they'll be able to change things in the next year or two, but I doubt it.

In a similar study, sentences with an initial main clause (e.g., (iv)) and sentences with an initial subordinate clause (e.g., (v)) were tested. When the sentences did not contain pronouns, sentences with an initial subordinate clause actually tended to be processed slightly faster (35.4 msec versus 38.5 msec) though the effect was not significant ($p < .23$). However, in sentences containing a pronoun in either the first or second clause, there was a significant interaction between the order of main and subordinate clauses and the position of the pronoun.

(iv)   Mary was laughing because the girls tickled the cat.
 (v)   Because the girls tickled the cat Mary were laughing.

Thus differences in processing complexity were not due to the branching pattern per se and thus do not accord with the predictions of the depth hypothesis.

9.   The preposition in (36) will also be associated with a high (3/1) nonterminal count in both (36a) and (36b) and this will occur shortly before the possessive marker attached to *Milwaukee*, accounting for the intuition that there is a locus of complexity in both (36a) and (36b) at this point in the phrase. However, in (36a), unlike (36b), this locus of complexity is immediately followed by another point of high complexity due to the high nonterminal count associated with the possessive marker attached to *friend*. Thus the examples in (36) provide support for Yngve's hypothesis that complex phrases (now defined in terms of high local density count) are more difficult to comprehend when they occur at or adjacent to points of high complexity than when they occur at points of low complexity.

10.   Notice that the complexity of extraposed relative clauses (relative to their nonextraposed counterparts) also supports the hypothesis that S nodes contribute more to complexity than do other node types. Assuming that extraposed relative clauses are Chomsky-adjoined to S and that the NP node dominating the head of the relative is pruned after extraposition (according to the principle of indistinguishability of immediately self-dominating nodes in the theory of Lasnik and Kupin, 1977) a new S node will be introduced by extraposition, though an NP node will be "lost." Given the hypothesis that S nodes contribute more to complexity than NP nodes do, the complexity of extraposed relatives will follow from the local nonterminal count. It is likely, however, that nonsyntactic factors also contribute to the complexity of extraposed relative clauses. Janet Fodor (private communication) has suggested that perceivers may be semantically garden-pathed in sentences with extraposed relative clauses.

11. In an unpublished study, K. Rayner, M. Carlson, and I tested sentences like those in (i) and (ii) using the eye movement recording technique. Sentences with an extraposed relative clause (e.g., (i)) systematically took longer to read than did their nonextraposed counterparts as indicated by the average reading time per character (43.7 versus 37.3 msec, $p < .002$).

(i) Any girl could break the table easily who takes karate lessons.
(ii) Any girl who takes karate lessons could break the table easily.

12. Though the local nonterminal count correctly captures the relative complexity of the examples in (44) it is not clear that it will by itself correctly capture the size of the differences in complexity between the various sentence forms. The Semantic Replacement Hypothesis proposed in section 4.5 predicts that sentence (44d) should be more complex than is predicted on the basis of its local nonterminal count alone and thus will account for the extreme complexity of this sentence form.

Nevertheless, numerous questions remain concerning the complexity of the sentence structures in (44). It is not clear, for example, whether introducing an adjective in a position where it drastically lowers the local nonterminal count of the sentence facilitates the comprehension of these sentences in the dramatic fashion predicted by an account that invokes only the local nonterminal count to explain the complexity of these sentence types. On the other hand, introducing an overt relative pronoun does not seem to drastically improve comprehension of these sentences. This observation argues in favor of the claim that the local nonterminal count contributes to the complexity of these structures, since many alternative garden path and gap-filling explanations of their complexity predict that insertion of a relative pronoun should radically alter the complexity of the sentence.

13. Emmon Bach has pointed out to me that the second-position constraints occasionally found in syntax may be viewed as another mechanism available for the demarcation of phrase boundaries; phrase boundaries may be signaled not only by markers occurring at the boundary but also by items whose position is fixed with reference to the phrase boundary. If this view ultimately proves to be revealing, say, in explaining the particular class of items that tend to be subject to second-position constraints, then the analogy between the role of the peripheries of domains in the determination of basic syntactic patterns and basic stress patterns becomes more striking.

14. There may appear to be a resemblance between the three-item buffer implied by the local nonterminal count and the three item buffer of PARSIFAL (Marcus, 1977). However, the resemblance is in fact totally superficial. The buffer in PARSIFAL is not length dependent (a 30-word constituent could count as one item, for example) and the role of this buffer in PARSIFAL guarantees that it does not impose the strict adjacency conditions that would be crucial to any buffer that might be implicated in an explanation for the local nonterminal count.

15. Intuitive judgments of processing complexity do in general seem to correlate with experimental measures of complexity, though certainly there are cases where experimentally observed differences in complexity exist which are too subtle or too brief to be accessible to intuition. What is not commonly found, however, are cases where systematic intuitive differences in complexity exist that cannot be confirmed experimentally or that actually reverse the complexity ranking established on experimental grounds. (Though see Perfetti and Goodman (1971) for one example where subjects' actual performance on a recall task did not correlate with subjects' ratings of recall difficulty.) It seems that intuitions about sentence complexity are heavily influenced by the point of maximal complexity in a sentence and not as heavily influenced by the average complexity of the entire sentence (as measured, say, by the average reading time per word or character). If this observation is correct, it calls for an explanation – perhaps along the lines suggested in the text – and warrants serious attention, because it may help reveal the relation between conscious and unconscious mental activities.

16.   Janet Fodor has also suggested to me that the absence of ancestor and offspring constraints might follow from the observation that grammars do not exhibit counting properties. Though this might account for the absence of certain restrictions discussed in the text, it does not explain the absence of restrictions involving vertical rather than horizontal restrictions demanding that a particular construction appear somewhere in the family of ancestors or cousins (offspring of sisters) of a lexical item.

17.   In keeping with the discussion in Frazier (1978), it will be assumed that in cases of phrase boundary ambiguity the processor does not explicitly attempt to make a decision about the position of a phrase or clause boundary per se. Rather it simply attaches each incoming item in the lexical string into a constituent structure representation of the sentence and thus the determination of phrasal and clausal boundaries is simply a consequence of the constituent structure representation that results from these attachment decisions. The relevant consequence of this is simply that the processor will typically decide that it is at the end of a minimal governing category only after it has determined that a following item is not a constituent of that (minimal governing) category. This will be important in preventing premature closure of clauses in cases where an optional constituent has been moved to the end of a clause.

18.   In a rather inconclusive study conducted by Charles Clifton, Peter Sells, and myself, sentences like the following were presented visually one word at a time. Response times were measured to determine how long it took subjects to detect a visually presented "#" which occurred at various points throughout the sentence.

  (i)   [. . . [Annette's tapes of herself] . . .]$_S$
  (ii)   [. . . [Annette's tapes of the concert] . . .]$_S$
  (iii) [. . . [casette tapes of herself] . . .]$_S$
  (iv)   [. . . [casette tapes of the concert] . . .]$_S$

The study was designed to investigate the effects of the Specified Subject Condition during sentence processing and thus we compared sentences containing noun phrases with specified subjects (e.g., (i) and (ii)) or without specified subjects (e.g., (iii) and (iv)); half of the noun phrases contained bound anaphors (as in (i) and (iii)) and half did not. Originally we had hypothesized that the Specified Subject Condition defined a binding domain that also demarcated a processing domain and thus we expected to find indications of longer processing times at the end of noun phrases containing specified subjects (compared to noun phrases lacking subjects) and longer processing times at the end of the sentence in cases where the noun phrase did not contain a subject (since in this case the entire sentence would compose a single processing domain). These predictions were not confirmed. This may perhaps be of some interest in the present context since the

Semantic Replacement Hypothesis proposed here draws no distinction between the processing domains of these four sentence types.

19. Note that this definition will imply an across-the-board convention in sentences containing conjoined clauses (Williams, 1978).

20. The Semantic Replacement Hypothesis would lead us to expect a correlation between the "squishiness" of the island constraints in some language and the availability of intersecting filler-gap dependencies in that language. The syntactic information that would be needed to revise an initial nested assignment of dependencies should be available for a longer period of time in languages with squishy island constraints, since no island will form an absolutely secure semantic replacement unit if the unit does on occasion permit extractions and the processor does on occasion make errors in its initial filler-gap decisions.

References

Bever, Thomas G. 1970. The cognition basis for linguistic structures. In: John R. Hayes (ed.), *Cognition and the development of language.* New York: John Wiley and Sons.

Bever, Thomas G., and C. Terence Langendoen. 1971. A dynamic model of the evolution of language. *Linguistic Inquiry* 2:433–63.

Bever, Thomas G., and D. J. Townsend. 1979. Perceptual mechanisms and formal properties of main and subordinate clauses. In: William E. Cooper and Edward C. T. Walker (eds.), *Sentence processing.* Hillsdale, N.J.: Lawrence Erlbaum.

Boomer, Donald S. 1965. Hesitation and grammatical encoding. *Language and Speech* 8:145–58.

Bordelois, Ivonne. 1974. The grammar of Spanish causative complements. Unpublished Ph.D. dissertation, Massachusetts Institute of Technology, Cambridge, Mass.

Butler, Milton C. 1977. Reanalysis of object as subject in Middle English impersonal constructions. *Glossa* 11:155–70.

Chomsky, Noam. 1981. *Lectures on government and binding.* Dordrecht, Holland: Foris.

Chomsky, Noam, and Howard Lasnik. 1977. Filters and control. *Linguistic Inquiry* 8:425–504.

Crain, Stephen. 1980. Pragmatic constraints on sentence comprehension. Unpublished Ph.D. dissertation, University of California at Irvine.

Crain, Stephen, and Henry Hamburger. 1981. A cognitive vs. a syntactic explanation of an acquisition error: an empirical test. Presented at Boston University Conference on Language Acquisition.

Cutler, Anne. 1976. Phoneme monitoring reaction time as a function of preceding intonation pattern. *Perception and Psychophysics* 20:55–60.

Davison, Alice. 1982. On the function and definition of "sentence topic" in sentence processing. Unpublished manuscript, University of Illinois (Champaign-Urbana).

Eady, J., and Janet D. Fodor. 1981. Is center embedding a source of processing difficulty? Presented at Linguistic Society of America annual meeting.

Ehrlich, Kate. 1980. Comprehension of pronouns. *Quarterly Journal of Experimental Psychology* 32:247–55.

Ehrlich, Kate, and Keith Rayner. 1982. Pronoun assignment and semantic integration during reading: eye movements and immediacy of processing. *Journal of Verbal Learning and Verbal Behavior* 22:75–87.

Engdahl, Elisabet. 1979. The nested dependency constraint as a parsing strategy. In: Elisabet Engdahl and Mark J. Stein (eds.), *Papers presented to Emmon Bach by his students.* Amherst, Mass.: University of Massachusetts Department of Linguistics.

Fodor, Janet D. 1978. Parsing strategies and constraints on transformations. *Linguistics Inquiry* 9:427–73.

 ——— 1979. Superstrategy. In: William E. Cooper and Edward C. T. Walker (eds.), *Sentence processing*. Hillsdale, N.J.: Lawrence Erlbaum.

 ——— (ms.) Parsing, constraints and freedom of expression. Unpublished manuscript, University of Connecticut, Storrs.

Fodor, Janet D., and Lyn Frazier. 1980. Is the human sentence parsing mechanism an ATN? *Cognition* 8:417–59.

Ford, Marilyn, and V. M. Holmes. 1978. Planning units and syntax in sentence production. *Cognition* 6:35–53.

Forster, Kenneth. 1966. Left-to-right processes in the construction of sentences. *Journal of Verbal Learning and Verbal Behavior* 5:285–91.

 ——— 1968. Sentence completion in left- and right-branching languages. *Journal of Verbal Learning and Verbal Behavior* 7:296–99.

Frazier, Lyn. 1978. On comprehending sentences: syntactic parsing strategies. Unpublished Ph.D. dissertation, University of Connecticut, Storrs.

 ——— 1979. Parsing and constraints on word order. In: Jean Lowenstamm (ed.), *University of Massachusetts occasional papers in linguistics*, vol. 5, pp. 177–98.

 ——— 1982. Shared components of production and perception. In: Michael Arbib, David Caplan, and John Marshall (eds.), *Neural models of language processes*. New York: Academic Press.

Frazier, Lyn, Charles Clifton, and Janet Randall. 1983. Filling gaps: decision principles and structure in sentence comprehension. *Cognition*, 13:187–222.

Frazier, Lyn, and Janet D. Fodor. 1978. The Sausage Machine: a new two-stage parsing model. *Cognition* 6:291–325.

Frazier, Lyn, and Keither Rayner. 1982. Making and correcting errors during sentence comprehension: eye movements in the analysis of structurally ambiguous sentences. *Cognitive Psychology* 14:178–210.

Frazier, Lyn, Marcia Carlson, and Keith Rayner. (In progress). Parameterizing the language processing system: branching patterns within and across languages.

Goodluck, Helen, and Susan Tavakolian. 1982. Competence and processing in children's grammar of relative clauses. *Cognition* 11:1–28.

Greenberg, Joseph H. 1965. Some universals of grammar with particular reference to the language of meaningful elements. In: Joseph H. Greenberg (ed.), *Universals of language*. Cambridge, Mass.: MIT Press.

Grosjean, François, Lysiane Grosjean, and Harlan Lane. 1979. The patterns of silence: performance structures in sentence production. *Cognitive Psychology* 11:58–81.

Hankamer, Jorge. 1970. Constraints on deletion in syntax. Unpublished Ph.D. dissertation, Yale University, New Haven, Conn.

Kimball, John. 1973. Seven principles of surface structure parsing in natural language. *Cognition* 2:15–48.

Langendoen, D. Terence, Nancy Kalish-Landon, and John Dore. 1974. Dative questions: a study of the relation of acceptability to grammaticality of an English sentence type. *Cognition* 2:451–78.

Lasnik, Howard, and Joseph Kupin. 1977. A restrictive theory of transformational grammar. *Theoretical Linguistics* 4(3).

Levin, H., J. Grossman, E. Kaplan, and R. Yang. 1972. Constraints and the eye voice span in right and left embedded sentences. *Language and Speech* 15:30–39.

Marcus, Mitchell. 1977. A theory of syntactic recognition for natural language. Ph.D. dissertation, Massachusetts Institute of Technology, Cambridge, Mass. Published in 1980 by MIT Press.

Marslen-Wilson, William. 1975. The limited compatibility of linguistic and perceptual explanations. *CLS parasession on functionalism.* Chicago: Chicago Linguistics Society.

Martin, E., and K. H. Roberts, 1966. Grammatical factors in sentence retention. *Journal of Verbal Learning and Verbal Behavior* 5:211–18.

1967. Sentence length and sentence retention in the free learning situation. *Psychonomic Science* 8:535.

Matthei, Edward. 1982. The acquisition of prenominal modifier sequences. *Cognition* 11:301–32.

Miller, George A., and Noam Chomsky. 1963. Finitary models of language users. In: R. Duncan Luce, R. R. Bush, and Eugene Galanter (eds.), *Handbook of mathematical psychology,* vol. 2. New York: Wiley.

Perfetti, Charles A. 1969. Sentence retention and the depth hypothesis. *Journal of Verbal Learning and Verbal Behavior* 8:101–4.

1969. Lexical density and phrase structure depth as variables in sentence retention. *Journal of Verbal Learning and Verbal Behavior* 8:719–24.

Perfetti, Charles A., and D. Goodman. 1971. Memory for sentences and noun phrases of extreme depth. *Quarterly Journal of Experimental Psychology* 23:22–23.

Potter, M. C., and B. A. Faulconer. 1979. Understanding noun phrases. *Journal of Verbal Learning and Verbal Behavior* 18:509–22.

Prince, Alan. 1982. Relating to the grid. Unpublished manuscript, University of Massachusetts. (Paper presented at "Trilateral Conference on Phonology," Austin, Texas, April 1981.)

Quintero, Carlos. (ms.). Multiple *wh*-extraction in Spanish. Unpublished manuscript, University of Massachusetts, Amherst, Mass.

Rayner, Keith, Marcia Carlson, and Lyn Frazier. 1983. The interaction of syntax and semantics during sentence processing: eye movements in the analysis of semantically biased sentences. *Journal of Verbal Learning and Verbal Behavior* 22:358–74.

Roeper, Thomas, and Susan Tavakolian. 1977. A limit on LAD: S-node attachment. Presented at 1977 Annual Meeting of the Linguistic Society of America.

Smith, K., and L. McMahon. 1970. Understanding order information in sentences: some recent work at Bell Laboratories. In: G. B. Flores d'Arcais and W. J. M. Levelt (eds.), *Advances in psycholinguistics.* Amsterdam: North Holland.

Solan, Lawrence. 1979. Language acquisition and language variation. Unpublished manuscript, Harvard University, Cambridge, Mass.

Tanenhaus, Michael K., and Mark S. Seidenberg. 1981. Discourse context and sentence perception. *Discourse Processes* 26:197–220.

Tavakolian, Susan. 1978. The conjoined-clause analysis of relative clauses and other structures. In: Helen Goodluck and Lawrence Solan (eds.), *Papers in the structure and development of child language.* University of Massachusetts occasional papers in linguistics, vol. 4.

Tomlin, Russell S. 1979. An explanation of the distribution of basic constituent orders. Unpublished Ph.D. dissertation, University of Michigan, Ann Arbor.

Wanat, Stanley F. 1971. Linguistics structure and visual attention in reading. Unpublished Ph.D. dissertation, Cornell University, Ithaca, N.Y.

Wanner, Eric. 1980. The ATN and the Sausage Machine: which one is baloney? *Cognition* 8:209–25.

Williams, Edwin. 1978. Across-the-board rule application. *Linguistic Inquiry* 9:31–43.

Williams, Edward. 1982. The NP cycle. *Linguistic Inquiry* 13:277–96.

Wright, P. 1966. Two studies of the depth hypothesis. *British Journal of Psychology* 60:63–69.

Yngve, Victor H. A. 1960. A model and an hypothesis for language structure. *Proceedings of the American Philosophical Society* 104:444–66.

5   Processing of sentences with intrasentential code switching

ARAVIND K. JOSHI

Speakers of certain bilingual communities systematically produce utterances in which they switch from one language to another possibly several times, in the course of an utterance, a phenomenon called *code switching*. Production and comprehension of utterances with intrasentential code switching is part of the linguistic competence of the speakers and hearers of these communities. Much of the work on code switching has been sociolinguistic or at the discourse level, but there have been few studies of code switching within the scope of a single sentence.[1] And until recently, this phenomenon has not been studied in a formal or computational framework.[2]

The discourse level of code switching is important; however, it is only at the intrasentential level that we are able to observe with some certainty the interaction between two grammatical systems. These interactions, to the extent they can be systematically characterized, provide a nice framework for investigating some processing issues both from the generation and the parsing points of view.[3]

There are some important characteristics of intrasentential code switching which give hope for the kind of work described here. These are as follows. (1) The situation we are concerned with involves participants who are about equally fluent in both languages. (2) Participants have fairly consistent judgments about the "acceptability" of mixed sentences. (In fact it is amazing that participants have such acceptability judgments at all.) (3) Mixed utterances are spoken without hesitation, pauses, repetitions, corrections, etc., suggesting that intrasentential code switching is not some random interference of one system with the other. Rather, the switches seem to be due to systematic interactions between the two systems. (4) The two language systems seem to be simultaneously active. (5) Intrasentential code switching is sharply distinguished from other interferences, such as borrowing, learned use of foreign words, and filling lexical gaps, all of which could be exhibited by monolingual speakers. (6) Despite extensive intrasentential switching, speakers and hearers usually

190

agree on which language the mixed sentence is "coming from." We call this language the *matrix language* and the other language the *embedded language*.[4] These interesting characteristics of the mixed sentences suggest that the two language systems are systematically interacting with each other in the production (and recognition) of the mixed sentences.

Our main objectives in this paper are (1) to formulate a system in terms of the grammars of the two languages and a switching rule, and (2) to show that a variety of observable constraints on intrasentential code switching can be formulated in terms of constraints on the switching rule. The main result of this paper is that a large number of constraints can be derived from a general constraint on the switchability of the so-called closed class items (determiners, quantifiers, prepositions, tense morphemes, auxiliaries, complementizers, pronouns, etc.). This result is of interest because the differential behavior of closed class items (as compared to the open class items) has been noted in various aspects of language processing (in the monolingual case). There are for example,[5] (1) certain types of speech errors stranding the closed class items; (2) resistance of the inventory of closed class items to loss and to the incorporation of new items; (3) frequency-independent lexical decision for closed class items (as compared to open class items, for which lexical decision is frequency-dependent); (4) the absence of frequency independence for closed class items in certain types of aphasia (see Bradley, Garrett, and Zurif, 1979); (5) closed class items that aid in comprehension strategies. It is not clear what the relationship is between the behavior of closed classes in intrasentential code switching and these other behaviors (in monolingual situations). I believe, however, investigating this relationship may give some clues concerning the organization of the grammar and the lexicon, and the nature of the interface between the two language systems.

The paper is organized as follows. In section 5.1 I describe the overall framework, and in section 5.2 I formulate a variety of constraints on the switching rule and their relationship to the closed class items. In section 5.3 I discuss some related work and compare it with mine. Although most of the paper is written from the point of view of generation, I will discuss briefly some issues concerning recognition, in section 5.4, and then summarize the major conclusions in section 5.5.

The examples in this paper are all from the language pair, Marathi (*m*) and English (*e*). Marathi (*m*) is the *matrix language* and English (*e*) is the *embedded language*.[6] (The coincidence of the abbreviation *m* for the matrix language, which is Marathi and *e* for the embedded language, which is English, is an accident, but a happy one!) A few facts about Marathi will be useful. It is an Indo-European language (spoken by about 60 million people on the west coast of India near Bombay and in parts of central

India). It is an SOV language. Adjectives and relative clauses appear prenominally, and it has postpositions instead of prepositions. It uses a rich supply of auxiliary verbs. Other facts about Marathi will become apparent in the examples (see section 5.2).

5.1. Formulation of the system

Let L_m be the *matrix language* and L_e be the *embedded language*. Further let G_m and G_e be the corresponding grammars; that is, G_m is the *matrix grammar* and G_e is the *embedded grammar*. A *mixed* sentence is one containing lexical items from both L_m and L_e. Let L_x be the set of all mixed sentences that are judged to be acceptable. Note that a mixed sentence is not a sentence of either L_m or L_e. However, it is judged to be "coming from" L_m. The task is to formulate a system characterizing L_x. My approach is to formulate a system for L_x in terms of G_m and G_e and a "control structure" that permits shifting control from G_m to G_e but not from G_e to G_m. I assume a "correspondence" between categories of G_m and G_e, for example, NP_m corresponds to NP_e (written as $NP_m \approx NP_e$). Control is shifted by a switching rule of the form

(1) $A_m \times A_e$

where A_m is a category of G_m, A_e is a category of G_e, and $A_m \approx A_e$. At any stage of the derivation, (1) can be invoked, permitting A_m to be switched to A_e. Thus further derivation involving A_m will be carried out by using rules of G_e, starting with A_e. The switching rule in (2.1) is *asymmetric*, which means that switching a category of the matrix grammar to a category of the embedded grammar is permitted, but not vice versa. This asymmetry can be stated directly in the rule itself, as I have done, or it can be stated as a constraint on a more generalized switching rule that will permit switching from A_m to A_e or the other way round. I have chosen to state the asymmetry by incorporating it in the rule itself because the asymmetry plays such a central role in our formulation. This asymmetric switching rule together with the further constraints described in section 5.2 is intended to capture the overpowering judgment of speakers about a mixed sentence "coming from" the matrix language L_m.

The switching rule in (1) is neither a rule of G_m nor a rule of G_e. It is also not a rule of a grammar, say G_x for L_x. As I have said before, I will construct a system for L_x in terms of G_m and G_e and a switching rule and not in terms of a third grammar, say G_x. Although formally this can be done, there are important reasons for not doing so. The issue will be discussed in section 5.3.

Using this general framework I will now show that the system for L_x can be formulated by specifying a set of constraints on the switching rule (beside the asymmetry constraint). These further constraints primarily pertain to the closed class items.

5.2. Constraints on the switching rule

Our hypothesis is that L_x can be completely characterized in terms of constraints on the switching rule (1). The types of constraints can be characterized as follows.

5.2.1. Asymmetry

I have already discussed this constraint. In fact it has been incorporated in the definition of the switching rule itself. The main justifications for asymmetry are as follows.

1. We want to maintain the notion of matrix and embedded languages and the asymmetry associated with this distribution.
2. Arbitrarily long derivations would be possible in a symmetric analysis – for example, allowing back and forth switching of A_m and A_e along a nonbranching path. There appears to be no motivation for allowing such derivations.
3. The asymmetry constraint, together with certain constraints on the non-switchability of closed class items, seems to allow a fairly complete characterization of L_x.

5.2.2. Nonswitchability of certain categories

Rule (1) permits switching any category A_m to A_e if $A_m \approx A_e$. However, certain categories cannot be switched. Although all major categories can be switched, we must exclude the root node S_m. Obviously, if we permit S_m to be switched to S_e, we can derive a sentence in L_e starting with S_m in a trivial manner. Hence, we need the following constraint:[7]

(2) Root node S_m cannot be switched.

5.2.2.1. Constraint on closed class items

(3) Certain closed class items (such as *Tense*, *Aux*, and *helping verb*) cannot be switched when they appear in main VP.

The italicized items in examples (4) and (5) are from L_m.

(4) a. *mula khurcyā rangawtāt.*
         'boys chairs   paint'
     b. *mula khurcyā* paint *kartāt.*
                      do(+ Tense)

In (4b) the root verb has been switched from Marathi to English. The closed class item *tāt* is not switched; however it is attached to an auxiliary *kar*, since it cannot be stranded. This phenomenon appears in mixed sentences of other language pairs (see Pfaff, 1979). It is not possible to switch both the verb and the tense in (4a).

(4) c. **mula khurcyā* paint.

It is also not possible to switch the entire VP in (4a).

   d. **mula* paint chairs.

Note that (7) could be derived by starting with S_e (i.e., by starting to derive a sentence of L_e) and then switching NP_e to NP_m, but this is not permitted by the asymmetry constraint. One cannot start with the S_e node because this requires switching S_m to S_e, which is blocked by the constraint on the switchability of the root node.

(5) Closed class items (e.g., *determiners, quantifiers, prepositions, possessive, Aux, Tense, helping verbs*, etc.) cannot be switched.

   Thus, for example, Det_m cannot be switched to Det_e. This does not mean that a lexical item belonging to Det_e cannot appear in the mixed sentence. It can indeed appear if NP_m has already been switched to NP_e and then NP_e is expanded into Det_e N_e according to G_e.

(6) a. *kāhi khurcyā* Det_m N_m
         some chairs

   b. some chairs Det_e N_e

   c. *kāhi* chairs $Det_m N_e$

   d. *some *khurcyā*   *$Det_e N_m$

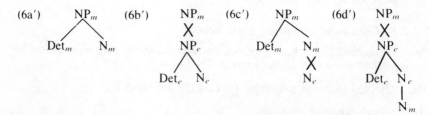

Adjectives do not constitute a closed class; hence all four combinations below are possible.

Note that (7d′) is a Marathi NP_m in which both the A_m and N_m have been switched. It is not derived from NP_e, because if it were, it would have a determiner. (Determiners are optional in Marathi.)

(7) a. *unca peṭi*
     tall box

    b. *unca* box

    c. tall *peṭi*

    d. tall box

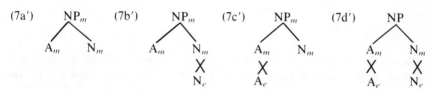

(7a′) NP_m — A_m N_m (7b′) NP_m — A_m N_m / N_e (7c′) NP_m — A_m / A_e, N_m (7d′) NP — A_m / A_e, N_m / N_e

Prepositions and postpositions are closed class items. Marathi has postpositions while English has prepositions.

(8) a. *kāhi khurcyāwar*
     some chairs on

    b. *kāhi* chairs*war*

    c. *some chairs*war* (This case is problematic; see comment below.)

    d. *some chairs on
    e. **kāhi khurcyā* on
    f.   on some chairs
    g. *on *kāhi khurcyā*
    h. **war kāhi khurcyā*
    i. **war* some chairs

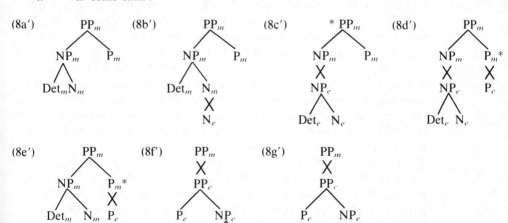

(8a′) PP_m: NP_m ($Det_m N_m$), P_m

(8b′) PP_m: NP_m (Det_m N_m / N_e), P_m

(8c′) *PP_m: NP_m / NP_e (Det_e N_e), P_m

(8d′) PP_m: NP_m / NP_e (Det_e N_e), P_m* / P_e

(8e′) PP_m: NP_m (Det_m N_m), P_m* / P_e

(8f′) PP_m / PP_e : P_e, NP_e (Det_e N_e)

(8g′) PP_m / PP_e : P_e, NP_e / NP_m (Det_m N_m)

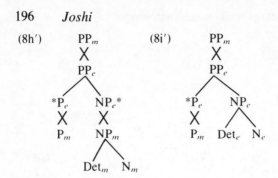

(8a'–i') all follow from the asymmetry constraint and the constraint on closed items, except for (8c'), which cannot be accounted for by the constraints described so far. A processing constraint such as the left corner constraint or the early determination strategy outlined in section 5.4 also does not account for this case without disturbing the analysis of (8a', b') or (8d'–i'). One way out (as suggested by Doron, 1981) is to regard prepositions as grammatical markers of case and not to allow case markers from one language to be coupled with an NP from another language. I would like to see (8c') follow from some more general principle, but I have no specific proposal at this time.

5.2.3. Constraints on complementizers

Complementizers are closed class items and therefore cannot be switched in the same sense as in the preceding section. However, often we have a choice of a complementizer. This choice depends both on the matrix verb V_m and the embedded verb V_e ($V_m \approx V_e$) to which V_m has been switched. Let the complementizers of V_m ($\approx V_m$) be $Comp_m = \{C_1, C_2, C_3\}$ and the complementizers of V_e ($\approx V_m$) be $Comp_e = \{C'_1, C'_2, C'_4\}$ where $C_1 \approx C'_1$, $C_2 \approx C'_2$. Now if V_m is switched to V_e (i.e., the verb is lexically realized in the embedded language), then the choice of the complementizer is constrained in the following manner. Since complementizers are closed classes, they cannot be switched. Hence, the choice is C_1, C_2, or C_3; however, only C_1 and C_2 are permitted, as the equivalent lexical verb V_e permits C'_1 and C'_2, which are the equivalents of C_1 and C_2, respectively. C_3 is not permitted because its equivalent C'_3 is not permitted for V_e, and C_4, which is the equivalent of C'_4, is not permitted because it is not allowed by V_m. Thus the only complementizers that are permitted, if V_m is switched to V_e, are those that are permitted by V_m and the equivalents of which are permitted by V_e ($V_m \approx V_e$). Thus the choice is contrained not only to the complementizers of V_m (because of nonswitchability of complementizers), but it is further constrained by the choice of complementizers of V_e as explained before.

(9) a. *tō parat jāyca ṭharawtō.*   ca:ing
         he back going decides
     b. **tō parat jāyla ṭharawtō*   lā:to
         he back to go decides

The Marathi verb *ṭharaw* ('decide') takes the complementizer *ca* ('ing') but not the complementizer *lā* (to). The corresponding English verb *decide* takes both the complementizers *to* and *ing* (after *on*). We now switch the Marathi verb V_m (*ṭhraw*) to V_e (*decide*) in both (9a) and (9b). Because the tense in the main VP cannot be switched (as we have seen in (4a) and (4b) earlier) a helping verb *kar* ('do') has to be introduced so that the tense can be attached to it. Thus we have

(10) a. *tō parat jāyca* decide *kartō.*   ca:ing
          he back going   do(+Tense)
      b. **tō parat jāyla* decide *kartō.*   la:to
          he back to go   do(+Tense)

Note that although *decide* takes both the complementizers *to* and *ing*, only (10a) is allowed. Sentence (10b) is blocked because the Marathi verb *ṭharaw* does not allow the complementizer *to*. Thus the only complementizer that appears in the mixed sentence is *ing*.

There are several interesting issues concerning the generation and recognition of sentences like (10a) and (10b). For example, at what point is the decision to switch the main verb made? (This issue could have been raised earlier, in the discussion of (4a) and (4b).) Since a new helping verb has to be introduced when the switch is made, does it mean that some "local" structural change has to be made along with the switching of the verb? Another point is that the choice of the complementizer (which comes before the matrix verb) also determines whether the verb can be switched or not. The machinery we have provided so far may have to be augmented to provide systematic answers to these questions. For example, we may have to introduce additional constraints on the switching rules.

An additional example:

(11) a. *mi tyālā ghar ghyāylā paṭawla*   lā:to
          I   to him house to buy persuaded
      b. *mi tyālā ghar ghyāycā paṭṭawla*   ca:ing

The Marathi verb *paṭaw* ('persuade') takes the complementizers *lā* ('to') and *ca* ('ing'). The corresponding English verb *persuade* only takes the complementizer *to*. Hence, when V_m (*paṭaw*) is switched to V_e (*persuade*) only the complement *lā* is allowed. Thus we have

(12) a. *mi tyālā ghar ghyāylā* persuade *kela*
          I   to him house to buy   did
      b. **mi tylālā ghar ghyāyca* persuade *kela*

5.2.4. Structural constraints

In the previous section, I mentioned that there may be a need for some structural constraints (in terms of some local context) on the switching rule. There is another (somewhat marginal) situation where a structural constraint may be necessary. The situation is as follows. In Marathi a relative clause is prenominal; that is, it appears before the head noun. There are four cases to be considered, since the head noun N and the relative clause R can be either in Marathi or English.

(13) a. $R_m N_m$
      b. $R_m N_e$

(14) a. $R_e N_e$
      b. $R_e N_m$

(15) a. $*N_m R_m$
      b. $?N_m R_e$

(16) a. $N_e R_e$
      b. $*N_e R_m$

Cases (13a) and (16a) are clear cases because they come from NP_m and NP_e, respectively. Case (13b) comes from NP_m, where the head noun is switched to N_e. Case (15a) is unacceptable because it cannot come from NP_m, and if it came from NP_e, then N_e would have to be switched to N_m, which is not permissible. Similarly, (16b) cannot come from NP_m, and if it came from NP_e, then R_e would have to be switched to R_m, which is not permissible. Cases (14a) and (14b) can be blocked only by preventing a switch of R_m to R_e – by not recognizing R_m and R_e as "corresponding categories." There are good reasons for this claim: (1) R_m is prenominal and R_e is postnominal. (2) Deletion of the shared NP in R_m is optional; these clauses are called correlative clauses. (Tony Kroch also brought to my attention the fact that no resumptive pronouns appear in R_m.) Doron (1981) has also made a similar claim. This leaves (15b), which is perhaps marginal. However, if one wants to generate it (as I tried to do in Joshi, 1981), then one needs a structural constraint. Case (15b) cannot clearly come from NP_m. If it came from NP_e, then N_e would have to be switched to N_m, which is not permissible. One way to account for (15b) is to say that R_m can be switched to R_e, but the switch is then accompanied by a local structural change, taking (14a) to (15b). This is not a very satisfactory solution. Doron (1981) has proposed another solution, which requires special rules beyond the rules of G_m and G_e, a solution that is not consistent with the approach that I have taken in this paper.

5.3. Related work

Although there has been considerable work on code switching, it is primarily sociolinguistic and also at the discourse level. The fact that there are constraints at the intrasentential level has also been noted in some recent works.[8] However, there has been no work on this phenomenon in a formal or computational framework, until very recently (cf. note 2).

For a detailed critical review of these works, see Doron (1981). As described in section 6.1, my approach keeps the two grammars independent, and the switching is accomplished by a switching rule satisfying a variety of constraints. Sankoff and Poplack do not keep the grammar disjoint. Rather, they attempt to construct a third grammar for the set of mixed sentences. The fact that intrasentential code switching is not just an interference but a systematic interaction of the two language systems is used as a justification by Sankoff and Poplack for constructing a third grammar. Doron has correctly pointed out that the fact that code switching is not an erratic phenomenon cannot bear directly on the question of having a single grammar; in fact, it suggests that there should be a uniform mechanism for switching, as for example, the switching mechanism in our approach. Sankoff and Poplack also treat the two languages symmetrically; in fact, they take this to be an empirical finding. As Doron has observed, there is little justification for symmetry from the data provided by Poplack; rather, the symmetry is simply assumed by them. Sankoff and Poplack also assume that there are two switches in x–y–z where segments x,y are in L_1 and segment y is in L_2. Such a formulation already assumes symmetry. The switch can be easily formulated as only one switch from L_1 to L_2 (see Doron for further details).

Sankoff and Poplack formulate their third grammar in the following manner. Given G_1 and G_2, they construct G_3 by taking the union of the category symbols of G_1 and G_2. We will call this the *marked union*, because the markers "1" and "2" identify the grammars to which the symbols belong; thus, we will have NP_1, NP_2, and the like in the union. Rewrite rules are then constructed so that the right-hand sides of the rules contain symbols of both G_1 and G_2, the symbols being marked by the index 1 or 2 as necessary to account for the observed constraints. This approach creates some serious problems (see Doron, 1981). To avoid them, Sankoff and Poplack introduce a further device of superscripting, e.g., VP_1^V meaning that the V of VP_1 must be obligatorily realized in L_1. Woolford (1980) has shown very convincingly that Sankoff and Poplack essentially described the relevant data case by case; their approach does not follow in any principled way from the observable constraints. They also fail to show how to build the third grammar in a systematic way from the two monolingual grammars. The main difficulty with the Sankoff and Poplack approach is that they attempt to formulate code switching purely in terms of some local constraints that refer to the points of transition.

There is yet another problem with their approach: it predicts unnecessary complications in the processing of monolingual sentences. Assume that G_1 has a rule A → B C D and G_2 has the rule A → B C D, and A →

B C E. Following Sankoff and Poplack, the prediction would be that in parsing a constituent of category A, even if it is a part of a monolingual sentence of L_1, there would be indeterminacy as long as D or E have not been reached, because we would not know whether the correct parse is $[_A BCD]$ or $[_A BCE]$. This is counterintuitive, there being no reason to believe that the processing of monolingual sentences should be affected in some way just because the speaker or hearer can also process mixed sentences.

In her recent work Woolford (1983) has proposed a model with two grammars, G_1 and G_2 (for Spanish and English, respectively), which share certain phrase structure rules. These shared phrase structure rules are said to belong to both the grammars "simultaneously." One could interpret this as a third grammar consisting of the shared rules plus the rules of G_1 and G_2 that are not in the intersection. However, this is not what is intended by Woolford. Her formulation is not quite precise yet on this point. The problem with this approach is that it is not clear what is meant by a terminal node created by a rule of G_1. Thus, for example, if A $\rightarrow$ B C is a rule of G_1 and B $\rightarrow$ D and C $\rightarrow$ E are rules in both G_1 and G_2 and therefore in G, then in the derivation below, it is not clear whether we should treat the terminal nodes (preterminal nodes) D, E as belonging to L_1, L_2 or one to L_1 and the other to L_2.

(17)

Besides providing a critical review of Sankoff and Poplack (1980), Woolford (ms., 1980) (Doron's comments are on Woolford, ms., 1980 only and not on Woolford, 1983) and Joshi (1981), Doron in her work further develops the asymmetric approach of Joshi (1981) and suggests some parsing strategies to account for the observed constraints. We will return to this discussion in section 6.4.

In summary, I believe that the approach described in Joshi (1981) and in this paper captures the constraints in a more principled manner, and that further investigation of the phenomenon of intrasentential code switching in this framework will prove to be very fruitful. (See Doron, 1981 for such an attempt.)

5.4. Parsing considerations

In this paper, an account has been given of the constraints on intrasentential code switching in a generative framework. The formal model and the constraints on switching proposed here clearly have implications for the kind of parser that can be constructed. I will not develop this aspect in this paper. However, I would like to point out that by adopting some parsing strategies, I can account for some of the constraints described earlier. A preliminary attempt was made in Joshi (1981), by proposing a strategy involving a so-called left corner constraint. This strategy has some serious drawbacks, as was pointed out by Doron (1981). She proposed an alternative strategy called "early determination," according to which the parser tries to determine as early as possible the language of the major constituent it is currently parsing. Thus upon encountering a Marathi (m) determiner, Det_m, the parser would predict a Marathi NP_m. The Marathi N_m could be then realized lexically in Marathi, or the N_m would be switched to N_e and then lexically realized in English.

(18)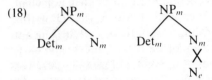

If NP_m is expanded into Det_m Nom_m, where Nom_m is expanded into A_m N_m, then we have

(19)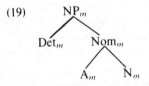

Note that A_m and N_m could be independently switched to A_e and N_e, respectively, thus giving four possible sequences

(20) a. Det_m A_m N_m
      b. Det_m A_m N_e
      c. Det_m A_e N_m
      d. Det_m A_e N_e

all of which are permissible.

If the parser encountered an English determiner, Det_e, then it would predict NP_e, but now N_e or A_e N_e (into which NP_e can expand) cannot be switched to N_m or A_m because of the asymmetry constraint. Thus the only permissible sequence is

(21) Det_e (A_e) N_e

and the following are excluded, among others:

(22) a. *Det_e N_m
      b. *Det_e A_e N_m

c. *$\text{Det}_e\ A_m\ N_e$
d. *$\text{Det}_e\ A_m\ N_m$

These predictions check with the data.

Of course, so far we have the same predictions as we had with the constraint on the nonswitchability of closed class items. However, there is some evidence to the effort that a strategy like early determination may be in effect.

The following distribution is correctly predicted by this strategy.

(23) a. *tall *peṭya*
      b. tall boxes
      c. *unca peṭya*
      d. *unca* boxes

Case (23a) is disallowed, because upon encountering an English adjective, A_e, the parser predicts Nom_e, which is expanded into $A_e\ N_e$. However, N_e cannot be realized lexically in Marathi, unless N_e is switched to N_m, which is disallowed. Note that (23a) cannot be disallowed by invoking nonswitchability of adjectives, because these are not closed classes. This early determination strategy does not help, however, in accounting for the distribution of phrases involving postpositions (see section 5.2).

Our conclusion at present is that the framework described in section 5.2, along with the constraints on closed class items, is the proper way to formulate the code switching system.[9] A parsing strategy as discussed here is perhaps also operative (see examples (23a–d) and when a closed class item is the leftmost constituent of a major category, then the two formulations make the same predictions.

It should be possible to come up with a parsing strategy that naturally captures the asymmetry constraint and the constraints on the closed class items. I do not have a specific proposal at this time, as some of my preliminary attempts have not been too successful. It is clear, however, that to account for asymmetry and the closed class constraints, the parser would have to operate much more in a top-down fashion. Since it is unlikely that the overall parsing strategies for mixed sentences can be radically different from those for monolingual sentences, this work on intrasentential code switching gives some support to the claim that parsing strategies for monolingual sentences must be heavily top-down also.

5.5. Conclusion

A formal model for characterizing intrasentential code-switching has been presented. The main features of this model are that (1) the model treats the two grammars (languages) asymmetrically, (2) there is no third grammar, and (3) the constraints on intrasentential code switching are stated in terms of the asymmetry of the switching rule and constraints on the switchability of closed class items.

We believe that further investigation of code switching in the proposed framework will be very productive, as it captures some essential aspects of intrasentential code switching.

Another interesting result concerns the role of closed class items. Since several important characteristics of closed class items are well known in the context of processing of monolingual utterances, I think that further investigation of the role of closed class items in the context of code switching will give us some insights into the processing of monolingual utterances.

My investigation of intrasentential code mixing can also be considered as a small contribution toward the larger problem of determining the nature of the interface between the two language systems of a bilingual speaker or hearer.

Notes

I wish to thank Ken Church, Lila Gleitman, Tony Kroch, Judy Klavans, Mitch Marcus, Ellen Prince, Ken Ross, S. N. Sridhar, Bonnie Webber and Ellen Woolford for valuable comments at various stages of this work. I am particularly indebted to Edit Doron for carefully reading an earlier version, making a critique of my approach and some other recent approaches, and finally making a draft of her paper available to me, which was immensely helpful in the preparation of this paper.

This work was partially supported by a grant from the National Science Foundation, MCS 81-07290.

1. Sridhar (1980) provides a good review. See also Pfaff (1979). For work in code-switching in Hindi and English, see for example Kachru (1978) and Singh (1981).
2. See Sankoff and Poplack (1980), Woolford (1983), Joshi (1981), and Doron (1981).
3. Most of this paper deals with generation. See section 6.4 for some discussion about recognition. A more detailed treatment of parsing will be presented at a later date.
4. In my earlier paper, Joshi (1981), I used the terms, *host language* and *guest language*. Sridhar (1980) uses this terminology also. In fact, it was Sridhar's paper that convinced me of the need for asymmetry in the system. Sridhar uses the terms *host* and *guest* in a rather general manner, but at the sentence level and at the discourse level. The notions of *matrix* and *embedded* languages are technical, and I use them instead of *host* and *guest* in order to avoid confusion with the notions of *host* and *guest* in the code-switching literature. Clearly, these two notions are related.
5. This list is based on a talk given by Mary-Louise Kean at the University of Pennsylvania in October 1981.
6. The data presented here come from my own judgments as well as that of two informants. I am keenly aware that these data are not the result of extensive field

work. They are judgmental, which is not unlike the data used in theoretical linguistic work in the monolingual case. The data used in this paper represent fairly solid and stable judgments, which, in fact, was a surprise to me and is what led me to investigate the mechanism of code switching. I have not heard any great disagreements with my data, although, of course, I have heard disagreements with my formulation and sometimes even with my assumption that any such formulation is possible at all.

7.   It should be noted that this constraint does not rule out the possibility of generating a sentence with only English words. This can happen if all the nodes below the root node are switched from *m*-nodes to *e*-nodes, as there is no constraint against switching all the daughter nodes of the root node. This will lead to a sequence of English words with Marathi word order. Such strings are neither sentences of L_m nor L_e, but, more important, they are not *mixed* sentences. I do not have, at present, a very good suggestion for constraining switches in the horizontal direction other than stating that the final sentence must have at least one Marathi word. Usually, this will be a closed class item. For the Marathi-English pair, the lack of a horizontal constraint is not a problem, but for language pairs with the same word order, it could be a problem. I am indebted to Ken Church for some remarks on this problem.

8.   See note 1 above.

9.   There is, of course, an approach (similar to that proposed by Marcus, 1982) which incorporates the closed class items directly into the rules (thereby, no doubt, multiplying the rules). With this move, the question of switching a closed class item does not arise, because the item is introduced in the rule itself and not via lexical insertion for a preterminal category. Thus we will have rules for NP_m and NP_e as follows (these are only some of the rules).

(i) $NP_m \rightarrow k\bar{a}hi\ N_m$
(ii) $NP_e \rightarrow$ some N_e

The reader can easily check that we will get the correct predictions from these rules. This move has two problems. First, the number of rules are multiplied immensely and second, it looks like a brute force approach. It also leads to the conclusion (as Marcus, 1982, has noted) that the functional role of closed class items is inverted. "Normally, the closed class items serve as the 'glue' that holds the content of sentence together; these words are known as function words exactly because they typically serve to indicate the function of the surrounding more contentful grammatical structures in larger syntactic entities." In the approach described in this note, these items "serve to divide rather than connect the surrounding structures; where they served before as connectors, here they serve as wedges" (Marcus, 1982). (See Miller et al., 1958, for the role of closed class items in supporting sentence structure.)

References

Bradley, Diane C., Merrill F. Garrett, and E. B. Zurif. 1979. Syntactic deficits in Broca's aphasia. In: D. Caplan (ed.), *Biological studies of mental processes*. Cambridge, Mass.: MIT Press.
Doron, Edit. 1981. On formal models of code-switching. Unpublished manuscript, University of Texas at Austin.

Joshi, Aravind K. 1981. Some problems in processing sentences with intrasentential code switching. Extended abstract of a paper read at the *University of Texas Parsing Workshop*, March.

Kachru, Braj. 1978. Toward structuring code-mixing, an Indian Perspective. *International Journal of the Sociology of Language* 16:28–46.

Marcus, Mitchell P. 1982. Consequences of functional deficits in a parsing model: implications for Broca's aphasia. In: *Neural models of language processing*. New York: Academic Press.

Miller, George A., E. B. Newman, and E. A. Friedman. 1958. Length-frequency statistics for written English. *Information and Control* 1:370–89.

Pfaff, Carol. 1979. Constraints on language switching. *Language* 55:291–318.

Sankoff, David, and Shana Poplack. 1980. A formal grammar for code-switching. *Centro de Estudios Aurtorriqueños Working Papers*, 8:1–55.

Singh, R. 1981. Grammatical constraints on code-mixing. *Recherches Linguistiques à Montréal* 17:155–63.

Sridhar, S. N. 1980. The syntax and psycholinguistics of bilingual code-mixing. *Studies in the Linguistic Sciences* 10 (no. 1, Spring) (University of Illinois, Urbana, Ill.).

Woolford, Ellen. 1980. A formal model of bilingual code-switching. Unpublished manuscript.

——— 1983. Bilingual code-switching and syntactic theory. *Linguistic Inquiry* 14(no. 3).

6   Tree adjoining grammars: How much context-sensitivity is required to provide reasonable structural descriptions?

ARAVIND K. JOSHI

Since the late 1970s there has been vigorous activity in constructing highly constrained grammatical systems by eliminating the transformational component either totally or partially. There is increasing recognition of the fact that the entire range of dependencies that transformational grammars in their various incarnations have tried to account for can be captured satisfactorily by classes of rules that are *nontransformational* and at the same time highly constrained in terms of the classes of grammars and languages they define.

Two types of dependencies are especially important: subcategorization and filler-gap dependencies. Moreover, these dependencies can be unbounded. One of the motivations for transformations was to account for unbounded dependencies. The so-called nontransformational grammars account for the unbounded dependencies in different ways. In a tree adjoining grammar (TAG) unboundedness is achieved by factoring the dependencies and recursion in a novel and linguistically interesting manner. All dependencies are defined on a finite set of basic structures (trees), which are bounded. Unboundedness is then a corollary of a particular composition operation called *adjoining*. There are thus no unbounded dependencies in a sense.

This factoring of recursion and dependencies is in contrast to transformational grammars (TG), where recursion is defined in the base and the transformations essentially carry out the checking of the dependencies. The phrase linking grammars (PLGs) (Peters and Ritchie, 1982) and the lexical functional grammars (LFGs) (Kaplan and Bresnan, 1983) share this aspect of TGs; that is, recursion builds up a set a structures, some of which are then filtered out by transformations in a TG, by the constraints on linking in a PLG, and by the constraints introduced via the functional structures in an LFG. In a generalized phrase structure grammar (GPSG) (Gazdar, 1982), on the other hand, recursion and the checking of the dependencies in a sense go together. In a TAG, dependencies are defined initially on bounded structures and recursion simply preserves them.

206

TAGs have the following important properties: (1) We can represent the usual transformational relations more or less directly in TAGs; (2) the power of TAGs is only slightly more than that of context-free grammars (CFGs) in what appears to be just the right way; and (3) TAGs are powerful enough to characterize dependencies (e.g., subcategorization, as in verb subcategorization, and filler-gap dependencies, as in the case of moved constituents in *wh*-questions), which might be at unbounded distance and nested or crossed. It should be noted that the extra power of TAGs (beyond that of CFGs) is not due to some ad hoc modification of the context-free rewriting rule, but rather it is a direct consequence of factoring recursion and dependencies in a special way.

In the next section TAGs are defined and some of their properties are stated. TAGs with *links* are introduced later, and then TAGs with *local constraints*. Some of the the formal properties of TAGs, GPSGs, PLGs, and LFGs are compared with respect to three issues: the types of languages (reflecting different patterns of dependencies) that can or cannot be generated by the different grammars, a certain growth property, and parsing complexity. After some detailed linguistic examples illustrating the use of TAGs, some problems that need further investigation are listed.

In this paper excessive notation and formal proofs have been avoided for several reasons: (1) some of the notation and proofs have already appeared (see Joshi, Levy, and Takahashi, 1975); (2) detailed notation is not necessary to get across the main ideas of this paper; (3) some of the new results can be obtained using the formalism set up by Joshi, Levy, and Takahashi (1975); and (4) the main purposes of the paper are to examine the structure of TAGs and the structural descriptions they can support and to evaluate their linguistic adequacy. In summary, TAGs provide significant insight into the problem of identifying the necessary and sufficient power for a grammar to characterize adequately natural language structures.

6.1. Tree adjoining grammars

I will introduce tree adjoining grammar (TAG) by first describing an alternative way of looking at the derivation of the strings and the corresponding derivation trees of a context-free grammar (CFG). Later I will introduce TAGs in their own right. TAGs are more powerful than CFGs both weakly and strongly. Grammars *G1* and *G2* are *weakly equivalent* if the string language of *G1*, L(G1), is identical to the string language of *G2*, L(*G2*). *G1* and *G2* are *strongly equivalent* if they are weakly equivalent and for each *w* in L(*G1*) = L(*G2*), *G1* and *G2* assign the same structural description to *w*.

A grammar G is *weakly adequate* for a (string) language *L* if L(*G*) = *L*. G is *strongly adequate* for *L* if L(*G*) = *L* and for each *w* in *L*, *G* assigns an "appropriate" structural description to *w*. The notion of strong adequacy is undoubtedly not precise because it depends on the notion of appropriate structural descriptions.

Example 6.1.1. Let *G'* be a context-free grammar with the following productions.

$S \rightarrow a\ T\ b$
$T \rightarrow S\ a$
$T \rightarrow TT$
$T \rightarrow a\ b$

S is the start symbol, *S* and *T* are the nonterminals, and *a* and *b* are the terminal symbols.

We can now define a *tree adjoining grammar* (*TAG*) *G* that is both weakly and strongly equivalent to *G'*. Let *G* = (*I,A*), where *I* and *A* are finite sets of *elementary trees*. The trees in *I* will be called the *initial trees* and the trees in *A*, the *auxiliary trees*.

A tree α is an initial tree if it is of the form in (1).

(1)   α =   *S*

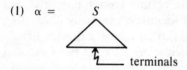

That is, the root node of α is labeled *S* and the frontier nodes are all terminal symbols. The internal nodes are nonterminals. A tree β is an auxiliary tree if it is of the form in (2).

(2)   β =   *X*

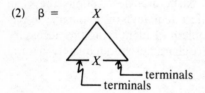

That is, the root node of β is labeled *X*, where *X* is a nonterminal and the frontier nodes are all terminals except one labeled *X*, the same label as that of the root. The node labeled by *X* on the frontier will be called the *foot* node of β. The internal nodes are nonterminals.

As defined, the initial and the auxiliary trees are not tightly constrained. The idea, however, is that both the initial and the auxiliary trees will be *minimal* in some sense. An initial tree will correspond to a *minimal* sentential tree (i.e., without recursion on any nonterminal) and an auxiliary tree, with root and foot node labeled *X*, will correspond to a *minimal* recursive structure that must be brought into the derivation, if there is recursion on *X*.

For the grammar in Example 6.1.1, we can define a TAG, $G = (I,A)$ as in (3).

(3) I: $\alpha_1 =$

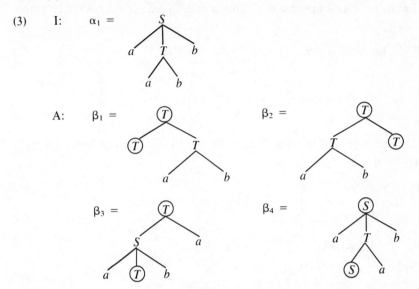

A: $\beta_1 =$ ... $\beta_2 =$

$\beta_3 =$ ... $\beta_4 =$

The root node and the foot node of each auxiliary tree are circled for convenience.

We will now define a composition operation called *adjoining* (or *adjunction*), which composes an auxiliary tree β with a tree γ. Let γ be a tree with a node labeled X and let β be an auxiliary tree with the root labeled X also. (Note that β must have, by definition, a node – and only one – labeled X on the frontier.) Adjoining can now be defined as follows. If β is adjoined to γ at the node n, then the resulting tree γ_1^i is as shown in (4).

(4) $\gamma =$ ... $\beta =$ ... $\gamma' =$

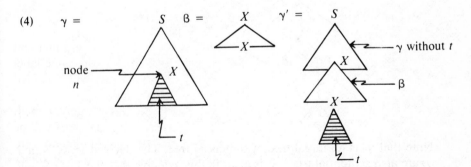

The tree t dominated by X in γ is excised, β is inserted at the node n in γ and the tree t is attached to the foot node (labeled X) of β; that is, β

is inserted or *adjoined* to the node *n* in γ, pushing *t* downward. Note that adjoining is not a substitution operation.

Let us now look at some derivations in the TAG, $G = (I,A)$ of Example 6.1.1.

(5)   Let $\gamma_0 = \alpha_1 =$ $\beta = \beta_3 =$

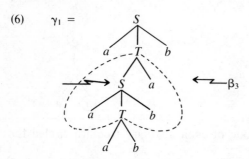

β_3 will be adjoined to γ_0 at T as indicated in γ_0. The resulting tree γ_1 is then as in (6).

(6) $\gamma_1 =$

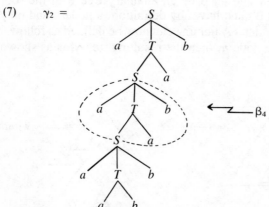

We can continue the derivation by adjoining, say, β_4, at S as indicated in γ_1. The resulting tree γ_2 is then as in (7).

(7) $\gamma_2 =$

Note that γ_0 is an initial tree, a sentential tree. The derived trees γ_1 and γ_2 are also sentential trees. It is clear in this example that the TAG G will derive all and only the sentential trees of the CFG G', starting from the initial tree of G. Thus G will also generate the string language $L(G')$ of G'.

We have introduced the TAG, G, in Example 6.1.1 with reference to the context-free grammar G'. We will now consider the TAGs in their own right. That is, *a TAG $G = (I,A)$ will be a grammar with a finite set of initial trees, a finite set of auxiliary trees, and the adjoining operation as defined before.* We will now define $T(G)$ and $L(G)$.

Definition 6.1.1. $T(G)$ is the set of all trees derived in G starting from initial trees in I. This set will be called the *tree set* of G.

Definition 6.1.2. $L(G)$ is the set of all terminal strings of the trees in $T(G)$. This set will be called the *string language* (*or language*) of G.

The relationship between TAGs, context-free grammars, and the corresponding string languages can be summarized as follows (Joshi, Levy, and Takahashi, 1975).

Theorem 6.1.1. For every context-free grammar G' there is TAG G' equivalent to G, both weakly and strongly.

In Example 6.1.1, G is strongly (and therefore weakly) equivalent to G'. It can be shown also that the equivalent TAG G can be obtained effectively.

Theorem 6.1.2. Each of the following statements holds of some TAG, G.

(a)   there is a context-free grammar G' that is both weakly and strongly equivalent to G;

(b)   there is a context-free grammar G' that is weakly equivalent to G but not strongly equivalent to G;

(c)   there is no context-free grammar G' that is weakly equivalent to G.

Parts (a) and (c) of Theorem 6.1.2 appear in Joshi, Levy, and Takahashi, 1975. Part (b) is implicit in that paper, but it is important to state it explicitly as done here. Example 6.1.1 illustrates part (a). Parts (b) and (c) will now be illustrated.

Example 6.1.2. Let $G = (I,A)$, where

(8)   I: $\alpha_1 =$ S
                               |
                               e

A: $\beta_1 =$ $\beta_2 =$

Let us look at some derivations in G.

(9) $\gamma_0 = \alpha_1 = S$ $\gamma_2 =$

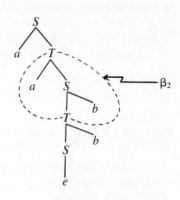

$\gamma_1 = \gamma_0$ with β_1 adjoined at S
as indicated in γ_0.

$\gamma_2 = \gamma_1$ with β_2 adjoined at T
as indicated in γ_2.

Clearly, $L(G)$, the string language of G, is

(10) $L = \{a^n \, e \, b^n \mid n \geq 0\}$

which is a context-free language. Thus there must exist a context-free grammar G' that is at least weakly equivalent to G. It can be shown, however, that there is no context-free grammar G' that is strongly equivalent to G; that is, $T(G) = T(G')$. This follows from the fact that the set $T(G)$ (the tree set of G) is *unrecognizable*; that is, no finite state bottom-up tree automaton can recognize precisely $T(G)$ (see Bresnan et al., 1982; sec. 4). *Thus a TAG may generate a context-free language, yet assign structural descriptions to the strings that cannot be assigned by any context-free grammar.*

Example 6.1.3. Let $G = (I, A)$, where

(11)   I: $\alpha_1 = S$

                        e

    A: $\beta_1 = S$ $\beta_2 = T$

The string language of G, $L(G)$, can be characterized as follows. We start with the language (which is a CFL)

(12) $L = \{ (a \, b)^n \, e \, c^n \mid n \geq 0 \}$.

$L(G)$ is then obtained by taking strings in L and moving (dislocating) some a's to the left. The precise definition of $L(G)$ is as follows:

(13) $L(G) = L_1 \{ w \ e \ c^n \mid n \geq 0,$ w is a string of a's and b's such that
    (i)   the number of a's = the number of b's = n, and
    (ii) for any initial substring of w, the number of a's $\geq$ the number of b's.}

L is a strictly context-sensitive language (a context-sensitive language that is not context free). This can be shown as follows. Intersection L with the finite state language $a^* \ b^* \ e \ c^*$ results in the language

(14) $L_2 = \{ a^n \ b^n \ e \ c^n \mid n \geq 0 \} = L_1 \cap a^* \ b^* \ e \ c^* .$

L_2 is a well-known, strictly context-sensitive language. The result of intersecting a context-free language with a finite-state language is always a context-free language; hence, L_1 is not a context-free language. It is thus a strictly context-sensitive language. Example 6.1.3 thus illustrates part (c) of Theorem 6.1.2. (In example (14), if the dislocated a's are all moved to the left of all b's, then we obtain another strictly context-sensitive language (Peters and Ritchie, 1982). See section 6.3 for a TAG with local constraints for this language. This language can be generated by the phrase linking grammar of Peters and Ritchie. See section 6.3 for further details.)

TAGs have more power than CFGs; however, the extra power is quite limited. Both the qualitative and quantitative characterization of this limitation will be discussed in detail in section 6.3. The language L_1 has equal number of a's, b's, and c's; however, the a's and b's are mixed in a certain way. The language L_2 is similar to L_1, except that all a's come before all b's. TAGs are not powerful enough to generate L_2. This can be seen as follows. Clearly, for any TAG for L_2, each initial tree must contain equal number of a's, b's, and c's (including zero), and each auxiliary tree must also contain equal number of a's, b's, and c's. Further, in each case the a's must precede the b's. Then it is easy to see from the grammar of Example 6.1.3, that it will not be possible to avoid getting the a's and b's mixed. (It will be shown subsequently how L_2 can be generated by a TAG with local constraints, but in a rather special way.) The so-called copy language

(15) $L_3 = \{ w \ e \ w \mid w \in \{a,b\}^* \}$

also cannot be generated by a TAG (although it can be generated by TAG with local constraints). The reason for this is somewhat similar to that for L_2, but it is not so obvious. It is thus clear that TAGs can generate more than context-free languages but cannot generate all context-sensitive languages.

Theorem 6.1.3. (Joshi, Levy, and Takahashi, 1975)

CFL $\subsetneq$ TAL $\subsetneq$ Indexed Languages $\subsetneq$ CSL

214   *Joshi*

where CFL, TAL, and CSL are the classes of context-free, tree adjoining, and context-sensitive languages, respectively.

Indexed languages correspond to the indexed grammars (Aho, 1969). The fact that TAGs cannot generate L_2 and L_3 is important, because it shows that TAGs are only slightly more powerful than context-free grammars. The way TAGs acquire this power is linguistically significant and will be commented upon later. With some (linguistically motivated) modifications of TAGs, or rather the operation of adjoining, it is possible to generate L_2 and L_3, but only in some special ways. Thus L_2 and L_3 in some ways characterize the limiting cases of context sensitivity that can be achieved by TAGs and their slight extensions.

6.2. TAGs with "links"

The elementary trees (initial and auxiliary trees) are the appropriate domains for characterizing certain dependencies (e.g., subcategorization dependencies and filler-gap dependencies). This characterization is achieved by introducing a special relationship between certain specified pairs of nodes of an elementary tree. This relationship is pictorially exhibited by an arc (a dotted line) from one node to the other. For example, in tree (16), the nodes labeled B and Q are linked.

(16)
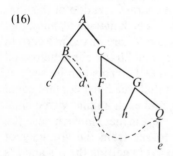

We will require the following conditions to hold for a link in an elementary tree.

If a node n_1 is linked to a node n_2 then
(i) n_2 c-commands n_1 (i.e., n_2 precedes n_1 and there exists a node m that immediately dominates n_2 and also dominates n_1).
(ii) n_1 dominates a null string (represented as a terminal symbol in the non-linguistic formal grammar examples).

Linking is thus an asymmetric relation. In the linguistic context both n_1 and n_2 will be of the same category and only n_1 will dominate a null string.

A TAG with links is a TAG where some of the elementary trees may have links as defined before. Henceforth, a TAG with links will often be called just a TAG.

Links are defined on the elementary trees. However, the important point is that the composition operation of adjoining will *preserve* the links. Links defined on the elementary trees may become *stretched* as the derivation proceeds. Example 6.2.1 will illustrate this point.

Example 6.2.1. Let $G = (I,A)$, where

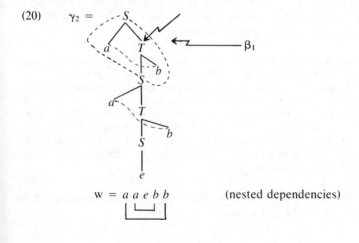

(17)   I: $\alpha_1 = S$ A: $\beta_1 =$ S $\beta_2 =$ T

Let

(18) $\gamma_0 = \alpha_1 =$ S

Adjoining β_1 at S as indicated in γ_0, we have

(19) $\gamma_1 =$

$w = a\,e\,b$

The terminal string corresponding to γ_1 is $a\ e\ b$, where the dependency is indicated by the solid line.

Adjoining β_1 again at S as indicated in γ_2, we have

(20) $\gamma_2 =$

$w = a\,a\,e\,b\,b$ (nested dependencies)

Adjoining β_2 at T as indicated in γ_2, we have

(21) $\gamma_3 =$

S
a T
a S
b
T
b
S
a T
b
S
e

$\leftarrow\!\!\!\!\!\!\!\!- \beta_2$

$$w = a\,a\,a\,e\,b\,b\,b \qquad \text{(cross-serial and nested dependencies)}$$

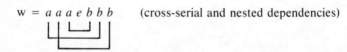

β_1 and β_2 each have one link. γ_2 and γ_3 show how the linking is preserved in adjoining. In γ_3 one of the links is stretched. It should be clear now how, in general, the links will be preserved during the derivation. I will not give a formal definition here.

Also note in this example that in γ_2 the dependencies between the a's and b's, as reflected in the terminal string, are properly nested, while in γ_3 two of them are properly nested, and the third one is cross-serial and it is crossed with respect to the nested ones (this, of course, is not a unique description). The two elementary trees β_1 and β_2 have only one link each. The nestings and crossings in γ_2 and γ_3 are the result of adjoining. There are two points to note here.

1.   TAGs with links can characterize certain cross-serial dependencies (as well as, of course, nested dependencies, which is not a surprise).
2.   The cross-serial dependencies (as well as the nested dependencies) arise as a result of adjoining. But this is not the only way they can arise. It is possible to have two links in an elementary tree representing cross-serial or nested dependencies, which will then be preserved during the derivation. Thus cross-serial dependencies, as well as nested dependencies, will arise in two distinct ways – either by adjoining or by being present in some elementary trees to start with.

It is clear from Example 6.2.1 that the string language of TAG with links is not affected by the links; that is, we have

Theorem 6.2.1. Let G be a TAG with links. Then $L(G) = L(G')$, where G' is a TAG that is obtained from G by removing all the links in the elementary trees of G.

Thus links do not affect the weak generative capacity. However, they make certain aspects of the structural description explicit, which is implicit in the TAG without links. Thus the trees derived in G of Example 6.2.1 show the dependencies explicitly. The trees derived in G' (i.e., G with the links removed) also have these dependencies, but they are implicit. In the following section, the use of links is illustrated in the context of a linguistic example.

6.3. TAGs with constraints on adjoining

The adjoining operation as defined in section 5.1 is context free. An auxiliary tree, say,

(22) $\quad \beta = \quad X$

is adjoinable to a tree t at a node, say, n, if the label of that node is X; the adjoining does not depend on the context (tree context) around the node n. In this sense, adjoining is context free.

We will now consider certain types of constraints that must be checked in order that an auxiliary tree is adjoinable at a node n. These constraints are similar to those called *local constraints* (Joshi and Levy, 1978). These constraints are a generalization of the context-sensitive constraints studied by Peters and Ritchie, 1969.

A TAG with local constraints is a TAG $G = (I,A)$, where I is the set of initial trees and A is the set of auxiliary trees and for each auxiliary tree there is a local constraint (possibly null). Rather than define local constraints precisely (for a detailed definition see Joshi and Levy, 1978), I will give some examples of TAGs with local constraints, which should be adequate to convey the main idea. First, consider a rather general example.

Example 6.3.1. Let $G = (I,A)$, where

(23) $\quad I: \alpha_1 = \quad S$

$\quad A: \beta_1 = \quad A$

$\qquad :LR(\phi_1 - \psi_1) \wedge TB(\phi_2 - \psi_2)$

For the auxiliary tree β_1 there is a local constraint specified to the right of β_1. This constraint can be treated as a predicate that must be true of a node, say, n, of a tree t in order that β_1 is adjoinable to t at n. In our example the predicate $LR(\phi_1 - \psi_1)$ is a *proper analysis* predicate that is true of the node n in tree t if there exists a proper analysis (a cut) of the tree t that passes through the node n and that is of the form

(24) $\rho_1 \, \phi_1 \, A \, \psi_1 \, \rho_2,$

where ρ_1 and ρ_2 are arbitrary strings of terminals and nonterminal symbols, ϕ_1 and ψ_1 are some specified strings of terminals and nonterminals, and A is the label of the node n. What this means is that if the predicate $LR(\phi_1 - \psi_1)$ holds at n, then there is a *left* context ϕ_1 and a *right* context ψ_1, around the node n.

The predicate $TB(\phi_2 - \psi_2)$ is called a *domination predicate*, which is true of the node n in the tree t if there is a path from the root to the frontier of t passing through n, which is of the form

(25) $\rho_1 \, \phi_2 \, A \, \psi_2 \, \rho_2,$

where ρ_1 and ρ_2 are arbitrary strings of terminals and nonterminals, ϕ_2 and ψ_2 are some specified strings of terminals and nonterminals, and A is the label of the node n. If the predicate $TB(\phi_2 - \psi_2)$ holds at n, this means that there is a *top* context ϕ_2 and a *bottom* context ψ_2 around the node n.

The set of trees $T(G)$ and the string language of G, $L(G)$ are defined in the same way as for a TAG without local constraints. In Example 6.3.1 we have only one auxiliary tree. In general, there will be more than one auxiliary tree and each tree will have a local constraint associated with it (possibly null). The local constraint associated with the auxiliary tree β_1 is a conjunction of a LR and a TB predicate. In general, a local constraint can be a Boolean combination of LR and TB predicates.

Example 6.3.2. Let $G(I,A)$, where

(26)   J: $\alpha_1 =$ S
                               |
                               e

A: $\beta_1 =$ S

$(LR(a-\ ) \wedge TB(T-b)$
$\vee(\neg LR(b-\ ) \wedge TB(\ -e))$

$\beta_2 =$ T

$:LR(a-\ ) \wedge TB\ (S-b)$

This TAG is the same as that in Example 6.1.3, except that β_1 and β_2 have local constraints associated with them. For example, in order for β_1 to be adjoinable to a node labeled S, we must have a left context a and a top context T and a bottom context b (or we must *not* have a left context b and must have a bottom context e; this part of the local constraint is to take care of the initial adjoining of β_1 to α_1). Similarly, for β_2 to be adjoinable to a node labeled T, we must have a left context a, a top context S, and a bottom context b. Some of the trees derived in G are

(27) $\quad \gamma_1 = \alpha_1 = S$

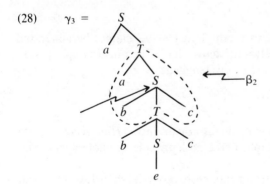

γ_2 is derived by adjoining β_1 to γ_1 at the indicated node S in γ_1. Note that β_1 cannot be adjoined now to the lowermost S node in γ_2 because the local constraint is not satisfied. Note also that β_1 cannot be adjoined to the top node S in γ_2.

(28) $\quad \gamma_3 =$

γ_3 is derived from γ_2 by adjoining β_2 to the indicated node labeled T in γ_2. Note that β_1 can be adjoined to γ_3 only at the node S in the middle of γ_3, but not at the top S node or the bottom S node of γ_3 because the local constraint is not satisfied. Also β_2 cannot be adjoined to either one of the T nodes of γ_3.

Joshi

(29) $\gamma_4 =$

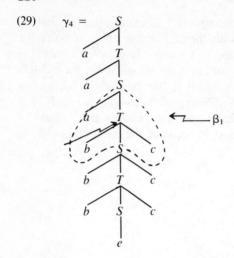

γ_4 is derived by adjoining β_1 to the indicated S node in γ_3. The only adjunction that is possible for γ_4 is a β_2 adjoined at the indicated T node in γ_4.

It is clear that in this grammar at each stage of the derivation the only node that receives adjunction is the center node of the tree, which will be either S or T (compare the derivations in Example 6.1.3). Since the adjoining always takes place at the center node, the string language $L(G)$ of G is

(30) $L_2 = \{a^n\, b^n\, e\, c^n \mid n \geq 0\}$

(compare the string language in Example 6.1.3). L_2 cannot be generated by a TAG without local constraints, as we have seen in Example 6.1.3.

Similarly, the string language (copy language)

(31) $L_3 = \{w\, e\, w \mid w \in \{a,b\}^*\}$

can be generated by a TAG with local constraints. (*Hint*: Use a TAG similar to the TAG in Example 6.1.2 and provide suitable local constraints.)

Thus TAGs with local constraints are more powerful than TAGs without local constraints. However, this extra power is very limited and it is much less than the full power of context-sensitive grammars, as will be shown later.

TAGs have three important properties, which restrict their generative power severely, but apparently in just the right way from the point of view of language structure.

6.3.1. Limited cross-serial dependencies

First let us look at the derivations in Example 6.3.2 somewhat more carefully. Let us call the a, b, and c in each auxiliary tree the *dependent* set
of elements. Alternatively, we can assume that in the auxiliary tree, β_1,
there is a link between b and a, and between c and a. Thus

(32) $\beta_1 =$

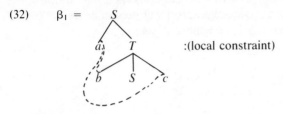

:(local constraint)

and similarly for β_2.
   If we write the terminal string of γ_4 indicating the dependencies by the
solid lines, we will have

(33)
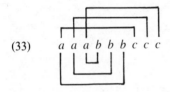

Thus the a's and b's have nested dependencies and the a's and c's have
cross-serial dependencies. If in β_1 we had a link between c and b, and
between c and a, then the b's and c's would be nested and the a's and
c's would be cross-serially dependent as shown below.

(34)
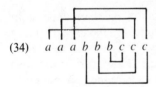

It should be clear that it will not be possible to construct a TAG with
local constraints that will generate

(35) $L = \{a^n\, b^n\, e\, c^n \mid n \geq 0\}$,

where the dependencies between a's, b's and c's are all cross-serial; for
example,

(36)
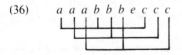

Thus although L_2 can be generated by a TAG with local constraints, the only permissible structure descriptions are of the form where the *a*'s and *b*'s (or the *b*'s and *c*'s) are nested and the *a*'s and *c*'s are cross-serially dependent, but not of the form where the *a*'s, *b*'s, and *c*'s are all cross-serially dependent. This property can be cast in a somewhat general form as a property of TAGs (with or without local constraints) as follows.

A context-free grammar allows characterizing dependencies between two sets when these dependencies are nested, as in

(37)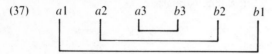

Further, there may be arbitrarily many such pairs of dependent sets; however, their dependencies do not cross. *Two pairs of dependent sets are either disjoint or else one pair is properly nested inside the other.* Thus we have either

(38)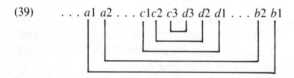

or

(39)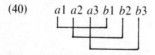

Similarly, TAGs can characterize arbitrarily many pairs of dependent sets, where the dependencies are nested, and two pairs of such dependent sets such that they are either disjoint or one is properly nested inside the other, just as in the case of context-free grammars. However, in the case of TAGs we can also have a pair of dependent sets where the dependencies are cross-serial, as in

(40)   *a*1 *a*2 *a*3 *b*1 *b*2 *b*3

(Actually, we can have the dependencies mixed, i.e., some nested and some cross-serial. Here we will consider only cross-serial ones to keep the discussion simple. However, the statements below apply for this general case also.)

In a TAG we can characterize cross-serial dependencies between only two dependent sets and not more than two; hence, we cannot represent the cross-serial dependencies as in

(41)   *a*1 *a*2 *b*1 *b*2 *c*1 *c*2

(involving three dependent sets). As long as the cross-serial dependencies involve only two dependent sets, as in the case of context-free grammars, we can have arbitrarily many such pairs of dependent sets, each with its cross-serial dependencies; however, any two pairs of such dependent sets are either disjoint or one is properly nested inside the other. Thus we have either

(42)   . . . *a*1 *a*2 *b*1 *b*2   . . .   *c*1 *c*2 *c*3 *d*1 *d*2 *d*3 . . .

or

(43)   . . . *a*1 *a*2   . . .*c*1 *c*2 *c*3 *d*1 *d*2 *d*3 . . .   *b*1 *b*2 . . .

Thus TAGs allow a limited amount of cross-serial dependencies, and the dependent sets have the nesting properties as in the case of context-free grammars.

In the preceding discussion the dependent sets consisted of single letters, *a*'s and *b*'s for example. Since the substitution property holds for context-free languages (CFLs) and the languages of TAGs (TALs)(i.e., a CFL or a TAL continues to be a CFL or a TAL, respectively, if a terminal symbol is substituted by a CFL or a TAL, respectively), the elements of the dependent sets can be strings from CFLs or TALs. We will not consider this more complex situation; single letters are enough for our purpose.

As further examples, we note that the language

(44) $L_4 = \{a^n\ b^n\ e\ c^n d^n \mid n \geq 0\}$

can be generated by a TAG with local constraints but with the structural descriptions of the form where *a*'s and *b*'s are nested, *c*'s and *d*'s are nested, and the *a*'s and *c*'s are cross-serially dependent (alternatively, *a*'s and *d*'s are nested, *b*'s and *c*'s are nested, and the *a*'s and *c*'s are cross-serially dependent) but not of the form where the *a*'s, *b*'s, *c*'s, and *d*'s are all cross-serially dependent.

As shown earlier, two pairs of dependent sets with cross-serial dependencies are either disjoint or one is properly nested inside the other; hence, languages such as

(45) $L_5 = \{a^n\, b^n\, c^n\, e\, d^n\, f^n \mid n \geq 0\}$

and

(46) $L_6 = \{w\, e\, w\, e\, w \mid w \in \{a,b\}^*\}$ (double copy language)

cannot be generated by a TAG with local constraints. Both L_5 and L_6 are strictly context-sensitive languages.

6.3.2. *Constant growth property*

This property is connected with the so-called semilinear property, a property also possessed by context-free languages. It can be shown that languages of TAGs also have this property, but I will not give the proof here (Joshi and Yokomori, 1983). Rather, I will give an informal discussion in terms of the constant growth property.

In a TAG, at each step of the derivation, we have a sentential tree so that the terminal string therefore is a sentence. The derivation thus proceeds from a sentential tree to a sentential tree, and, therefore, from a sentence to a sentence. Let γ_{i+1} be derived from γ_i by adjoining β_j to γ_i. Then the terminal strings of γ_i and γ_{i+1}, say, w_i and w_{i+1}, are both sentences, and the length of w_{i+1} is equal to the length of w_i plus the length of the terminal string of β_j, say, w_j (not counting the single nonterminal symbol in the frontier of β_j), i.e.,

(47) $|w_{i+1}| = |w_i| + |w_j|$

where $|x|$ denotes the length of x. Thus the lengths of the terminal strings (which are sentences) increase by a constant (from a fixed set of constants corresponding to the lengths of the terminal strings of the auxiliary trees of the given TAG).

It is thus clear that for any string, w, of $L(G)$, we have

(48) $|w| = |w_k| + a_1 |w_1| + a_2 |w_2| + \cdots$
$$+ a_i |w_i| + \cdots + a_m |w_m| \qquad a_i \geq 0, \quad 1 \leq i \leq m$$

where w_k is the terminal string of some initial tree and w_i, $1 \leq i \leq m$, the terminal string of the ith auxiliary tree, assuming there are m auxiliary trees. Thus w is a linear combination of the length of the terminal string of some initial tree and the lengths of the terminal strings of the auxiliary trees.

The constant growth property severely restricts the class of languages generated by TAGs. Languages such as

(49) $L_7 = \{a^{2^n} \mid n \geq 1\}$

(50) $L_8 = \{a^{n^2} \mid n \geq 1\}$

are not languages of any TAG. They do not satisfy the constant growth property.

Tree adjoining languages (TALs) have the constant growth property, as we have just seen. Now if we consider a TAG with local constraints, it is also the case that the corresponding TAL has the constant growth property. *The local constraints filter out some strings, but those that remain still satisfy the constant growth property.*

It can thus be seen that TAGs (with or without local constraints) are only slightly more powerful than CFGs. This extra power is highly constrained, at least because of the two properties discussed before.

6.3.3. Polynomial parsing

TAGs also have the following property.

Polynomial parsing. TAGs can be parsed in time $O(n^4)$ (Joshi and Yokomori, 1983). Whether or not an $O(n^3)$ algorithm exists for TAGs is not known yet. Thus the parsing performance of TAGs is comparable to that of CFGs, possibly only slightly worse.

It should be noted that the extra power of TAGs (beyond that of CFGs) is not due to some ad hoc modification of the context-free rewriting rule, but, rather, it is the direct consequence of factoring recursion and the domains of dependencies in a particular manner, which is linguistically significant (see section 6.4 for linguistic examples). I would like to propose that the three properties

1.   limited cross-serial dependencies,
2.   constant growth, and
3.   polynomial parsing

roughly characterize a class of grammars (and associated languages) that are only slightly more powerful than context-free grammars (context-free languages). I will call these *mildly context-sensitive grammars (languages)*, MCSGs (MCSLs). This is only a rough characterization because conditions 1 and 3 depend on the grammars, while condition 2 depends on the languages; further, condition 1 needs to be specified much more precisely than I have done so far. I now would like to claim that grammars that are both weakly and strongly adequate for natural language structures will be found in the class of MCSGs. TAGs are a specific instantiation of such a class of grammars. PLGs and TAGs are so different in their formulations that it has been difficult to compare them directly. However, on the basis of the work done so far (see examples in sections 6.1 and 6.2 and this section thus far; see also the examples in the remarks at the end of this section), I believe that PLGs and TAGs have nearly the same power; that is, they are both MCSGs. LFGs, on the other hand, have much more power than CFGs, TAGs and PLGs. Indexed languages ap-

Table 6.1. *Comparison of generalized phrase structure grammar (and context-free grammar), tree adjoining grammar, phrase linking grammar, and lexical functional grammar*

Languages	GPSG (and CFG)	TAG[a]	PLG	LFG
1. Language obtained by starting with $L = \{(ba)^n c^n \mid n \geq 1\}$ and then dislocating some a's to the left.	no	yes	yes	yes
2. Same as language 1 except that the dislocated a's are to the left of all b's.	no	yes	yes	yes
3. $L = \{w \mid w$ is string of equal number of a's, b's and c's but mixed in any order$\}$.	no	no(?)	yes	yes
4. $L = \{x\, c^n y \mid n \geq 1, x,y$ are strings of a's and b's such that the number of a's in x and $y =$ the number of b's in x and $y = n\}$.	no	no	yes	yes
5. Same as language 4 except that the length of $x =$ length of y.	no	yes	no(?)	yes(?)
6. $L = \{w\, c^n \mid n \geq 1, w$ is string of a's and b's and the number of a's in $w =$ the number of b's in $w = n\}$.	no	yes	yes(?)	yes(?)
7. $L = \{a^n\, b^n\, c^n \mid n \geq 1\}$.	no	yes	no	yes
8. $L = \{a^n\, b^n\, c^n\, d^n \mid n \geq 1\}$.	no	yes	no	yes
9. $L = \{a^n\, b^n\, c^n\, d^n\, e^n \mid n \geq 1\}$.	no	no	no	yes
10. $L = \{w\, w \mid w$ is string of a's and b's$\}$ (copy language).	no	yes	no(?)	yes
11. $L = \{w\, w\, w \mid w$ is string of a's and b's$\}$ (double copy language).	no	no	no(?)	yes
12. $L = \{a^n\, c^m\, b^n\, d^m \mid m \geq 1, n \geq 1\}$.	no	no	no(?)	?
13. $L = \{a^n\, b^n\, c^p \mid n \geq 1, p \neq n\}$.	no	yes	?	yes(?)
14. $L = \{a^{2^n} \mid n \geq 1\}$.	no	no	no(?)	yes
15. $L = \{a^{n^2} \mid n \geq 1\}$.	no	no	no(?)	yes
16. Limited cross-serial dependencies.	no	yes	?	no(?)
17. Constant growth property	yes	yes	yes(?)	no
18. Polynomial parsing	yes	yes	?	no(?)

Note: ?: answer unknown to the author; yes(?): conjectured yes; no(?): conjectured no.
[a] With or without local constraints.

pear to be generable by LFGs (as communicated by Robert Berwick) and some nonindexed languages are also generable by LFGs (as communicated by Fernando Pereira). I believe that LFGs as formulated at present are far more powerful than required. It has not been shown, to the best of my knowledge, that this extra power of LFGs is really needed. Whether meaningful ways of constraining LFGs exist so that the corresponding grammars will be in MCSGs is an open problem. (See Table 6.1.)

6.3.4. Formal remarks

Let L_9 be the language obtained from the language

(51) $\{(b\ a)^n\ c^n \mid n \geq 1\}$

by dislocating some number of a's and moving them to the left; all dislocated a's precede all b's. (This language is described in Peters and Ritchie, 1982, and can be generated by a phrase linking grammar.) Note that this language is different from that in Example 6.1.3, because here we require that all dislocated a's precede all b's. Let us now consider a TAG with local constraints that generates L.

Let $G = (I,A)$, where

(52) *I*:

A:

:$TB(S-T)$

This is not the simplest TAG for L_9. Note also that β_2 has a local constraint that requires a top context S and a bottom context T for β_2 to be adjoinable. The bar over some a's serves to indicate the dislocated a's. The TAG, G, above not only generates L, but also generates the appropriate linked tree sets of the corresponding PLG (see Peters and Ritchie, 1982). It is not clear yet whether a TAG without local constraints can be constructed for L_9; this is probably not possible.

Those familiar with PLGs may be interested in the following PLG for the language in Example 6.1.3.

(53) $G':S \rightarrow \overline{a}\ S$
      $S \rightarrow \overline{a}\ b\ S\ c$
      $S \rightarrow e$

The a's with bars have to be properly linked as defined by Peters and Ritchie (1982).

Example 6.3.4. The language L_{10} is of considerable interest. (This language was suggested by William Marsh (private communication) and some of his students. This language is also referred to as Bach language. Marsh has shown that this language can be generated by a PLG.)

(54) $L_{10} = \{w/w \in \{a,b,c\}^*$ and the number of a's = the number of b's = the number of c's}.

That is, L_{10} has the same number of a's, b's, and c's, but the a's, b's and c's appear in all possible orders. L_{10} can be generated by a phrase linking grammar (PLG).

This language is interesting because, in a sense, it represents the extreme case of the degree of free word order permitted in a language. This extreme case is linguistically not relevant. Languages 1–6 in Table 6.1 represent different degrees of free word order, the language in 3 being the extreme case. Indicated in the table is the degree of free word order permitted by each type of grammar in terms of these languages. GPSGs cannot generate this language. TAGs also cannot generate this language, although for TAGs the proof is not in hand yet. LFGs can generate this language.

In a TAG, for each elementary tree, we can add more elementary trees, systematically generated from the given elementary trees to provide additional free word order (in a somewhat similar fashion to Pullum, 1982). Since the adjoining operation in a TAG gives some additional power to a TAG beyond that of a CFG, this device of augmenting the elementary trees should give more freedom, for example, by allowing some limited scrambling of an item outside of the constituent to which it belongs. Even then a TAG does not seem to be capable of generating the language in the preceding example (the language in 3 in Table 6.1). Thus there is extra freedom, but it is quite limited. The extra power of TAGs may be just adequate to handle the free word order phenomenon; however, we need to know much more about this phenomenon before we can be sure of the claim.

Table 6.1 lists (1) a set of languages reflecting different patterns of dependencies that can or cannot be generated by different types of grammars, and (2) the three properties of TAGs mentioned earlier.

6.4. Some linguistic examples

In this section, which gives some detailed linguistic examples of TAGs, many details that do not serve the purpose of illustrating the power of TAGs have been ignored or simplified. (For a more detailed account of linguistic relevance of TAGs, see Joshi and Kroch, 1984.)

6.4.1. An English example

Example 6.4.1. Let $G = (I,A)$, where I is the finite set of initial trees and A is the finite set of auxiliary trees. Only some of these trees in I and A will be listed, especially those relevant to the derivations of certain sentences. Rather than introducing all the trees at once, I will introduce them a few at a time and make some appropriate remarks as we go along. Later I will show some sample derivations.

(55)   *I(Initial Trees):*

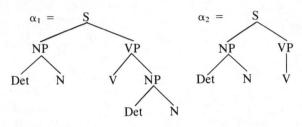

Note that α_1 corresponds to a "minimal sentence" with a transitive verb, e.g.,

(56)   The man met the woman.

and α_2 corresponds to a minimal sentence with an intransitive verb; for example,

(57)   The man fell.

The initial trees, as defined earlier, require terminal symbols on the frontier. In the linguistic context, the nodes on the frontier will be preterminal symbols such as N, V, A, P, Det, etc. The lexical items are inserted for each one of the preterminal symbols as each elementary tree enters the derivation. Thus if we choose α_1 as the initial tree, then

(58) $\gamma_1 = \alpha_1$ (with lexical items inserted) =

```
                    S
                  /   \
               NP      VP
              /  \     /  \
           Det    N   V    NP
            |     |   |    /  \
           the  man  met Det   N
                          |    |
                         the woman
```

As we continue the derivation by selecting auxiliary trees and adjoining them appropriately, we follow the same convention; that is, as each auxiliary tree is chosen, we make the lexical insertions. *Thus in a derivation in a TAG, lexical insertion goes hand in hand with the derivation.* Each step in the derivation selects an elementary tree together with a set of appropriate lexical items.

Note that as we select the lexical items for each elementary tree we can check a variety of constraints, e.g., agreement and subcategorization constraints on the set of lexical items. Thus, for example, the following choices of lexical items will not be permitted.

(59)

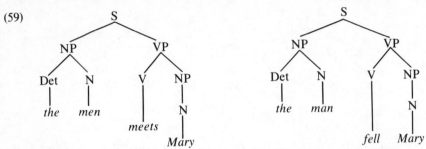

This is because, in the first case, the number agreement is violated and in the second case, *fell* does not take NP object. The point here is that these constraints can be easily checked because the entire elementary tree which is the domain of these constraints is available as a single unit at each step in the derivation. If we had started with α_2, then the choice of lexical items as shown in (60) would be permitted.

(60)

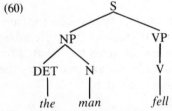

When an auxiliary tree enters the derivation, similar considerations hold. In addition, further constraints, both contextual and lexical, can be checked by means of *local constraints*. We will illustrate some of these later as we proceed with our example.

(61) $\alpha_3 =$

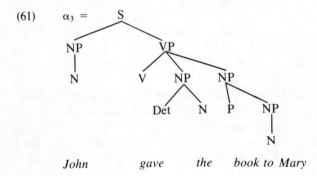

Note that henceforth a possible lexical choice will be stated by giving an example below each tree. It is clear that for each subcategorization frame we will have an initial tree. We could, of course, represent this finite set of trees by some schema. This is only a matter of convenience and it is not relevant to our current purpose.

(62) $\alpha_4 =$

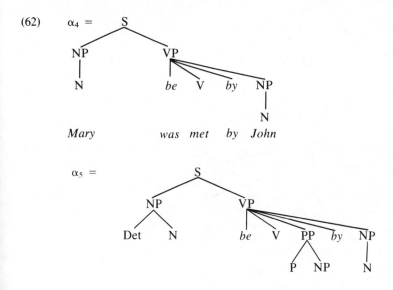

Note that α_4 and α_5 are the passive forms of α_1 and α_3, respectively. I have shown a flat structure for passive for convenience only. Nothing in this section hangs on this particular structure for passive. (For further details about the analysis of passive with respect to TAGs, see Joshi and Kroch, 1984.)

(63) $\alpha_{10} =$

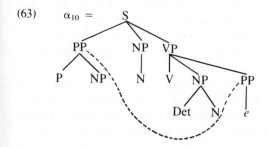

In α_{10}, a link is shown from the lower PP node to a higher PP node. It should be noted that when lexical items are inserted for the preterminal nodes in α_{10}, not only can we check that a verb requiring NP PP object has been inserted, but also that the preposition P is *to* as required by the verb, for example.

(64) $\alpha_{15} =$

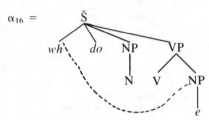

Who met Mary?

$\alpha_{16} =$

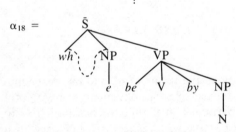

Who did John meet?

⋮

$\alpha_{18} =$

Who was met by John?

⋮

Each one of the finite sets *I* and *A* can be quite large. The set of initial trees contains so far all the *minimal* sentential trees corresponding to different subcategorization frames together with their *transforms*. It should be noted that this set is finite and these trees have been listed explicitly.

We could, of course, provide rules for obtaining some of these trees from a given subset of trees. These rules will achieve the effect of conventional transformational rules; however, they need not be formulated as the usual transformational rules. We can formulate them directly as tree rewriting rules, especially since both the domains and the co-domains of the rules will be finite. *These rules will be abbreviatory in the sense that they will generate only finite sets of trees. Hence, incorporation of such rules will be only a matter of convenience and will not affect the TAG in any essential manner.*

So far, all the initial trees defined correspond to minimal sentences. I will now introduce some initial trees that are minimal but are not matrix sentences. The motivation for introducing these trees will be clear from the examples and the subsequent use of these trees in the derivations. Some problems associated with the introduction of these trees will be discussed in the next section.

(65) $\alpha_{25} =$

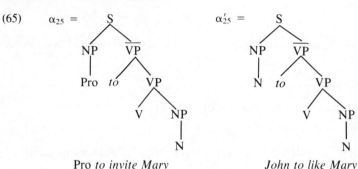

Pro *to invite Mary*   *John to like Mary*

Note that α_{25} and α'_{25} are similar, except that in the first case the subject NP is realized as Pro and in the second case by a lexical item. α_{25} will be used in the derivation of sentences such as

(66)   John persuaded Bill Pro to invite Mary.
        John tried Pro to invite Mary.

α'_{25} will be used in deriving sentences such as

(67)   John seems to like Mary

(68) $\alpha_{26} =$

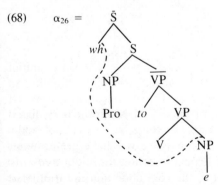

Who Pro *to invite*

$$\alpha'_{26} =$$

α_{26} and α'_{26} differ in the same way α_{25} and α'_{25}. α_{26} will be used in deriving sentences such as

(69)   Who did John try to invite?

α'_{26} will be used in deriving sentences such as

(70)   Who did John expect Bill to invite?

So far we have considered some initial trees. Now let us examine auxiliary trees.

(71)   An auxiliary tree $\beta_1 =$

who met Mary

The terminal nodes of an auxiliary tree should all be terminal symbols, except one that is a nonterminal identical to the label of the root node. In the linguistic context, instead of terminals we will have preterminals on the frontier. (See the remarks on lexical insertion for initial trees.) In β_1 the circled NP nodes correspond to the root node and the foot node of an auxiliary tree. These nodes have been circled for convenience.

β_1 will be used to build a subject relative clause around an NP as in

(72)   The boy who met Mary left.

The link in β_1 links the extracted NP node to *wh*.

(73) $\beta_2 =$

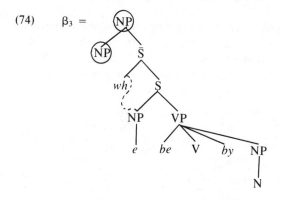

who Mary met

β_2 corresponds to the object relative clause.

(74) $\beta_3 =$

who was met by Mary

β_3 corresponds to a subject relative clause where the verb is in the passive form. It is clear that we will have a large number of auxiliary trees; however, the set is finite. As in the case of initial trees, it is possible to write rules for obtaining some of the auxiliary trees, say for example, β_3 from β_1, or even all of the auxiliary trees, say for example, β_1 from α_1, etc. These *rules* will correspond more or less directly to the usual transformations. However, there are important differences: (1) The rules will be only abbreviatory in the sense that only a finite set of trees will be derivable from a finite set of trees. (2) The rules can be defined directly as tree rewriting rules, where both the domain and the co-domain are trees, unlike the transformational rules, which are mediated by structural descriptions based on proper analyses. *It is in this sense that the trees in I and A capture the usual transformational relations more or less directly.*

It should be pointed out that the so-called Island Constraints do not have to be stated as constraints in a TAG. They are simply corollaries of the TAG formulation. This observation is due to Tony Kroch (see Joshi and Kroch, 1984, for further details). Thus

(75)   *To whom what did John do?

is disallowed if there is no elementary tree (an initial tree) corresponding to (75). Then (76) is automatically prevented

(76)   *To whom did you wonder what John did?

The prevention of (75) is a matter of what elementary trees (initial trees, in this case) and what links are allowed on them. Once the elementary trees are defined, the links are *preserved* throughout the derivation in a TAG, as shown in section 6.3. No new linking relations are added between a tree and an auxiliary tree that is being adjoined. The so-called Island Constraints then follow as corollaries. Similar considerations hold for the Complex-NP Constraint.

The *preservation* of the linking relations during the derivation in a TAG accounts for the so-called *unbounded movements*. In a sense, in a TAG, there are no unbounded movements. All movements are defined on the elementary trees; thus they are bounded. The unboundedness then is a

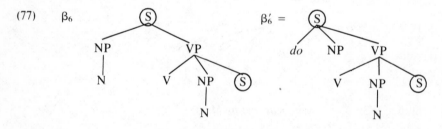

(77) β_6 ... John persuaded Bill S ... $\beta_6' = $ ... Did John persuade Bill S

(78) $\beta_7 = $ ... John expected S ... $\beta_7' = $ ... Did John expect S

(79)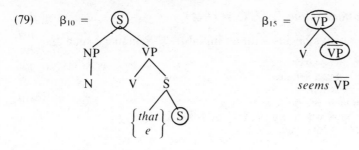

John knew that S

corollary of the fact that the links are *preserved* during the derivation in a TAG.

β_6, β_6', β_7, β_7', and β_{10} correspond to the sentences involving sentential complements. For example,

(80)   John persuaded Bill to invite Mary.

would be derived starting with an initial tree corresponding to

(81)   Pro to invite Bill

to which β_6 is adjoined giving

(82)   John persuaded Bill Pro to invite Mary.

β_6' would be used in deriving

(83)   Who did John persuade Bill to invite?

β_7 and β_7' will be used in a similar fashion. β_{15} will be used in deriving

(84)   John seems to like Mary.

Sentence (82) will not be derived in the same way as

(85)   John tried to invite Mary.

So far I have not shown any local constraints for any one of the auxiliary trees. This was done for simplicity. Clearly, many of the auxiliary trees listed will be accompanied by local constraints. As I illustrate some of the derivations in the above TAG, I will point out some of the local constraints needed and how they can be stated for particular auxiliary trees. These examples should be adequate to show the use of the local constraints in a TAG.

6.4.2. *Derivations in the TAG, G = (I, A)*

A derivation always begins with an initial tree. Sentences such as

(86) a. John met Mary.
      b. The girl is a senior.
      c. The rock fell.
      d. John gave the book to Mary.
      e. The book was given to Mary by John.
      f. To Mary John gave the book.

$$\vdots$$

correspond directly to initial trees. In particular, (84b) corresponds to α_1 (with appropriate lexical insertions).

(87) $\gamma_1 = \alpha_1 =$

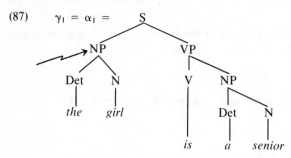

The girl is a senior.

I will now derive several sentences.

(88)   The girl who met Bill is a senior.

Let us take β_1 (with appropriate lexical insertions).

(89) $\beta_1 =$

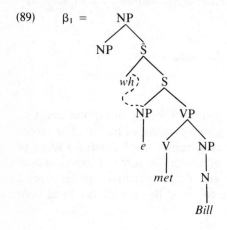

β_1 is then adjoined to α_1 at the indicated node labeled NP resulting in γ_2.

(90) $\gamma_2 =$

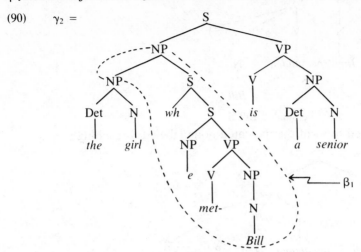

The girl who met Bill is a senior.

(91)   John persuaded Bill to invite Mary.

We will start with the initial tree α_{25}.

(92) $\gamma_1 = \alpha_{25} =$

Pro to invite Mary

Then we take β_6.

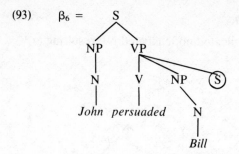

(93) $\beta_6 =$

John persuaded Bill S

β_6 is adjoined to γ_1 of the indicated node labeled S resulting in γ_2.

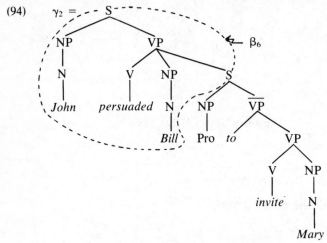

(94) $\gamma_2 =$

John persuaded Bill to invite Mary.

Note that if we start with α'_{25}, which is like α_{25} except that instead of Pro, we have a lexical NP

(95) $\gamma'_1 = \alpha'_{25} =$

Jim to invite Mary

Adjoining β_6 to α'_{25} at the indicated node labeled S, we get γ'_2.

240

(96) $\gamma'_2 =$

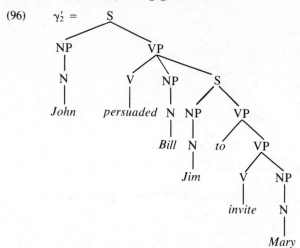

* John persuaded Bill Jim to invite Mary.

γ'_2 can be disallowed if while adjoining β_6 to γ_1 (or γ'_1) we can check whether the subject NP is a Pro and allow adjoining only in that case. This can be achieved by associating a local constraint with β_6 as follows.

(97) $\beta_6 =$ ⑤

           NP   VP   :*TB* (—NP Pro)

            N   V   NP   ⑤

                      N

(98)   Who did John persuade Bill to invite?

We will start with the initial tree α_{26}.

(99) $\gamma_1 = \alpha_{26} =$ $\bar{S}$

              wh   S   ←⌐

                 NP $\overline{VP}$

                 Pro   *to*   VP

                         V   NP

                       invite   *e*

            Who Pro to invite

Then we take β'_6.

242   *Joshi*

(100) $\beta_6' =$

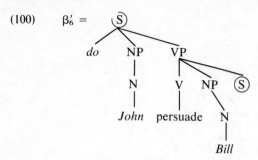

did John persuade Bill S

β_6 is adjoined to γ_1 at the indicated node labeled S, resulting in γ_2.

(101) $\gamma_2 =$

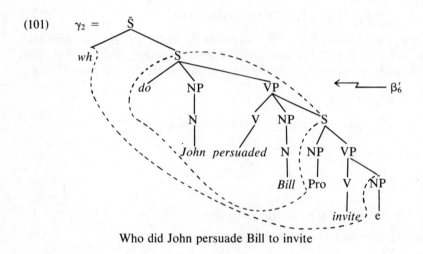

Who did John persuade Bill to invite

Note that the link in γ_1 is *preserved* in γ_2; it is *stretched* resulting in the so-called unbounded dependency.

It is now easy to see that starting from α_{25}' and then adjoining β_7 to α_{25} at the root node S, we obtain

(102)   John expected Bill to invite Mary.

Starting with α_{26}' and adjoining β_7' to α_{26}' at the node labeled S, we obtain

(103)   Who did John expect Bill to invite?

By setting up further auxiliary trees such as, for example,

(104) β_{30} =

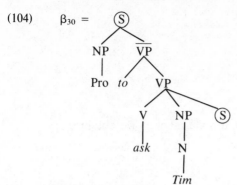

we can obtain (105) as follows.

(105)   John persuaded Bill to ask Tim to invite Mary.

We will start with α_{25} corresponding to

(105a)   Pro to invite Mary.

Then we adjoin β_{30} to the S node in α_{25}, giving

(105b)   Pro to ask Tim Pro to invite Mary.

Finally, adjoining β_6 to the root node S of the tree corresponding to (105b), we obtain

(105c)   John persuaded Bill Pro to ask Tim Pro to invite Mary.

A very important aspect of TAGs is that *we can provide distinct derivations for sentences containing the so-called equi and raising verbs.* This observation is due to Tony Kroch. (For further details, see Joshi and Kroch, 1984.) Thus

(106)   John tried to please Mary.

will be derived as follows. We will start with α_{25}

(107) $\gamma_1 = \alpha_{25}$ =   S

```
                       S ←↰___
                      / \
                    NP   VP
                    |    / \
                   Pro  to  VP
                           / \
                          V   NP
                          |   |
                       please N
                              |
                             Mary
```

Pro to please Mary

We then take β_7.

(108) $\beta_7 =$

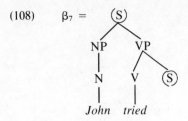

John tried S

Adjoining β_7 to γ_2 at the indicated node label S, we obtain γ_2.

(109) $\gamma_2 =$

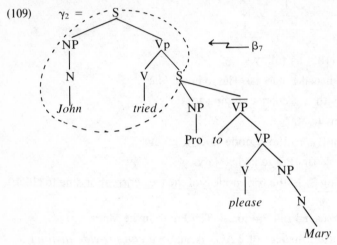

John tried Pro to please Mary.

On the other hand

(110)   John seems to like Mary.

will be derived as follows. We will start with α'_{25}

(111) $\gamma_1 = \alpha'_{25} = $ S

John to like Mary

We then take β_{15}.

244

(112)   β₁₅ =

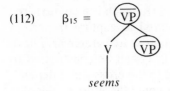

Adjoining β₁₅ to γ₁ at this indicated node labeled VP, we obtain γ₂.

(113)   γ₂ =

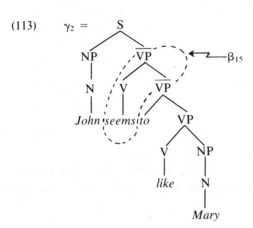

John seems to like Mary.

6.4.3. *Cross-serial dependencies in Dutch*

There are infinitely many sentences in Dutch that are of the following form (Bresnan et al., 1983).

(114)   . . . *Jan Piet Marie zag helpen zwemmen*

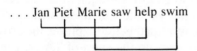

. . . Jan saw Piet help Marie swim

where the dependencies are as indicated by the solid lines. Thus we have strings of the form

(115)   . . . *a1 a2 a3 b1 b2 b3* . . .

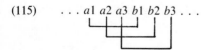

The string language is of the form $\{a^n b^n \mid n \geq 1\}$, which is a context-free language, but the structural description required to capture the cross-serial dependencies cannot be achieved by a context-free grammar. I have already shown in the preceding test how a TAG can be constructed to provide structural descriptions corresponding to the cross-serial dependencies. The TAG in Examples 6.1.1 and 6.2.1 could therefore be adapted for characterizing dependencies in (114). However, a TAG in which the elementary trees correspond to

(116) (a) *Jan zag.*
       (b) *Piet helpen.*
       (c) *Marie zwemmen.*

with the derivation beginning with

(117) *Jan zag.*

will not do because, although the TAG will give the correct cross-serial dependencies, the resulting derivation will be linguistically defective and also will not be quite in the spirit of TAGs. It is clear that we must construct a TAG in which the derivation will begin with an initial tree corresponding to

(118) *Marie zwemmen.*

and, of course, we must get the appropriate cross-serial dependencies. Bresnan et al. (1983) have stated certain facts about conjoining verbs and conjoining NP PP sequences, and they have proposed a structure to account for these facts. Their structure is characterized by the fact that the corresponding Ns and Vs branch out from two distinct paths from the root to the frontier. Such a structure can be regarded as having two spines, one to support the Ns and the other to support the Vs. (The unrecognizability of such tree sets follows directly, if we require that the Ns and the Vs match.) TAGs as defined so far will allow us to construct only structures with one spine. The TAG described below captures the cross-serial dependencies, and the derivations are in the spirit of TAGs. I must emphasize that the TAG given here is primarily for the purpose of illustrating how a TAG can be constructed to capture the cross-serial dependencies in the right manner, keeping the derivations in the spirit of TAGs. I do not wish to claim any detailed linguistic justification for the structure proposed here; however, the dependencies are correctly represented.

In Joshi, Levy, and Takahashi, 1975, a variant of TAG was considered. This variant will allow construction of structures with two (or even more) spines, as described in Bresnan et al., 1983. The matter will not be discussed here.

Let $G = (I,A)$ be a TAG, where

(119)   I: $\alpha_1 =$

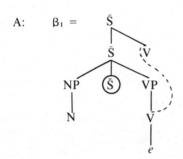

    A: $\beta_1 =$

Let us look at some derivations. We will start with α_1. (The Ns and Vs are indexed for reading convenience.)

(120) $\gamma_1 = \alpha_1 =$

Marie zwemmen.

Adjoining β_1 to γ_1 at the indicated node we obtain γ_2.

Note that in the TAG described, in each step of the derivation the corresponding Ns and Vs enter the derivation at the same time. Also even if one goes bottom-up on the tree γ_3, the corresponding Ns and Vs are together.

(121) $\gamma_2 =$

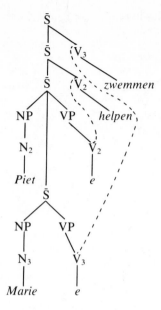

Piet Marie helpen zwemmen.

6.5. Some further problems

A number of issues are only lightly treated in this paper. In particular, some of the discussion of linguistic relevance is very brief. A fuller discussion is given in Joshi and Kroch, 1984. Some other problems need further investigation. I will only mention these here.

1. Some initial trees are not matrix sentences. Thus they have to have an auxiliary tree adjoined before they become sentences. This requires filtering out those derivation trees where such adjoining has not taken place. It is easy to set up a mechanism for achieving this, without affecting the general character of TAGs, especially with respect to their generative capacity.

2. To accommodate coordination, both *I* and *A* sets have to be enlarged by introducing some schemas. The *I* and *A* sets then can become potentially infinite, an extension that will not affect generative capacity in any essential way. However, this aspect needs much further investigation, which has not been carried out yet.

3. Each step in the derivation in a TAG introduces an elementary tree (a large structural chunk) together with the associated lexical items. This property of TAGs may turn out to be highly relevant for modeling some aspect of sentence production. I am currently studying this suggestion.

Adjoining β_1 at the indicated node in γ_2 we get γ_3.

(122) $\gamma_3 =$

Jan Piet Marie zag helpen zwemmen.

Acknowledgments

This work is partially supported by the NSF Grant MCS 81-07290.

I wish to thank Bob Berwick, Jean Gallier, Gerald Gazdar, Ron Kaplan, Lauri Karttunen, Tony Kroch, Mitch Marcus, Bill Marsh, Stan Peters, Ellen Prince, Geoff Pullum, Bob Ritchie, Stu Shieber, R. Shyamasundar, Hans Uszkoreit, Bonnie Webber, Scott Weinstein, and Takashi Yokomori for their valuable comments. I am particularly indebted to Tony Kroch for comments on certain lingustic issues and to Takashi Yokomori for comments on some formal aspects. Some forthcoming publications will discuss these issues in greater detail (see Joshi and Kroch, 1984, and Joshi and Yokomori, 1984).

250   *Joshi*

References

Aho, Alfred. 1969. Indexed grammars. *Proceedings of the 8th IEEE meeting on Switching and Automata Theory.*

Bresnan, Jean W., Ronald Kaplan, Stanley Peters, and Annie Zaenen. 1982. Cross-serial dependencies in Dutch. *Linguistic Inquiry.*

Gazdar, Gerald. 1982. Phrase structure grammars. In: Pauline Jacobson and Geoffrey Pullum (eds.), *The nature of syntactic representations.* Dordrecht, Holland: D. Reidel.

Joshi, Aravind K., and Leon Levy. 1982. Phrase structure trees bear more fruit than you would have thought. *American Journal of Computational Linguistics.*

Joshi, Aravind K., Leon S. Levy, and M. Takahashi. 1975. Tree adjunct grammars. *Journal of the Computer and System Sciences.*

Joshi, Aravind K., and Takashi Yokomori. 1983. Parsing of tree adjoining grammars. Technical Report. Department of Computer and Information Science, University of Pennsylvania.

Joshi, Aravind K., and Leon S. Levy. 1978. Local constraints. *SIAM Journal of computing.*

Joshi, Aravind K., and Takashi Yokomori. 1983. Some characterization theorems for tree adjoining grammars and recognizable sets. Technical Report. Department of Computer and Information Science, University of Pennsylvania.

Joshi, Aravind K., and Tony Kroch. Forthcoming 1984. Linguistic significance of TAG's. (tentative title).

Kaplan, Ronald, and Joan W. Bresnan. 1983. Lexical functional grammar – a formal system for grammatical representation. In Joan Bresnan (ed.), *The mental representation of grammatical relations.* Cambridge, Mass.: MIT Press.

Peters, Stanley, and Robert Ritchie. 1969. Immediate constituent analysis revisited. *Proceedings of the ACM Symposium on Theory of Computing.*

Peters, Stanley, and Robert Ritchie. 1982. Phrase linking grammars. Technical Report. Department of Linguistics, University of Texas at Austin.

Pullum, Geoffrey K. 1982. Free word order and phrase structure rules. In J. Pustejovsky and P. Sells (eds.), *Proceeding of NELS 12.* Amherst, Mass.

7 Parsing in functional unification grammar

MARTIN KAY

Language is a system for encoding and transmitting ideas. A theory that seeks to explain linguistic phenomena in terms of this fact is a *functional* theory. One that does not misses the point. In particular, a theory that shows how the sentences of a language are all generable by rules of a particular formal system, however restricted that system may be, does not explain anything. It may be suggestive, to be sure, because it may point to the existence of an encoding device whose structure that formal system reflects. But, if it points to no such device, it simply constitutes a gratuitous and wholly unwelcome addition to the set of phenomena to be explained.

A formal system that is decorated with informal footnotes and amendments explains even less. If I ask why some phenomenon, say relativization from within the subject of a sentence, does not take place in English and am told that it is because it does not take place in any language, I go away justifiably more perplexed than I came. The theory that attempts to explain things in this way is not functional. It tells me only that the source of my perplexity is more widespread than I had thought. The putative explanation makes no reference to the only assertion that is sufficiently self-evident to provide a basis for linguistic theory, namely that language is a system for encoding and transmitting ideas.

But, surely there is more to functionalism than this. To fill their role as systems for encoding and transmitting ideas, languages must first be learnable. Learnability is a functional property and language learning needs to be explained. But what is involved here is a derivative notion of function. A satisfactory linguistic theory will at least make it plausible that children could learn to use language as a system for encoding and transmitting ideas. It will *not* show how a child might learn to distinguish sentences from nonsentences, a skill with little survival value and one for which evolution probably furnished no special equipment.

It follows that any reasonable linguistic theory will be functional. To use the word to characterize one particular theory, as I shall shortly do,

251

must therefore be accounted pretentious. However, while it is true that the label has been used before, it is manifestly untrue that linguistic theories have typically been functional. Just recently, there has been a partial and grudging retreat from the view that to formalize is to explain. This has not been because of any widespread realization of the essential vacuity of purely formal explanations, but for two other reasons. The first is the failure of the formalists to produce workable criteria on which to distinguish competing theories, and the second is the apparent impossibility of constructing theories whose most cogent remarks are made within the formalism rather than in footnotes and amendments. The search for sources of constraint to impose on formal grammar has led to an uneasy alliance with the psychologists and a belated rekindling of interest in parsing and other performance issues (for some discussion, see Gazdar, 1982; Kaplan, 1972, 1973, 1978; Kay, 1973, 1977, 1979).

My aim in this polemic is not to belittle the value of formalisms. Without them linguistics, like most other scientific enterprises, would be impotent. It is only to discredit them as an ultimate basis for the explanation of the contingent matters that are the stuff of science. What I shall describe under the banner of functional unification grammar is indeed a formalism, but one that has been designed to accommodate functionally revealing, and therefore explanatorily satisfying, grammars.

7.1. Functional unification grammar

A functionally adequate grammar must either be a particular transducer, or some kind of data structure that more general kinds of transducer – generators and parsers – can interpret. It must show not only what strings can be associated with what meanings, but how a given meaning can be expressed and a given utterance understood. Furthermore, it cannot take logic as the measure of meaning, abjuring any responsibility for distinctions that are not readily reflected in the predicate calculus. The semantic side of the transducer must traffic in quantifiers and connectives, to be sure, but also in topic and emphasis and given and new. Functional grammar will, therefore, at the very least, adopt some form of *functional* sentence perspective.

In practice, I take it that the factors that govern the production of a sentence typically come from a great variety of different sources, logical, textual, interpersonal, and so forth. In general, each of these, taken by itself, underdetermines what comes out. When they jointly overdetermine it, there must be priorities enabling a choice to be made among the demands of the different sources. When they jointly underdetermine the outcome, the theory must provide defaults and unmarked cases. The point is that we must be prepared to take seriously the claim that language in general, and individual utterances in particular, fill many different *functions* and that these all affect the theory, even at the syntactic level.

I have outlined a broad program for linguistic theory, and the possibility of carrying it through rests on our being able to design clean, simple formalisms. This applies to the formal descriptions by which words, phrases, sentences, grammars, and languages are known and also to the operations that the theory allows to be performed on these descriptions.

Much of the character of the theory I shall outline comes from the set-.heoretic properties that are imputed to descriptions of all kinds in every-day life. These properties do not, in fact, carry over to the descriptions provided for in most linguistic formalisms. In this theory, there is no limit on how detailed a description can be and no requirement that everything in it should serve some grammatical end. Generally speaking, to add more detail to a description is to narrow the class of objects described, and to remove material from a description is to widen its coverage. In fact, descriptions and the sets of things they refer to are mathematical duals of one another with respect to the operations of set theory. In other words, the intersection of a pair of descriptions describes the union of the sets of objects that they describe separately and the union of a pair of descriptions describes the intersection of the corresponding pairs of sets. These are properties we are entitled to look for in anything to which the term "description" is seriously applied.

Descriptions are sets of *descriptors* and prominent among the kinds of object that go to make up the sets are pairs consisting of an attribute, like *number*, with an associated value, like *singular*. An important subclass of attributes consists of grammatical *functions* like *Subject*, *Modifier*, and *Connective*.

The claim that this theory makes on the word "functional" in its title is therefore supported in three ways. First, it gives primary status to those aspects of language that have often been called functional; logical aspects are not privileged. Second, it describes linguistic structures in terms of the function that a part fills in a whole, rather than in terms of parts of speech and ordering relations. Third, and most important for this paper, it requires its grammars to *function*; that is, they must support the practical enterprises of language generation and analysis.

7.1.1. Compilation

The view that a grammar is a data structure that can be interpreted by one or more transducers has some attractions over the one that would have it actually be a transducer. On the one hand, while the grammar itself remains the proper repository of linguistic knowledge, and the formalism, an encapsulation of formal linguistic universals, the language-independent transducer becomes the embodiment of a theory of performance. But there is no reason to suppose that the same transducer should be reversible, taking responsibility for both generation and parsing. While the strongest hypothesis would indeed provide only one device, a more conservative position would separate these functions. This paper takes the conservative position. Given that generation and parsing are done by different transducers, a strong hypothesis would have both transducers interpret the same grammar; a more conservative position would associate a different formalism with each transducer and provide some mechanism for ensuring that the same facts were represented in each. This paper takes the conservative position. Specifically, the position is that the generator operates directly on the canonical form of the grammar – the competence grammar – and that the parser operates on a translation of this grammar into a different formalism. This paper will concentrate on how this translation is actually carried out; it will, in short, be about machine translation between grammatical formalisms.

The kind of translation to be explored here is known in computer science as *compilation*, and the computer program that does it is called a *compiler*. Typically, compilers are used to translate programs from so-called *high-level* programming like FORTRAN or ALGOL, into the *low-level* languages that directly control computers. But, compilers have also proved very useful in other situations.

Whatever the specific application, the term "compilation" almost always refers to a process that translates a text produced by a human into a text that is functionally equivalent, but not intended for human consumption. There are at least two reasons for doing this. One is that those properties of a language that make for perspicuity and ease of expression are very different from those that make for simple, cheap, reliable computing. Put simply, computers are not easy to talk to and it is sometimes easier to use an interpreter. It is economical and efficient for man and machine to talk different languages and to interact through an intermediary. The second reason has to do with flexibility and is therefore also economic. By compilation, the programming enterprise is kept, in large measure, independent of particular machines. Through different compilers, programs can be made to run on a variety of computers, existing or yet to be invented. All in all, compilers facilitate the business of writing programs for computers to execute. The kind of compiler to be described here confers practical benefits on the linguist by facilitating the business of obtaining parsing grammars. It does this by making the enterprise essentially indistinguishable from writing competence grammars.

It is possible to say things in the native language of a computer that never should be said, because they are either redundant or meaningless. Adding zero to a number, or calculating a value that is never used, is redundant and therefore wasteful. Attempting to divide a number by zero makes no sense and an endless cycle of operations prevents a result ever being reached. These things can almost always be assumed to be errors on the part of the programmer. Some of these errors are difficult or impossible to detect simply by inspecting the program and emerge only in the course of the actual computation. But some errors can be dealt with by simply not providing any way of committing them in the higher-level language. Thus, an expression $n/0$, meaning the result of dividing n by 0, would be deemed outside the language, and the compiler would not be able to translate a program that contained it. The general point is this: compiling can confer additional benefits when it is used to translate one language into a *subset* of another. In the case of programming languages, the idea is to exclude from the subset useless constructions.

This benefit is easy to appreciate in the linguistic case. As I have said, competence grammars are written in a formal language designed to enshrine restrictions that have been found characteristic of the human linguistic faculty, in short, linguistic universals. The guarantee that performance grammars reflect these same universals can be provided by embedding them in the language of those grammars. But it can also be provided by deriving the performance grammars from the competence grammars by means of a process that is guaranteed to preserve all important properties. The language of the performance grammar is relatively unconstrained and would allow the expression of theoretically unmotivated things, but the translation procedure ensures that only a properly motivated subset is used. This strategy clearly makes for a stronger theory by positing a close connection between competence and performance. It has the added advantage of freeing the designer of the performance formalism of any concern for matters already accounted for in the competence system.

7.1.2. Attributes and values

As I have already pointed out, functional unification grammar knows things by their *functional descriptions*, (FDs). A *simple* FD is a set of *descriptors* and a descriptor is a *constituent set*, a *pattern*, or an attribute with an associated value. I shall come to the form and function of constituent sets and patterns shortly. For the moment, we consider only attribute-value pairs.

The list of descriptors that make up an FD is written in square brackets, no significance attaching to the order. The attributes in an FD must be distinct from one another so that if an FD F contains the attribute a, it is always possible to use the phrase "the a of F" to refer unambiguously to a value.

An attribute is a *symbol*, that is, a string of letters. A value is either a symbol or another FD. The equal sign, " = ", is used to separate an attribute from its value so that, in α = β, α is the attribute and β the value. Thus, for example, (1) might be an FD, albeit a simple one, of the sentence *He saw her.*

(1)
$$
\begin{bmatrix}
\text{CAT} & = \text{S} \\[4pt]
\text{SUBJ} & = \begin{bmatrix} \text{CAT} & = \text{PRON} \\ \text{GENDER} & = \text{MASC} \\ \text{CASE} & = \text{NOM} \\ \text{NUMBER} & = \text{SING} \\ \text{PERSON} & = 3 \end{bmatrix} \\[4pt]
\text{DOBJ} & = \begin{bmatrix} \text{CAT} & = \text{PRON} \\ \text{GENDER} & = \text{FEM} \\ \text{CASE} & = \text{ACC} \\ \text{NUMBER} & = \text{SING} \\ \text{PERSON} & = 3 \end{bmatrix} \\[4pt]
\text{VERB} & = \text{SEE} \\
\text{TENSE} & = \text{PAST} \\
\text{VOICE} & = \text{ACTIVE}
\end{bmatrix}
$$

(2)
$$
\begin{bmatrix}
\text{CAT} & = \text{S} \\[4pt]
\text{PROT} & = \begin{bmatrix} \text{CAT} & = \text{PRON} \\ \text{GENDER} & = \text{MASC} \\ \text{NUMBER} & = \text{SING} \\ \text{PERSON} & = 3 \end{bmatrix} \\[4pt]
\text{GOAL} & = \begin{bmatrix} \text{CAT} & = \text{PRON} \\ \text{GENDER} & = \text{FEM} \\ \text{NUMBER} & = \text{SING} \\ \text{PERSON} & = 3 \end{bmatrix} \\[4pt]
\text{VERB} & = \text{SEE} \\
\text{TENSE} & = \text{PAST}
\end{bmatrix}
$$

If the values of SUBJ and DOBJ are reversed in (1), and the value of VOICE changed to PASSIVE, it becomes an FD for the sentence *She was seen by him.* However, in both this and the original sentence, *he* is the protagonist (PROT), or logical subject, and *she* the goal (GOAL) of the action, or logical direct object. In other words, both sentences are equally well described by (2). In the sense of transformational grammar (2) shows a *deeper* struc-

(3)

$$
\begin{bmatrix}
\text{CAT} & = \text{S} \\[4pt]
\text{SUBJ} = \text{PROT} = &
\begin{bmatrix}
\text{CAT} & = \text{PRON} \\
\text{GENDER} & = \text{MASC} \\
\text{CASE} & = \text{NOM} \\
\text{NUMBER} & = \text{SING} \\
\text{PERSON} & = 3
\end{bmatrix} \\[4pt]
\text{DOBJ} = \text{GOAL} = &
\begin{bmatrix}
\text{CAT} & = \text{PRON} \\
\text{GENDER} & = \text{FEM} \\
\text{CASE} & = \text{ACC} \\
\text{NUMBER} & = \text{SING} \\
\text{PERSON} & = 3
\end{bmatrix} \\[4pt]
\text{VERB} & = \text{SEE} \\
\text{TENSE} & = \text{PAST} \\
\text{VOICE} & = \text{ACTIVE}
\end{bmatrix}
$$

ture than (1). However, in functional unification grammar, if a given linguistic entity has two different FDs, a single FD containing the information in both can be constructed by the process of *unification*, which we shall examine in detail shortly. The FD (3) results from unifying (1) and (2).

A pair of FDs is said to be *incompatible* if they have a common attribute with different symbols, or incompatible FDs, as values. Grammatically ambiguous sentences have two or more incompatible FDs. Thus, for example, the sentence *He likes writing books* might be described by (4) or (5). Incompatible simple FDs $F_1 \cdots F_k$ can be combined into a single *complex* FD $\{F_1 \cdots F_k\}$ which describes the union of the sets of objects that its components describe. The notation allows common parts of components to be factored in the obvious way, so that (6) describes all those objects that are described by *either* (4) or (5).

The use of braces to indicate alternation between incompatible FDs or sub-FDs provides a compact way of describing large classes of disparate objects. In fact, as we shall see, given a few extra conventions, it makes it possible to claim that the grammar of a language is nothing more than a single complex FD.

7.1.3. Unification

A string of atoms enclosed in angle brackets constitutes a *path* and there is at least one that identifies every value in an FD. The path $\langle a_1\, a_2 \cdots a_k \rangle$ identifies the value of the attribute a_k in the FD that is the value of $\langle a_1 a_2$

$\cdots a_{k-1}\rangle$. It can be read as *The a_k of the a_{k-1} $\cdots$ of the*

(4)
$$
\begin{bmatrix}
\text{CAT} & = \text{S} \\
\text{SUBJ} & = \text{he} \\
\text{DOBJ} & = \begin{bmatrix}
\text{CAT} & = \text{NP} \\
\text{HEAD} & = \text{books} \\
\text{MOD} & = \begin{bmatrix} \text{CAT} = \text{PRESP} \\ \text{LEX} = \text{WRITE} \end{bmatrix}
\end{bmatrix} \\
\text{VERB} & = \text{LIKE} \\
\text{TENSE} & = \text{PRES} \\
\text{VOICE} & = \text{ACTIVE}
\end{bmatrix}
$$

(5)
$$
\begin{bmatrix}
\text{CAT} & = \text{S} \\
\text{SUBJ} & = \text{he} \\
\text{DOBJ} & = \begin{bmatrix}
\text{CAT} & = \text{NP} \\
\text{HEAD} & = \begin{bmatrix}
\text{CAT} & = \text{S} \\
\text{VERB} & = \begin{bmatrix} \text{CAT} = \text{PRESP} \\ \text{LEX} = \text{WRITE} \end{bmatrix} \\
\text{DOBJ} & = \begin{bmatrix} \text{CAT} & = \text{NP} \\ \text{HEAD} & = \text{books} \end{bmatrix}
\end{bmatrix}
\end{bmatrix} \\
\text{VERB} & = \text{LIKE} \\
\text{TENSE} & = \text{PRES} \\
\text{VOICE} & = \text{ACTIVE}
\end{bmatrix}
$$

(6)
$$
\begin{bmatrix}
\text{CAT} & = \text{S} \\
\text{SUBJ} & = \text{he} \\
\text{DOBJ} & = \left\{
\begin{bmatrix}
\text{CAT} = \text{NP} \\
\begin{bmatrix}
\text{HEAD} = \text{books} \\
\text{MOD} = \begin{bmatrix} \text{CAT} = \text{PRESP} \\ \text{LEX} = \text{WRITE} \end{bmatrix}
\end{bmatrix}
\end{bmatrix}
\begin{bmatrix}
\text{HEAD} = \begin{bmatrix}
\text{CAT} = \text{S} \\
\text{VERB} = \begin{bmatrix} \text{CAT} = \text{PRESP} \\ \text{LEX} = \text{WRITE} \end{bmatrix} \\
\text{DOBJ} = \begin{bmatrix} \text{CAT} = \text{NP} \\ \text{HEAD} = \text{books} \end{bmatrix}
\end{bmatrix}
\end{bmatrix}
\right\} \\
\text{VERB} & = \text{LIKE} \\
\text{TENSE} & = \text{PRES} \\
\text{VOICE} & = \text{ACTIVE}
\end{bmatrix}
$$

a_1. Paths are always interpreted as beginning in the largest FD that encloses them. Attributes are otherwise taken as belonging to the smallest enclosing FD. Accordingly,

(7) $\quad [A = [B = \langle C \rangle = X]] \equiv \begin{bmatrix} A = [B=X] \\ C = \langle A\ B \rangle \end{bmatrix}$

A pair consisting of a path in an FD and the value that the path leads to is a *feature* of the object described. If the value is a symbol, the pair is a *basic feature* of the FD. Any FD can be represented as a list of basic features. For example, (8) can be represented by the list (9).

It is in the nature of FDs that they blur the usual distinction between features and structures. Example (8) shows FDs embedded in other FDs, thus stressing their structural properties. Rewriting (8) as (9) stresses the componential nature of FDs.

It is the possibility of viewing FDs as unstructured sets of features that makes them subject to the standard operations of set theory. However, it is also a crucial property of FDs that they are not *closed* under set-

(8)

$$
\begin{bmatrix}
\text{CAT} & = \text{S} \\[4pt]
\text{SUBJ} = \text{PROT} = \begin{bmatrix} \text{CAT} & = \text{PRON} \\ \text{GENDER} & = \text{MASC} \\ \text{CASE} & = \text{NOM} \\ \text{NUMBER} & = \text{SING} \\ \text{PERSON} & = 3 \end{bmatrix} \\[4pt]
\text{DOBJ} = \text{GOAL} = \begin{bmatrix} \text{CAT} & = \text{PRON} \\ \text{GENDER} & = \text{FEM} \\ \text{CASE} & = \text{ACC} \\ \text{NUMBER} & = \text{SING} \\ \text{PERSON} & = 3 \end{bmatrix} \\[4pt]
\text{VERB} = \begin{bmatrix} \text{CAT} & = \text{VERB} \\ \text{WORD} & = \text{SEE} \end{bmatrix} \\[4pt]
\text{TENSE} & = \text{PAST} \\
\text{VOICE} & = \text{ACTIVE} \\
\text{ASPECT} = \begin{bmatrix} \text{PERFECT} & = + \\ \text{PROGRESSIVE} & = - \end{bmatrix}
\end{bmatrix}
$$

theoretic operations. Specifically, the union of a pair of FDs is not, in general, a well-formed FD. The reason is this: The requirement that a given attribute appear only once in an FD implies a similar constraint on the set of features corresponding to an FD. A path must uniquely identify a value. But, if the FD F_1 has the basic feature $\langle \alpha \rangle = x$ and the FD F_2 has the basic feature $\langle \alpha \rangle = y$, then either $x = y$ or F_1 and F_2 are incompatible and their union is not a well-formed FD. So, for example, if F_1 describes a sentence with a singular subject and F_2 describes a sentence with a plural subject, then $S_1 \cup S_2$, where S_1 and S_2 are the corresponding sets of basic features, is not well formed because it would contain $\langle \text{SUBJ NUMBER} \rangle = \text{SINGULAR}$ and $\langle \text{SUBJ NUMBER} \rangle = \text{PLURAL}$.

When two or more simple FDs are compatible, they can be combined into one simple FD describing those things that they both describe, by the process of unification. Unification is the same as set union except that it yields the null set when applied to incompatible arguments. The "$=$" sign is used for unification, so that $\alpha = \beta$ denotes the result of unifying α and β. Examples (10)–(12) show the results of unification in some simple cases.

(9)

$$\langle CAT \rangle = S$$

$$\langle SUBJ\ CAT \rangle = PRON$$

$$\langle SUBJ\ GENDER \rangle = MASC$$

$$\langle SUBJ\ CASE \rangle = NOM$$

$$\langle SUBJ\ NUMBER \rangle = SING$$

$$\langle SUBJ\ PERSON \rangle = 3$$

$$\langle PROT\ CAT \rangle = PRON$$

$$\langle PROT\ GENDER \rangle = MASC$$

$$\langle PROT\ CASE \rangle = NOM$$

$$\langle PROT\ NUMBER \rangle = SING$$

$$\langle PROT\ PERSON \rangle = 3$$

$$\langle OBJ\ CAT \rangle = PRON$$

$$\langle OBJ\ GENDER \rangle = FEM$$

$$\langle OBJ\ CASE \rangle = ACC$$

$$\langle OBJ\ NUMBER \rangle = SING$$

$$\langle OBJ\ PERSON \rangle = 3$$

$$\langle GOAL\ CAT \rangle = PRON$$

$$\langle GOAL\ GENDER \rangle = FEM$$

$$\langle GOAL\ CASE \rangle = FEM$$

$$\langle GOAL\ NUMBER \rangle = SING$$

$$\langle GOAL\ PERSON \rangle = 3$$

$$\langle VERB\ CAT \rangle = VERB$$

$$\langle VERB\ WORD \rangle = SEE$$

$$\langle TENSE \rangle = PAST$$

$$\langle VOICE \rangle = ACTIVE$$

$$\langle ASPECT\ PERFECT \rangle = +$$

$$\langle ASPECT\ PROGRESSIVE \rangle = -$$

The result of unifying a pair of complex FDs is, in general, a complex FD with one term for each compatible pair of terms in the original FDs. Thus $\{a_1 \cdots a_n\} = \{b_1 \cdots b_m\}$ becomes an FD of the form $\{c_1 \cdots c_k\}$ in which each c_h ($1 \le h \le k$) is the result of unifying a compatible pair $a_i = b_j$ ($1 \le i \le m$, $1 \le j \le n$). This is exemplified in (13).

(10)
$$
\begin{bmatrix} \text{CAT} & = \text{VERB} \\ \text{LEX} & = \text{RUN} \\ \text{TENSE} & = \text{PRES} \end{bmatrix} = \begin{bmatrix} \text{CAT} & = \text{VERB} \\ \text{NUM} & = \text{SING} \\ \text{PERS} & = 3 \end{bmatrix} \Rightarrow \begin{bmatrix} \text{CAT} & = \text{VERB} \\ \text{LEX} & = \text{RUN} \\ \text{TENSE} & = \text{PRES} \\ \text{NUM} & = \text{SING} \\ \text{PERS} & = 3 \end{bmatrix}
$$

(11)
$$
\begin{bmatrix} \text{CAT} & = \text{VERB} \\ \text{LEX} & = \text{RUN} \\ \text{TENSE} & = \text{PRES} \end{bmatrix} = \begin{bmatrix} \text{CAT} & = \text{VERB} \\ \text{TENSE} & = \text{PAST} \\ \text{PERS} & = 3 \end{bmatrix} \Rightarrow \text{NIL}
$$

(12)
$$
\begin{bmatrix} \text{PREP} = \text{MIT} \\ \text{CASE} = \text{DAT} \end{bmatrix} = \begin{bmatrix} \text{CAT} & = \text{PP} \\ \text{HEAD} & = \begin{bmatrix} \text{CAT} & = \text{NP} \\ \text{CASE} & = \langle\text{CASE}\rangle \end{bmatrix} \end{bmatrix} \Rightarrow \begin{bmatrix} \text{CAT} & = \text{PP} \\ \text{PREP} & = \text{MIT} \\ \text{CASE} & = \text{DAT} \\ \text{HEAD} & = \begin{bmatrix} \text{CAT} & = \text{NP} \\ \text{CASE} & = \langle\text{CASE}\rangle \end{bmatrix} \end{bmatrix}
$$

(13)
$$\left\{ \begin{matrix} \begin{bmatrix} \text{TENSE} & = & \text{PRES} \\ \text{FORM} & = & \text{is} \end{bmatrix} \\ \begin{bmatrix} \text{TENSE} & = & \text{PAST} \\ \text{FORM} & = & \text{was} \end{bmatrix} \end{matrix} \right\} = \begin{bmatrix} \text{CAT} & = & \text{VERB} \\ \text{TENSE} & = & \text{PAST} \end{bmatrix} \Rightarrow \begin{bmatrix} \text{CAT} & = & \text{VERB} \\ \text{TENSE} & = & \text{PAST} \\ \text{FORM} & = & \text{was} \end{bmatrix}$$

Unification is the fundamental operation underlying the analysis and synthesis of sentences using functional unification grammar.

It is important to understand the difference between saying that a pair of FDs are *equal* and saying that they are *unified*. Clearly, when a pair of FDs has been unified, they are equal; the inverse is not generally true. To say that a pair of FDs A and B are unified is to say that A and B are *two names for one and the same description*. Consequently, if A is unified with C, the effect is to unify A, B, and C. On the other hand, if A and B, though possibly equal, are not unified, then unifying A and C does not affect B and, indeed, if A and C are not equal, a result of the unification will be to make A and B different. A crucial consequence of this is that the result of unifying various pair of FDs is independent of the order in which the operations are carried out. This, in its turn, makes for a loose coupling between the grammatical formalism as a whole and the algorithms that use it.

7.1.4. Patterns and constituent sets

We come now to the question of recursion in the grammar and how constituency is represented. I have already remarked that functional unification grammar deliberately blurs the distinction between structures and sets of features. It is clear from the examples we have considered so far that some parts of the FD of a phrase typically belong to the phrase as a whole, whereas others belong to its constituents. For example, in (8), the value of SUBJ is the FD of a constituent of the sentence, whereas the value of ASPECT is not. The purpose of constituent sets and patterns is to identify constituents and to state constraints on the order of their occurrence. Example (14) is a version of (8) that specifies the order. (SUBJ VERB DOBJ) is a pattern stating that the values of the attributes SUBJ, VERB, and DOBJ are FDs of constituents and that they occur in that order. As the example illustrates, patterns appear in FDs as the values of attributes. In general, the value is a list of patterns, and not just one as in (14). The attribute *pattern* is distinguished, its value being the one used to determine the order of the immediate constituents of the item being described. The attribute *C-set* is also distinguished, its value being a single list of paths identifying the immediate constituents of the current item, but imposing

(14)

$$
\begin{bmatrix}
\text{C-set} & = & \text{(SUBJ VERB OBJ)} \\[4pt]
\text{Pattern} & = & \text{(SUBJ VERB OBJ)} \\[4pt]
\text{CAT} & = & \text{S} \\[4pt]
\text{SUBJ = PROT} & = & \begin{bmatrix} \text{CAT} & = & \text{PRON} \\ \text{GENDER} & = & \text{MASC} \\ \text{CASE} & = & \text{NOM} \\ \text{NUMBER} & = & \text{SING} \\ \text{PERSON} & = & 3 \end{bmatrix} \\[4pt]
\text{DOBJ = GOAL} & = & \begin{bmatrix} \text{CAT} & = & \text{PRON} \\ \text{GENDER} & = & \text{FEM} \\ \text{CASE} & = & \text{ACC} \\ \text{NUMBER} & = & \text{SING} \\ \text{PERSON} & = & 3 \end{bmatrix} \\[4pt]
\text{VERB} & = & \begin{bmatrix} \text{CAT} & = & \text{VERB} \\ \text{WORD} & = & \text{SEE} \end{bmatrix} \\[4pt]
\text{TENSE} & = & \text{PAST} \\[4pt]
\text{VOICE} & = & \text{ACTIVE} \\[4pt]
\text{ASPECT} & = & \begin{bmatrix} \text{PERFECT} & = & + \\ \text{PROGRESSIVE} & = & - \end{bmatrix}
\end{bmatrix}
$$

no order on them. Here, as elsewhere in the formalism, one-step paths can be, and usually are, written without enclosing angle-brackets.

The patterns are templates that the string of immediate constituents must match. Each pattern is a list whose members can be

1. *A path.* The path may have as its value
    a. *An FD.* As in the case of the constituent set, the FD describes a constituent.
    b. *A pattern.* The pattern is inserted into the current one at this point.
2. *A string of dots.* This matches any number of constituents.
3. *The symbol #.* This matches any one constituent.
4. *An FD.* This will match any constituent whose description is unifiable with it. The unification is made with a *copy* of the FD in the pattern, rather than with the FD itself, because the intention is to impute its properties to the constituent, but not to unify all the constituents that match this part of the pattern.
5. *An expression of the form (* fd), where fd is an FD.* This matches zero or more constituents, provided they can all be unified with a copy of *fd*.

The ordering constraints in (14) could have been represented by many other sets of patterns, for example, those in (15).

(15) (SUBJ VERB ⋯) (⋯ VERB DOBJ)
      (SUBJ ⋯ DOBJ) (⋯ VERB ⋯)
      (⋯ SUBJ ⋯ DOBJ) (# VERB ⋯)
      (⋯ SUBJ ⋯ VERB ⋯ DOBJ)
      (⋯ SUBJ ⋯ VERB ⋯) (⋯ DOBJ)

The pattern (16) requires exactly one constituent to have the property [TRACE = NP]; all others must have the property [TRACE = NONE].

(16) ((* [TRACE = NONE]) [TRACE = NP] (* [TRACE = NONE]))

Clearly, patterns, like attribute-value pairs, can be incompatible thus preventing the unification of FDs. This is the case in examples in (17).

(17) (⋯ SUBJ ⋯ VERB ⋯) (⋯ VERB ⋯ SUBJ ⋯)
      (# SUBJ ⋯) (SUBJ ⋯)
      (⋯ SUBJ VERB ⋯) (⋯ SUBJ DOBJ ⋯)

The last of these could be a compatible pair just in case VERB and DOBJ were unified, but the names suggest that the first would have the feature [CAT = VERB] and the other [CAT = NP], ruling out this possibility.

The value of the *C-set* attribute covers all constituents. If two FDs are unified, and both have *C-set* attributes, the *C-set* attribute of the result is the intersection of these. If a member of the pair has no such attribute, the value is taken from the other member. In other words, the universal set of constituents can be written by simply omitting the attribute altogether. If there are constituents, but no patterns, then there are no constraints on the order in which the constituents can occur. If there are patterns, then each of the constituents must be assimilated to all of them.

7.1.5. Grammar

A functional unification grammar is a single FD. A sentence is well formed if a constituent-structure tree can be assigned to it each of whose nodes is labeled with an FD that is compatible with the grammar. The immediate descendents of each node must be properly specified by constituent-sets and patterns.

Generally speaking, grammars will take the form of alternations, each clause of which describes a major category; that is, they will have the form exhibited in (18).

(18)
$$\left\{ \begin{array}{l} \begin{bmatrix} \text{CAT} = c_1 \\ \quad\quad\vdots \end{bmatrix} \\ \begin{bmatrix} \text{CAT} = c_2 \\ \quad\quad\vdots \end{bmatrix} \\ \begin{bmatrix} \text{CAT} = c_3 \\ \quad\quad\vdots \end{bmatrix} \\ \quad\quad\vdots \end{array} \right\}$$

Example (19) shows a simple grammar, corresponding to a context-free grammar containing the single rule (20).

(19)
$$
\left\{
\begin{array}{l}
\left[
\begin{array}{l}
\text{(SUBJ VERB . . .)} \\
\text{CAT} = \text{S} \\
\text{SUBJ} = [\text{CAT} = \text{NP}] \\
\left\{
\begin{array}{l}
[\text{SCOMP} = \text{NONE}] \\
\left[
\begin{array}{l}
\text{(· · · SCOMP)} \\
\text{SCOMP} = [\text{CAT} = \text{S}]
\end{array}
\right]
\end{array}
\right\}
\end{array}
\right] \\
[\text{CAT} = \text{NP}] \\
[\text{CAT} = \text{VERB}]
\end{array}
\right\}
$$

(20) S → NP VERB (S)

FD (19) describes *either* sentences *or* verbs *or* noun phrases. Nothing is said about the constituency of the verbs or noun phrases described – they are treated as terminal constituents. The sentences have either two or three constituents depending on the choice made in the embedded alternation. All constituents must match the FD (19). Since the first constituent has the feature [CAT = NP], it can only match the second term in the main alternation. Likewise, the second constituent can only match the third term. If there is a third constituent, it must match the first term in the alternation, because it has the feature [CAT = S]. It must therefore also have two or three constituents also described by (19). If (19) consisted only of the first term in the outer alternation, it would have a null extension because the first term, for example, would be required to have the incompatible features [CAT = NP] and [CAT = S]. On the other hand, if the inner alternation were replaced by its second term, so that [SCOMP = NONE] were no longer an option, then the FD would correspond to the rule (21), whose derivations do not terminate.

(21)   S → NP VERB S

7.2. The parser

7.2.1. The General Syntactic Processor

As I said at the outset, the transducer that is used for generating sentences operates on grammars in essentially the form in which they have been given here. The process is quite straightforward. The input is an FD that constitutes the specification of a sentence to be uttered. The more detail it contains, the more closely it constrains the sentence that will be produced. The transducer attempts to unify this FD with the grammar. If this cannot be done – that is, if it produces a null result because of incompatibilities between the two descriptions – there is no sentence in the language that meets the specification. If the unification is successful, the result will, in general, be to add detail to the FD originally provided. If the FD that results from this step has a constituent set, the process is repeated, unifying each constituent in turn with the grammar. A constituent that has no constituents of its own is a terminal that must match some entry in the lexicon.

Parsing is by no means so straightforward. Grammars, as I have characterized them, do not, for example, enable one to discern, in any immediate way, what properties the first or last word of a sentence might have. It is mainly for this reason that a compiler is required to convert the grammar into a new form. Compilation will result in a set of *procedures*, or miniature programs, designed to be embedded in a general parsing program that will call upon it at the appropriate time.

The general program, a version of the *General Syntactic Processor*, has been described in several places. The basic idea on which it is based is this. There are two principal data structures, the *chart*, and the *agenda*. The chart is a directed graph each of whose edges maps onto a substring of the sentence being analyzed. The chart therefore contains a vertex for each of the possible end points of such substrings, $k + 1$ vertices for a sentence of k words. Vertices are directed from left to right. The only loops that can occur consist of single edges incident from and to the same vertex.

Each word in the sentence to be parsed is represented by an edge labeled with an FD obtained by looking that word up in the lexicon. If the word is ambiguous, that is, if it has more than one FD, it is represented by more than one edge. All the edges for the ith word clearly go from vertex $i - 1$ to vertex i. As the parser identifies higher order constituents, edges with the appropriate FDs are added to the chart. A particular analysis is complete when an edge is added from the first to the last vertex and labeled with a suitable FD, say one with the feature [CAT = S].

The edges just alluded to are all *inactive*; they represent words and phrases. *Active* edges each represent a step in the recognition process. Suppose a phrase with c constituents is recognized. Since the only knowledge the parser has of words and phrases is recorded in the chart, it must be the case that the constituent edges are entered in the chart before the process of recognizing the phrase is complete, though the recognition process can clearly get underway before they are all there. If the phrase begins at vertex v_i, the chart will contain c vertices (possibly among others) beginning at v_i, each ending at a vertex where one of the constituents ends. The one that ends where the final constituent ends is the one that represents the phrase itself. That one is inactive. The remainder are *active* edges and each records what is known about a phrase when only the first of so many of its constituents have been seen, and also what action must be taken to incorporate the next constituent to the right. The label on an active edge therefore has two parts, an FD describing what is known about the putative phrase, and a *procedure* that will carry the recognition of the phrase one step further forward. It is these procedures that constitute the parsing grammar and that the compiler is responsible for constructing.

Parsing proceeds in a series of steps in each of which the procedure on an active edge is applied to a pair of FDs, one coming from that same active edge, and the other from an inactive edge that leaves the vertex where the active edge ends. In other words, if a and i are an active and an inactive edge respectively, a being incident to the vertex that i is incident from, the step consists in evaluating $P_a(f_a, f_i)$, where f_a and f_i are the FDs on a and i, and P_a is the procedure. The step is successful if f_i meets the the requirements that P_a makes of it, one of which is to unify it with the value of some path in a copy of f_a. This copy then becomes part of the label on a new edge beginning where f_a begins and ending where f_i ends. The requirements imposed on f_i, the path in the copy of f_a with which it is unified, and the procedure to be incorporated in the label of the new edge, are all built in to P_a. The last step completes the recognition of a phrase, and the new edge that is produced is inactive and therefore has no procedure in its label.

This process is carried out for every pair consisting of an active followed by an inactive edge that comes to be part of the chart. Each successful step leads to the introduction of one new edge, but this edge may result in several new pairs. Each new pair produced therefore becomes a new item on the agenda which serves as a queue of pairs waiting to be processed.

The initial step in the recognition of a phrase is one in which the active member of the pair is incident from and to the same vertex – the same vertex from which the inactive edge is also incident. This is reasonable because active edges are like a snapshot of the process of recognizing a phrase when it is still incomplete. The initial active edge is therefore a snapshot of the process before any work has been done. These edges constitute the only cycles in the chart. Their labels clearly contain a process, but no FD. The question that remains to be answered is how these initial active edges find their way into the chart.

Suppose the first step in the recognition of all phrases, of whatever type, is carried out by a single procedure. I leave open, for the moment, the question of whether this is true of the output of the functional grammar compiler. This process will be the only one that is ever found in the label of initial, looping, active edges. If a looping edge is introduced at every vertex in the chart labeled with this process, then the strategy I have outlined will clearly cause all substrings of the string that are phrases to be analyzed as such, and all the analyses of the string as a whole will be among them. This technique corresponds to what is sometimes called undirected, bottom-up parsing.[1] If there is a number of different processes that can begin the recognition of a phrase, then a loop must be introduced for each of them at each vertex. Undirected top-down parsing is modeled by a strategy in which the only loops introduced initially are at the first vertex and the procedures in their labels are those that can initiate the search for a sentence. Others are introduced as follows: when the FD that a given procedure is looking for on an inactive edge corresponds to a phrase rather than a lexical item, and there is no loop at the relevant vertex that would initiate the search for a phrase of the required type, one is created.

7.2.2. The parsing grammar

The parsing grammar, as we have seen, takes the form of a set of procedures, each of which operates on a pair of FDs. One of these FDs, the *matrix FD*, is a partial description of a phrase, and the other, the *constituent FD*, is as complete a description as the parser will ever have of a candidate for inclusion as constituent of that phrase. There may be various ways in which the constituent FD can be incorporated. Suppose, for example, that the matrix is a partial FD of a noun phrase and that it already contains the description of a determiner. Suppose, further, that the edge representing the determiner ends where the current active edge ends. The current procedure will therefore be a specialist in noun-phrase constituents that follow initial determiners. Offered a constituent FD that describes an adjective, it will incorporate it into the matrix FD as a modifier and create a new active edge whose label may contain itself – on the theory that what can follow a determiner can also follow a determiner and an adjective. But, if the constituent FD describes a noun, that must be incorporated into the matrix as its head. At least two new edges will be produced in this case, an inactive edge representing a complete noun phrase and an active edge labeled with a procedure that specializes in incorporating prepositional phrases and relative clauses.

We have seen that the process of recognizing a phrase is initiated by an active edge that loops back to its starting vertex, and which has a null FD in its label. For the case of functional grammar, all such loops will be labeled with the same procedure, one capable of recognizing initial members of all constituents and building a matrix FD that incorporates them appropriately. Thus, for example, if this procedure is given a constituent FD that is a determiner description, it will put a new active edge

270   *Kay*

in the chart whose FD is a partial NP description incorporating that determiner FD.

The picture that emerges, then, is of a network of procedures, akin in many ways to an augmented transition network (ATN) (Wood, 1969). The initial procedure corresponds to the initial state and, in general, there is an arc connecting a procedure to the procedures that it can use to label the new active edges it introduces. The arc that is followed in a particular case depends on the properties that the procedure finds in the constituent FD it is applied to.

Consider the situation that obtains in a simple English sentence in the active voice after a noun phrase, a verb, and a second noun phrase have been seen. Three different grammar procedures are involved in getting this far. Let us now consider what would face a fourth procedure. If the verb is of the appropriate kind, the question of whether the second noun phrase is the direct or the indirect object is still open. If the current constituent FD is a noun phrase, then one possible way to continue the analysis will accept that noun phrase as the direct object and the preceding one as the indirect object. But, regardless of what the constituent FD is, another possibility that must be explored is that the preceding noun phrase was in fact the direct object. Let us assume that what can follow is the same in both cases; in ATN terms, a transition is made to the same state. A grammar procedure that does this is given below in (22).

```
(22)  [1]    (PROG ((OLDMATRIX MATRIX)
      [2]           S1)
      [3]       (SELECTQ (PATH 4 CAT)
      [4]           (NP)
      [5]           (NIL (SETQ S1 T))
      [6]           (GO L1))
      [7]       (AND S1 (NEWPATH 4 CAT)
      [8]                   (QUOTE NP)))
      [9]       (ASSIGN 3 IOBJ)
      [10]      (ASSIGN 4 DOBJ)
      [11]      (TO S/DOBJ)
      [12]  L1  (SETQ MATRIX OLDMATRIX)
      [13]      (ASSIGN 3 DOBJ)
      [14]      (TO S/DOBJ)
      [15]  OUT)
```

The procedure is written in Interlisp, a general programming language, but only a very small subset of the language is used, and the salient points about the example will be readily understood with the help of the following remarks. The major idiosyncracy of the language for present expository purposes is that the name of a function or procedure, instead of being written before a parenthesized list of arguments, is written as the first item within the parentheses. So what would normally be written as $F(x)$ is written (F x).

The heart of the procedure is in lines 3 through 6, which constitute a call on the function SELECTQ. SELECTQ examines the value of the CAT attribute of the constituent FD, as specified by the first argument (PATH 4 CAT). This returns the value of the ⟨CAT⟩ path of the fourth, that is, the current constituent.[2] The SELECTQ function can have any number of arguments, and the remaining ones give the action to be taken for various values of the first one. All but the last give the action for specific values, or sets of values, and the last says what is to be done in all other cases. In (22), the specific values are NP (line 4), and NIL (line 5). The nonspecific case is given in line 6: (GO L1). Now let us examine these cases more closely.

The last case is the most straightforward. If the value of the constituent FD has some value other than NP, or NIL for its CAT attribute, then it must describe something other than a noun phrase. NP is the value it would have if it did describe a noun phrase, and NIL is a purely conventional value that the procedure finds when the attribute is absent altogether. The only other possibility is that the attribute has some other substantive value, like VP. If this happens, the instruction (GO L1) is executed, causing processing to resume at line 12. The first thing that is done here, (SETQ MATRIX OLDMATRIX), is of minor interest, and we will return to it shortly. After this, only two instructions remain, on lines 13 and 14. The effect of the first of these, (ASSIGN 3 DOBJ), is to unify the description of the third constituent of the phrase – the noun phrase immediately preceding the phrase that this procedure examines – with the value of the path DOBJ. In short, it implements the hypothesis that that constituent was the direct object. The instruction (TO S/DOBJ), intentionally reminiscent of the language of ATNs, causes a new active edge to be created, labeled with the procedure S/DOBJ.

In the remaining cases, the constituent either has, or could be given, the feature [CAT = NP]. These are the cases in which the current constituent could be the direct, and the preceding constituent the indirect, object. However, if the value of the CAT attribute of the current constituent is NIL, it must be assigned the value NP before the hypothesis is acted upon and the procedure sets the local variable S1 to T (Interlisp's own name for "true") in line 5 to remind it to do this. It is actually done in by the instructions on lines 7 and 8; if S1 has a nonnull value, the instruction (NEWPATH 4 CAT) (QUOTE NP)) is carried out, causing NP to become the new value of the CAT attribute of the constituent FD. Setting and testing the local variable S1 is an efficiency measure, enabling the cost of the NEWPATH operation to be avoided when the required value is already in place.

The instructions on lines 9 and 10 are similar to the one on line 13. They cause the third and fourth constituents to be assigned the functions IOBJ and DOBJ, respectively. (TO S/DOBJ) then causes a new active edge to be created as before. The procedure then goes on to do what it would have done in the default case described above. But it must first restore the FDs to the condition they were in when the procedure was entered, and this is the purpose of the instruction (SETQ MATRIX OLDMATRIX) on line 12.[3] The original matrix FD was preserved as the value of the temporary variable OLDMATRIX in line 1 and the constituent FD is embedded in the same data structure by a subterfuge that is best left unexamined.

If, in the case we have just examined, the grammar made no provision for constituents following the direct object, the instruction (TO S/DOBJ) appearing on lines 11 and 14 would have been replaced by (DONE). This has the effect of creating an inactive edge labeled with the current matrix FD. More realistically, the procedure should probably have both instructions in both places, on the theory that material can follow the direct object, but it is optional.

Before going on to discuss how procedures of this kind can be compiled from functional grammars, a few words are in order on why procedures like (22) have the particular structure they have. Why, in particular, is the local variable s1 used in the way it is rather than simply embedding the (NEWPATH 4 CAT) (QUOTE NP)) in the (SELECTQ) instruction? The example at (23) will help make this clear. The procedure succeeds, and a transition to the state NEXT is made, just in case the current constituent has the features [CAT = NP] and [ANIMATE = NONE]. If attribute CAT in the constituent FD has the value NIL, then as we have seen, the function NEWPATH must be called to assign the value NP to this attribute. However, there is no point in doing this if the other requirements of the constituent are not also met. Accordingly, in this case, the procedure verifies the feature [ANIMATE = NONE] before making any reassignments of values.

```
(23)   [1]    (PROG ((OLDMATRIX MATRIX)
       [2]           S2 S1)
       [3]      (SELECTQ (PATH 1 CAT)
       [4]                (NP)
       [5]                (NIL (SETQ S1 T))
       [6]                (GO OUT))
       [7]      (SELECTQ (PATH 1 ANIMATE)
       [8]                (NONE)
       [9]                (NIL (SETQ S2 T))
       [10]               (GO OUT))
       [11]     (AND S2 (NEWPATH 1 ANIMATE)
       [12]                      (QUOTE NONE)))
       [13]     (AND S1 (NEWPATH 1 CAT)
       [14]                      (QUOTE NP)))
       [15]        (TO NEXT)
       [16]   OUT)
```

A second point that may require clarification involves instructions like (ASSIGN 3 DOBJ), which can cause the assignment of constituents other than the current one to grammatical functions – attributes – in the matrix FD. In principle, all such assignments could be made when the constituent in question is current, in which case no special instruction would be required and it would not be necessary to use numbers to identify particular constituents. These devices are the cost of some considerable gains in efficiency. A situation that illustrates this is now classic in discussions of ATN grammars. Suppose that the first noun phrase in a sentence is to be assigned to the SUBJ attribute if the sentence is active, and to the DOBJ attribute if it is passive. The voice is not known at the time the noun phrase is encountered what the voice of the sentence is. A perfectly viable solution to the problem this raises is to make both assignments, in different active edges, and to unify the corresponding value with that of the VOICE attribute. When the voice is eventually determined, only the active edge with the proper assignment for the first noun phrase will be able to continue. But, in the meantime, parallel computations will have been pursued redundantly. The numbers that appear in the ASSIGN instructions serve as a temporary label and enable us to defer the decision as to the proper role for a constituent.

7.3. The compiler

The compiler has two major sections. The first part is a straightforward application of the generation program to put the grammar, effectively, into disjunctive normal form. The second is concerned with actually building the procedures.

A grammar is a complex FD, typically involving a great many alternations. As with any algebraic formula involving *and* and *or*, it can be restructured so as to bring all the alternations to the top level. In other words, if F is a grammar, or indeed any complex FD, it is always possible to recast it in the form $F_1 \lor F_2 \cdots F_n$, where the F_i $(1 \le i \le n)$ each contain no alternations. This remains true even when account is taken of the alternations implicit in patterns, for if the patterns in an FD do not impose a unique ordering on the constituents, then each allowable order is a different alternative.

Now, the process of generation from a particular FD, f, effectively selects those members of $F_1 \cdots F_n$ that can be unified with f, and then repeats this procedure recursively for each constituent. But F is, in general, a conjunct containing some atomic terms and some alternations. Ignoring patterns for the moment, the procedure is as follows:

1. Unify the atomic terms of F with f. If this fails, the procedure as a whole fails. Some number of alternations now remain to be considered. In other words, that part of F that remains to be unified with f is an expression F' of the form $(a_{1,1} \lor a_{1,2} \cdots a_{1,k_1}) \land (a_{2,1} \lor a_{2,2} \cdots a_{2,k_2}) \cdots (a_{n,1} \lor a_{n,2} \cdots a_{n,k_n})$.

2.   Rewrite as an alternation by *multiplying out* the terms of an arbitrary alternation in F', say the first one. This gives an expression F'' of the form $(a_{1,1} \wedge (a_{2,1} \vee a_{2,2} \cdots a_{2,k_2}) \wedge (a_{n,1} \vee a_{n,2} \cdots a_{n,k_n})) \vee (a_{1,2} \wedge (a_{2,1} \vee a_{2,2} \cdots a_{2,k_2}) \wedge (a_{n,1} \vee a_{n,2} \cdots a_{n,k_n})) \cdots (a_{1,k_1} \wedge (a_{2,1} \vee a_{2,2} \cdots a_{2,k_2}) \wedge (a_{n,1} \vee a_{n,2} \cdots a_{n,k_n}))$.

3.   Apply the whole procedure (steps 1–3) separately to each conjunct in F''.

If f is null, then there are no constraints on what is generated and the effect is to enumerate all the sentences in the language, a process that presumably only terminates in trivial cases. Unconstrained generation does terminate, however, if it is applied only to a single level in the constituency hierarchy and, indeed, the effect is to generate precisely the disjunctive normal form of the grammar required by the compiler.

It remains to spell out the alternatives that are implicit in the patterns. This is quite straightforward and can be done in a separate part of the procedure applied to each of the FDs that the foregoing procedure delivers. The basic idea is to generate all permutations of the constituent set of the FD and to eliminate those that do not match all the patterns. This process, like the one just described, can be considerably streamlined. Permutations are generated in an analog of alphabetical order, so that all those that share a given prefix are produced together. But, if any such prefix itself violates the requirements of the patterns, the process is truncated and the corresponding suffixes are not generated for them.

The result of this phase of the compilation is a list of simple FDs, containing no alternations, and having either no pattern, or a single pattern that specifies the order of constituents uniquely. Those that have no pattern become lexical entries and they are of no further interest to the compiler. It seems likely that realistic grammars will give rise to lists which, though quite long, are entirely manageable. If a little care is exercised and list-processing techniques are used in a thoroughgoing manner, a great deal of structure turns out to be shared among members of the list.

When FDs are simplified in this way, an analogy between them and phrase structure rules begins to emerge. In fact, a simple FD F of this kind could readily be recast in the form $F \rightarrow F_1 \cdots F_k$ where $F_1 \cdots F_k$ are the subdescriptions identified by the terms in the pattern taken in the order given there. The analogy is not complete because the items that make up the right-hand side of such a rule cannot be matched directly against the left-hand sides of other rules. A rule of this kind can be used to expand a given item, not if its left-hand side is that item, but if it can be *unified* with it.

The second phase of the compiler centers around a procedure which, given a list of simple FDs, and an integer n, attempts to find an attribute, or path, on the basis of which the *n*th constituent of those FDs can be distinguished. In the general case, the result of this process is (1) a path *A*, (2) a set of values for *A*, each associated with the subset of the list of FDs whose *n*th constituent has that value of *A*, and (3) a residual subset of the list consisting of FDs whose *n*th constituent has no value for the attribute *A*. The procedure attempts to find a path that minimizes the size of the largest of these sets. The residual set cannot be distinguished from the other sets on the basis of the chosen path; in other words, for each member *R* of the residual set, a new member can be added to each of the other sets by adding a path with the appropriate value to a copy of *R*. The same procedure is applied to each of the resulting sets, with the same constituent number, until the resulting sets cannot be discriminated further. The overall result of this is to construct a discrimination tree that can be applied to an FD to determine in which of the members of the list it could be incorporated as the *n*th constituent.

The discrimination procedure also has the responsibility of detecting features that are shared by all the FDs in the list provided to it. For this purpose, it examines the whole FD and not just the *n*th constituent. Clearly, if the list is the result of a previous discrimination step, there will always be at least one such feature, namely the path and value on the basis of which that previous discrimination was made. The discrimination procedure thus collects almost all the information required to construct a grammar procedure. All that is lacking is information about the other procedures that a given one must nominate to label active chart edges that it produces. This in its turn is bound up with the problem reducing equivalent pairs of procedures to one. Before going on to these problems, we shall do well to examine one further example of a grammar procedure to see how the operation of the discrimination process is reflected in its structure.

The procedure below, (24), shows the reflexes of all the important parts of the procedure. It is apparent that two sets of FDs have been discriminated on the basis that the discriminating path was CAT. If the value of the path is VERB, a further discrimination is made on the basis of the TRANSITIVE attribute of the third constituent. If the constituent is a transitive verb, the next active arc will be labeled with the procedure V-TRANS, and if intransitive with V-INTRANS. If the category is AUX, the next procedure will be AUX-STATE. This discrimination is reflected in lines 5–23. Lines 3 and 4 reflect the fact that all the FDs involved have the subject in first position, and that subject is singular. The instruction (OR (UNIFY (SUBJ) (1)) (GO OUT)), for example, say that either the value of the subject attribute can be unified with the first constituent or the procedure terminates without further ado.

```
(24)  [1]    (PROG ((OLDFEATURES FEATURES)
      [2]           S1 S2)
      [3]         (OR (UNIFY (SUBJ) (1)) (GO OUT))
      [4]         (OR (UNIFY SING (SUBJ NUM)) (GO OUT))
      [5]         (SELECTQ (PATH (3 CAT))
      [6]                  (VERB (GO L2))
      [7]                  (AUX (GO L1))
      [8]                  (NIL (SETQ S1 T))
      [9]                  (GO OUT))
      [10]        (NEWPATH 3 CAT (QUOTE VERB))
      [11]  L2    (SELECTQ (PATH (3 TRANSITIVE))
      [12]                 (PLUS (GO L4))
      [13]                 (MINUS (GO L3))
      [14]                 (NIL (SETQ S2 T))
      [15]                 (GO OUT))
      [16]        (NEWPATH 3 TRANSITIVE (QUOTE PLUS))
      [17]  L4    (TO V-TRANS)
      [18]        (SETQ FEATURES OLDFEATURES)
      [19]        (AND S2 (NEWPATH 3 TRANSITIVE (QUOTE MINUS)))
      [20]  L3    (TO V-INTRANS)
      [21]        (OR S1 (GO OUT))
      [22]        (NEWPATH 3 CAT (QUOTE AUX))
      [23]  L1    (TO AUX-STATE)
      [24]  OUT)
```

It remains to discuss how a procedure is put in touch with its successor procedures. In the examples I have shown, instructions like (TO V-IN-TRANS), provide more or less mnemonic names for the procedures that will be used to label new active edges, but, in doing so, I was exercising expository license. When the time comes to insert a name like this into the procedure, the discrimination process is invoked recursively to compile the procedure in question. Having done this, it compares the result with a list of previously compiled procedures. If, as frequently happens, it finds that the same procedure has been compiled before, it uses the old name and throws away the result of the compilation just completed; otherwise it assigns a new name. The effect of this is to substantially reduce the total number of procedures required. In ATN terms, the effect is to conflate similar tails of the transition networks. If this technique were not used, the network would in fact have the form of a tree.

7.4. Conclusion

The compilation scheme just outlined is based on the view, expressed at the outset, that the competence grammar is written in a formalism with theoretical status. This is the seat of linguistic universals. Since the parsing grammar is tightly coupled to this by the compiler, the language that it is written in is of only minor theoretical interest. The obvious choice is therefore a standard programming language. It is not only relatively straightforward to compile the grammar into such a language, as I hope to have shown, but the result can then be further compiled into the language of a particular computer. The result is therefore an exceedingly efficient parser. But there is a concomitant inefficiency in the research cycle involved in developing the grammar. This comes from the fact that the compilation itself is a long and very time-consuming enterprise.

Two things can be said to mitigate this to some extent. First, the parsing and generation grammars do indeed describe exactly the same languages, so that much of the work involved in testing prototype grammars can be done with a generator that works directly and efficiently off the competence grammar. The second point is this: it is not in fact necessary to compile the whole grammar in order to obtain an entirely satisfactory parser. Suppose, for example, that every constituent is known to have a value for the attribute CAT. Some such assumption is almost always in order. Suppose, further, that a parsing grammar is compiled ignoring completely all other attributes; in other words, the compiler behaves as though any attribute-value pair in the grammar that did not mention CAT was not there at all. The resulting set of parsing procedures clearly recognizes at least all the sentences of the language intended, though possibly others in addition. However, the results of the parsing process can be unified with the original grammar to eliminate false analyses.

Notes

1. See Kay (1980) for a fuller discussion of these terms.

2. The functions PATH, NEWPATH, and ASSIGN all take an indefinite number of arguments which, since the functions are all FEXPRS, are unevaluated. The first argument is a constituent number and the remainder constitute a path.

3. Argumentative LISP programmers may find this construction unconvincing on the grounds that OLDMATRIX in fact preserves only a pointer to the data structure and not the data structure itself. They should subside, however, on hearing that the data structure is an association list and the only changes made to it involve CONSing new material on the beginning, thus masking old versions.

References

Gazdar, Gerald. 1982. Phrase structure grammar, In: Pauline Jacobson and Geoffrey K. Pullum (eds.), *The nature of syntactic processing*. Dordrecht, Holland: D. Reidel, pp. 131–86.

Kaplan, Ronald M. 1972. Augmented transition networks as psychological models of sentence comprehension. *Artificial Intelligence* 3:77–100.

　　1973. A General Syntactic Processor. In: Rustin (ed.), *Natural language processing*, Englewood Cliffs, N.J.: Prentice-Hall.

　　1978. Computational resources and linguistic theory. *Theoretical Issues in Natural Language Processing 2*.

Kay, Martin. 1973. The mind system. In: Rustin (ed.), *Natural language processing.* Englewood Cliffs, N.J.: Prentice-Hall.

1977. Morphological and syntactic analysis. In: A. Zampolli (ed.), *Syntactic structures processing.* Amsterdam: North Holland.

1979. Functional grammar. *Proceedings of the Fifth Annual Meeting of the Berkeley Linguistic Society.*

1980. *Algorithm schemata and data structures in syntactic processing.* CSL-80-12 Xerox Palo Alto Research Center.

Woods, William A. 1969. Transition network grammars for natural language analysis. *Communications of the Association for Computing Machinery* 13:591–602.

8   Parsing in a free word order language

LAURI KARTTUNEN and MARTIN KAY

We will start with a review of some facts about Finnish. The conventional wisdom about Finnish word order is that it is free because the language has a rich inflectional system. The syntactic role that a given constituent plays in the sentence is often uniquely determined by its form. It is not necessary for comprehension to mark it with position. The standard reference book on Finnish gives only one general directive concerning word order: "One should avoid ordering words in a way that may lead to a misunderstanding or give rise to distracting associations in the mind of the hearer or the reader" (Ikola, 1968:301). This conversational maxim suggests that syntax itself places no constraints on word order. This is seemingly true for major constituents at sentence level. For example, all the six possible permutations of the three words *Esa* (Sg Nom), *luki* 'read' (Past Sg 3rd), and *kirjan* 'book' (Sg Gen) are grammatical sentences in Finnish. Only the last of the six sounds a bit strange in isolation, but one can imagine contexts where it might fit.

(1)   *Esa luki kirjan.*   *Kirjan Esa luki.*   *Luki Esa kirjan.*
       Esa kirjan luki.   *Kirjan luki Esa.*   *?Luki Kirjan Esa.*

       Esa read a/the book.

The looseness of ordering constraints on sentence level does not extend to all syntactic categories. The order of constituents in a noun phrase, for example, is almost as fixed in Finnish as it is in English. There are constraints on sentence level as well. They just happen not to rule out any of the permutations in a case as simple as (1). The fact that one can distinguish the subject from the object in these examples by looking at the case endings is certainly not unrelated to the fact that the language allows the order to vary, but the two properties do not always go together.

It would be a mistake to conclude from this data that the order does not matter. In fact it matters a great deal. Although the examples in (1) are equivalent in the sense that they express the same proposition, it is obvious to anyone who speaks the language that these sentences are generally not interchangeable. In particular discourse situations some sound

279

more natural than others. There are also intonational differences. We leave out the last example because we are not sure of its status. The remaining five seem to fall naturally into two groups. We have tried to find translations that have roughly the same conversational function in English as their counterparts in Finnish.

(2) NEUTRAL: (a) *Esa luki kirjan.*   Esa read a book.
                    (b) *Kirjan luki Esa.*   The book was read by
                                                 Esa.
    CONTRASTIVE: (c) *ESA kirjan luki.*   It was ESA who read the
                                                 book.
                    (d) *KIRJAN Esa luki.*   It was a BOOK that Esa
                                                 read.
                    (e) *LUKI Esa kirjan.*   Esa DID read a book.

The capitals here indicate that the contrastive sentences seem to require an emphatic stress and intonation peak on their first constituent. The presence and the location of emphasis in (2c–e) is made obligatory by word order. These sentences sound distinctly un-Finnish if one emphasizes some noninitial constituent: ?*Esa KIRJAN luki.* ?*Esa kirjan LUKI.* (Heinamaki, 1980). In that respect (2a,b) are different. They allow optional emphasis on any constituent: e.g., *ESA luki kirjan, Kirjan LUKI Esa, Esa luki KIRJAN,* etc.

There are also subtler differences. Although the examples in (2a,b) are synonymous, and in some intuitive sense *neutral*, they address different topics. Sentence (2a) would be a natural answer to the question *What did Esa read?*; (2b) would sound right only as an answer to *Who read the book?* In contexts where there is no recent mention of either Esa or the book, for example, in answering a question like *What happened?*, (2a) sounds more natural.

In Finnish word order and emphasis obviously encode distinctions that in English are associated with other sorts of structural differences. The alternation between the SVO and OVS orders in (2a) and (2b) has intuitively very much the same feel to it as the difference between active and passive in English. The two sentences express the same fact but differ with respect to how that fact is viewed, whether it is seen as a fact about Esa or as a fact about the book. We use the term *topic* to describe the discourse function of the first constituent in (2a,b). Another word for the same concept is *theme*.[1]

The conclusion that we draw from examples of this sort is that it would not be very interesting to write a grammar for Finnish that postulates some fixed underlying order from which various surface orders are generated by means of an uninterpreted scrambling transformation. It would be equally unilluminating to account for the variation by means of numerous phrase structure rules even if they are derived from a small set of basic rules in a systematic way. In either case one is left with the task of indicating how the ultimate surface configurations differ from one another with regard to topic, emphasis, and other such matters. It is not difficult to produce a grammar that generates all the possible orders. It is more challenging to try to explain what the different configurations express.

Discourse functions like topic are notoriously fuzzy, but they are more relevant for word order in Finnish than structural categories, such as NP, V, VP, or traditional syntactic functions, subject and object and the like. The observations we have made here are hardly new, but we are not familiar with any grammars of Finnish that successfully integrate the description of word order phenomena with the rest of syntax. The problem is particularly difficult in standard transformational grammar. In that framework basic syntactic functions are associated with fixed positions in the underlying phrase structure trees. There is no natural way to assign discourse roles, because they depend not on the application of particular transformations but on the resulting surface configuration.

It seems to us that an adequate solution should have two features. First of all, it should have a system of syntactic representation that does not assign syntactic roles exclusively on the basis of structural configurations. Second, it should provide a way to constrain configuration variation by statements that mention discourse roles in addition to principles that refer to syntactic functions and categorial properties of constituents. The framework we use has been described in a number of papers by Martin Kay under the label *functional grammar*. We refer to it here as *functional unification grammar* in order to avoid confusion with other uses of the old term and because unification plays a central role in our grammar.

The organization of this paper is as follows. First, we present some data from Finnish with an informal account of word order phenomena. Then comes a formal grammar for the same data written in the style and notation discussed in Kay's paper "Parsing in functional unification grammar" (in this volume). We illustrate the workings of the grammar by showing some output from a generator that takes as input a functional description of a sentence and produces from it every realization of the sentence that the grammar allows. Finally, we describe briefly how one turns the generator into a parser that does the reverse operation, that is, a machine that produces for any input sentence all and only the functional descriptions allowed by the grammar.

8.1. Data

Let us start by looking at the data more closely. We concentrate here on simple transitive sentences and discuss the positioning of subject and object, adverbs, and auxiliary verbs. There are of course many other types of sentences in Finnish, but the principles that determine word order do not vary significantly from one type to another.

8.1.1. Topic

The data in (2) seem to pattern as follows. Each sentence has a topic: some nominal constituent that is located immediately in front of the finite verb. In a simple transitive sentence the subject and the object noun phrase are equally eligible to serve as topics. Because it is more common in Finnish for subjects to be topics than for objects, the SVO order

(2a) *Esa luki kirjan.*   Esa read the book

is statistically more frequent than the OVS order[2]

(2b) *Kirjan luki Esa.*   The book was read by Esa.

We see no reason to assume that either one of the two sentences should be syntactically derived from the other or from some canonical underlying configuration by changing the order. It would certainly be mistaken to argue that the OVS order must be transformationally derived from SVO because it is less frequent. This would be analogous to saying that there must be a passive transformation in English because active sentences are more common than passive.

Nevertheless, a grammar of Finnish would be incomplete if it did not in some manner give preference to the SVO order. We do this by designating subject as the default topic of this construction. There are obviously many discourse contexts that are neutral with regard to the choice of topic. For example, if one is using the sentence *Esa read the book* to answer the question *What happened yesterday?*, there need not be any reason at all to take Esa as topic except a bias in the language itself. It is in such cases where default assignments play a role in determining word order. By making subject be the default topic, we give the SVO order preference over OVS whenever the context allows it. We do not assume that there is a single underlying order or an underlying pairing of syntactic and discourse roles.

It is important to recognize in this context that the assignment of default topic depends on particular constructions. For example, in existential sentences (e.g., *There are books on the table*) the subject is not the default topic in Finnish (or English) and its natural place is at the end of the sentence rather than in the beginning.

8.1.2. Contrast

In addition to a topic, a sentence may have an initial emphatic constituent that plays a different role. For the lack of a better term, we call it *contrast*.

Contrasted focus (Chafe, 1976) and *initial focus* are other names for the same function.

(2) (c) *ESA kirjan luki.*   It was ESA who read the book.
   (d) *KIRJAN Esa luki.*   It was the BOOK that Esa read.
   (e) *LUKI Esa kirjan.*   Esa DID read the book.

In some contexts it might be better to translate the first two sentences in English as *topicalized* constructions: 'By ESA the book was read', 'The BOOK Esa read'. The initial constituents in these sentences play a conversational role that is very similar to the focus NP in the cleft construction.

Like the corresponding English sentences, (2c) and (2d) implicate that the contrasted NP picks out one individual from some contextually determined set of alternatives. It does not introduce a new individual to the discourse. There is an implication that the referent and the set of other possible choices are already part of the context of discourse. By saying that the sentence is true of the particular individual, (2c) and (2d) imply it is not true of the others. For example, (2c) implicates that, of the people under consideration, only Esa read the book. (2d) suggests that Esa read just the book and not any of the other things.

It is not clear how this account should be extended to cover (2e), where the emphasis is on the verb.[3] The alternatives here consist of Esa either reading or not reading the book. Sentence (2e) is an emphatic way of saying that the former is the true one. The appearance of the finite verb in the contrast position is always a mark of disagreement. It implies that the addressee holds the opposite view.

Because of the implied contrast, sentences of this sort are commonly used in rebuttals. For example, (2d) could be uttered to deny a preceding assertion that Esa read something other than the book. It could also be used to continue a sentence like *Esa had a magazine and a book*, with the implication that Esa did not read the magazine.

Note that in a framework that postulates SVO as the underlying word order for Finnish, it would not be possible to attribute the parallel contrastive interpretations of (2c) and (2d) to any particular transformation. The SOV order in (2c) would have to be generated by a rule that moves the verb to the end of the sentence, the OSV order of (2d) by a rule that moves the object to the beginning. This is essentially what is proposed by Hakulinen and Karlsson (1979:308–9). They use the term *Topicalization* for the preposing rule and *Verb Movement* for the postposing rule. We regard this as an unfortunate choice of terminology, because it doesn't indicate that the discourse role associated with the first position in these cases is one of contrast. What intuitively is the topic (theme) of the sentence is designated not by the initial constituent but by the immediately following one. We will discuss the question of verb placement shortly.

It is interesting in this connection that the contrasted constituent can also take on a number of clitics that occur only in sentence-initial position. Of these the most important one is the question clitic-*ko* shown in (3).

(3) (a) *ESAKO kirjan luki?*   Was it ESA who read the book?
     (b) *KIRJANKO Esa luki?*   Was it a BOOK that Esa read?
     (c) *LUKIKO Esa kirjan?*   Did Esa read a book?

Only the last one is a neutral *yes/no* question; the others carry the same implication as their declarative counterparts. They present the referent of the initial NP as a member of some contextually determined range of alternatives and implicate the sentence is true only of one of them. Because the same order of constituents exists even without the question particle, there is no reason to assume that there is a special fronting rule for *yes/no* questions in Finnish. This also applies to *wh*-questions:

(4) (a) *KUKO luki kirjan?*   Who read a book?
     (b) *KUKA kirjan luki?*   Who was it who read the book?
     (c) *MINKÄ Esa luki?*   What did Esa read?

In all of these cases the same word order can be found in noninterrogative sentences.

8.1.3. Nonemphatic contrast

Sentential adverbs, such as *eilen* "yesterday" and *kotona* "at home," and *sangyssa* "in bed," can occur anywhere except between the verb and topic.

(5) (a) *Esa luki kirjan eilen.*   Esa read the book yesterday.
     (b) *Esa luki eilen kirjan.*   Esa read the book yesterday.
     (c) *??Esa eilen luki kirjan.*
     (d) *Eilen Esa luki kirjan.*   Yesterday Esa read a book.

As the last example indicates, they can also occur in contrast position preceding topic without necessarily being emphatic. In principle a sentence can contain any number of such adverbs and they can occur alone scattered in allowable adverb positions or in groups of two or more, as in (6).

(6) (a) *Eilen Esa luki kotona kirjan sangyssa.*   Yesterday Esa read at
     (b) *Esa luki eilen kotona sangyssa kirjan.*   home a book in bed.

The prosodic pattern in sentences like (5d) and (6a) is sensitive to the position of the verb. If the verb is nonfinal, as in these examples, the contrasted adverb need not carry any special emphasis. But if the verb is moved to the end of the sentence, the adverb becomes emphatic and the prosodic pattern changes accordingly.

(7) *EILEN Esa kirjan luki.*   It was YESTERDAY that Esa read the book.

Emphatic contrast signals that (7) is a rebuttal of a preceding contrary statement. Emphasis on the contrasted constituent and the final position of the verb are a sign of disagreement.

The question now arises whether examples like (2c) and (2d) have initial emphasis because they begin with a contrasted element or because they end with the verb. If it is the latter, then the sentences in (8) should be just as good as those in (9).

(8)　(a)　*Kirjan Esa luki eilen.*　　The BOOK Esa read yesterday.
　　　(b)　*?Esa kirjan luki eilen.*　It was Esa who read the book yesterday.

(9)　(a)　*KIRJAN Esa eilen luki.*　　The BOOK Esa read yesterday.
　　　(b)　*ESA kirjan eilen luki.*　　It was ESA who read the book yesterday.

The contrasted element clearly carries obligatory emphasis in (9), where the verb is final. All of the verb-final cases, (9a), (9b), and (7), are sentences that one would say only to contradict another speaker. Of the two examples in (8), where the verb is nonfinal, at least the former could be uttered without special emphasis on the first noun phrase, and it need not be a case of disagreement. It seems that the difference between emphatic and nonemphatic contrast is a matter of degree. The more emphasis there is, the stronger the suggestion that the statement would become false if the contrasted term were replaced by something else, say the term just mentioned by the other speaker.

8.1.4. *Final position*

There is a tendency in Finnish as well as English for heavy constituents to gravitate to the end of the sentence.

(10)　*Esa luki eilen Chomskyn uuden kirjan Hallitsemisesta ja Sitomisesta.*
　　　Esa read yesterday Chomsky's new book about Government and Binding.

The end is also the unmarked position for constituents that introduce some new individual or put some already mentioned character to a surprising new relation. Heavy phrases that contain a lot of descriptive material typically also introduce new things to the discourse. They could be expected to come at the end for that reason alone.

Although final noun phrases do not necessarily designate novel individuals, that is a clear preference for new things to be introduced last. This tendency is exploited in Finnish to make up for the lack of definite and indefinite articles. Because a reference to a new entity would appear in the final position, one way to mark something as old is not to mention it there. Although the two sentences in (11) are actually both ambiguous from the point of view of English, it is likely that 'the book' is the correct translation in (11a) and 'a book' in (11b).

(11)　(a)　*Esa luki kirjan eilen.*　Esa read the book yesterday.
　　　(b)　*Esa luki eilen kirjan.*　Esa read a book yesterday.

286   Karttunen and Kay

8.1.5. Order of verbs

There are two auxiliaries in Finnish: the negative verb *ei*, which is inflected for person and number but not for tense, and the verb *ole* for perfect tense. The latter is similar to *have* in English. *Ei* and *ole* control the form of the next element in the verbal chain very much as English auxiliaries do. The negative verb requires that next verb to be either a present negated form or a past participle. The choice depends on whether the tense of the sentence is present or past. The perfect auxiliary requires that the main verb be a past participle. A sentence may thus have three inflected verbs.

(12) *Esa ei ole lukenut kirjaa.*   Esa hasn't read the book.

The order is fixed: Negative < Perfect < Main Verb, but the elements do not have to be contiguous. The chain may be broken by intervening adverbs or noun phrases as in (13).

(13) *El Esa ole kirjaa lukenut.*   No, Esa hasn't read the book.

Except for the fact that *ei* and *ole* often do occur next to each other, there does not seem to be any motivation in Finnish to regard the string *ei ole* as a constituent analogous to Aux in English. There also does not seem to be any evidence for a structure involving stacked VPs or Vs. There is no phenomenon in Finnish similar to VP-deletion in English. Other elements in the sentence can freely intervene between *ei ole* and *lukenut* as long as their order remains the same. We assume that the structure is flat and consists maximally of three elements: FiniteVerb, TensedVerb, and MainVerb. The negative verb can only be FiniteVerb. If that role is played by *ole*, it is also TensedVerb at the same time, but it is never MainVerb. Anything that can serve as MainVerb can also play the other two roles. Thus in a simple sentence the same verb is simultaneously FiniteVerb, TensedVerb, and MainVerb.

It is interesting to note that it is the main verb rather than the negative or perfect auxiliary that has to appear in the final position in sentences such as (14) that show emphatic contrast.

(14) (a) *EILEN Esa oli kirjan lukenut.* It was YESTERDAY that Esa had read the book.
(b) *KIRJAA Esa ei eilen lukenut.* It was the BOOK that Esa didn't read yesterday.

8.1.6. Focus of negation

One important feature of negative sentences is that the focus of the negation may be marked by emphasis. This is the case also when the negative verb itself is in the initial contrasted position, as in (15). In that position

it carries emphasis only in the absence of any marked focus, as in (15a).
If the sentence contains an emphasis peak to mark the focus of negation
(15b–d), the negative verb itself is unstressed regardless of its position.
The data here suggest that the focus peak can be anywhere in the sentence,
but actually there are restrictions.[4]

(15) (a) *El Esa kirjaa lukenut.*   No, Esa DIDN't read a book.
      (b) *Ei ESA kirjaa lukenut.*   No, ESA didn't read the book.
      (c) *Ei Esa KIRJAA lukenut.*   No, Esa didn't read the BOOK.
      (d) *Ei Esa kirjaa LUKENUT.*   No, Esa didn't READ the book.

It is important for the semantics to distinguish the cases in (15) from
those in (16), where the sentence does contain negation but the contrast
is on some other constituent.

(16) (a) *ESA kirjaa ei lukenut.*   ESA is the one who didn't read
                                        the book.
      (b) *KIRJAA Esa ei lukenut.*   The BOOK Esa didn't read.

One indication of the difference is that (16b) could be used in a dialogue
like (17), where (15c) could not appear.

(17) Speaker A: *Esa ei lukenut lehtea.*   Esa didn't read the paper.
      Speaker B: *KIRJAA Esa ei lukenut.*   The BOOK Esa didn't read.
                 (**Ei Esa KIRJAA lukenut.*)   (No, Esa didn't read the
                                               BOOK.)

In this context (15c) would be out of place. Sentences with contrasted
negation are appropriate responses only to affirmative statements. Sentence (15c) could be used as a partial denial of (18); so could (16b).

(18) *Esa luki kirjan ja lehden.*   Esa read the book and the paper.

In a context like this one, (15c) and (16b) are equally appropriate. They
both entail that (18) is false, but only the former signals that it is in direct
conflict with the preceding statement.

Because initial negation is in many ways a special case, it may be a
mistake to view it as contrast. A better analysis remains to be worked
out.

8.1.7. Crossing clause boundaries

Objects and adverbs from infinitival and participial clauses can also appear in the beginning of the main sentence as topics or in the contrast
position, but they do not play any syntactic role in the main clause. For
example, cases like (19b) and (19c) show that the object of the infinitive

can be the topic or the contrast of the entire sentence. (There is no good English translation for sentence (19b)).

(19) (a) *Esa halusi lukea kirjan.*   Esa wanted to read the book.
      (b) *Kirjan halusi lukea Esa.*   The one who wanted to read the book was Esa.
      (c) *KIRJAN Esa lukea halusi.*   The BOOK Esa wanted to read.

More than one element can be outside of the rest of the infinitival clause, at least as long as they occupy designated positions (contrast, topic) in the main sentence. However, it does not seem possible to freely interleave constituents from infinitival clauses with elements of the main clause. Examples such as (20b) sound very marginal if not completely unacceptable.

(20) (a) *Esa halusi lukea kirjan kotona.*   Esa wanted to read the book at home.
      (b) *?Kirjan halusi kotona Esa lukea.*

If it is true that the mixing of elements from different clauses is possible only in cases like (19b) and (19c), which can be described in the same way as long-distance dependencies in English, then configurational variation in Finnish is clause-bound and affects only sister constituents. It would obviously be much harder to account for examples such as (20b), where the elements of the infinitival clause *lukea kirjan kotona* "to read the book at home" are scattered all over the main sentence. We leave the matter open for the time being.

8.1.8. Other sentence types

So far we have discussed only simple transitive sentences, because they are sufficient to illustrate all the word order phenomena that we are trying to account for in our sample grammar. There are of course many other sentence types in Finnish. The most important are as follows:

(21) Simple intransitive   *Esa nukkuu kotona.*   Esa sleeps at home.
      Impersonal transitive   *Kirja luettiin.*   The book was read.
      Impersonal intransitive   *Taalla tanssitaan.*   There is dancing here.
      Existential   *Pihalla juoksee poikia.*   There are boys running in the yard.
      Possessive   *Esalla on rahaa.*   Esa has money.
      Necessive   *Esan taytyy mukkua.*   Esa must sleep.

Each of these sentence types shows just as much variation in word order as simple transitive sentences do in accordance with the same principles. The differences arise from the fact that in some cases the default topic of the construction is something other than the subject. For example, in possessive sentences the possessor, which syntactically is an adverbial, usually plays the role of the topic. In existential sentences it is most often the locative phrase, although the subject is in principle just as eligible. Because the subjects of existential sentences typically introduce new individuals to the discourse, they tend to occur in the last position leaving the topic slot for the locative phrase. The default order for *There are boys running in the yard*, composed of *poikia* "boys" (Pl Partitive), *juoksee* "run" (Pres Sg 3rd), and *pihalla* "in the yard," is LOC V S, as shown in (21). However, the S V LOC order in (22a) and LOC S V in (22b) orders are just as grammatical.

(22) *Poikia juoksee pihalla.*   As for boys, there are some running in the yard.

   PIHALLA poikia juoksee.   It is in the YARD where there are some boys running.

In both cases the topic is boys, in the latter case the adverb is contrasted. We expect that our grammar of simple transitive sentences could easily be extended to include these types of constructions.

8.1.9. Summary

From the foregoing discussion of Finnish it is possible to disengage four propositions that are important to our present concerns.

1.   There are languages whose word order is substantially free, if, by that, we mean that once it has been established that a certain sequence of phrases constitutes a sentence, it is also known that most of their permutations have the same status.

2.   Finnish and other free word order languages also have a strong permutation property in that the members of a set of permutations are equivalent in more than simple wellformedness. In particular, they are logically equivalent, although they may differ with respect to the preferred resolution of quantifier scope ambiguities and other such matters we have not discussed here.

3.   In Finnish, and, as far as we know, in other free word order languages, the members of a set of permutations are rarely if ever equivalent in all respects. In particular, there are important functional properties relating to topic, contrast, and the distinction between given and new which distinguish them.[5] In that respect, Finnish is a configurational language.

4.   The placement of constituents may be constrained by a mixed set of criteria. Some may refer to discourse roles, others to syntactic roles or just to grammatical categories. It seems unlikely that one can make sense of the configurational variation in a language like Finnish except as an interplay of many different principles.

We distinguish two discourse roles: topic and contrast. We interpret *Topic* in the traditional way. An expression in that role serves to identify an individual or individuals that is to be tagged with the proposition expressed by the sentence. It indicates what the sentence is about. The underlying intuition is that, whenever possible, we tend to associate a proposition with some individual that it involves and view it as a fact about *Theme*, which is often used in the same sense.

There is no standard term corresponding to our *Contrast*, but similar characterizations have been given elsewhere for the role itself. There is a suggestion that the expression in that role designates one of several mutually exclusive alternatives. These may but need not be explicitly given in the discourse. By referring to only one of them, the sentence creates an implication that the others lack whatever the relevant property happens to be.

The same two discourse roles, topic and contrast, are of course just as relevant for English as they are for Finnish. Topic is one of the differences between active and passive. Contrast is needed, for example, to explain the fact that *The BOOK John read* can be used as a correction but not as a continuation to *John read the magazine*. The difference is that surface configurations in English encode syntactic relations as well as discourse functions, whereas in Finnish they are for the most part only used for the latter purpose.

Our findings about constituent order in Finnish can be summarized as follows:

(23) (a) Topic immediately precedes FiniteVerb.
      (b) Contrast (if any) is first and immediately precedes Topic.
      (c) Contrast is more emphatic if MainVerb comes last.
      (d) Only final NPs introduce new discourse referents.
      (e) FiniteVerb precedes TensedVerb, if they are distinct.
      (f) TensedVerb precedes MainVerb, if they are distinct.
      (g) Adverbs can occur in any position not ruled out by other constraints.

These principles account for the data we have considered, but we are aware that some of them need to be refined further and there are other constraints we are not going to pursue here. Instead, we will show how ordering constraints of this sort are integrated with the rest of syntax in functional unification grammar.

8.2. A unification grammar for Finnish

We use the notation described in Kay's paper in this book. In functional unification grammar, each grammatical phrase of a language has a functional representation or description (FD) consisting of attribute-value pairs. The set of possible attributes ranges from phonological to semantic properties. Here are some of the properties that appear in our grammar for Finnish.

(24) Phonological: Emphasis
     Morphological: Case, Number, Person, Tense, Voice
     Semantic: Positive, Aspect, Quantity
     Structural: Cat(egory), Pattern (alias $), Branching
     Syntactic: Subject, Object, Adverb
     Pragmatic: Topic, Contrast, New

The values can be either atomic designators (Yes, No, Nom, Sg, Past, NP, etc.) or functional descriptions. They can be designated indirectly by specifying paths that lead to them. For example, the FD of FiniteVerb might contain the pair [Number = Sg]. If the grammar requires Subject to agree with FiniteVerb in Number, then the FD of Subject may contain the pair [Number = ⟨FiniteVerb Number⟩] (pronounced: "Number is FiniteVerb's Number"). Alternatively, Subject might be specified with [Number = Sg] and FiniteVerb with [Number = ⟨Subject Number⟩]. These are equivalent ways expressing the fact that the two constituents have been unified with respect to Number.

The values of syntactic and functional attributes are typically FDs. For example, the FD of the sentence *John read the book* would contain the pair

$$(25) \quad \begin{bmatrix} \text{SUBJECT} = \begin{bmatrix} \text{CAT} = \text{NP} \\ \text{LEX} = \text{JOHN} \end{bmatrix} \end{bmatrix}$$

The similarities between our framework and lexical functional grammar (Kaplan and Bresnan, 1980) are obvious. One important difference is that in functional unification grammar the information about constituent structure is not expressed by means of phrase structure rules in the grammar. The dominance hierarchy of mother and daughter nodes is represented separately from the left-to-right order of sister nodes. The latter is encoded as the value of a special pattern attribute ($). This results in a deliberate blurring of the distinction between constituents and properties. It is not important as far as phrases are concerned, because it is a trivial matter to recover a unique phrase structure tree from a fully specified functional representation. It does make a difference in the grammar. Since patterns can be arbitrarily loose or strict with respect to order, it is easy to allow configurational variation. In that respect unification grammar is similar to the immediate-dominance/linear-precedence (ID/LP) variant of generalized phrase structure grammar (Gazdar and Pullum, 1982).

The complete functional description for *Esa slept* is given in (26).

(26)

TYPE	=	Non Terminal
Cat	=	S
$	=	((Subject) (MainVerb))
Tense	=	Past
Perfect	=	No
Positive	=	Yes
Polarity	=	Positive
Contrast	=	NONE
Topic	=	⟨Subject⟩

Subject =

TYPE	= Terminal
Cat	= NP
Quantity	= All
Nominal	= NONE
Determiner	= NONE
Branching	= No
New	= No
Emphasis	= No
ProDrop	= No
Person	= ⟨MainVerb Person⟩
Number	= ⟨MainVerb Number⟩
Case	= Nom
LEX	= Esa

FiniteVerb	=	⟨TensedVerb⟩
TensedVerb	=	⟨MainVerb⟩

MainVerb =

TYPE	= Terminal
Cat	= Verb
Tense	= Past
Positive	= Yes
Polarity	= Positive
Subject	= ⟨Subject⟩
TenseMood	= Past
Branching	= No
Person	= 3rd
Number	= Sg
Emphasis	= No
Subcat	= Intransitive
Voice	= Active
Object	= ⟨Object⟩
LEX	= sleep

Abverb	=	NONE
Branching	=	Yes
Emphasis	=	No
LEX	=	NONE
Object	=	NONE

The functional description in (26) is fully specified in the sense that it specifies a single sentence. An important feature of unification grammar is that removing parts of such specifications results in FDs that describe sets of sentences. For example, if the properties [Perfect = NO], [Positive = Yes] are left out, the resulting FD describes a set of sentences containing *Esa slept, Esa didn't sleep, Esa has slept, Esa hasn't slept*. Another way to loosen up a description is to introduce alternations. If we change (246) by replacing [Contrast = NONE] with the alternation

$$(27) \quad \left\{ \begin{array}{l} [\text{Contrast } = \text{ NONE}] \\ [\text{Contrast } = \langle \text{FiniteVerb} \rangle] \end{array} \right\}$$

we get an FD representing the set *Esa slept*, Esa DID sleep.

Loosely specified patterns that do not prescribe a unique order or constituents have the same effect as explicit alternations. For example, the pattern (... FiniteVerb ... TensedVerb ... MainVerb...) specifies that the three constituents it mentions have to occur in the given order, but they need not be contiguous. The ellipses marked by three dots match any sequence of constituents. Thus the pattern actually matches a large set of possible sequences.

One can think of a grammar as a very loose functional description that simultaneously describes all the phrases of the language. There is no formal distinction in this theory between a grammar and an FD for a single unambiguous phrase except that the latter by definition contains no alternations.

A section of our Finnish grammar is given in (28). It deals for the most part with verb inflection and subject-verb agreement. The top of the description, [Cat = S], indicates that it pertains to sentences. The first alternation says in effect that a sentence either has the property [Tense = Present] or [Tense = Past]. The second alternation forces a choice between two clusters of properties, one headed by [Positive = Yes], the second by [Positive = No]. In the former case FiniteVerb and TensedVerb are the same, in the latter case FiniteVerb is the tenseless negative verb. The last alternation in the diagram involves a choice between person (active) and impersonal (passive) voice. In the active, the sentence must have a grammatical subject with certain agreement properties. In the passive, there is no such requirement. The pattern ((#[New = No]) #1) in the middle of (28) incorporates the idea that NPs introduce new discourse referents only in the last position. It attributes the property [New = No] to all but the last immediate constituent. This is not a satisfactory solution, but it serves us here as example of a nontrivial pattern.

One way to test the correctness of a grammar of this sort is to take a partial description of a sentence and to produce from it all realizations that the grammar allows. We have used such a generator extensively in

(28)

$$
\begin{bmatrix}
\text{Cat} = \text{S} \\[4pt]
\left\{
\begin{array}{l}
\textit{Present} \\
[\text{Tense} = \text{Present}] \\
\textit{Past} \\
[\text{Tense} = \text{Past}]
\end{array}
\right\} \\[4pt]
\$ = (\ldots \text{FiniteVerb} \ldots \text{TensedVerb} \ldots \text{MainVerb} \ldots) \\[4pt]
\left\{
\begin{array}{l}
\textit{Positive} \\
\begin{bmatrix}
\text{Positive} & = \text{Yes} \\
\text{Polarity} & = \text{Positive} \\
\text{FiniteVerb} & = \text{TensedVerb}
\end{bmatrix} \\[6pt]
\textit{Negative} \\
\begin{bmatrix}
\text{Positive} = \text{No} \\
\text{Polarity} = \text{Negative} \\
\text{FiniteVerb} = \begin{bmatrix} \text{LEX} & = \text{not} \\ \text{Tense} & = \text{NONE} \end{bmatrix}
\end{bmatrix}
\end{array}
\right\} \\[4pt]
\left\{
\begin{array}{l}
\textit{NonPerfect} \\
\begin{bmatrix}
\text{Perfect} & = \text{No} \\
\text{TensedVerb} & = \text{MainVerb}
\end{bmatrix} \\[6pt]
\textit{Perfect} \\
\begin{bmatrix}
\text{Perfect} = \text{Yes} \\
\text{TensedVerb} = [\text{LEX} = \text{have}] \\
\text{MainVerb} = \begin{bmatrix} \text{Tense} & = \text{NONE} \\ \text{TenseMood} & = \text{PastPart} \\ \text{Number} & = \langle \text{TensedVerb Number} \rangle \end{bmatrix}
\end{bmatrix}
\end{array}
\right\} \\[4pt]
\$ = ((\#[\text{New} = \text{No}]) \#1) \\[4pt]
\text{FiniteVerb} = \begin{bmatrix} \text{Cat} & = \text{Verb} \\ \text{Positive} & = \langle \text{Positive} \rangle \end{bmatrix} \\[4pt]
\text{TensedVerb} = \begin{bmatrix} \text{Cat} & = \text{Verb} \\ \text{Tense} & = \langle \text{Tense} \rangle \\ \text{Positive} & = \langle \text{Positive} \rangle \\ \text{Number} & = \langle \text{FiniteVerb Number} \rangle \end{bmatrix} \\[4pt]
\text{MainVerb} = \begin{bmatrix} \text{Cat} & = \text{Verb} \\ \text{Subject} & = \langle \text{Subject} \rangle \\ \text{Object} & = \langle \text{Object} \rangle \end{bmatrix}
\end{bmatrix}
$$

$$
\left[
\left\{
\begin{array}{l}
\textit{Personal} \\
\left[
\begin{array}{l}
\text{MainVerb} = [\text{Voice} = \text{Active}] \\[4pt]
\text{Subject} =
\begin{bmatrix}
\text{Case} & = & \text{Nom} \\
\text{Number} & = & \langle\text{FiniteVerb Number}\rangle \\
\text{Person} & = & \langle\text{FiniteVerb Person}\rangle
\end{bmatrix} \\[4pt]
\$ = (\dots \text{Subject} \dots)
\end{array}
\right] \\
\textit{Impersonal} \\
\left[
\begin{array}{l}
\text{MainVerb} =
\begin{bmatrix}
\text{Voice} & = & \text{Passive} \\
\text{Number} & = & \text{Pl}
\end{bmatrix} \\[4pt]
\text{Subject} = \text{NONE}
\end{array}
\right]
\end{array}
\right\}
\right]
$$

the course of our investigation. The generator takes as input an incomplete FD and systematically explores every admissible way of expanding it. It produces a sequence of fully specified FDs from which one can extract a constituent structure tree or just a list of FDs that represent the words, as our generator does. These are turned over to another generator, which augments the stem with appropriate morphological suffixes and prints out the actual Finnish word. Our syntactic generator was written by Martin Kay; the morphological generator for Finnish is the work of Lauri Karttunen, Rebecca Root, and Hans Uszkoreit (1981).

A sample of output from the generator is given in (29). It shows (to a Finn) that the subject-verb agreement part of the grammar in (28) is descriptively adequate. The input description for the generator leaves the

(29)   Input description:

$$
\begin{bmatrix}
\text{Cat} & = \text{S} \\
\text{Tense} & = \text{Past} \\
\text{Contrast} & = \text{NONE} \\
\text{Topic} & = \langle\text{Subject}\rangle \\
\text{Subject} & =
\begin{bmatrix}
[\text{Cat} & = & \text{NP}] \\
\text{Nominal} & = &
\begin{bmatrix}
\text{Nominal} & = & [\text{LEX} = \text{child}] \\
\text{Attribute} & = & [\text{LEX} = \text{small}]]
\end{bmatrix} \\
\text{Determiner} & = & \text{NONE}
\end{bmatrix} \\
\text{Main Verb} & = [\text{LEX} = \text{sleep}] \\
\text{Object} & = \text{NONE} \\
\text{Adverb} & = \text{NONE}]
\end{bmatrix}
$$

Output:

Pieni lapsi nukkui
Pienet lapset nukkuivat
Pieni lapsi oli nukkunut
Pienet lapset olivat nukkuneet
Pieni lapsi ei nukkunut
Pienet lapset eivät nukkuneet
Pieni lapsi ei ollut nukkunut
Pienet lapset eivät olleet nukkuneet

values of Positive, Perfect, and Subject's Number unspecified. Since these three attributes are required by the grammar and each has two possible values, the generator produces eight sentences: *The small child sleeps. The small children sleep. The small child doesn't sleep*, etc. The most striking feature of the example is that the two auxiliary verbs, *ei* and *ole* that are not mentioned in the input FD at all, appear in the output where they should with the right inflectional endings.

The FD in (30) contains the part of the grammar that deals with Topic and Contrast. Except for the given/new distinction, discussed previously, it incorporates all the ordering principles listed in (23).

The section of grammar displayed in (30) consists of two alternations, one for Topic, the other for Comment. The first part says that a sentence either has a topic or it does not. The latter alternative is for constructions we have not discussed here, for example, imperatives. If there is a Topic, it can be either Subject, Object, or Adverb. The preferred choice is listed first; it is the one that the generator tries out first. (In that sense, Subject is the default selection for Topic.) Furthermore, the choice of Object or Adverb for that role is limited by an additional requirement. Either there is no Subject, or Subject serves as Contrast, or Subject introduces a new individual to the discourse. The position of Topic depends on whether FiniteVerb serves as Contrast. If it does, then FiniteVerb comes first and Topic immediately behind it. Otherwise they come in the opposite order.

The second alternation in (30) pertains to Contrast. If there is Contrast, either FiniteVerb, Subject, Object, or Adverb serves in that role. If the verb is selected, it is always emphasized. Otherwise emphasis depends on the position of the MainVerb. If MainVerb comes last, Contrast carries emphasis. The position of Contrast is immediately in front of Topic. The expression "PART(Topic NIL)(Contrast NIL)" at the end means that Contrast and Topic have to be distinct, unlike FiniteVerb, TensedVerb, and MainVerb.

As one can see by comparing the two sections of the grammar in (28) and (30), the information of the left-to-right order of constituents comes from several places in the grammar. The value of the pattern attribute typically is a list of patterns, such as (. . . MainVerb . . .), (. . . Finite-Verb . . . TensedVerb . . . MainVerb . . .), (Subject . . .), each of which

(30)

$$
\begin{bmatrix}
\begin{cases}
\begin{bmatrix}
Topic \\[4pt]
\begin{cases}
\begin{bmatrix}
[Topic = Subject] \\[4pt]
\begin{cases}
[Subject = NONE] \\
[Subject = Contrast] \\
[Subject = [New = Yes]]
\end{cases} \\[10pt]
\begin{cases}
[Topic = Object] \\
[Topic = Adverb]
\end{cases}
\end{bmatrix} \\[20pt]
\begin{cases}
No\ VerbContrast \\
[\$ = (\ldots\ Topic\ FiniteVerb\ \ldots)] \\
VerbContrast \\
[\$ = (FiniteVerb\ Topic\ \ldots)]
\end{cases}
\end{cases} \\[30pt]
\begin{matrix}
NoTopic \\
\begin{bmatrix}
Topic = NONE \\
\$\quad = (FiniteVerb\ \ldots)
\end{bmatrix}
\end{matrix}
\end{cases} \\[30pt]
\begin{cases}
\begin{matrix}
NoContrast \\
\begin{bmatrix}
Contrast = NONE \\
Emphasis = No \\
\$\quad = (Topic\ \ldots)
\end{bmatrix}
\end{matrix} \\[20pt]
\begin{matrix}
Contrast \\
\begin{cases}
\begin{matrix}
VerbContrast \\
\begin{bmatrix}
Contrast = FiniteVerb = [Emphasis = Yes] \\
Emphasis = Under
\end{bmatrix}
\end{matrix} \\[16pt]
\begin{matrix}
OtherContrast \\
\begin{cases}
\begin{cases}
[Contrast = Subject] \\
[Contrast = Object] \\
[Contrast = Adverb]
\end{cases} \\[16pt]
\begin{cases}
\begin{matrix}
NoEmphasis \\
\begin{bmatrix}
Emphasis = No \\
\$\quad = (\ldots\ MainVerb\ \#1)
\end{bmatrix}
\end{matrix} \\[16pt]
\begin{matrix}
Emphasis \\
\begin{bmatrix}
Contrast = [Emphasis = Yes] \\
Emphasis = Under \\
\$\quad = (\ldots\ MainVerb)
\end{bmatrix}
\end{matrix}
\end{cases}
\end{cases}
\end{matrix}
\end{cases}
\end{matrix} \\[20pt]
\$ = (Contrast\ Topic\ \ldots) \\
PART\ (Topic\ NIL)(Contrast\ NIL)
\end{cases}
\end{bmatrix}
$$

expresses some ordering constraint. These need to be checked for consistency and merged into a single pattern in order to extract a phrase structure tree for the sentence. In our system this is done by the generator as the phrase is produced. If the patterns are inconsistent, the merge fails and nothing is generated. Sometimes the merge produces alternatives. If the position of some constituent is not uniquely determined, the generator tries out all possibilities and produces multiple output.

The first part of (31) contains an FD for *Esa read the book* which leaves Topic and Contrast unspecified. The second part shows the output from the generator, which contains all the six possible permutations. (The morphological analyzer prints words that have the feature [Emphasis = Yes] in capitals.)

(31)   Input Description:

$$
\begin{bmatrix}
\text{Cat} & = \text{S} \\
\text{Tense} & = \text{Past} \\
\text{Perfect} & = \text{No} \\
\text{Positive} & = \text{Yes} \\
\text{Subject} & = [\text{LEX} = \text{Esa}] \\
\text{MainVerb} & = \begin{bmatrix} \text{LEX} & = \text{read} \\ \text{Aspect} & = \text{Perfective} \end{bmatrix} \\
\text{Adverb} & = \text{NONE} \\
\text{Object} & = \begin{bmatrix} \text{Cat} & = \text{NP} \\ \text{Nominal} & = [\text{LEX} = \text{book}] \\ \text{Determiner} & = \text{NONE} \\ \text{Quantity} & = \text{All} \\ \text{Number} & = \text{Sg} \end{bmatrix}
\end{bmatrix}
$$

Output:

Esa luki kirjan
LUKI Esa kirjan
LUKI kirjan Esa
KIRJAN Esa luki
ESA kirjan luki
Kirjan luki Esa

One useful aspect of the grammar we have sketched is its modularity. Although the grammar can be represented as a single FD with many alternations, the parts are relatively independent from one another and can be constructed separately.

8.3. Parser

We now turn to the question of what provisions, if any, a parser must make in order to accommodate a language like Finnish. We begin by considering this question from the point of view of context-free phrase structure grammar without arguing the merits of this kind of grammar for these or any other languages. We are interested in it because it is the simplest and best understood kind of grammar, and one for which a great variety of parsing strategies have been proposed. Functional unification grammar, while it is not context free, does belong to the class of phrase structure grammars in the sense that sentences are assigned recursive constituent structures directly, and these are not modified in the course of the generation process as they would be in, for example, transformational grammar. The daughters of a given node are determined by the label of the parent node without reference to context. The formalism fails to be context free because node labels are not taken from a closed set. As we shall see, the parsing strategies devised for context-free grammar can therefore be carried over virtually unchanged to grammars of this new kind.

At the heart of any context-free parsing algorithm is a step in which it must be decided of a particular string of words and phrases, or of a prefix of such a string, whether or not it matches the right-hand side of a rule in the grammar. Let us call this the *matching step*. Parsers differ considerably in how the many matching steps that must be taken are scheduled relative to one another and in the schemes used for representing the strings of words and phrases. Matching steps, however, differ only in minor details such as the number of rules considered at a time and possible special treatment for sets of rules whose right-hand sides begin the same way, thus allowing for some economy in the matching process.

If free word order languages present a special problem in the design of parsing strategies, it is clearly in the matching step that the problem arises. But it is not difficult to see that what these languages present is in fact more of an opportunity than a fundamental problem because, in the last analysis, it is always possible to provide a separate rule for each possible order of constituents. The opportunity is to work with a much smaller grammar by embodying the permutation property in the algorithm itself. This also provides no fundamental problem.

Let us assume that the parser gains access to the grammar through the intermediary of a set of functions that obtain rules with particular properties on demand. Thus, if a rule is required to match a string beginning with a determiner or to expand a node labeled NP, these requirements are supplied as arguments to the proper function and any rules meeting them are returned as the value. This much is standard practice. It is clearly a straightforward matter to arrange for the function to manufacture ordered context-free rules of the familiar kind from a data base containing rules whose right-hand sides are not completely specified as to order. There is no reason why a parser should be restricted to a single way of accessing the rules in its grammatical data base. A rule that allows one constituent ordering can be represented in the usual way, while the set that would result from generating all permutations of unordered rules could be stored in the more compact form and expanded only as required. The artifice of access functions serves to dissociate these essentially administrative concerns from the body of the parsing program.

The fact that the permutations of a given sequence of constituents generally are not equivalent in all respects seems to support the view that the grammar of free word order languages should not be treated in any special way in parsing. Although permuting the constituents of a sentence leaves its logical form unchanged, it does affect other semantic or pragmatic properties so that the rules for the different permutations would have to differ otherwise than in their order. This is not an entirely convincing argument, because the semantic and pragmatic distinctions do not necessarily have to be associated with individual rules of grammar but can be assigned to an interpretive component that works on the resulting constituent structures. This point was well made in respect of lexical functional grammar by P-K. Halvorsen (1983).

Functional unification grammar has the property – which some will consider an advantage and some a liability – of leaving open a large number of different approaches to the parsing of free word order languages. As we have seen, it is convenient within this formalism to separate a grammar into a number of components. The categorial component can be separated from the logical component, and both of these can be distinct from a functional component. Compositional semantics can be described within the formalism, and this can constitute a separate component of the grammar. In this last case, the advantages of keeping the components separate are particularly clear because we should expect the semantic component to be largely universal, allowing itself to be combined through unification with categorial and other components from the grammars of particular languages.

The designer of a parsing strategy for functional unification grammar has the option of obtaining initial structures for sentences using only one of the components and of obtaining more complete descriptions by later unifying these with other components of the grammar. The only requirement is that the component, or components, used in the first stage of the analysis should contain information on constituent sets because, without these, it is impossible to tell which functional roles are filled by distinct constituents. Notice that the components incorporated in the first-order parser need not contain the ordering information represented in patterns even if the word order of the language concerned is narrowly specified. The result of putting these patterns in a component of the grammar with which structures are unified later is that the initial parsing will be conducted as though there were no constraints on word order, and analysis in which the constraints were violated would be eliminated in later steps. This would almost certainly not be the recommended strategy because of the large number of pseudo-ambiguities that would remain after the end of the first stage. Generally speaking, the parser that incorporates only one component will be less constrained and will therefore recognize a greater number of spurious structures, which will fail to unify with other components of the grammar. On the other hand, these structures will be simpler and more easily identified than if the grammar were of the more highly constrained variety resulting from the unification in advance of several components.

A context-free rule has the form $A \rightarrow B_1 \cdots B_n$, where A is a nonterminal category label and $B_1 \cdots B_n$ are arbitrary category labels. A functional unification grammar is not made up of rules, but it is possible to extract a set of rules from it which are very similar to that of context-free rules. These rules have the form $F \rightarrow P_1 \cdots P_n$, where F is a functional description and $P_1 \cdots P_n$ are paths identifying parts of that description. For example, the following would be a possible rule.

$$
(32) \quad \begin{bmatrix} \text{Cat} & = \text{S} \\ \text{Subject} & = [\text{Cat} = \text{NP}] \\ \text{Verb} & = \begin{bmatrix} \text{Cat} & = \text{V} \\ \text{Number} & = \langle \text{Subject Number} \rangle \\ \text{Person} & = \langle \text{Subject Person} \rangle \end{bmatrix} \end{bmatrix} \rightarrow \langle \text{Subject} \rangle \langle \text{Verb} \rangle
$$

This says that any phrase whose description can be unified with the one given can be accommodated in the constituent structure in such a way as to dominate a pair of other constituents, the first of which is its subject and the second of which is its verb. Each of these can, of course, have a description of arbitrary complexity, which will also be part of the description of the dominating node. There are therefore indefinitely many labels that a phrase could have while still meeting the conditions required for the application of this rule. Notice that this rule provides for agreement in person and number between the subjects and the verb. Although this does not require essentially non-context-free devices, it does suggest a way in which the formalism might incorporate them. The reader may wish to verify, for example, that the following grammar generates the well-known non-context-free language $a^n b^n c^n$. In this case the essential property is the Daughter feature, which must have the same value for all nodes at the same level in the structure of any sentence, but a different one for each level. The description of a node dominating three terminals, for example, must have the feature [Daughter = [Daughter = [Daughter = NONE]]].[6]

(33)

$$
\left\{
\begin{array}{l}
\textit{Top} \\
\left[
\begin{array}{ll}
\text{Cat} & = \text{Top} \\
\text{A} & = \begin{bmatrix} \text{Cat} & = \text{Middle} \\ \text{Char} & = \text{a} \end{bmatrix} \\[2ex]
\text{B} & = \begin{bmatrix} \text{Cat} & = \text{Middle} \\ \text{Char} & = \text{b} \end{bmatrix} \\[2ex]
\text{C} & = \begin{bmatrix} \text{Cat} & = \text{Middle} \\ \text{Char} & = \text{c} \end{bmatrix} \\[2ex]
\$ & = \text{(A B C)} \\[1ex]
\text{TYPE} & = \text{NonTerminal}
\end{array}
\right] \\[2ex]
\textit{Middle} \\
\left[
\begin{array}{ll}
\text{Cat} & = \text{Middle} \\
\text{Daughter} & = \langle \text{Daughter Daughter} \rangle \\
& \left\{
\begin{array}{l}
\textit{NonBranching} \\
\begin{bmatrix}
\text{Daughter} & = \text{NONE} \\
\text{x} & = [\text{Cat} = \text{Terminal}] \\
\$ & = \text{(x)}
\end{bmatrix} \\[2ex]
\textit{Branching} \\
\begin{bmatrix}
\text{Daughter} & = \text{ANY} \\
\text{x} & = [\text{Cat} = \text{Terminal}] \\
\text{X} & = \begin{bmatrix} \text{Cat} & = \text{Middle} \\ \text{Char} & = \langle \text{Char} \rangle \end{bmatrix} \\
\$ & = \text{(x X)}
\end{bmatrix}
\end{array}
\right\} \\[2ex]
\text{TYPE} & = \text{NonTerminal}
\end{array}
\right] \\[2ex]
\textit{Terminal} \\
\begin{bmatrix}
\text{Cat} & = \text{Terminal} \\
\text{TYPE} & = \text{Terminal} \\
\text{LEX} & = \langle \text{Char} \rangle
\end{bmatrix}
\end{array}
\right\}
$$

Although the form of these rules is not identical to that of a context-free rule and although grammars can be written with them that have more generative power, they can clearly be incorporated in a parser of essentially the same design as would be used with a context-free grammar. It is perhaps worth noting an implication of this, namely that functional unification grammar has less generative power than context-sensitive grammar because it is well known that the same parsing strategies are not applicable to these. The question we now briefly address is that of deriving a set of rules of the kind just suggested, with or without ordered right-hand sides, from a grammar expressed in the standard way.

It turns out that an algorithm that will produce rules from a functional unification grammar is a minor variant of the unification algorithm itself. The simplest kind of unification algorithm produces a result in disjunctive normal form. To produce a result in a more compact form would require the use of complex algebraic simplification techniques. However, as a model of human sentence production, a generator of descriptions in disjunctive normal form may be particularly apt because we assume that the speaker will abandon the process as soon as the first term has been produced. While the grammar will generally allow a variety of ways of expressing a given idea, the speaker is interested in finding only one of them, which is to say that he is only interested in one term of the expression. This assumes, of course, that a careful speaker controls the quality of his linguistic output by providing more complete descriptions to the linguistic generator and not by generating several alternatives among which he then makes a choice.

For the present purposes, in any case, a generator of disjunctive normal forms will be ideal and we shall indeed need all the terms in the expressions that it produces. However, the essentially recursive step in which the grammar is unified with constituents below the top-level node is disabled. The result is a device that does nothing more than reduce the grammar itself to disjunctive normal form, providing a separate description of each possible phrase type. These descriptions can be made into the rules we require by simply extracting their patterns and making them the right-hand sides of the rules. Unordered rules are obtained by curtailing the normal unification process so as not to include the patterns. In this case the right-hand sides of the rules are provided by the constituent sets.

The details of the process by which a functional description is reduced to disjunctive normal form need not concern us here. They are part of the stock in trade of computer scientists, especially in artificial intelligence. The following broad outline will be sufficient. The functional description has the structure of a tree with attribute-value pairs labeling terminal nodes and either "and" or "or" labeling the nonterminal nodes. Each term in the disjunctive normal form also has such a tree structure, but since all the nonterminals are labeled "and," it would be possible to replace them all with a single nonterminal node. Each tree that represents one of these terms can be derived from the tree for the original expression by simply selecting certain arcs and nodes from it. The top node must be included. If a node labeled "and" is included, then the arcs extending downward from it, and the nodes to which these lead, must also be included. If a node labeled "or" is included, then exactly one of the arcs leading downward from it, and the node to which this leads, must be included. Arcs and nodes must be included only if they satisfy these requirements. It emerges that the terms of the resulting expression, and therefore the rules of the parsing grammar, differ from one another with respect to the choice of a downward arc from at least one "or" node.

What, then, is the appropriate strategy for a "mildly configurative" language like Finnish, where many, but not all, of the orderings of a constituent set are generally allowable? We have outlined straightforward procedures for automatically constructing more or less traditional rules spelling out each possible order individually. Such rules can then be compiled into a transition network that can be made the basis of very efficient analysis procedures. However, the number of such rules that would have to be generated, and the storage space they would consume, would make this an attractive alternative only if all the rules were very short. But we have seen that Finnish has largely flat structures at the sentence level where word order is least constrained; the rules would therefore be long and the size of the corresponding set of ordered rules unthinkably large.

The preferred analysis strategy for a language like Finnish would therefore make use of unordered rules, each annotated with the corresponding patterns taken from the functional unification grammar. Those patterns are then brought into play by the parser at the time the rule is matched against a segment on the string. Let us suppose that each of the patterns associated with a rule is converted into the form of a finite-state machine. Since patterns are written in the language of regular expressions, we know that automata theory has standard techniques for doing this. These are now used in the parser's matching step as follows. The first item in the string to be matched is first compared with the members of the constituent set for the rule to verify that, considerations of order aside, it could belong to a phrase sanctioned by this rule. If it is found, the matching member of the constituent set is removed so that it will not also be allowed to match against subsequent items. Needless to say, this is done in a nondeterministic manner so that what is done in this matching step does not affect others. It is next verified that each of the finite-state machines produced from the patterns associated with the rule can be advanced to a new state over this item. If this can be done for each of the machines, the matching step proceeds to the next character with the reduced constituent set and new states for each of the pattern machines. A string meeting the specifications of the rule has been identified when the constituent set is empty and each of the finite-state machines is in a final state.

What is in fact being done in this procedure is that that particular part of the fully expanded set of rules required for the particular case on hand is computed on demand and the string to be matched is used to direct the computation in a straightforward way so that it can proceed quite efficiently. In fact, in all but the most perverse situations, which must be especially constructed to make a point, this version of the matching step required very little more computation than one that worked from a grammar containing the fully expanded set of ordered rules. The number of patterns associated with a given rule is quite small and each of them can be made deterministic using algorithms that are a standard part of automata theory. On occasion, it may even be possible to combine some of the finite-state machines associated with a rule into a single machine without encountering much of a combinatorial explosion. In short, the overall strategy leaves room for space versus time trade-offs of several kinds so that it is readily adapted to a variety of practical needs.

We conclude that formalisms like that of functional unificational grammar justify two of the principal claims made for them, namely that they enable a perspicuous account to be given of the so-called *functional* aspects of language and that they provide a firm basis for performance models and computational procedures. Free word order languages like Finnish cannot be described in a revealing way within a framework that contains only ordered rules or that does not allow separate statements to be made about logical and functional aspects of the language that nevertheless interact so that each constrains the other in a well-defined way. In addition to this, we have shown that a framework in which revealing descriptions of the languages are possible does not lead to intractable parsing problems.

Notes

Most of the research for this paper was conducted while the first author was a fellow at the Center for Advanced Study in the Behavioral Sciences.

1. Preposed constituents in English sentences such as *The BOOK Esa read* are not topics in this sense of the term, although the preposing rule is commonly known as *Topicalization* (Chafe 1976; Prince 1981).
2. According to Hakulinen and Karlsson (1982) there are about five instances of SVO for one occurrence of OVS in Finnish texts.
3. Heinamaki (1980) and Hakulinen and Karlsson (1981) do not mention finite verbs among constituents that can be contrasted (focused on) but we are inclined to think that they should be included here.
4. As Heinamaki (1980) points out, negation cannot focus on the topic in cases like **Ei KIRJAA Esa lukenut* 'No, the BOOK Esa didn't read', although (15b) and (15c) are both grammatical. The initial placement of negation is irrelevant here because the judgments remain the same even if "ei" comes after the topic: **KIRJAA ei lukenut Esa* versus *ESA ei lukenut kirjaa Esa ei lukenut KIRJAA*. Similar asymmetries in the assignment of negative focus show up in other constructions, for example in existential clauses: *Ei TAI OSSA kissoja ole* 'There are no cats in the HOUSE' verses *Ei KISSOJA talossa ole* 'There are no CATS in

the house'. The latter proposition can only be expressed by changing the order to *Ei talossa KISSOJA ole*. It appears that negation cannot focus on the topic unless it is the unmarked default topic – that is, the subject in transitive sentences, locative in existential sentences. This is an interesting problem for future research.

5. The distinction between logical and functional aspects of meaning can be nicely drawn in *situation semantics* – see Barwise and Perry, 1982. The basic idea is that meanings are relations between types of situations. In particular, the meaning of a declarative sentence S is a relation between situations that are assertions of S and situations that are described by them. In Finnish, changes of word order typically affect only the domain but not the range of this relation. The set of situations described by a sentence is unaffected by configurational changes, but the set of discourse situations varies.

6. The feature Char assures that only *a* appears as a terminal under *A*, similarly for *B* and *C*. All lower level constituents agree with their dominating node with respect to this feature except for terminal nodes, which pick it up as their lexical realization. Every nonterminal node has a Daughter property whose value is a list that in effect encodes the length of the longest branch it dominates. Thus a node that dominates only a terminal symbol has the feature [Daughter = NONE]; the node immediately above has the feature [Daughter = [Daughter = NONE]], and so on.

References

Barwise, Jon, and John Perry. 1982. Meanings and attitudes. Unpublished manuscript.

Chafe, Wallace L. 1976. Givenness, contrastiveness, definiteness, subjects, topics, and point of view. In: Charles N. Li (ed.), *Subject and topic*. New York: Academic Press, pp. 25–26.

Gazdar, Gerald, and Geoffrey Pullum. 1982. Subcategorization, constituent order, and the notion of 'head'. In: M. Moortgat, H. v. d. Hulst, and T. Hoekstra (eds.), *The scope of lexical rules*. Dordrecht, Holland: Foris, pp. 107–24.

Hakulinen, Auli, and Fred Karlsson. 1979. *Nykysuomen lauscoppia*. Helsinki, Finland: Suomalaisen Kirjallisuuden Seura.

Hakulinen, Auli, and Fred Karlsson. 1980. Finnish syntax in text: Methodology of a quantitative study. *Nordic Journal of Linguistics* 3, 2:93–129.

Halvorsen, Per-Kristian. 1983. Semantics for lexical-functional grammar. *Linguistic Inquiry* 14, 4:567–615.

Heinamaki, Orvokki. 1980. Problems of basic word order. In: *Proceedings of the Fourth International Congress of Fenno-Ugrists*. Turku, Finland: University of Turku.

Ikola, Osmo. ed. 1968. *Suomen kielen kasikirja*. Helsinki, Finland: Weilin and Goos.

Kaplan, Ronald, and Joan Bresnan. 1982. Lexical-functional grammar: A formal system for grammatical representation. In: Joan Bresnan (ed.), *The mental representation of grammatical relations*. Cambridge, Mass.: MIT Press, pp. 173–281.

Karttunen, Lauri, Rebecca Root, and Hans Uszkoreit. 1981. Morphological analysis of Finnish by computer. Paper presented at the 1981 winter meeting of the Linguistic Society of America.

Prince, Ellen. 1981. Topicalization, focus-movement, and Yiddish-movement: A pragmatic differentiation. BLS 7. *Proceedings of the Seventh Annual Meeting of the Berkeley Linguistics Society*. Berkeley, Calif.

9　A new characterization of attachment preferences

FERNANDO C. N. PEREIRA

Kimball's parsing principles (Kimball, 1973), Frazier and Fodor's Sausage Machine (Frazier and Fodor, 1978; Fodor and Frazier, 1980) and Wanner's augmented transition network (ATN) model (Wanner, 1980) have tried to explain why certain readings of structurally ambiguous sentences are preferred to others, in the absence of semantic information. The kinds of ambiguity under discussion are exemplified by the following two sentences.

(1)　Tom said that Bill had taken the cleaning out yesterday.

(2)　John bought the book for Susan.

For sentence (1), the reading 'Yesterday Bill took the cleaning out' is preferred to 'Tom spoke yesterday about Bill taking the cleaning out.' Kimball (1973) introduced the principle of Right Association (RA) to account for this kind of preference. The basic idea of the Right Association principle is that, in the absence of other information, phrases are attached to a partial analysis as far right as possible.

For sentence (2), the reading 'The book was bought for Susan' is preferred to 'John bought a book that had been beforehand destined for Susan.' To account for this preference, Frazier and Fodor (1978) introduced the principle of Minimal Attachment (MA), which may be summarized as stating that, in the absence of other information, phrases are attached so as to minimize the complexity of the analysis.

Much of the debate about the formulation and interaction of such principles is caused by their lack of precision and, at the same time, by their being too specific. I propose a simple, precise, and general framework in which improved versions of Right Association and Minimal Attachment can be formulated. It will turn out that the two principles correspond to two precise rules on how to choose between alternative parsing actions in the parsing model.

Apart from the concrete results shown, this article has two further purposes. First, to show that it is possible to describe principles such as RA and MA starting from very few assumptions about grammar and pars-

307

ing mechanisms. Second, that, by making all the assumptions clear, the principles are much easier to formulate and to discuss.

From the material I present, one should not infer that I am proposing certain specific mechanisms as models of human sentence processing. Rather, I am presenting a possible general framework within which precise falsifiable models can be formulated.

Underlying the proposed framework is the assumption of a bottom-up parsing mechanism. This is much less restrictive than it may appear from the literature. Both Kimball and Frazier and Fodor discount purely bottom-up mechanisms on the basis that they are not "predictive" enough. This criticism is founded on the incorrect assumption that bottom-up parsers cannot take account of left context, and in particular of top-down predictions, to narrow their choice of parsing actions. Frazier and Fodor (1978) state that: "Since higher nodes cannot be entered until after all the words they dominate have been received, these nodes cannot be made use of for the 'forwards' prediction of words or nodes within that portion of the lexical string." Their formulation assumes that the parser has no internal state and that its only sources of information are the partially built phrase marker and the input. Of course, this need not be so. For example, the LR ("left-to-right scan, rightmost derivation") context-free parsing theory (Aho and Ullman, 1972), which I will discuss in more detail in section 9.3, provides a very powerful method to encode possible left contexts into a finite set of parser states, even for ambiguous languages (Aho and Johnson, 1974). I am not suggesting that LR parsing is a suitable model for people's performance. I am just pointing out that the world of bottom-up parsers is much wider than is all too often assumed.

9.1. Shift-reduce parsing

The class of bottom-up parsers that I will use to demonstrate the proposals in this paper is the shift-reduce parsers, which are well understood in the theory of context-free parsing (Aho and Ullman, 1972). The shift-reduce method is a general framework for bottom-up parsing, which can in fact be used for grammar formalisms other than context-free grammars, such as type-O grammars (Deussen, 1978) and definite-clause grammars (Pereira and Warren, 1980). In the present discussion, however, it is enough to look at context-free parsing.

Any shift-reduce method has two basic ingredients: a *stack* and an *oracle*. The stack is a string of grammar symbols, which is empty when analysis starts and which becomes empty again at the end of a successful analysis. The stack is only accessed at its right end, called the *top* of the stack. The left end is the *bottom*. Symbols can be appended or *pushed* onto the top of the stack, and removed or *popped* from the top of the stack. A string is said to *match* the top of the stack if it is a final segment of the stack. The combination of a current stack and a partially consumed input string is called a *configuration* or *point*. I will write a stack with its top to the right of the page. Empty stacks or strings will be denoted by □.

A shift-reduce parser changes its configuration by doing *moves*. There are two kinds of moves: a single *shift* move and, for each grammar rule, a *reduce* move. The shift move consists in reading the next terminal from the input, and pushing it onto the stack. A reduce move consists in taking a grammar rule whose right-hand side matches the top of the stack, and substituting the matched string on the stack by the left-hand side of the rule.

For example, given the grammar

(3) 1. S → NP VP
     2. NP → Det N
     3. VP → V NP
     4. Det → the
     5. N → cat
     6. N → dog
     7. V → loves

and the input string

(4) The cat loves the dog.

the table below shows a sequence of valid moves. The move at the end of each line is applied to the configuration in that line to give the configuration on the next line.

(5)

Stack	Remaining input	Move
□	the cat loves the dog	shift
the	cat loves the dog	reduce by rule 4
Det	"	shift
Det cat	loves the dog	reduce by rule 5
Det N	"	reduce by rule 2
NP	"	shift
NP loves	the dog	reduce by rule 7
NP V	the dog	shift
NP V the	dog	reduce by rule 4
NP V Det	dog	shift
NP V Det dog	□	reduce by rule 6
NP V Det N	"	reduce by rule 2
NP V NP	"	reduce by rule 3
NP VP	"	reduce by rule 1
S		

A shift-reduce parser is said to reach the *success* state (or to succeed), after some sequence of moves on some input, when the stack contains only the initial symbol of the grammar and the input is exhausted. In the previous example, the sequence of moves given leads to the success state. If some sequence of moves cannot lead to the success state and cannot be extended by some new moves, it has *blocked*.

9.2. Oracles and conflicts

A shift-reduce parser based only on the preceding definitions would, of course, be impractical, because it would have no means of choosing moves that lead to success on a well-formed input. There are just too many possible moves for any sizable grammar. That is the reason why we need the previously mentioned oracle. An oracle examines the moves that are possible in a configuration and forbids moves that it knows will only lead to blocking move sequences. It allows all the other moves. Notice that an oracle is not allowed to forbid moves that may lead to success. Therefore, all the analyses of a given string according to the given grammar correspond to some sequence of allowed moves from the initial configuration.

If oracles were unrestricted, it would be trivial to provide good oracles (just explore all possible move sequences until a successful one is found). Therefore, I will restrict oracles to finite-state machines, and this is assumed from now on. Of course, the existence of suitable oracles is a precondition for accepting shift-reduce parsing as a reasonable model. In general, this is a difficult question, which requires substantial further research.

There are important classes of grammars for which good oracles are possible. I call an oracle *exact* when it allows, at most, one move in any configuration. The context-free languages which can be parsed with exact oracles are called deterministic languages (Aho and Ullmann, 1972). Clearly, deterministic languages must be unambiguous, so they are too small a class of languages for our purposes. Nevertheless, the methods developed for handling deterministic languages, suitably relaxed,[1] may be useful to derive plausible oracles for natural language analysis. In particular, the LR parser theory, because of its close connection with the general parsing method of Earley (1970), is an interesting candidate for investigation. I use LR theory to derive the example of an oracle in the next section.

The connection between LR parsing and the Earley algorithm shows, in an instructive way, how predictions and left context are incorporated in an oracle. The finite automaton that implements the oracle in an LR parser has states corresponding to sets of partially applied rules – called *dotted rules* or *items* – in the Earley parsing algorithm. A dotted rule is just a grammar rule with a dot in the right-hand side separating the symbols to its left, which have been found, from the symbols to its right, which are still needed for the rule to be applied. A state transition in the LR automaton corresponds to moving the dot in the dotted rules for the old state over the symbols that might be on the top of the stack after the parsing action, to get the dotted rules for the new state.

The dotted rules in the Earley algorithm are generated by a combination of top-down predictions and bottom-up reductions. All the dotted rules that are generated for a given input are compatible with an analysis of some string that shares an initial segment with the input. Therefore, the states in the LR oracle are finite encodings of sets of partial parse trees for initial segments of the input. In the case of deterministic languages, this encoding can be exact, but in the case of ambiguous languages, the finite encoding will collapse incompatible partial parse trees into a single state, thus making the oracle inexact. Furthermore, by restricting the number of states, more incompatible partial analyses would be merged, giving a potential model for the effects of limited memory (see Marcus's theory of deterministic parsing (Marcus, 1980)).

Given that any oracle for a natural language grammar is, in general, going to allow more than one move at each point, when the parser wants to make a move it will have to solve *conflicts*. Two kinds of conflicts can occur: a *shift-reduce* conflict, in which the shift move and some reduce move are allowed at the same point, and a *reduce-reduce* conflict, in which no shift but several reduce moves are allowed at the same point. From these definitions, it follows that shift-reduce and reduce-reduce conflicts are mutually exclusive. If a parser is to avoid backtracking or parallel elaboration of analyses, it must resolve conflicts in some way. Of course, by doing so, it may be excluding exactly those moves that lead to success. On the other hand, if backtracking is allowed, conflict resolution may be used to specify an order in which moves are to be tried.

9.3. Example of an oracle

To make the notion of an oracle more concrete, I will now give a simple example, consisting of an inexact oracle for the grammar

(6) 1. S → NP VP
     2. NP → Det N
     3. NP → ProperN
     4. VP → V NP
     5. Det → Art
     6. Det → NP 's

As noted before, oracles are finite-state devices. The particular oracle presented here is a nondeterministic finite automaton. At any configuration during an analysis, the oracle takes its current state and the grammar symbol currently on top of the parser's stack (or □ if the stack is empty) and produces a set of pairs (*parser move, oracle stack*). From this set, the parser chooses a pair that defines its next move and the next state of the oracle. This mapping can be described by transitions of the form

(7)   state : top of stack ⇒ parser move, next state

where ": top of stack" is omitted if the transition applies for any symbol on the top of the stack.

The example oracle is given by the following transitions, where A is the initial state:

(8)   A ⇒ shift, B
      B : Art ⇒ reduce by rule 5, C
      B : ProperN ⇒ reduce by rule 3, D
      C ⇒ shift, E
      †D ⇒ shift, F
      †D ⇒ reduce by rule 4, G
      E ⇒ reduce by rule 2, D
      F : 's ⇒ reduce by rule 6, C
      F : V ⇒ shift, B
      G ⇒ reduce by rule 1, success

In constructing this oracle, I have used the methods outlined in section 9.2. Each state corresponds to a set of dotted rules, and state transitions correspond to shift or reduce moves that advance the dot in the dotted rules in a state. More precisely, the states are the "LP(0) sets of items" (Aho and Ullmann, 1972) for the grammar.

This oracle is exact but for a shift-reduce conflict in state D, from which there are the two alternative transitions marked with †. This conflict can be solved by adding look-ahead to the oracle, and, in fact, the grammar can be parsed deterministically with one symbol of look-ahead. A suitable exact oracle can be derived using a specialization of the LR techniques known as LALR(1) parsing (Aho and Johnson, 1974; Pereira and Shieber, forthcoming).

I will now give an example of the oracle's operation with the input sentence

(9)   The boy stole Mary's cat.

(10)

State	Stack	Move	Remaining input
A	□	shift	the boy stole Mary's cat
B	Art	reduce by rule 5	boy stole Mary's cat
C	Det	shift	boy stole Mary's cat
E	Det N	reduce by rule 2	stole Mary's cat
† D	NP	shift	stole Mary's cat
F	NP V	shift	Mary's cat
B	NP V ProperN	reduce by rule 3	's cat

† D	NP V NP	shift	's cat
F	NP V NP 's	reduce by rule 4	cat
C	NP V Det	shift	cat
E	NP V Det N	reduce by rule 2	□
D	NP V NP	reduce by rule 4	□
G	NP VP	reduce by rule 1	□
H	S		

At the points in the analysis marked with †, the oracle allows a shift or a reduction by rule 4. The parser has to choose between (or develop in parallel) those moves. In the example, shift moves are preferred. This is the right choice for a nonblocking sequence of moves. (I am here behaving as an additional oracle.)

9.4. Preference

Precise versions of the Right Association and Minimal Attachment strategies can now be presented.

- Right Association corresponds to solving all shift-reduce conflicts in favor of shifting;
- Minimal Attachment corresponds to solving all reduce-reduce conflicts in favor of the reduce move that pops the most symbols from the stack.[2]

To see how these definitions work, I assume that the oracle will produce exactly the conflicts that correspond to the intuitively perceived ambiguities in the examples. To avoid uninteresting detail, I will also assume the context-free rules necessary to analyze the relevant part of each example, and I will enter words in the stack as their lexical categories. The reader should not assume that the particular rules chosen have any particular merit apart from reflecting reasonably the intuitive structure of the examples.[3]

I will first discuss the following shift-reduce conflict:

(11)   (FF1-1) Tom said that Bill had taken the cleaning out‿yesterday.
   1. S → NP VP
   2. VP → V $\overline{S}$
   3. S → S Adv
   4. $\overline{S}$ → that S

   Stack: NP V that S

When the input has been read up to the caret (ˆ), after some necessary reductions that have to be done at this point (the oracle must see to that), the parser will have the choice of reducing by rule 4 or of shifting the Adv *yesterday* onto the stack. The preference for shifting will lead to the configuration

(12)   Tom said that Bill had taken the cleaning out yesterday‿.

   Stack: NP V that S Adv

At this point, only rule 3 may be used, and the adverb is therefore attached to the lower S.

A reduce-reduce conflict occurs in (FF1-13)[4]:

(13) (FF1-13) John bought the book for Susan.
      5. NP → NP PP
      6. VP → V NP (PP)

      Stack: NP V NP PP

At this point in the analysis, the parser has to reduce either by rule 5 (and then rule 6 without the optional PP) or by rule 6 with the PP. The latter option consumes more from the stack, and therefore is chosen, causing the PP to be attached to the VP node.

Rules 5 and 6 are implicit both in Frazier and Fodor's and in Wanner's analyses for the sentence. Unfortunately, my view of MA is sensitive to the choice of grammar rules in the same way as Wanner's. If rule 5 was replaced by 5'.[5]

(14) 5'. NP → Det N PP*

the preference for shifting over reducing would cause the final PP to be attached to the NP.[6] Of course, my proposal still explains the data, but only together with certain grammar rules. And it might be argued that rule 5' is highly dubious, because it suggests that a NP node is only found when all the PPs that modify it have been found. This runs against the intuition that, at each stage through the string of PPs, one has a perfectly well-formed NP, which is the situation portrayed by rule 5.

The same problem would occur in Wanner's ATN, if he had used a right-recursive (or a loop) network to attach the PPs, instead of a left-recursive network analogous to rule 5. But whereas shift-reduce parsing has no problem with left-recursive constructions, the top-down regime implicit in Wanner's proposal is inadequate for the NP part of his network. In a phrase with the final analysis of (15),

(15)   *Left recursive analysis*

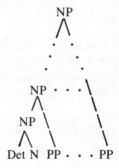

the ATN will attach every intermediate NP node as if it were the top NP, before finding that there are more PPs to include in the NP and that, therefore, the intermediate NP has been wrongly attached. This is very unreasonable behavior for a parser that purports to model human performance.

Wanner criticizes Frazier and Fodor's use of sentence length to explain the preferred reading of (FF1-15).

(16) (FF1-15) Joe bought the book that I had been trying to obtain for Susan.

Like Wanner's, my proposals make that preference independent of sentence length.

(17) 7. NP → NP $\bar{\text{S}}$/NP
    8. VP → V to VP
    9. PP → Prep NP

    4a. $\bar{\text{S}}$/NP → Comp S/NP
    1a. S/NP → VP
    1b. S/NP → NP VP/NP
    6a. VP/NP → V (PP)
    8a. VP/NP → V to VP/NP
    Stack: NP V NP Comp NP V to V

The rules use X/Y nonterminals to represent "an X with a Y hole." This is an approximation, sufficient for the purposes of this paper, of Gazdar's (1981) "derived category" description of relative clauses. In (FF1-15), there is a noun phrase gap for the object of *obtain* in *obtain – for Susan*, which must thus be analyzed as a VP/NP, a verb phrase missing a noun phrase.

In the given configuration, there is a shift-reduce conflict, where the parser may either reduce by rule 6a (without the optional PP) or shift the word *for*. After the shift, there is only one possible sequence of moves, sketched in (18).

(18)

Stack	Remaining input	Move
NP V NP Comp NP V to V Prep	Susan	shift
NP V NP Comp NP V to Prep NP	□	reduce by (9)
NP V NP Comp NP V to V PP		reduce by (6a)
NP V NP Comp NP V to VP/NP		reduce by (8a)
NP V NP Comp NP VP/NP		...

We see thus that the PP *for Susan* is attached to the lower VP, giving the preferred reading 'It was for Susan that I was trying to obtain the book,' rather than the reading 'John bought for Susan the book I had been trying to obtain.'

Although Wanner's model can explain this example, it cannot, as noted in Fodor and Frazier (1980), explain the RA-induced preference in

(19)   (FF2-27) Joe took the book that I had wanted to include in my birthday gift
         for Susan

The problem with Wanner's proposal is that his top-down model is forced to apply his preference rules *before* the phrases being attached have been scanned. Wanner's rule for enforcing MA, the CAT-before-SEEK rule in which looking for a word takes precedence over looking for a complex phrase, operates before the parser has seen what follows *a birthday gift*. The original proposals of Frazier and Fodor cannot explain (FF2-27) either, and so they are forced to go into a rather complicated explanation of a new principle of "local association."

In contrast, (FF2-27) causes no problem to the present formulation. The preposition *for* is reached with the following configuration

(20)   Stack: NP V NP Comp NP V to V Prep NP   Input: for Susan

At this point, there will be a shift-reduce conflict between shifting *for* onto the stack or reducing Prep NP to PP. The shift move is preferred, leading to the following sequence of moves.

(21)

Stack	Input	Move
NP V NP Comp NP V to V Prep NP Prep	Susan	shift
NP V NP Comp NP V to V Prep NP Prep NP		reduce by (9)
NP V NP Comp NP V to V Prep NP PP		reduce by (5)
NP V NP Comp NP V to V Prep NP		reduce by (9)
NP V NP Comp NP V to V PP		reduce by (6a)
NP V NP Comp NP V to VP/NP		reduce by (8a)
NP V NP Comp NP VP/NP		reduce by (1b)
NP V NP Comp S/NP		reduce by (4a)
NP V NP Sbar/NP		reduce by (7)
NP V NP		reduce by (6)
NP VP		reduce by (1)
S		success

This example shows that, in the shift-reduce model, conflicts between MA and RA are automatically eliminated because the two principles operate necessarily at different points in the analysis. This is a consequence of general properties of bottom-up parsers that will be discussed in the next section.

Another case of reduce-reduce conflict happens in example (FF2-12). The initial segment given there can be extended in two different ways that force different lexical category assignments for *that*. The preferred reading seems to be 'That silly old-fashioned hat is cheap', in which the fragment is the initial segment of a noun phrase, in contrast with the reading 'That silly old fashioned hats are cheap is well known,' for which *that* is a complementizer. Frazier and Fodor argue that Wanner's CAT-before-SEEK principle for ATNs cannot explain the preferred reading because the example does not involve a conflict between looking for a word and looking for a phrase, but a conflict between two different phrase types, which could be called a SEEK-SEEK conflict in ATN terminology.[7] Choosing the largest reduction again fits the data.

(22)   (FF2-12) That silly old-fashioned.

    10. NP → (Det) Adj* N

    Stack: that Adj Adj (N)

Reducing by rule 10 with the optional Det will pop the most from the stack, so that will be the preferred move. I am assuming here that a word is only given a lexical category when it is needed for a reduction, otherwise the choice between Det or Comp for *that* would have to be done immediately after shifting *that* onto the stack. Delaying the choice of lexical category seems reasonable and fits the general notion that bottom-up parsing avoids making decisions too early.

9.5. In defense of bottom-up parsers

The examples of the last section show the crucial difference between top-down and bottom-up models of sentence parsing. Although there is a superficial similarity between arc preferences in an ATN and shift-reduce conflict resolution, the two mechanisms operate in entirely different ways: whereas in the top-down ATN model preferences are exercised before the phrases to which they apply are scanned, in the shift-reduce formulation preferences operate only when phrases could be closed by a reduce move. Because of this, situations that appear as a conflict between two preference principles in the ATN model do not arise in a shift-reduce parser: the conflict has disappeared by the time the parser has parsed the relevant phrases.

I have also shown in the last section that two important preference principles are naturally described as conflict resolution rules in a very general bottom-up parsing framework.[8] The effects of these conflict resolution rules are only indirectly dependent on the actual grammar used, and, in fact, the rules I used are consistent with the phrase markers used in the discussion of the examples by Frazier and Fodor and Wanner.

As I explained in section 9.2, the criticism that bottom-up parsers have no predictive capabilities is unfounded. The predictive ability of a shift-reduce parser is embodied in its oracle, which will take note of the left context in its internal finite-state network. This finite-state network encodes that "after such and such phrases have been found, and given that the next few words are such and such, we are building such and such phrase, and therefore such and such shifts or reduces are required." In fact, shift-reduce parsing as a model of performance might be criticized not because it can predict too little, but because it can predict too much:

the class of languages that can be parsed bottom-up without backtracking[9] is strictly larger than the class of languages parsable top-down without backtracking (Aho and Ullmann, 1972).

The fact that an oracle tries to encode, in a finite (and necessarily small) number of states, an infinity of situations means that there may be some loss of information. That is, when deep down in the analysis of some subphrase, the detail of the higher found or predicted nodes of the left context may be lost. This is precisely the effect of limited memory that Frazier and Fodor try to model in the Sausage Machine.

Shift-reduce parsers require more stack for deep right branching constructions than for deep left branching ones. This has been used by Kimball to discount them as useful in modeling performance. However, his argument depends crucially on what grammar rules are chosen, whereas the arguments here are of a more general nature and less dependent on the grammar used.

9.6. Conclusion

I have explained how it is possible to describe rigorously the attachment preferences of Right Association and Minimal Attachment in a way that seems to satisfy both Frazier and Fodor's and Wanner's requirements, and that clarifies the interaction between the two principles. I have started from very limited assumptions that clearly distinguish between parsing strategy (the oracle), grammar, and preferences. In contrast, Frazier and Fodor's Sausage Machine mixes strategy and preferences, and Wanner's ATN mixes preferences with grammar formulation.

My formulation of the principles, however, is not totally independent of the grammar rules. This dependence on the grammar might be caused by the shift-reduce strategy making decisions too early. It would be interesting to investigate extending the idea of delayed assignment of lexical categories used in example (FF2-12) into a method for delaying certain reductions. A careful discussion of the role of delayed reductions in handling lexical preferences in a shift-reduce parsing model has been given by Shieber (1983). His model gives the correct predictions for some cases in which the mechanisms presented here are too coarse.

Notes

This research was partially supported by the Defense Advanced Research Projects Agency under Contract N00039-80-C-0575 with the Naval Electronic Systems Command. The views and conclusions contained in this document are those of the author and should not be interpreted as representative of the official policies, either expressed or implied, of the Defense Advanced Research Projects Agency or the United States Government.

1. Relaxation might mean using the theory to produce an imperfect oracle and supplementing it with preference rules (see below).
2. What about several allowed productions popping the same amount? This means that there are several rules with the same right-hand sides, undistinguishable by the oracle. Apart from terminal rules (those with only terminals in the right-hand side) for homographs, such rule conflicts do not seem to occur in natural language grammars. In particular, if an $\overline{X}$ grammar is used, right-hand sides will at least differ in their head words.
3. All the examples are taken from Frazier and Fodor (1978) and Fodor and Frazier (1980) and Wanner (1980). To simplify the references, they will be numbered by (A-N), where A is FF1 for Frazier and Fodor (1978), FF2 for Fodor and Frazier (1980) and ATN for Wanner's article, and N is the number within the article.
4. A nonterminal in parenthesis is optional.
5. The notation X^* denotes any string of zero or more Xs.
6. I am indebted to David Warren for pointing this out.
7. A SEEK action is the top-down ATN counterpart of a reduction in a bottom-up, shift-reduce, parser.
8. The resolution of shift-reduce conflicts in favor of shifting is actually used when parsing ambiguous programming language constructs, such as dangling ELSE statements in ALGOL-like languages, to achieve the analysis users find most natural (Aho and Johnson, 1974).
9. Or parallel elaboration.

References

Aho, Alfred V., and S. C. Johnson. 1974. LR parsing. *Computing Surveys*, 6(2):99–124.
Aho, Alfred V., and Jeffrey D. Ullman. 1972. *The theory of parsing, translation and compiling.* Englewood Cliffs, N.J.: Prentice-Hall.
Deussen, P. 1978. A unified approach to the generation and the acception of formal languages. *Acta Informatica* 9:377–90.
Earley, Jay. 1970. An efficient context-free parsing algorithm. *Communications of the Association for Computing Machinery* 13(2):94–102.
Fodor, Janet D., and Lyn Frazier. 1980. Is the human sentence parsing mechanism an ATN? *Cognition* 8:417–59.
Frazier, Lyn, and Janet D. Fodor. 1978. The Sausage Machine: a new two-stage parsing model. *Cognition* 6:291–25.
Gazdar, Gerald. 1981. Unbounded dependencies and coordinate structure. *Linguistic Inquiry* 12(2):155–84.
Kimball, John. 1973. Seven principles of surface structure parsing in natural language. *Cognition* 2(1):15–47.
Marcus, Mitchell. 1980. *A theory of syntactic recognition for natural language.* Cambridge, Mass.: MIT Press.
Pereira, Fernando C. N., and Stuart Shieber. Forthcoming. Shift-reduce scheduling and syntactic closure.
Pereira, Fernando C. N., and David H. D. Warren. 1980. Definite clause grammars for language analysis – a survey of the formalism and a comparison with augmented transition networks. *Artificial Intelligence* 13:231–78.
Shieber, Stuart. 1983. Sentence disambiguation by a shift-reduce parsing technique. In: *Proceedings of the 21st Annual Meeting of the Association for Computational Linguistics*, pp. 113–118.
Wanner, Eric. 1980. The ATN and the Sausage Machine: Which one is baloney? *Cognition* 8:209–25.

10   On not being led up the garden path: the use of context by the psychological syntax processor

STEPHEN CRAIN and MARK STEEDMAN

It is odd that natural languages show such massive syntactic ambiguity in comparison with the artificial languages of logic and computer programming. It is particularly odd that natural languages show so many *local* syntactic ambiguities. At any point in processing a sentence, there is frequently a choice as to which of two or more rules of the grammar has been applied and which "path" in the analysis should be followed. To take an example from Marcus (1980), when a left-to-right processor has encountered the words *have the policemen . . .* , it is faced with a local ambiguity between interrogative and imperative constructions, as in

(1)   a.   Have the policemen whom you saw arrived?
       b.   Have the policemen whom you saw dismissed!

The point in the sentence at which the ambiguity is syntactically resolved may be indefinitely delayed by such intervening material as relative clauses. Some local ambiguities may even be *mis*resolved, and make human sentence processors fail to find an analysis for a perfectly well-formed sentence. Bever's (1970) "garden path" sentences provide examples, such as

(2)   a.   The horse raced past the barn fell.
       b.   The boat floated down the river sank.
       c.   The dealer sold the forgery complained.

Such sentences are perfectly grammatical, as the comparison with analogues like *The horse driven past the barn fell* reveals. But the local ambiguity of *raced* (as opposed to *driven*) between a past participle and a tensed verb is for some reason so irrevocably misresolved in favor of the latter that subjects typically fail entirely to find the grammatical reading.

The source (whether conscious or not) of models or metaphors for the psychological process of local ambiguity resolution has usually been computer science, and in particular the techniques that have been developed for compiling computer programming languages. Computer languages do typically involve a very limited kind of local ambiguity – presumably

320

because this makes them comfortable for human users, who are used to that sort of thing. But designers of computer languages always take care that such ambiguities can quickly be resolved by the compiler. Typically, these languages are designed so that a structural criterion, such as "looking ahead" to the next word or symbol is enough. Such languages can be extremely efficiently processed syntactically, and provide a tempting model for those interested in the psychological ambiguity-resolving mechanism. It is possibly for this reason that, while virtually all the psychological theories admit that semantics and context may intervene with greater or lesser degrees of intimacy in syntactic processing, most have nevertheless assumed that the *primary* responsibility for resolving local ambiguities lies with mechanisms that are similarly structural. Examples are the limited look ahead of Marcus (1980), and the attachment strategies and rule orderings variously used by Kimball (1973), Frazier (1978), Frazier and Fodor (1978), Fodor and Frazier (1980), Kaplan (1972), Wanner and Maratsos (1978), Wanner (1980), and Ford, Bresnan, and Kaplan (1981), among others.

The argument that natural language processors are as straightforward as artificial language processors like compilers is an appealing one, and the work just referred to has been immensely fruitful in producing a taxonomy of local ambiguity resolution phenomena. However, there is a grave danger inherent in the analogy. No compiler in existence appeals to semantics, much less to context, in resolving local ambiguities, but this should not be allowed to obscure the possibility that the human processor does so. If such is the case, the simple empirical question of the proportional responsibilities of structural and semantic criteria for resolving ambiguities becomes a pressing one. We believe that the experiments described below reveal that the human language processor is *not* really like the artificial ones. We shall argue for the proposal (by no means a novel one) that the primary responsibility for the resolution of local syntactic ambiguities in natural language processing rests not with structural mechanisms, but rather with immediate, almost word-by-word interaction with semantics and reference to the context.

The argument will proceed as follows. In the "Preliminaries" section, the concept of *autonomy* and the possible nature of contextual influences upon syntactic processing will be discussed. Some arguments for and against certain kinds of interaction will be reviewed, followed by an argument in favor of interaction on purely linguistic grounds. In the following section, certain varieties of definite and indefinite referring expressions and their presuppositions[1] are discussed, and a hypothesis concerning the way such reference might interact with parsing processes is advanced. It is argued that the so-called null or neutral context, used in many experiments claiming to support the view that human syntactic processing is autonomous, is in fact far from neutral with respect to these processes. The paper next presents some experiments in which reference and context are manipulated, and subjects' ability to comprehend "garden path" sentences is shown to depend on them as the theory predicts. The results suggest that there may be no such thing as an intrinsically garden-pathing sentence *structure*, but rather that for a given sentence, certain *contexts*, (possibly including the null context) will induce a garden path effect, while others will not. Our conclusion is a tentative one, for the experiments that will reveal the residual contribution (if any) of structural mechanisms have not yet been done. But there is a growing body of evidence to suggest that the importance of semantics and reference in parsing has been seriously underestimated in recent theories.

10.1. Preliminaries

It is important to begin by stressing that the term *semantics* is used here in its widest sense. Many of the theories which we shall discuss below allow semantics in the restricted form of lexical entries to guide parsing. An example is the use of semantic features of nouns and control properties of verbs (Winograd, 1972; Bresnan, 1978; Fodor, 1978; Ford, Bresnan, and Kaplan, 1981; cf. also Woods's 1973 proposal of "selective modifier placement," and Marcus's 1980 extension of it). However, we consider lexical guidance of parsing to come under the heading of structural or syntactic guidance. The interaction that we have in mind allows more general world knowledge to be accessed (cf. unimplemented proposals by Winograd and Marcus concerning noun-noun modification) and (most important) reference to a context or "mental model," of which Winograd's (1972) parser provided an early (though simplified) illustration to which we shall return below. We shall include these latter domains in the term *semantics*, distinguishing between them where necessary.

It is also worth stressing from the start that the notion of "plausibility," as it is usually used in discussing this question, plays a very minor role in the present proposal. The term is usually used to refer to the assessment of plausibility according to general world knowledge, such as that which tells us that it is more usual for doctors to cure patients than the reverse. It has reasonably been pointed out (Forster, 1979) that the use of such a criterion in parsing is bound often to be unreliable, since the reason for having syntax at all is presumably that real events frequently contradict such expectations (especially the events that people choose to comment upon). We are arguing here instead for the influence of *specific* conversational context, which may be "plausible" or "implausible" in the more restricted sense and still show a strong effect upon syntactic processing.

10.1.1. On the concept of autonomy

The position that has been sketched in the introduction stands in opposition to a number of theories of psychological sentence processing that have been advanced under the banner of "autonomy of syntax," such as those of Forster (1979), Frazier (1978), and more recently Frazier, Clifton, and Randall (1983). However, considerable confusion has been engendered by the several quite distinct senses in which the term *autonomy* has been used in the literature. It is in fact necessary to distinguish three such senses in order to define the position of the current paper with respect to these other proposals.

All of the models that we discuss here, including our own, assume autonomy in the sense that syntactic and semantic components are distinguished *in the theory*. Autonomy in this sense could be termed *formal autonomy*. There is really no alternative to formal autonomy in a theory of language, but to postulate radical nonautonomy in processing is not to deny that there is a place for syntax in the theory.

A second sense of the term *autonomy* might be called *representational autonomy*, and refers to the extent to which, at some level of analysis, purely syntactic representations are built which are only subsequently translated into semantic representations. The "level" at which there is such autonomy may be as high as the sentence (see Forster, 1979:55) or some intermediate level, such as the clause or phrase (Chapin, Smith, and Abrahamson, 1972; Fodor, Bever, and Garrett, 1974), in which case there is "modified" or partial representational autonomy.[2] The alternative is total or "radical" representational nonautonomy, according to which the semantic interpretation is assembled directly, without any intervening nonsemantic representation. In such theories, including the present one, rules of syntax describe what a processor *does* in assembling a semantic interpretation. The difference from more standard theories is simply that the rules do not describe a class of structures that are *built*.[3] (Of course, the semantic interpretation, as distinct from the process of its evaluation, must be represented *somehow*; and it might be appropriate to think of that representation as a structure. However, according to the radical version of the doctrine of representational nonautonomy, it is a structure that neither *can* be inspected or changed, nor *needs* to be, in order to produce an object that can be evaluated. Indeed, it may permit the evaluation of subexpressions while syntactic processing of higher expressions remains incomplete.)

In this sense of the term, both autonomous and nonautonomous processors are, a priori, equally practicable. For example, compilers for programming languages may be of either kind. (See Bolliet, 1968, for a discussion of nonautonomous compiling, and Davies and Isard, 1972, for an early proposal to extend such mechanisms to natural language processing.) Since the primary use of an autonomous syntactic structure is for translation into a semantic interpretation, there is an obvious parsimony in the proposal that such interpretations can as well be built directly. Nevertheless, it has generally been assumed that some degree of representational autonomy obtains in psychological sentence processing. The reason has presumably been the widespread belief that natural language grammars, unlike their artificial counterparts, include rules which operate over nonadjacent elements and which have usually been described in the framework of transformational grammar (TG), where transformational rules are defined as mappings between entire phrase markers, rather than between nodes.

The most obvious realization (not of course the only one) of such rules in a processor implies the building of an autonomous surface structure, which can only be transformed and hence interpreted once it is complete. We shall return to the question of natural language grammar and its implications for autonomy below, but it should be noted at this point that any theory which, contrary to transformational grammar, assumes what Bach has called the "rule-to-rule" hypothesis concerning the relation of syntax and semantics renders this version of the autonomy hypothesis empirically vacuous. The rule-to-rule hypothesis is simply that in natural languages there is a functional correspondence between syntactic and semantic rules, as there is in the formal logical semantics devised by Carnap and Tarski. In theories embodying this hypothesis, of which Montague (1974) and the theory discussed in section 10.1.3 provide examples, syntactic and semantic *representations* may be identical. In fact, representational autonomy is essentially a notion of *grammar*, rather than of semantic ambiguity resolution, and could as well be called *grammatical autonomy*.[4]

The term *autonomy* has also been used to refer to one pole of the dimension that we have referred to in the introduction under the heading of *interaction* of semantics and syntax during local ambiguity resolution. This sense of the term might be called *local ambiguity resolution autonomy*, but we shall continue here to refer to the relevant dimension of processing simply as *interaction*. As in the case of representational autonomy, theories are free to be either entirely noninteractive, forbidding any interaction before the sentence is complete, or partially interactive at some intermediate level such as the clause or phrase, or entirely interactive down to the level of the word or morpheme.

It is often not appreciated that the parameter of interaction during local ambiguity resolution is essentially independent of the question of representational autonomy. Representationally nonautonomous models may be (and frequently are) interactive. (That is, although syntactic processing may be no more than the process by which a semantic representation is built, the syntactic process itself, and the resolution of local ambiguities in that process, may call upon semantics, say by evaluating rival interpretations of some fragment of the sentence such as a phrase.) But a representationally nonautonomous model may equally well be fully *non-interactive*. (For example, it may develop all interpretations in parallel and only select among them once the processing is complete, or use some structural criterion to produce a single interpretation, perhaps backtracking later if necessary.) Representationally autonomous and partially autonomous theories are similarly free to be interactive or noninteractive.[5] To compound the confusion, two quite different proposals as to the nature of this interaction are currently proposed under the confused banner of nonautonomy, and it is to these that we now turn.

10.1.2. *"Strong" and "weak" interaction*

It is important to distinguish between two forms of the interactive hypothesis, which can be termed the *strong* and the *weak* versions. The weak form of the hypothesis is simply that from time to time the syntactic processor may allow the semantic component to decide whether to abandon or continue with a given analysis, perhaps even to the extent of comparing evaluations or referents of alternative analyses, in order to resolve a local syntactic ambiguity. (Of course, theories differ in their assumptions concerning the occasions on which such appeals to semantics may be made.) Thus under the weak hypothesis, syntactic processing independently "proposes" alternatives, either serially or in parallel, while semantics "disposes" among these alternatives. According to the strong form of the hypothesis, on the other hand, semantics and context actually influence *which* syntactic entities get proposed in the first place, perhaps by adjusting the order in which alternative syntactic rules are applied, or by temporarily making certain rules entirely unavailable.

Some models which have avowed the strong version of the interactive hypothesis do not in fact embody strong interaction in any form. For example, Winograd (1972) claimed to use the strong interaction in his program. However, the nature of the interaction was simply that the top-down parsing of the verb phrase was guided by the lexical entry for the verb, rather than by a general expansion of VP. As was noted earlier, this is not a semantic criterion at all, but rather a syntactic one. Other researchers who have been associated with the strong hypothesis (Tyler and Marslen-Wilson, 1977; Crain, 1980) have in fact shown a certain equivocation between the strong and the weak versions (cf. Marslen-Wilson and Tyler, 1980). This is probably just as well. There are not as far as we know any working programs that employ the strong interaction, and such systems promise to be computationally extremely complex. It is not even really clear that they could work at all.[6] (Of course, if semantics and syntax can interact on a very intimate basis, perhaps almost word-by-word as we shall argue below, then it becomes very difficult to tell the difference empirically between the strong and the weak versions.)

The models that allow some form of semantic interaction of the weak variety, among which the present proposal is to be numbered, are by far the most numerous and deserve the most attention. They are most importantly classified according to the intimacy with which semantics is allowed to intervene – that is, according to the size of the chunks in which the purely syntactic processes propose their analyses for disposal by semantics. In some models this unit is an entire sentence. More commonly it is a clause. In others it is held to be some smaller unit such as the noun phrase or even something closer to the word. In this last case there is total or "radical" (but still weak) interaction.

One argument that is sometimes raised against the whole principle of interaction between semantic and syntactic processing does not apply to theories that propose what we are calling the *weak* interaction. The argument is an instance of one that has been advanced most clearly and most generally by Simon (1969). If sentence comprehension is not a "nearly decomposable" system – that is, if syntax, semantics, and context are not discrete subsystems whose interactions are very limited – then there is very little chance that anyone will ever understand it, because it will be impossible to pursue the basic scientific strategy of holding everything constant whilst making a minimal change to one component. In other words, we may as well proceed as if it *were* nearly or totally decomposable, because if it is not, we cannot succeed anyway. Simon's argument probably has considerable force against what we have distinguished above as the "strong" form of the interactive hypothesis. (It certainly is the overwhelming argument in favor of what we have called "formal" autonomy of syntax.) However, a radical version of what we term the *weak* interactive hypothesis, which postulates frequent and immediate appeals from syntax to semantics and context to accept or reject alternative analyses on an almost word-by-word basis, is no less "nearly decomposable" than one that limits such appeals to complete clauses.

10.1.3. A linguistic argument for nonautonomy and weak interaction

There is a quite different kind of argument that can be adduced in favor of nonautonomy in representation and the weak version of the interactionist position. This argument is not based on processing grounds at all, but on the peculiarities of natural language grammar. We began the paper by asking why natural languages should appear to allow a much more extreme degree of local syntactic ambiguity than is tolerated in artificial languages. It is equally puzzling that they appear to require grammatical rules of a power and complexity that appear to be similarly unnecessary for the artificial language of logic and computation, whose grammars are basically context-free.[7] For of course one of the most important contentions of transformational grammar has been that natural languages cannot usefully be described without such powerful grammatical devices as transformations.[8]

A number of "base-generative" theories of natural language grammar have recently proposed ways of replacing transformational rules with rules of lesser power, such as context-free phrase structure rules (cf. Brame, 1978; Bresnan, 1978; Gazdar, 1981, 1982; Peters, 1980). By contrast, most theories of grammatical performance in sentence comprehension currently incorporate grammars that potentially allow operations equivalent to (various restricted classes of) transformations. However, the possibility of base-generative natural language grammar may have very strong implications for parsing. For it was argued above that one of the reasons for the predominance of autonomous syntactic representations in processing theories has been the belief that the complexities of human grammars required them.

In one version of the base-generative hypothesis, proposed by Ades and Steedman (1982), the generalizations that have in the past been captured in various "unbounded movement" transformations are captured instead by augmenting a categorial grammar of context-free power (Ajdukiewicz, 1935; Bar Hillel et al., 1960) with a novel type of rule schema called "partial combination," which has the effect of allowing the grammar to acknowledge as a kind of constituent certain incomplete fragments of sentences and phrases like *She must have, She might have been, She might have been dreaming she loved* and so on.[9] It is only by treating such fragments as in some sense constituents that the context-free apparatus of categorial grammar can be extended to handle the apparent discontinuity of constituency in constructions like Topicalization, as in (3).

(3) [[That man] [she might have been dreaming she loved]]

The arguments for extending categorial grammar (or phrase structure grammar) in this way are purely linguistic, and of no direct concern for the present paper. However, Ades and Steedman point out that the grammar is directly compatible with a class of processors known as *shift-reduce* parsers (Pereira, this volume), and that the schema in question can be viewed as a rule of processing. They show that the partial combination rule can be associated with a well-defined semantic operation of "function composition,"[10] which will allow such a parser to perform an immediate word-by-word assembly of a fully interpreted semantic representation of such a fragment. They point out the compatibility of this operation with representationally fully nonautonomous syntactic processing and the potential usefulness of such fully interpreted fragments in the resolution of local syntactic ambiguities by the weak interaction. If these proposals are correct, then it is tempting to speculate that *both* of the anomalies of natural language that were noted at the beginning of this section have a common origin in the fact that human sentence processors are nonautonomous and interactive in the sense defined here. That is, the involvement of such processors (perhaps as a necessary consequence of some psychological or practical consideration, such as the comparative slowness of speech with respect to a rapidly and often dangerously changing world) could be seen as having the following two consequences. First, the grammar comes to include just a few extra constructions, involving so-called extraction, over and above the ones that are defined by the ordinary context-free grammar implicated by the semantics. Second, since fully interpreted semantic entities corresponding to incomplete fragments of the sentence have anyway to be produced by the processor, and the context in which they can be evaluated is a very powerful source of redundancy, they can be used to handle a degree of ambiguity that in purely syntactic processing terms would be intolerable.

10.1.4. Summary

The theory that is proposed here, while remaining completely committed to the formal autonomy of syntax and semantics, is equally committed to total nonautonomy of the representational kind and to an extreme version of the weak interaction, or nonautonomy in ambiguity resolution. The next section considers the way in which the weak interaction might be implemented.

10.2. Local ambiguity resolution by the weak interaction

In order to show how the weak interaction might actually work, it is necessary to specify both the way in which the alternative analyses are proposed, and the way in which semantics disposes of these proposals.

10.2.1. Serial versus parallel models

It seems inevitable that a weakly interactive model, relying on plausibility and reference to context to decide which parse route to follow, would have initially to construct such interpretations in parallel, rather than considering them serially. Whereas wellformedness and some structural considerations can be treated as all-or-none judgments, the use of context seems only to allow comparison of analyses, because by definition no felicitous utterance is entirely predictable from context. (It is significant in this connection that on the limited occasions on which Marcus, 1980, proposes to allow lexical features and co-occurrence restrictions to decide ambiguities in the application of a rule within his look ahead buffer, he too proposes the corresponding structures in parallel. Swinney, 1979, has found experimental evidence of short-term parallel activation of all senses of ambiguous words in context, followed by very rapid elimination of all but contextually appropriate senses.) It seems inconceivable that there could exist an *absolute* criterion by which plausibility in this broader sense could be assessed. It would have to be a pragmatic, context-dependent criterion, such as one specifying the amount of "new information" (in the sense used by Halliday, 1967) that an utterance should contribute. However, if it did exist, such a criterion could be applied to alternative analyses proposed in series under a strictly structural criterion, such as the Minimal Attachment strategy of Frazier and Fodor (1978), until one proved acceptable. Under this hypothesis, the prediction would be that the structures proposed first would show a lesser processing load – that is, even in a weakly interactive model of the kind proposed here, there would be a residual effect of structure. If alternative analyses are proposed in parallel for disposal by semantics, on the other hand, then no such residual effects should appear. These contrary predictions are investigated in experiment III below.

   In what does the "disposal" among alternative analyses by semantics consist? We take it that the very existence of garden path phenomena shows that eventually one alternative is selected according to goodness of fit to the context,[11] and that at least on some occasions it is not possible for the processor to later back up to try a previously rejected alternative. Like any processor that commits itself to one analysis of a local ambiguity via a possibly fallible heuristic, this one predicts increased difficulty on the occasions where the heuristic goes wrong. However, rather than predicting difficulty for a given *structure*, the present theory predicts difficulty for certain sentences when they are used *in given contexts*. The account does not of itself imply any distinction between blind alleys that can be recovered from and those (implied in the term *garden path*) from which recovery is impossible, although there will certainly be occasions on which the dissonance between the context and the sentence is so great that the hearer cannot find his or her way to any grammatical parse. The implication is that there will be no purely structural garden paths – that is, ones that cannot be eliminated by the manipulation of semantics and context. These predictions also are investigated in the experimental section of the paper. But first it will be necessary to show how the weak interaction might exploit context and reference.

10.2.2. Plausibility, reference, and presupposition

The simplest weak interaction between context and processing rests on a basis of a priori plausibility, based on semantics and world-knowledge, both specific and general. Winograd's and Marcus's unimplemented proposals of this kind have already been mentioned. We might embody this interaction in the following principle:

(4) *The Principle of A Priori Plausibility.* If a reading is more plausible in terms either of general knowledge about the world, or of specific knowledge about the universe of discourse, then, other things being equal, it will be favored over one that is not.

What the "other things" that have to be equal are, and how "plausibility" is assessed, are discussed next. However, we may note at this point that, in case of a conflict between general and specific knowledge, then the latter must clearly take precedence.

One kind of specific knowledge about the universe of discourse is embodied in the particular referents that are present in the listener's mental model of the universe of discourse, and several mechanisms have been proposed for the weak interaction between syntactic processes and reference to a mental model.

An early and particularly interesting proposal of this kind for present purposes is that of Winograd (1972). He proposed that ambiguities in the closure of definite noun phrases in parsing sentences like

(5) a. Put [the block in the box]$_{NP}$ [on the table]$_{PP}$
     b. Put [the block]$_{NP}$ [in the box on the table]$_{PP}$

could be resolved on the basis of the candidate NP's success in referring to a simulated "mental model," which took the form of a data base representing the state of a simple universe of discourse and the previous conversation. If the state of this model showed that there was indeed a block in the box, and moreover that this block was uniquely identifiable either by virtue of being the only one, or by having been recently mentioned, then analysis (a) was adopted. However, if that analysis failed to produce any referent, and provided that the state of the model and the previous conversation was such as to make the expression *the block* produce a unique referent (again either by virtue of uniqueness in the model or of recent mention), then analysis (b) would be adopted.[12] It will be convenient to refer to a rather general form of this heuristic as the Principle of Referential Success, and define it as follows:

(6) *The Principle of Referential Success.* If there is a reading that succeeds in referring to an entity already established in the hearer's mental model of the domain of discourse, then it is favored over one that does not.

(This principle is a special case of the earlier Principle of A Priori Plausibility. It will later be subsumed under a more general principle.)

The way that referential success was evaluated by Winograd gave a dramatically simple "procedural" account of the concepts of "sense" and "reference" for this limited domain. The interpretation or sense of an expression like *the block in the box* was taken to be a LISP procedure that would search the data base for an appropriate object, producing (if successful) a value identifying the object in question. Such a procedure was assembled from smaller fragments of LISP corresponding to the senses of the components of the phrase. For example the sense of the word "block" was a procedure that tested whether a given entity in the world-model had the properties appropriate to blocks. The sense of the phrase "in the box," recursively assembled from the senses of its components, was a procedure to test whether a given entity was positioned in the box in question. The sense of the article "the" was a test to ensure either that the set of things in the model satisfying the procedure corresponding to the words "block in the box" contained one member, or that one of the set had recently been mentioned, and to deliver that unique member. Like the traditional concept of sense, the procedure produced in this way was the same every time the expression was used. The referent was simply the value, say BLOCK49, produced by running this program with the database in a certain state. This value was typically *not* the same on every occasion of use. The concept of reference itself corresponded to the execution of the sense-procedure. (See Woods, 1975, for a discussion of the relation of procedural semantics to traditional terminology.)

As an account of reference, Winograd's model was extremely simplified and failed to address many questions of the nature of indefinite reference, or of attributive and other uses of definite expressions. (See objections by Woods, 1975; Ritchie, 1977; Marcus, 1980. It will be noted that the interpretation of the "sense" of a referring expression adopted in the present paper is not the same as a search procedure. It is in fact much closer to the nonprocedural, logic-related variety of the semantics of such expressions. In common with Ritchie (1977), we regard the sense-as-procedure view of semantics as too narrow. The sense of an expression must of course be something more general, which can be *interpreted as* a procedure, *or* as a formula. Moreover, the process by which Winograd's program proposed and rejected alternative analyses was a serial one based on sheer length of the relevant substring. We have already suggested that in order to take account of the relative nature of goodness of fit to a context, such interactions would have to be parallel.) Nevertheless, this program remains an important example of the general feasibility of using reference to resolve syntactic ambiguities. More recent accounts of the interaction between parsing and semantics have not been limited to reference and the noun phrase as a unit. Steedman and Johnson-Laird (1978), in the context of a model of "functional sentence perspective" and "given" and "new" information, described a program that incrementally compared a sentence with a data base "mental model" as the successive arguments of the verb were encountered. Bobrow and Webber (1981) have also described a parser guided by such "incremental" semantics.

Most of the computational work that has been done on reference since Winograd's has concentrated upon the problem of deploying complex knowledge in order to establish reference, and in particular on the representation of knowledge about the conversation itself. Accounts such as those of Grosz (1977), Sidner (1979), and Webber (1978) have attempted to elaborate the concept of *focus*, and the way in which referents may be inferred on the basis of complex world knowledge, rather than being found among things which have received explicit mention in the previous discourse. Mellish (1981) has shown how much more complex varieties of quantified expression may be incrementally evaluated during parsing. However, much less has been done in the way of extending such mechanisms to deal with certain other varieties of referring expression – in particular, certain other uses of definite expressions. The following remarks concerning some extensions of this nature are therefore necessarily preliminary and tentative.

In explaining the kinds of effects of context that are investigated in the second, experimental half of the paper, we assume that the domain of reference in these models is a *mental representation* of a specific conversational context, including things that have been mentioned and (some) things that have been implied in the conversation, rather than the world itself.[13] The domain of reference cannot be the world alone since certain effects of context are due to the speaker's *introducing* referents into the hearer's model, rather than merely recognizing reference to items already introduced in the conversation. For example, there are uses of definite referring expressions other than the one discussed by Winograd. If someone asks "Did you see the man who just walked past the window?" of a hearer who in fact did not, then the hearer will evidently *not* have a preexisting referent for the definite expression in his or her model of the universe of discourse. Instead, the hearer, having detected the presupposition (or entailment) of that referent's existence in the speaker's mental model, and assuming that the speaker is conversationally cooperative (Grice, 1975), will set up such a referent in his or her own mental model, always provided that it does not positively contradict the rest of the model. (This process has been described by Lewis, 1979, with the "Rule of accommodation for presupposition,"[11] by Stalnaker, 1974, and by Kartunnen, 1974, as "extending" the context; and by Soames, 1982, as the "addition of presuppositions to the conversational context of an utterance." Hawkins, 1978, refers to such uses of restrictive relatives as "establishing" relative clauses.) The conversants will from then on be able to refer to the referent thus established, as for example when the first speaker says "Well, *he* wasn't wearing any clothes." It follows that in examining the effects of context upon processing it is necessary to consider, not only the actual content of the hearer's preestablished context, but also the ways in which expressions that initially have no referent there may themselves cause such referents to be added.

Winograd's and his followers' models of reference and its interaction with syntax do not handle the second kind of reference at all. (For example, the process that was described earlier for definite noun phrases would simply fail once it became clear that there was no previously established referent for the phrase *the man who just walked past the window*.) What would be involved in extending such a program to handle definite expressions more appropriately? Once it is clear that there is no alternative analysis that is consistent with the model, the program must modify the model itself, add into it a new element, MAN49 say, together with the information that this entity just walked past the window, perhaps as some formula such as [MAN49 WALK PAST WINDOW2 AT TIME1249]. There is considerable experimental support for this intuitively attractive view of the hearer's part in the process of reference and the dependence of that process on the state of the hearer's mental model. Seidenberg and Tanenhaus (1977) have shown definite expressions to take longer to comprehend when a referent has not been established by the preceding discourse, and Wason (1965, 1981) and Johnson-Laird (1968a, b) have shown that some increased comprehension latencies that used to be cited in support of the derivational theory of complexity were in fact an artifact arising from mismatches between the context and the presuppositions of the test sentences.

But what if there are *two* or more possible senses, neither of which succeeds in referring in the hearer's model? How does the hearer select which reading to allow to modify the model? We suggest the following heuristic, which we will call the Principle of Parsimony.

(7) *The Principle of Parsimony.* If there is a reading that carries fewer unsatisfied but consistent presuppositions or entailments than any other, then, other criteria of plausibility being equal, that reading will be adopted as most plausible by the hearer, and the presuppositions in question will be incorporated in his or her model.

(We conjecture that the reason for the principle is simply that each conversational participant only has *one* model of the universe of discourse.

The reading that involves fewest alterations to this model will be favored, perhaps simply because it is computed most quickly.) This principle is again a special case of the Principle of A Priori Plausibility, and subsumes the earlier Principle of Referential Success. If one or more readings successfully refer then by definition they implicate *no* changes to the model, and any other readings will be less parsimonious in their demands.

It is an immediate consequence of a model in which referring expressions can themselves change the model, and in which ambiguities may be resolved on grounds of presuppositional "loadedness," that some of the evidence that has been cited in support of purely structural influences on ambiguity resolution may need to be reexamined. Restrictive relative clauses by their nature carry more presuppositions or entailments than simple NPs, and so in a neutral context, which satisfies neither reading of a sentence that is ambiguous between these readings, we might expect the simple noun phrase to be preferred *on pragmatic grounds*, rather than on grounds of its structural simplicity as has been suggested in a number of structuralist strategies, such as Kimball's Closure Principle, Frazier and Fodor's Minimal Attachment, Ford, Bresnan, and Kaplan's Invoked Attachment and Marcus's Limited Lookahead.

The suggestion has strong empirical consequences. The garden path effect of the sentences in (2) such as

(8) The horse raced past the barn fell.   (= 2a)

has widely been supposed to arise from some structural peculiarity of the sentence, relative to some such strategy. However, we have suggested that the local ambiguity of the fragment *the horse raced past the barn*, as between an analysis as an S beginning with a simple NP and an analysis as a complex NP, could be resolved by reference to context, requiring the satisfaction of any presuppositions. If so, then we might expect that the garden path effect due to the simple NP analysis would be removed by making the use of a complex NP felicitous by embedding it in a story involving more than one horse and some racing. Similarly, one might expect the garden path effect to be exacerbated by a different story concerning only one horse, thus making felicitous the simple NP. This prediction is investigated in experiment II below.

It is important to note that we cannot assume that the so-called null context, in which no horses whatsoever have been mentioned, will be neutral with respect to the above sentence, for the following reason. Although the null context does not *provide* a referent for either the simple or the complex NP reading, it may still not be *neutral* with respect to the sentence, because the two readings may, because of the differential number of presupposition/entailments that they invoke, differ in the ease with which the hearer can *set up* their referents. The scenario corresponding to the restrictive relative reading of (8) involving *the horse (which was) raced* . . . is surely more presuppositionally complex than that for the usual garden path reading, which involves a simple NP. It includes several horses rather than one, and a number of further facts about the basis on which they can be distinguished. Otherwise the speaker would have said *The horse fell* or *A horse fell*. We need look no further than the sheer number of presuppositions in order to see grounds for distinguishing the two readings with respect to the so-called null context.

Nor is this a matter of a priori plausibility of the rival readings in terms of general world-knowledge. There is *no* absolute difference in plausibility between the two readings. In fact they provide a good example of our contention that the notion of plausibility is incomplete in the absence of a specification of a particular context, a point that has been made by Wason (1981) in connection with the comprehension of negatives.

The model has implications for other varieties of referring expressions, and makes equally strong predictions for them. For example, *non*restrictive relatives carry only the presuppositions that would be associated with the simple head nominal, since the subordinate clause supplies "new information," rather than restricting the reference set. The classical garden-pathing experiments do not allow subjects the alternative of the nonrestrictive analysis (since written nonrestrictive relatives are typically marked with commas). But Hamburger and Crain (1981) have provided some evidence that the nonrestrictive reading is favored in contexts that do not support the richer restrictive reading. Their results indicate that the reported difficulties in comprehension of (spoken) restrictive relatives by young children (Solan and Roeper, 1978; Sheldon, 1974, 1977; Tavakolian, 1978) are artifactual. Hamburger and Crain argue that the original experiments forced the children to adopt a nonrestrictive interpretation, by only offering a context containing one item of the appropriate category. Once such a possibility was excluded (by using context situations including several items of the relevant category), the children were capable of understanding and even producing sentences containing restrictives at an early age.

Similarly, speakers who utter indefinite noun phrases do not necessarily commit themselves to the presuppositions of the corresponding definites. The use of a referential definite like *the horse which was raced past the barn* presupposes (among other things): (1) that a set of individuals identified by the head nominal (in this case a set of horses) is already represented in the hearer's model; (2) that it is already given or implicit that the relative clause applies to some individual in that set; (3) that the whole expression identifies a *single* individual. The nonrestrictive interpretation of the referential definite lacks the second presupposition, while indefinites like *a horse which was raced past the barn* need presuppose none of these things. One can use the latter phrase if no particular set of horses has been mentioned, whether or not the question of racing has been raised, and of course there is no implication that there is only one individual who fits the description.

It is usual to distinguish between "generic" and "existential" uses of indefinites. The distinction is exhibited in the following pair of sentences.

(9) a. A bad workman blames his tools.
     b. A bad workman walked through the door.

The same distinction is exhibited by "bare plurals" (see Carlson, 1977).

(10) a. Bad workmen blame their tools.
     b. Bad workmen walked through the door.

The existential interpretation is favored in the (b) sentences because of the fact that (for reasons that are of no immediate concern) they induce a nonstative, nonhabitual reading, and generics by definition necessarily have stative predications made about them. The generic interpretation is favored (though not necessitated) in the (a) sentences because their simple present tense favors a stative reading; nonspecific existential sets of individuals do not commonly have stative predications made of them.

The existential interpretations of these indefinites cause an entity of some kind (individual or set) to be added to the mental model, and carry no further presuppositions or entailments. It follows that if indefinite noun phrases are substituted for their definite counterparts in Bever's sentences (2), fewer changes to the so-called neutral context will be associated with the choice of the restrictive relative interpretation of fragments like *a horse raced past a barn* . . . Both this analysis and the analysis interpreting this string as a complete sentence cause one individual to be added to the model, and on both analyses it must be noted that it is a horse, and that it raced or was raced past the barn.[14] Since the scores of changes to the model are equal, the Principle of Parsimony predicts that the garden pathing effect of the construction will be considerably reduced by changing the garden path sentences (2) to carry the existential readings as in (11) and (12), an operation that will leave their structural properties unchanged:

(11) a. A horse raced past a barn fell.
     b. A boat floated down a river sank.
     c. A dealer sold a forgery complained.

(12) a. Horses raced past barns fell.
     b. Boats floated down rivers sank.
     c. Dealers sold forgeries complained.

Garden path effects should therefore be less frequent than for definite noun phrases.

The other variety of indefinite reference under consideration here, the generic, similarly reduces the presuppositional imbalance between the rival local analyses. Utterances like the following do not seem to carry any presuppositions, but merely cause hearers to introduce into the focus of discourse the concept or set of all cows.

(13)   a.   Cows will often eat dandelions.
      b.   A cow will often eat dandelions.

Therefore, when generics are introduced into the garden path sentences (2), as in

(14)   a.   A horse raced past a barn falls.
      b.   A boat floated down a river sinks.
      c.   A dealer sold a forgery complains.

and, for the bare plurals

(15)   a.   Horses raced past barns fall.
      b.   Boats floated down rivers sink.
      c.   Dealers sold forgeries complain.

garden path effects are at least as unlikely to occur as with the existential indefinites. These predictions are investigated in experiment I below.

Our attempt to specify in detail the consequences that would ensue from using reference to guide parsing is very speculative.[15] However, even if our analysis should prove to be incorrect about the finer details of the existential and generic interpretations, this general approach does seem to imply, at the very least, that the replacement of definite NPs by indefinites or bare plurals should tend to reduce garden path effects. On a structuralist theory of garden pathing, in contrast, the indefinite versions of the Bever sentences are predicted to behave exactly like the corresponding definites in (2), since they are structurally identical.

10.2.3. Summary

The preceding sections of the paper have argued that local syntactic ambiguities are resolved by an interaction of the "weak" variety from semantics and reference, which can evaluate alternatives proposed by the syntactic processor. It has been suggested that these alternatives are proposed in parallel, rather than serially under some structural criterion. The manner in which such an interaction might involve reference to a mental model of a situation, via the evaluation of noun phrases, has been explored in some detail. Some ways in which specific differences in the context of utterance might have differing effects on processing choices have been proposed in the form of the Principle of A Priori Plausibility, and the successively more general principles of Referential Success and of Par-

338   *Crain and Steedman*

simony, and we have argued that the so-called neutral context is typically far from neutral with respect to this process. We have also suggested that such an interaction could occur with great intimacy, well before the processing of a clause, or even certain phrases, is completed.

In the next part of the paper we consider some experimental evidence for these proposals. There are three main predictions: (1) that referential context can influence garden path effects; (2) that it can do so even while the clause remains incomplete; (3) that residual structural effects, such as those predicted by a model in which alternative analyses are proposed in series under a structural criterion such as Minimal Attachment for disposal by semantics and reference, will not be apparent. The first and major prediction is investigated in experiment I, in which definiteness is manipulated in a so-called neutral context, and in experiment II, in which the context itself is manipulated. Prediction 2 is also investigated in the second experiment, while prediction 3 is investigated in the third experiment.

10.3. Experiments

Much current research has adopted the strategy of supposedly eliminating contextual effects by the use of the so-called null context; that is, by presenting sentences in isolation. However, we have argued that the context of sentence processing consists in a mental model that is actively constructed by the hearer, using inference on the basis of his or her knowledge of the way the world works. The fact that the experimental situation in question makes a null contribution to the context does not mean that the context is null. It is merely not under the experimenter's control.

A way of bringing the context under experimental control might seem to be to choose sentences whose ambiguous readings can be claimed to be balanced for plausibility, and this stratagem too has been widely adopted. However, because plausibility in the broad sense used in the present study can only be assessed with respect to a given context, and because the so-called null context is in fact simply an *unknown* context, this expedient is still subject to the objection that the set of assumptions under which the subject constructs a context are not under control. Any processing preferences that are observed may therefore be due to facts about the construction of that context, rather than about the structural properties of the different readings.

It is therefore necessary to control context in a much fuller sense, offering the target sentences in a matrix of preceding sentences that unambiguously establish a known set of assumptions under which the subject will approach the target sentence. In this way, minimal differences in such preliminary information that will lead to differences in ambiguity resolution can be discovered and distinguished from properties of the target sentences themselves.

The production of minimal pairs of conditions is the basis of all experimental scientific investigation. However, the method has not been widely used in the study of contextual effects. It is generally admitted that one can devise different contexts that result in different interpretations of an ambiguous sentence. But the differences between these contexts are usually so substantial that researchers have been unable to identify which of the several possible mechanisms are responsible for the variations in interpreting the ambiguity.

Garden path phenomena can be used to reflect the influence of minimal differences in referential context in two ways. One method is to use such differences to overcome garden path difficulties that would otherwise occur. The other is to use them to create garden paths where they *would not* otherwise occur. These are the methods used in the first two of the experiments that follow. (All the experiments are from Crain, 1980.) A third experiment investigates the question of whether structurally based strategies are also involved, in the following way. Suppose that two minimally differing contexts result in different analyses of an ambiguous sentence. If the presence of a certain feature in the first context caused the parser to select one analysis and another feature in the second caused the parser to pursue the alternative analysis, a new context containing both features then controls for them. In this context, any residual preference in the resolution of the ambiguity must either be the result of an inherent bias in the salience of those features, or be due to a purely structural preference for one analysis over the other. In cases where it can be argued that no pragmatic bias is present, any bias in the ambiguity resolution must be ascribed to structural criteria.

10.3.1. Experiment I: Avoiding garden paths

In the following experiment, manipulations of plausibility and referential character are used to overcome garden path effects that typically occur in their absence. By minimally changing classic garden path sentences and comparing these with the originals, it becomes possible to see what kind of semantic and pragmatic information is called on by the parser. The following sentences are structurally identical to *The horse raced past the barn fell.*

(16) a. The teachers taught by the Berlitz method passed the test.
      b. The children taught by the Berlitz method passed the test.
      c. Teachers taught by the Berlitz method passed the test.
      d. Children taught by the Berlitz method passed the test.

In examples (a) and (b), plausibility (that is, the likelihood of a particular reading in the light of general real-world knowledge) is manipulated in order to determine its effect during parsing. In sentences (c) and (d) what is manipulated is the definiteness, and hence the referential and presuppositional character, of the subject NPs.

Sentences like these were presented visually one word at a time across a CRT screen. The words remained on the screen until the end of the sentence, which was marked by the appearance of three asterisks. Eight subjects saw one of four lists. Each list contained one of the 4 versions (a–d) of each of 18 sentences like (16). Seven of the 18 sentences containing bare plurals used the present tense form for the final verb as in (e) and (f), allowing us to distinguish the effects of existential and generic uses of indefinite noun phrases upon garden paths.

(16) e.   Teachers taught by the Berlitz method pass the test.
      f.   Children taught by the Berlitz method pass the test.

Each of the 4 versions for a sentence was randomly assigned to a list. All versions appeared in the same position in each list, interspersed among 74 filler sentences, with at least 2 fillers appearing between any 2 target sentences. Eleven of the fillers were ungrammatical, as were 3 of the 11 practice sentences.

The subject's task was to decide whether or not each sentence was grammatical. Subjects were told that ungrammatical sentences would contain extra words, have words missing, or would exhibit violations of number agreement. They were instructed not to judge a sentence ungrammatical on the basis of its meaning.

Following Frazier (1979) a rather rapid presentation rate of 300 msec per word was used, which is slow enough to allow each word to be recognized accurately, but fast enough to pressure the subjects sufficiently to reveal processing difficulty. The sentences were removed from the screen 300 msec after completion, and subjects had only 2 seconds to give their response to each sentence before another sentence appeared.

Grammaticality decisions were analyzed with both subjects and sentences as random variables. The (b) and (d) sentences (plausible, definite/indefinite relative clause interpretation) were judged grammatical significantly more often than the (a) and (c) sentences, $F_1(1,31) = 12.95$, $p < .01$ and $F_2(1,17) = 11.18$, $p < .005$, showing the effect of semantic plausibility and real world knowledge on syntactic processing.

This result confirms the observation by Bever (1970) that a priori plausibility of the local S reading of the initial words reduces the garden path effect in such variants of the garden path sentence (3) as (17).

(17) The articles read in the paper stank.

Similar results have recently been confirmed by Crain and Coker (1978) and by Frazier (private communication).

The (c) and (d) sentences (indefinite, implausible/plausible relative clause reading; see (16c,d) above) were judged grammatical significantly more often than the definites (a) and (b), $F_2(1,31) = 19.10$, $p < .001$ and $F_2(1,17) = 17.06$, $p < .001$. This difference confirms one of the predictions of the preceding section, that the relative clause analysis of the ambiguous word string should be more accessible for indefinite than for definite noun phrases, because the indefinite examples make fewer extensions of the mental model.

Another prediction was confirmed. The seven generic (e) and (f) sentences combined evoked significantly fewer judgments of ungrammaticality than the eleven existential (c) and (d) sentences combined ($z = 1.82$; $p < .05$). Subjects found the generic sentences ungrammatical only 29 percent of the time, even at this fast rate of presentation. (Sentences (e) and (f) did not evoke significantly different judgments.) It is worth noting that, though the differences are not significant, the (d) sentences (which are both indefinite and plausible) were accepted slightly more often than either the (b) or the (c) sentences, as expected.

10.3.2. Experiment II: Creating garden paths

A second procedure for determining the effect of context on parsing decisions uses context to *induce* garden path effects as well as to overcome them (see Crain, 1980). For instance, in the following sentence there is a preference for analyzing the words *that John wanted to visit the lab* as a complement clause rather than as a relative clause attached to *the child*.

(18) It frightened the child that John wanted to visit the lab.

Such preferences have commonly been attributed to structural factors. However, when there is a referent for "it" in the context, the preference can be switched, as (19) shows.

(19) *Context:* There was an explosion.
      It frightened the child that John wanted to visit the lab.

By contrast, (20) shows how such a context can be used to induce a garden path effect. Since the target sentence follows a context that both establishes a referent for *it* and satisfies the presuppositions of the relative clause analysis, a garden path effect results.

(20) *Context:* Several children heard an explosion.
      It frightened the child that John wanted him to visit the lab.

Since the target sentence in (20) is *only* grammatical on a complement clause analysis, and a relative clause analysis is encouraged by the context, it appears to be ungrammatical. In this context it appears to exhibit the same sort of ungrammaticality as (21).

(21) *We frightened the child that John wanted him to visit the lab.

These examples suggest that referential context can be made to induce garden path effects where they do not occur otherwise, in the so-called null context. In a second experiment, minimal pairs of contexts were constructed to induce either relative or complement readings of locally ambiguous sentences in a similar way, as follows.

(22)   The psychologist told the wife that he was having

$$\text{trouble with}\begin{cases}\text{to leave her husband.}\\\text{her husband.}\end{cases}$$

Contexts in which the complement clause reading of the ambiguous substring *the wife that he was having trouble with . . .* is felicitous are easy to come by. Since it is the reading with the fewest presuppositions, even the so-called null context makes this reading felicitous, a fact that has arguably lent spurious support to a number of structural disambiguation strategies such as Minimal Attachment. But other contexts favoring the complement reading can be constructed in order to provide minimal pairs with contexts that make relative clause readings felicitous, as in (23a and b). If in such contexts the ambiguous substring is assigned a relative clause analysis, then when *her husband* is encountered it should evoke a garden path effect. If a complement clause analysis is pursued, *to leave her husband* should be unacceptable.

(23)   a.   *Complement-inducing context*
              A psychologist was counseling a married couple.
              One member of the pair was fighting with him but the other one was nice to him.

       b.   *Relative-inducing context*
              A psychologist was counseling two married couples.
              One of the couples was fighting with him but the other one was nice to him.

       c.   *Complement target sentence*
              The psychologist told the wife that he was having trouble with her husband.

       d.   *Relative target sentence*
              The psychologist told the wife that he was having trouble with to leave her husband.

The target sentences (c) and (d) both contain completing phrases that will produce garden path effects if the inappropriate context is used to decide the syntactic analysis of the ambiguous substring *the wife that he was having trouble with*. The presence of two married couples in the relative-inducing context establishes a set of wives, making the use of a restrictive modifying phrase felicitous. The simple NP *the wife* does not succeed in referring, while the complex NP *the wife that he was having trouble with* does. In the complement-inducing context only one woman has been introduced, so the simple NP analysis is felicitous, and the complex is not.

Four pairs of contexts comparable to (23) were constructed and were assigned to lists in the following way. Each list contained either a complement-inducing context like (23a) or a relative-inducing context like (23b), and each context was followed by either an appropriate or an inappropriate target sentence like (23c) and (23d), making four lists (given in Appendix 10B). These experimental contexts and their targets were randomly interspersed among 30 filler items, also consisting of contexts followed by target sentences, and either two or three of the experimental contexts and targets discussed below as experiment III. Two lists had a total of 35 items, and two had 36 items. Ten of the filler items contained ungrammatical target sentences. The 4 lists were presented to different subjects, 17 in each group (N = 68), so that no subject saw the same target sentence more than once. Each list was preceded by 5 practice items. Three of the target sentences in these practice trials were ungrammatical.

The materials were presented one word at a time 550 msec apart on a CRT screen in front of the subject. The subject was instructed to read the context sentences and the target sentences silently. The context sentences were erased from the screen before the target sentence appeared. A tone was presented between the context and target sentences to indicate that a target sentence would be presented one second later. Subjects were instructed to press a response key if the target sentence following the tone was ungrammatical. Subjects were told to use the context to help them make sense of the target sentences and to try to find a grammatical, coherent analysis of each target sentence if possible. The kind of ungrammaticality subjects were instructed to look for was defined by examples and by the description "sentences containing missing words; extra, unexpected words; and failures of agreement."[16, 17]

The complement target sentences produced garden path effects when preceded by a relative-inducing context (e.g., when *her husband* was the completing phrase) 54 percent of the time. When the same context was succeeded by the relative target sentence, 22 percent of the subjects' responses indicated that the sentence appeared to be ungrammatical. In the complement-inducing context, the complement target sentence produced garden path effects only 12 percent of the time. This is hardly surprising since this analysis is also preferred in the so-called null context. However, the relative target sentence evoked reports of ungrammaticality 50 percent of the time. That is, people took a garden path that they could not recover from about equally often in both contexts (when the completing phrase was inconsistent with the context). The interaction between context and target sentence was significant for both analyses (subjects: $F_1(1,50)$ = 39.29, p < .001; contexts: $F_2(1,3)$ = 14.53, p < .05).[18] We conclude that referential context is made use of during parsing and is the principal determinant of garden path effects.[19]

The question remains open whether the two analyses are pursued in series or in parallel. It also remains an open question whether the alternatives are *proposed* in parallel or in series. The experiment does not exclude the possibility that a structural strategy such as Minimal Attachment or Invoked Attachment proposes just one analysis, which semantics and reference then may reject (although we have indicated in our preliminary discussion that we do not regard this as very likely, in view of the fact that plausibility is a *relative* matter, and is therefore best suited to providing a ranking of alternative analyses). The question of whether structural strategies are *also* appealed to is considered in the next experiment.

10.3.3. Experiment III: Are structurally based strategies used as well?

If contexts can be devised which establish appropriate referents for both syntactic analyses, then in the absence of any difference in a priori plausibility between the rival analyses, any residual preference for one or the other would seem to require a structural explanation. An example of a first attempt at finding such a context is given below.

(24)   *Context-establishing sentences*
   a.   Three new players joined the baseball team.
   b.   Several older players picked one of the new players to join them for the first practice.
   c.   The other new players were upset by this.

Target sentence
The coach convinced the player that the old pros chose to practice by $\left\{ \begin{array}{l} \text{himself} \\ \text{themselves} \end{array} \right\}$ for the rest of spring training.

In this context there is a unique referent established in sentence (b) for the expression *the player*. (This much is evident from the fact that the word *him* can be substituted for the expression in the target sentence.) This feature of the context implies a complement clause in the target sentence – that is, one in which the old pros chose to practice by themselves. (Presumably, the fact that the other new players were upset led to this decision.) Alternatively, the word *that* could begin a restrictive relative clause in the target, since both the sets of felicity conditions mentioned before have been met. That is, there are a set of referents, a felicity condition for a restrictive modifying phrase, namely the players mentioned in (a) and (b), and the presupposition expressed by the singular definite article and the relative clause is established, because one of these players *was* chosen by the old pros.

Five pairs of context and target sentences comparable to (24) were assigned to the four lists of stimulus items described under experiment II. Two of these were assigned to two lists and three to the other two lists. These lists differed with respect to the target sentence that followed the context sentences, so that each context preceded each type of target sentence only once (the context and target sentences are given in Appendix 10C). The remaining items on the lists and the experimental procedures are presented in experiment II.

When the presuppositions of both the complement clause and relative clause analyses of the target sentences were fulfilled in this way subjects indicated no significant preference for either the complement clause or relative clause analysis of the target sentence. Both the relative and complement target sentences were judged grammatical 61 percent of the time following the five context sets.[20] While it is possible that there was a structural preference for the simple NP neatly counterbalanced by a lesser plausibility or increased difficulty associated with this analysis in this particular context, we see no particular reason to suppose that such was the case. In the absence of any evidence for such a bias, the result at least suggests that no parsing strategy based on relative structural complexity was used by subjects to decide upon the syntactic analysis to pursue in these sentences. In particular, it lends no support to the rival proposal considered in section 10.2.1 that, while semantics can *decide between* alternative analyses, they are nevertheless *proposed* serially on the basis of structural criteria.

10.4. Conclusion

In this paper, we have contrasted explanations of local ambiguity resolution which tap semantics and reference to context with those based solely on structural and lexical strategies. We have argued on theoretical and on experimental grounds that some of the phenomena that have led to the proposal of strategies such as Minimal Attachment (Frazier, 1979) and Lexical or Syntactic Preferences and Invoked Attachment (Ford, Bresnan, and Kaplan, 1981) are in fact due to the evaluation of the alternative analyses with respect to their plausibility in the context in which they are used. In these and many other experiments claiming the contrary, the only context used has been the so-called null context, which we have shown is far from neutral in these matters. The experiments presented here suggest that there may be *no* intrinsically garden-pathing structures whatever, but rather that, for any given sentence, there are certain contexts (including the null context) which induce garden paths, and certain others which do not.

We have also argued that such evaluations can be made well before the sentences are complete. The fact that the contextual cues seem to be used during the first pass through a sentence, often before the last words have been encountered at all, is important. The knowledge that the presuppositions of a relative clause have or have not been established appears to be used during (not following) sentence comprehension. This result is in conflict with previous accounts of comprehension, which claim that the division of a sentence into given and new information occurs only after its syntactic and semantic interpretation is completed (Clark and Haviland, 1974; Cutler, 1976; and Holmes, 1979). It also appears to be incompatible with noninteractive processing of syntax even in a "modified" version limiting interaction to the level of major phrases, at least on the reasonable assumption that the corresponding representationally autonomous units provide the input to semantic interpretation, for such models do not explain how the effects could be found before the constituent is complete.

Once context was controlled, no residual effects of structural mechanisms were apparent for the material in this study. However, the question of whether *anything* more than semantics is used for local ambiguity resolution remains open. A particularly interesting area for investigation will be the other major set of ambiguity resolution phenomena that have variously been ascribed to structural or lexical strategies like Right Association (Kimball, 1973), Late Closure (Frazier, 1978), or Final Arguments (Ford, Bresnan, and Kaplan, 1981). We believe that the systematic study of minimal pairs of contexts and the further refinement of theoretical accounts of reference will be crucial in such investigations.

APPENDIX 10A: MATERIALS FOR EXPERIMENT I

1. a. The teacher taught by the Berlitz method passed the test.
   b. The child taught by the Berlitz method passed the test.
   c. Teachers taught by the Berlitz method passed the test.
   d. Children taught by the Berlitz method passed the test.

2. a. The large corporation loaned money at low interest rates kept accurate records of its expenses.
   b. The small business loaned money at low interest rates kept accurate records of its expenses.
   c. Large corporations loaned money at low interest rates kept accurate records of their expenses.
   d. Small businesses loaned money at low interest rates kept accurate records of their expenses.

3. a. The assassin killed in the line of duty was mourned.
   b. The medic killed in the line of duty was mourned.

    c. Assassins killed in the line of duty were mourned.
    d. Medics killed in the line of duty were mourned.

4. a. The captain issued the pass used it to leave on the weekend.
    b. The visitor issued the pass used it to leave on the weekend.
    c. Captains issued the passes used them to leave on the weekend.
    d. Visitors issued the passes used them to leave on the weekend.

5. a. The fighter pushed into the crowd could not move.
    b. The youngster pushed into the crowd could not move.
    c. Fighters pushed into the crowd could not move.
    d. Youngsters pushed into the crowd could not move.

6. a. The manager charged for the repairs thought he was cheated.
    b. The customer charged for the repairs thought he was cheated.
    c. Managers charged for the repairs thought they were cheated.
    d. Customers charged for the repairs thought they were cheated.

7. a. The official warned about possible layoffs picketed the company's main office.
    b. The worker warned about possible layoffs picketed the company's main office.
    c. Officials warned about possible layoffs picketed the company's main office.
    d. Workers warned about possible layoffs picketed the company's main office.

8. a. The general presented the award returned to his place in line.
    b. The winner presented the award returned to his place in line.
    c. Generals presented the awards returned to their places in line.
    d. Winners presented the awards returned to their places in line.

9. a. The postman delivered the junk mail threw it in the trash.
    b. The tenant delivered the junk mail threw it in the trash.
    c. Postmen delivered the junk mail threw it in the trash.
    d. Tenants delivered the junk mail threw it in the trash.

10. a. The professors instructed about the assignments were confused.
    b. The students instructed about the assignments were confused.
    c. Professors instructed about the assignments were confused.
    d. Students instructed about the assignments were confused.

11. a. The soldiers dropped from the airplanes into the jungle were not seen by the enemy.
    b. The supplies dropped from the airplanes into the jungle were not seen by the enemy.
    c. Soldiers dropped from the airplanes into the jungle were not seen by the enemy.

    d. Supplies dropped from the airplanes into the jungle were not seen by the enemy.

12. a. The contestant wheeled onto the track watched the finish of the race.
    b. The invalid wheeled onto the track watched the finish of the race.
    c. Contestants wheeled onto the track can watch the finish of the race.
    d. Invalids wheeled onto the track can watch the finish of the race.

13. a. The host offered the tempting food gulped it down.
    b. The guest offered the tempting food gulped it down.
    c. Hosts offered tempting food gulp it down.
    d. Guests offered tempting food gulp it down.

14. a. The owner asked to have the food ready in advance could serve at any time.
    b. The chef asked to have the food ready in advance could serve at any time.
    c. Owners asked to have the food ready in advance can serve at any time.
    d. Chefs asked to have the food ready in advance can serve at any time.

15. a. The grandfather rocked to sleep finally woke up.
    b. The grandchild rocked to sleep finally woke up.
    c. Grandfathers rocked to sleep will eventually wake up.
    d. Grandchildren rocked to sleep will eventually wake up.

16. a. The instructors separated on the large dance floor chose new partners.
    b. The couple separated on the large dance floor chose new partners.
    c. Instructors separated on the large dance floor must choose new partners.
    d. Couples separated on the large dance floor must choose new partners.

17. a. The interviewer called during prime time programming interrupted normal broadcasting.
    b. The listener called during prime time programs interrupted normal broadcasting.
    c. Interviewers called during prime time programming may interrupt normal broadcasting.
    d. Listeners called during prime time programs may interrupt normal broadcasting.

18. a. The speaker lectured about the dangers of smoking often tried to help his own friends quit.
    b. The teenager lectured about the dangers of smoking often tried to help his own friends quit.
    c. Speakers lectured about the dangers of smoking often try to help their own friends quit.
    d. Teenagers lectured about the dangers of smoking often try to help their own friends quit.

APPENDIX 10B: MATERIALS FOR EXPERIMENT II

1. a. *Complement-inducing context*
      A psychologist was counseling a married couple.
      One member of the pair was fighting with him but the other one was nice to him.
   b. *Relative-inducing context*
      A psychologist was counseling two married couples.
      One couple was fighting with him but the other couple was nice to him.
   c. *Complement target sentence*
      The psychologist told the wife that he was having trouble with her husband.
   d. *Relative target sentence*
      The psychologist told the wife that he was having trouble with to leave her husband.

2. a. *Complement-inducing context*
      A bank robbery was committed.
      A policeman began investigating a neighborhood gang.
      Some of the gang members were militant but the others weren't.
   b. *Relative-inducing context*
      A bank robbery was committed.
      A policeman began investigating two neighborhood gangs.
      One of the gangs was militant but the other wasn't.
   c. *Complement target sentence*
      The officer warned the gang that he suspected them of the robbery.
   d. *Relative target sentence*
      The officer warned the gang that he suspected not to carry guns.

3. a. *Complement-inducing context*
      A teacher had three new girls in class.
      One of the new girls hated boys.

b. *Relative-inducing context*
   A teacher had three new girls in class.
   All the boys in the class hated two of the three girls.
c. *Complement target sentence*
   The teacher told the girl that the boys liked to help themselves
   to some paper.
d. *Relative target sentence*
   The teacher told the girl that the boys liked to help herself to
   some paper.

4. a. *Complement-inducing context*
      Three helicopters were used in the rescue mission.
      One of them had needed repair but some of it had already been
      finished by the mechanics.
   b. *Relative-inducing context*
      Three helicopters were used in the rescue mission.
      All of them had needed repair but two of them had already been
      finished by the mechanics.
   c. *Complement target sentence*
      The mechanics told the pilot of the helicopter that they were still
      working on the damages.
   d. *Relative target sentence*
      The mechanics told the pilot of the helicopter that they were still
      working on to show them the damages.

APPENDIX 10C: MATERIALS FOR EXPERIMENT III

1. *Context sentences*
   a. The league president handed out a new schedule for the season.
   b. Two teams were now required to play during Christmas vacation.
   c. The team members expressed their disappointment with the new
      schedule.

   Target sentence
   In response, the league president told the teams that he had re-
   scheduled

   $\begin{cases} \text{them to play the games on the original dates.} \\ \text{that they would play on the original dates.} \end{cases}$

2. *Context sentences*
   a. Three new players joined the baseball team.
   b. Several older players picked one of the new players to join them
      for the first practice.
   c. The other new players were upset by this.

Target sentence

The coach convinced the player that the old pros chose to practice by

$$\left\{ \begin{array}{l} \text{himself} \\ \text{themselves} \end{array} \right\} \text{ for the rest of spring training.}$$

3. *Context sentences*
   a. Several buyers were in town for the sale.
   b. One buyer was sent a special invitation by the store owners.
   c. The other buyers were outraged, and called a lawyer.

Target sentence

The lawyer notified the buyer that the store owners had requested to make

$$\left\{ \begin{array}{l} \text{themselves} \\ \text{himself} \end{array} \right\} \text{ available only at the sale.}$$

4. *Context sentences*
   a. Five minor league players were discussed as possible replacements for the injured catcher.
   b. One of them was selected by the coaches at a secret meeting with the owner.
   c. The entire team wondered how the selection had been made.

Target sentence

The owner convinced the player that the coaches had decided on

$$\left\{ \begin{array}{l} \text{him because he was the best hitting catcher.} \\ \text{that he was chosen because of his hitting.} \end{array} \right.$$

5. *Context sentences*
   a. Three guards had joined the night shift at the prison.
   b. One of the new guards was having trouble with the prisoners.
   c. The other new guards were treated with respect.

Target sentence

The warden convinced the guard that the prisoners hated to return to

$$\left\{ \begin{array}{l} \text{their duties on this shift.} \\ \text{his old job on the other shift.} \end{array} \right.$$

Notes

This paper was presented to the Sloan Conference on Modelling Human Parsing at the University of Texas at Austin, March 1981. We benefited from William Marslen-Wilson's discussion on the original paper, and from the comments of other participants and our colleagues in Texas. The paper was prepared while both authors were Visiting Fellows under a grant from the Sloan Foundation to the Center for Cognitive Sciences at the University of Texas, Austin. We are grateful to Gerry Altman, Gillian Brown, Chuck Clifton, Peter Culicover, Janet Fodor, Jerry Fodor, Lyn Frazier, Alan Garnham, Henry Hamburger, Stephen Isard, Dennis Norris, Phil Johnson-Laird, Terence Parsons, Nigel Shadbolt, Richard Shillcock, and Ken Wexler for helpful comments on earlier drafts.

1. It has been suggested (e.g., Wilson, 1975) that the concept of presupposition can entirely be subsumed under the broader concept of entailment. However, we shall continue to use "presupposition" in its more informal sense, in which it is a cover term for both presuppositions and entailments.

2. Where there is some degree of representational autonomy, there is a further question as to whether syntactic and semantic representations are built in series or to some extent in parallel. The latter alternative, which has to some extent been explored by Schank (1975), will be ignored here.

3. The notion of (surface) syntactic rules as representing what a processor does in constructing some other representation was implicit in many early computational parsers, such as the ATN.

4. While such a term is appealingly straightforward, we have avoided it here in order not to court confusion with yet another use of the term within transformational grammar to distinguish the "Generative Semantic" and "Standard Theoretic" positions. Both of these versions of TG are representationally autonomous within the definition just given.

5. It might appear that the level of constituent up to which their syntax is representationally autonomous places a lower bound on the intimacy with which the weak interaction can occur – that if the clause is the unit, then only complete clauses can affect syntactic processing, if major phrases, then only complete major phrases. However, a theory may involve autonomous modifiable structure at a high level such as the clause, while including nonautonomous representations at some lower level, such as the noun-phrase.

6. See Forster's criticism (1979:54) of Tyler and Marslen-Wilson (1977). Gerry Altman has pointed out to us that a further objection to strong interaction is implicit in our arguments in section 10.2.4, that "plausibility" cannot be the all-or-none criterion that the strong interaction would require.

7. It has been frequently noted that artificial languages like ALGOL *do* include constructions that cannot be described with CF rules alone. However, such constructions are not generally handled by purely syntactic mechanisms. (See Aho, 1968; Hopcroft and Ullman, 1979.)

8. Within the "revised" and "extended" versions of TG, it has been proposed that transformations themselves might be eliminated (Koster, 1978; Chomsky, 1981). But such proposals still involve comparably powerful devices, such as coindexing and filtering.

9. The scheme of Gazdar (1981) also represents certain similar "hole categories" within the grammar. The relation between these theories is discussed in Ades and Steedman (1982).

10. Ades and Steedman (1982: appendix, p. 552).

11. This observation does not exclude the possibility that more than one alternative might be developed in parallel for a little while. We take the experiments of Swinney (1979) to suggest that alternatives are proposed in parallel, but very rapidly reduced in number.

12. An objection that is frequently raised against Winograd's proposal to allow reference to guide syntactic processing should be mentioned at this point. The objection is based on questions of computational cost and efficiency, and some investigations by Woods (1973) using the ATN parsing program are often quoted in connection with it. Woods criticized Winograd's proposal on the ground that certain of the parser's attempts to evaluate potential NPs would concern analyses that would later turn out to be excluded on purely syntactic grounds. Because the process of establishing reference may in general involve arbitrary amounts of inference, it is comparatively costly. Woods argued that this cost would be avoided if the processor completed its syntactic analyses first, and only offered for evaluation noun phrases that were consistent with an analysis of the sentence as a whole. For example, the following sentence has only one overall analysis, since the verb requires both an object and a locative phrase among its complements. But there are two local analyses of noun phrases, indicated by the brackets, one of which fails to be consistent with any reading of the sentence as a whole.

(i) a. Put [the block]$_{NP}$ [in the box]$_{PP}$
    b. *Put [the block in the box]$_{NP}$

(An analogous false path would in fact arise in the more complex example (5), as *Put [the block in the box on the table]$_{NP}$.) Why go to the trouble and expense of evaluating the spurious NP in (b), Woods asked, since the analysis will eventually be abandoned anyway, and for the computers and inference systems that we are familiar with, syntactic processing is comparatively quick and cheap? This economy argument cannot of course be decisive for theories of the psychological mechanism, whatever its relevance to more purely engineering questions, and we shall demonstrate below that human listeners do in fact undertake very complex inferences during sentence processing. The question of whether human beings, faced with the sentence cited, consider the potential reference of the spurious noun phrase is a purely empirical question, which would have to be answered by a manipulation of context and an attempt to thereby induce difficulties in its comprehension. The fact that such a simple experiment has not, as far as we know, been done merely underlines the prevalent tendency to ignore potential contextual effects in experiments on sentence processing (but cf. Seidenberg and Tanenhaus, 1977).

13. These entities may be explicitly represented, or implicit, that is, inferable, cf. Mellish (1981). Sanford and Garrod (1981) have shown that referring expressions like *the clothes* take no longer to comprehend when the referent has been implied by a previous sentence like *Harry dressed the baby* than when it has received explicit mention, as in *Harry put the clothes on the baby*. This result is only explicable on the assumption that the inference from the act of dressing to the existence of some clothes has been made before the referring expression is encountered. Johnson-Laird and Garnham (1980) and Clark and Marshall (1982) also exploit mental models in accounting for certain varieties of definite reference.

14. In addition, each analysis gives rise to one presupposition that is unique to that reading. The sentence analysis, because of the "anaphoric" nature of the past tense that has been identified by McCawley (1971), Partee (1973) and Isard (1974), presupposes that a past reference time has been established. The reduced passive analysis presupposes that there is an agent of the racing, but does not specify its time. (Williams, 1970, has pointed out the temporal nonspecificity of reduced passives in this respect in connection with his critique of the "WHIZ-deletion" analysis of the construction.) In the absence of empirical evidence to the contrary, we assume that the costs of accommodating each of these presuppositions are comparable.

15. For example, finer differences in presuppositional character must be drawn between nongeneric and generic interpretations, for both indefinites and definites.

16. The following examples of ungrammatical sentences were used to provide subjects with a uniform criterion for ungrammaticality. (Each of these sentences followed a set of three context sentences. The sentences were taken from Frazier, 1979.)

(i) *Missing an obligatory constituent*
Nobody knew could play tennis so well.

(ii) *Extra constituent*
When Terry cooked the beans you there were never enough.

(iii) *Subject-verb agreement violations*
You sees the cat and dog.

17. Preliminary versions of this paper report data from Crain, 1980. The present set of experiments includes some additional judgments obtained at the University of Connecticut. The second set of data was sufficiently consistent with the first to justify pooling both sets for the purposes of this analysis. Reaction times were recorded only for the original subjects, and not for the Connecticut subjects. Discussion of the reaction time data appears in Crain, 1980, and in the earlier versions of this paper. It is omitted here for the following reason. Experiments II and III presented words at a slower rate than experiment I because preliminary explorations indicated that subjects failed to relate the target sentences to the contexts at faster rates. Slow presentation rates are not good indicators of on-line processing, however, and the reaction time measures would therefore contribute little to the present discussion.

18. With so few experimental contexts, the interpretation of the analysis by contexts should be confined to the specific items in this experiment. However, it is important to note that subjects responded alike to all four contexts, suggesting that other such contexts would yield similar results.

19. Altmann (in preparation) shows related effects of referential context upon the attachment of relative clauses and PP modifiers to NPs, using a reading time measure of processing load.

20. Janet Fodor and Lyn Frazier have pointed out to us that there is a third reading of the target sentences, one that makes a relative clause analysis appear ungrammatical (as opposed to the complement clause analysis). This may account, in part, for the large number of unacceptability judgments in this experiment. In addition, this may have been due to the sheer complexity of the contexts by comparison to the problems posed by the experimental contexts of experiment II.

References

Ades, Anthony E., and Mark J. Steedman. 1982. On the order of words. *Linguistics and Philosophy* 4:517–58.

Aho, Alfred V. 1968. Indexed grammars – an extension of context-free grammars. *Journal of the Association for Computing Machinery* 15:647–71.

Ajdukiewicz, Kazimierz. 1935. Die syntaktische Konnexität, *Studia Philosophica* 1:1–27. English translation in: Storrs McCall (ed.), *Polish logic 1920–1939*. London: Oxford University Press.

Altmann, Gerry T. M. 1984. Reference and the resolution of syntactic ambiguity: interaction in human sentence processing. Ph.D. dissertation, University of Edinburgh. (In preparation).

Bar-Hillel, Yehoshua, C. Gaifman, and E. Shamir. 1960. On categorial and phrase structure grammars. In: Y. Bar-Hillel (ed.), *Language and information*. Reading, Mass.: Addison-Wesley.

Bever, Thomas G. 1970. The cognitive basis for linguistic structures. In: John R. Hayes (ed.), *Cognition and the development of language*. New York: Wiley.

Bobrow, Robert, and Bonnie L. Webber. 1981. Parsing and semantic interpretation as an incremental recognition process. Paper presented at Conference on Modelling Human Parsing Strategies, University of Texas, Austin, March 1981.

Bolliet, L. 1968. Compiler writing techniques. In: F. Genuys (ed.), *Programming languages*. New York: Academic Press.

Brame, Michael K. 1978. *Base generated syntax*. Seattle: Noit Amrofer.

Bresnan, Joan. 1978. A realistic transformational grammar. In: Morris Halle, Joan Bresnan, and George Miller (eds.), *Linguistic structure and psychological reality*. Cambridge, Mass.: MIT Press.

Chapin, Paul G., T. S. Smith, and Arthur A. Abrahamson. 1972. Two factors in perceptual segmentation of speech. *Journal of Verbal Learning and Verbal Behavior* 11:164–73.

Chomsky, Noam. 1981. *Lectures on government and binding*. Dordrecht, Holland: Foris.

Clark, Herbert, and Susan Haviland. 1977. Comprehension and the given-new contract. In: Roy O. Freedle (ed.), *Discourse production and comprehension*. Norwood, N.J.: Ablex.

Clark, Herbert M., and Catherine R. Marshall. 1982. Definite references and mutual knowledge. In: Aravind K. Joshi, Ivan Sag and Bonnie Webber (eds.), *Elements of discourse understanding*. Cambridge, England: Cambridge University Press.

Crain, Stephen. 1980. Contextual constraints on sentence comprehension. Unpublished Ph.D. dissertation, University of California, Irvine.

Crain, Stephen, and Pamela L. Coker. 1978. A semantic constraint on syntactic parsing. Paper presented at the Linguistic Society of America Annual Meeting, Boston, Mass., December 1978.

Cutler, Anne. 1976. Beyond parsing and lexical look-up: an enriched description of auditory sentence comprehension. In: Roger J. Wales and Edward Walker (eds.), *New approaches to language mechanisms*. Amsterdam: North-Holland.

Davies, D. J. M., and Stephen D. Isard. 1972. Utterances as programs. In: Donald Michie (ed.), *Machine Intelligence 7*. Edinburgh: Edinburgh University Press.

Donnellan, Keith. 1966. Reference and definite descriptions. *Philosophical Review* 75:281–304.

Fodor, Janet D. 1978. Parsing strategies and constraints on transformations. *Linguistic Inquiry* 9:427–73.

Fodor, Janet D., and Lyn Frazier. 1980. Is the human sentence parsing mechanism an ATN? *Cognition* 8:417–59.

Fodor, Jerry A., Thomas G. Bever, and Merrill Garrett. 1976. *The psychology of language*. New York: McGraw-Hill.

Ford, Marilyn, Joan Bresnan, and Ronald Kaplan. 1981. A competence based theory of syntactic closure. In: Joan Bresnan (ed.), *The mental representation of grammatical relations*. Cambridge Mass.: MIT Press.

Forster, Kenneth I. 1979. Levels of processing and the structure of the language processor. In: William E. Cooper and Edward C. T. Walker (eds.), *Sentence processing: psycholinguistic studies presented to Merrill Garrett*. Hillsdale, N.J.: Lawrence Erlbaum.

Frazier, Lyn. 1978. On comprehending sentences: syntactic parsing strategies. Ph.D. dissertation, University of Connecticut. Bloomington: Indiana University Linguistics Club, 1979.

Frazier, Lyn, Charles Clifton, and Janet Randall. 1983. Filling gaps: decision principles and structure in sentence comprehension. *Cognition* 13:187–222.

Frazier, Lyn, and Janet Fodor, 1978. The Sausage Machine: a new two-stage parsing model. *Cognition* 6:291–325.

Gazdar, Gerald. 1981. Unbounded dependencies and constituent structure. *Linguistic Inquiry* 12:155–84.

1982. Phrase structure grammar. In: Pauline Jacobson and Geoffrey K. Pullum (eds.), *On the nature of syntactic representation*. Dordrecht: Reidel.

Grice, H. Paul. 1975. Logic and conversation. In: Peter Cole and Jerry L. Morgan (eds.), *Syntax and semantics*, vol. 3. New York: Academic Press.

Grosz, Barbara. 1977. The representation and use of focus in dialogue understanding. Stanford Research Institute Technical Note 151, Menlo Park, Calif.

Halliday, Michael A. K. 1967. Notes on transitivity and theme. *Journal of Linguistics* 3:177–244.

Hamburger, Henry, and Stephen Crain. 1981. Relative acquisition. In: Stan Kuczaj (ed.), *Language development: syntax and semantics*. Hillsdale, N.J.: Lawrence Erlbaum.

Haviland, Susan, and Herbert Clark. 1974. What's new? Acquiring new information as a process in comprehension. *Journal of Verbal Learning and Verbal Behavior* 13:512–21.

Hawkins, John A. 1978. *Definiteness and indefiniteness*. London: Croom Helm.

Holmes, V. M. 1979. Some hypotheses about syntactic processing in sentence comprehension. In: William E. Cooper and Edward C. T. Walker (eds.), *Sentence processing: studies presented to Merrill Garrett*. Hillsdale, N.J.: Lawrence Erlbaum.

Hopcroft, John E. and Jeffrey D. Ullman. 1979. *Introduction to automata theory, languages and computation*. Reading, Mass.: Addison-Wesley.

Isard, Stephen D. 1974. What would you have done if . . . *Theoretical Linguistics* 1:233–55.

Johnson-Laird, P. N. 1968a. The choice of the passive voice in a communication task. *British Journal of Psychology* 59:7–15.

1968b. The interpretation of the passive voice. *Quarterly Journal of Experimental Psychology* 20:69–73.

1977. Procedural semantics. *Cognition* 5:189–214.

Johnson-Laird, P. N., and Alan Garnham. 1980. Descriptions and discourse models. *Linguistics and Philosophy* 3:371–93.

Kaplan, Ronald. 1972. The ATN as a model of psychological sentence processing. *Artificial Intelligence* 3:77–100.

Karttunen, Lauri. 1974. Presupposition and linguistic context. *Theoretical Linguistics* 1:181–94.

Kimball, John. 1973. Seven principles of surface structure parsing in natural language. *Cognition* 2:15–47.

Koster, Jan. 1978. *Locality principles in syntax*. Dordrecht, Holland: Foris.

Lewis, David. 1970. General semantics. *Synthese* 22:18–67.

1979. Scorekeeping in a language game. *Journal of Philosophical Logic* 8:339–59.

Lyons, John. 1977. *Semantics*. Cambridge, England: Cambridge University Press.

Marcus, Mitchell P. 1980. A Theory of Syntactic Recognition for Natural Language. Cambridge, Mass.: MIT Press. (MIT Ph.D. dissertation, 1977.)

Marslen-Wilson, William D. 1973. Linguistic structure and speech shadowing at very short latencies. *Nature* 244:522–23.

Marslen-Wilson, William D., and Lorraine K. Tyler. 1980. The temporal structure of spoken language understanding: the perception of sentences and words in sentences. *Cognition* 8:1–74.

Marslen-Wilson, William D., and Alan Welsh. 1978. Processing interactions and lexical access during word recognition in continuous speech. *Cognitive Psychology* 10:29–63.

McCawley, James. 1971. Tense and time reference in English. In: Charles J. Fillmore and D. Terence Langendoen (eds.), *Studies in linguistic semantics*. New York: Holt, Rinehart and Winston.

Mellish, Christopher. 1981. Coping with uncertainty: noun-phrase interpretation and early semantic analysis. Unpublished Ph.D. dissertation, University of Edinburgh.

Montague, Richard. 1974. *Formal philosophy*. New Haven, Conn.: Yale University Press.

Partee, Barbara. 1973. Some structural analogies between tenses and pronouns in English. *Journal of Philosophy* 70:601–9.

Peters, Stanley. 1980. Linked tree grammars. Unpublished ms. University of Texas, Austin.

Ritchie, Grant. 1977. Computer modelling of English grammar. Unpublished Ph.D. dissertation, University of Edinburgh.

Sanford, J. A., and S. Garrod. 1981. *Understanding written language: explorations of comprehension beyond the sentence*. Chichester, England: Wiley.

Seidenberg, Mark, and Michael K. Tanenhaus. 1977. Psychological constraints on grammars: on trying to put the *real* back in "psychological reality." In: Woodford A. Beach, Sharon E. Fox, and Shulamith Philosoph (eds.), *CLS 13*. Chicago: Chicago Linguistic Society.

Sheldon, Amy. 1974. The role of parallel function in the acquisition of relative clauses in English. *Journal of Verbal Learning and Verbal Behavior* 13:272–81.

Sidner, Candace. 1979. Towards a computational theory of definite anaphora comprehension in English. TR 537, AI Laboratory, Massachusetts Institute of Technology, Cambridge, Mass.

Simon, Herbert. 1969. *The sciences of the artificial*. Cambridge, Mass.: MIT Press.

Slobin, Daniel I. 1966. Grammatical transformations and sentence comprehension in childhood and adulthood. *Journal of Verbal Learning and Verbal Behavior* 5:219–27.

Soames, Scott. 1982. How presuppositions are inherited: a solution to the projection problem. *Linguistic Inquiry* 13:483–545.

Solan, Lawrence, and Thomas Roeper. 1978. Children's use of syntactic structure in interpreting relative clauses. In: Helen Goodluck and Lawrence Solan (eds.), *Papers in the structure and development of child language*. University of Massachusetts Occasional Publications in Linguistics, vol 4.

Stalnaker, Robert L. 1974. Pragmatic presuppositions. In: Milton K. Munitz and Peter K. Unger (eds.), *Semantics and philosophy*. New York: New York University Press.

Steedman, Mark J., and P. N. Johnson-Laird. 1976. A programmatic theory of linguistic performance. In: P. Smith and R. Campbell (eds.), *Advances in the psychology of language – formal and experimental approaches*. New York: Plenum.

Swinney, David A. 1979. Lexical access during sentence comprehension: (Re) consideration of context effects. *Journal of Verbal Learning and Verbal Behavior* 15:681–89.

Tavakolian, Susan L. 1981. The conjoined clause analysis of relative clauses. In: Susan L. Tavakolian (ed.), *Language acquisition and linguistic theory*. Cambridge, Mass., MIT Press.

Tyler, Lorraine K., and William D. Marslen-Wilson. 1977. The on-line effects of semantic context on syntactic processing. *Journal of Verbal Learning and Verbal Behavior* 16:683–92.

Wanner, Eric. 1980. The ATN and the Sausage Machine: Which one is baloney? *Cognition* 8:209–25.

Wanner, Eric, and Michael Maratsos. 1968. An ATN approach to comprehension. In: Joan Bresnan, George A. Miller, and Morris Halle (eds.), *Linguistic structure and psychological reality*. Cambridge, Mass.: MIT Press.

Wason, Peter. 1965. The contexts of plausible denial. *Journal of Verbal Learning and Verbal Behavior* 4:7–11.

————. 1981. The verification task and beyond. In: David R. Olson (ed.), *The social foundations of language and thought*. New York: W. W. Norton.

Webber, Bonnie L. 1978. *A formal approach to discourse anaphora*. Report no. 3761, Bolt, Beranek, and Newman.

Williams, Edwin. 1970. Small clauses in English. In: John Kimball (ed.), *Syntax and semantics*, vol. 4. New York: Academic Press.

Wilson, Deirdre. 1975. *Presuppositions and non-truth-conditional semantics*. New York: Academic Press.

Winograd, Terry. 1972. *Understanding natural language*. Edinburgh: Edinburgh University Press.

Woods, William. 1973. Transition network grammars. In: Randall Rustin (ed.), *Natural language processing*. Courant Computer Science Symposium 8. New York: Algorithmics Press.

————. 1975. What's in a link? In: Daniel Bobrow and Bertram Raphael (eds.), *Representation and understanding*. New York: Academic Press.

11   Do listeners compute linguistic representations?

MICHAEL K. TANENHAUS, GREG N. CARLSON, and
MARK S. SEIDENBERG

In order to understand the relationship between syntactic theory and how
people parse sentences, it is first necessary to understand the more general
relationship between the grammar and the general cognitive system
(GCS). The Chomskyan view, adhered to by most linguists working within
the modern generative framework, is that the grammar is a cognitive
subsystem whose vocabulary and operations are defined independently
of the GCS and account for the structure of language (Chomsky, 1980).
Linguistics is thus the branch of theoretical cognitive psychology which
explains language structure.

There is another possible relationship between the grammar and the
GCS in which linguistics does not play a primary theoretical role in explaining language structure. On this view, the structure of language is
explained by basic principles of the GCS – for example, the nature of
concepts in interaction with basic properties of the human information
processing system. If this view is correct, grammars become convenient
organizational frameworks for describing the structure of language. Linguistics is then a descriptive rather than a theoretical branch of cognitive
psychology. The linguistics-as-descriptive position was held by the American Structuralists and is presently being revived from a somewhat different perspective in the form of "cognitive grammar" (Lakoff, in press).

These two frameworks for understanding the relationship between
grammars and the cognitive system – linguistics as explanation and linguistics as description – suggest different research strategies for answering the question posed by the theme of this book: namely, What is
the relationship between syntactic theory and how listeners parse sentences? If the linguistic system is primary, then the natural focus of parsing
research is on how linguistic representations as defined by the grammar
are recovered from a perceptual input during comprehension. Questions
such as whether the rules of grammar are actually realized as processing
operations become primary (e.g., Bresnan, 1978, 1982). However, if the
general cognitive system is basic, the focus of research shifts to questions

359

concerning the operation and organization of the cognitive system. Properly understood, the structure of language would fall out as a consequence of the structure of the cognitive system itself.

We should at the outset make clear that we are biased in favor of the linguistics-as-explanation position. There is at least one strong methodological reason for adopting this point of view as a working hypothesis: it places constraints on the nature of the language processing system. Let us assume that grammars, as presently construed, are psychologically explanatory models of language structure. If we further assume that the representation a grammar assigns to a sentence describes at least part of the message normally communicated when the sentence is spoken and understood (Fodor, Fodor, and Garrett, 1975), then the form of grammars places severe constraints on the form of language processing models (see Cairns, in press). If we further assume that grammatical knowledge must be represented in a form that is usable as a set of procedures by the language processor, then the form of grammars may be constrained by facts about language processing. It is hoped that these mutual constraints will be strong enough to lead to empirically testable models of language structure and language processing.

At least two types of evidence may be used to decide between linguistics as description and linguistics as explanation. One type of evidence involves demonstrating that the principles of grammar do or do not plausibly derive from processing or general cognitive principles. Frazier (this volume) provides excellent examples of this type of argument. However, arguments of this sort, pro and con, rely crucially on a detailed understanding of the general cognitive system which we do not at present possess, and require assumptions about the cognitive system whose chief support is plausibility. As our understanding of the cognitive system deepens, though, the significance of such arguments will become more apparent.

Another approach is also available to us, which we will examine in some detail. This is to determine whether or not linguistic representations[1] can be separated from other cognitive representations. If linguistic representations as characterized by the grammar can be isolated, then we have strong reason to hold that the way linguists conceive of language represents an explanatory theory rather than simply a convenient organizational scheme.

At this point it will be useful to present an overview of the organization of this paper. We begin by reviewing some recent psycholinguistic studies challenging Fodor, Bever, and Garrett's well-known conclusion (1974) that psycholinguistic experimentation provides evidence for the psychological reality of structural descriptions, and against the psychological reality of grammatical operations. These studies provide evidence against models that propose a temporally defined stage in processing in which the listener's representation of a sentence corresponds to the representation assigned the sentence by the grammar. However, these results do not necessitate abandoning the hypothesis that listeners compute linguistic representations. They are, we will argue, fully compatible with a model of language comprehension as found in Forster, 1979, in which the language processing system contains a set of autonomous processing modules each of which corresponds to a "level" in the grammar. The output of each of the processing modules is a linguistic representation.

The next section reviews evidence that one processing subsystem hypothesized by Forster, the lexical processor, operates as an autonomous processing module. Accepting the modular view presents a theoretical challenge, which is to specify what a theory of parsing is like in a modular system, as well as a methodological challenge, which is to develop methodologies that are sensitive to the outputs of processing modules.

The theoretical challenge is addressed in the next section, which explores some of the consequences of the modularity hypothesis for theories of parsing. We illustrate different classes of models that are compatible with modularity assumptions and the types of empirical claims each makes. We argue that deciding among the logical possibilities depends crucially on being able to observe the nature of the representations that listeners are developing in real time.

The methodological challenge is addressed in the final section. A central assumption of the modularity hypothesis is that listeners are computing different levels of linguistic representations that correspond to separate processing modules. We explore the possibility that priming methodologies can be extended to levels of representation beyond the word in a series of experiments using sentences with gaps and sentences with anaphors. These studies suggest that priming may be capable of distinguishing between two levels of linguistic representation – linguistic form and linguistic meaning – and a level of representation that integrates linguistic and nonlinguistic information, which we will term the *constructed representation*.

11.1. Comprehension and linguistic representations

In their summary of the psycholinguistic research of the 1960s and early 1970s, Fodor, Bever, and Garrett (1974) concluded that, "experimentation to date has provided evidence for the psychological reality of structural descriptions and against the psychological reality of grammatical operations" (p. 512). At the time that Fodor et al. drew this conclusion, psycholinguistic research had failed to find evidence that transformations corresponded to mental operations under the assumption that the perceptual complexity of a sentence ought to be correlated with its derivational complexity, where the derivational complexity of a sentence was defined by the number of currently assumed transformations that applied in its derivation. On the other hand, studies of sentence processing suggested that clauses defined the major boundary of segmentation points in sentence processing, and studies of sentence memory suggested that the memory representation of a sentence was strikingly similar to its deep structure. Given these results, it was perfectly reasonable to conclude that listeners assign linguistic representations to incoming sentences.

11.1.1. Evidence against a linguistic level

The stage was then set for a series of developments that would lead psycholinguists to progressively weaken their claims about the relationship between grammars and processing models (see Carlson and Tanenhaus, 1982). The claim that deep structures are stored in memory was undermined by a series of influential studies conducted by Bransford and Franks and their colleagues (see Bransford, 1979, for review). These studies demonstrated that the stored representation of a sentence combines information from the sentence with information drawn from real-world knowledge. For example, after hearing a sentence such as

(1)   Three turtles rested on a log and the fish swam beneath them.

subjects believed that they had heard (2) as often as (3).

(2)   The fish swam beneath the log.

(3)   The fish swam beneath the turtles.

The meaning of (2) is not in any sense represented in the deep structure of (1). Rather, it is inferred from the meaning of (1) by the use of knowledge of spatial relations in the real world.

Results like these are not incompatible with a model in which listeners compute linguistic representations during an initial stage in comprehension. For example, it is still possible to suggest that there is an initial message level representation (a purely linguistic level), which is then used in conjunction with extralinguistic knowledge to generate a *constructed* representation (Fodor, Fodor, and Garrett, 1975). However, models like this, in which there is a sequentially defined linguistic stage in comprehension, appear untenable in light of more recent psycholinguistic studies.

For example, a number of studies have demonstrated that the boundary points in sentence processing do not necessarily correspond to a particular level of linguistic structure (Carroll, Tanenhaus, and Bever, 1978; Marslen-Wilson, Tyler, and Seidenberg, 1978; Tanenhaus and Seidenberg, 1978). These studies found that a number of factors, including the length, completeness, and specificity of the grammatical relations within a clause – and even preceding context – interact in determining the boundary points in processing. As a consequence, the claim that listeners compute purely linguistic representations loses much of its empirical support because processing decisions appear to be guided more by general perceptual properties of the processor than by purely linguistic information (at points where one would expect only linguistic information about the sentence being processed to be available).

Other studies have underscored the general point that one cannot isolate a clearly defined temporal stage of linguistic processing in which only grammatical information is available to the processor. For instance, Marslen-Wilson (1975) and Marslen-Wilson and Welsh (1978) have provided evidence that lexical, syntactic, and nonlinguistic contextual information interact to determine the likelihood that shadowers will restore a distorted word. Marslen-Wilson and Tyler (1981) have also demonstrated the on-line availability of information from different levels of representation in a study on the resolution of anaphora. They used materials such as

(4) As Philip was walking back from the ship, he saw an old woman trip and fall flat on her face.

(5) She seemed unable to get up.

(6) a. Philip ran toward . . .
    b. He ran toward . . .
    c. Running toward . . .

Following each of the fragments, listeners were presented with a visual target word, which was either a pragmatically plausible or implausible continuation of the fragment, given that the subject had linked the anaphor to the appropriate antecedent *Philip* in (4). The plausible target was *her*, and the implausible target was *him*. Plausible continuations of the fragment were named faster than implausible continuations in all conditions, demonstrating that listeners had assigned a referent to the anaphor by the end of the fragment. Thus even pragmatic inferences seem to be drawn on-line and in parallel with the grammatical analysis of a sentence.[2]

Tanenhaus and Seidenberg (1981) reached the same conclusion in a study in which sentences that either began or ended with a definite noun phrase, (8a) and (8b), were preceded by either a context that established an antecedent for the noun phrase, or one that did not – (7a) and (7b), respectively.

(7) a. John died yesterday.
    b. John was murdered yesterday.

(8) a. *The murderer* was one of John's friends.
    b. One of John's friends was *the murderer*.

When the noun phrase came at the end of the target sentence, comprehension times were longer in the nonantecedent context than in the antecedent context, replicating Haviland and Clark (1974). The comprehension time difference presumably reflects the time it takes the listener to make an inference in order to create an antecedent for the definite noun phrase in the nonantecedent context. However, when the definite noun phrase came at the beginning of the sentence, there was no difference between comprehension times in the nonantecedent and the antecedent contexts, suggesting that subjects made the inference necessary to link the definite noun phrase to the previous sentence while they were processing the target sentence.

Recent research also suggests that various types of nonlinguistic information can guide parsing decisions. Carroll et al. (1978) and Crain and Steedman (this volume) have demonstrated that parsing biases for ambiguous sentences, including biases explained by Frazier and Fodor's (1978) Minimal Attachment Principle, can be overridden by context (see, however, Rayner, Carlson, and Frazier, 1983, who come to a different conclusion). Context may also reduce or eliminate on-line complexity differences due to syntactic structure. Object relative clauses such as (9a) are more difficult to process than subject relative clauses such as (9b). This is presumably due to the greater memory demands that object relatives place on the parser (Wanner and Maratsos, 1978).

(9) a. The girl who the boy kissed smiled.
     b. The girl who kissed the boy smiled.

Tanenhaus (1978) found that comprehension times to sentences such as (9a) were longer than comprehension times to (9b) when the sentences were preceded by a neutral context such as (10). When, however, the context provided the listener with information about the content of the relative clause, as in (11a) and (11b), the comprehension time difference between (9a) and (9b) was eliminated.

(10) The kids were playing spin the bottle.

(11) a. A boy kissed one of the girls.
      b. One of the girls kissed the boy.

Davison and Lutz (this volume) provide further experimental evidence that context alters the relative complexity of different types of sentences.

11.1.2. Modularity

Given the results reviewed above, what remains of the hypothesis that listeners compute purely linguistic representations? Clearly, we cannot identify a temporal stage in which the mental representation that the listener assigns to a complete sentence is in any reasonable sense a linguistic representation. Can we then preserve the claim that listeners compute linguistic representations as a hypothesis with empirical content? One remaining possibility, perhaps the only viable one, is the modularity hypothesis (Chomsky, 1980; J. A. Fodor, 1983; Forster, 1979; Marr, 1982).[3] Consider for now a model of language processing in which there are at least two distinct systems: a general cognitive system (GCS), which contains a general problem solver, and a linguistic system consisting of one or more linguistic modules. The general problem solver has access either to the output of the linguistic system or, quite plausibly, to the output of each of the modules. It also has access to the knowledge base stored in the cognitive system in what psychologists commonly refer to as the *episodic* and *semantic memory systems*. The general problem solver operates on the output of the linguistic modules to develop a constructed representation. This is essentially the model presented by Forster (1979).

The modules in the model just sketched are not defined in terms of the temporal sequence in which they appear, but rather as they are in linguistics. Each is defined by the vocabulary it uses and by the set of operations it performs. A module, given a certain input, will always compute the same output irrespective of the states or operations of other modules or the general cognitive system. We will assume for the moment that the output of each module corresponds to a level of linguistic representation; later on in this paper, however, we will explore some other possibilities.

This model clearly preserves the hypothesis that listeners compute linguistic representations. It also is compatible with data indicating that representations from different levels are simultaneously available since the modules are not necessarily arranged serially. The modules cannot operate in strict parallel, however, because there are certain dependencies between modules. For example, the syntactic module needs to know the possible syntactic categories of a lexical item before it can continue building a syntactic representation. The amount of serial staggering between modules will depend on the size of the units that each module accepts as input and the size of the units that it outputs. The smaller the units, the closer the approximation to a purely parallel model. The studies reviewed above suggest that the units are quite small, and that processing occurs very rapidly. Thus in the course of normal comprehension, representations from all levels will generally be present very shortly after a given portion of a sentence is received. If true, this presents a strong methodological challenge. In order to observe the outputs of the modules, it is necessary to devise experimental methodologies that are sensitive to different levels of linguistic representation. Moreover, these experimental procedures must also be capable of observing representations as they develop in real time, because for a given linguistic input the outputs of any module may be available only for an extremely short time, as work reviewed next seems to suggest.

We will now examine in some depth recent research on the interaction of context and lexical access. Our reasons for examining this research are twofold. First, the interaction of context and lexical access is one research domain where many investigators have concluded that the modular view is incorrect. We will argue that this conclusion is at best premature, given a number of recent results, including some from our laboratories. Second, the methodologies developed to examine the interaction of context and lexical access can be naturally extended to explore linguistic representations beyond the lexical level.

11.2. Modularity and lexical access

In an important paper, Forster (1976) outlined the hypothesis that lexical processing is a modular subsystem in language comprehension. Two predictions can be derived from the central claim underlying modularity, namely, that the operations and outputs of a processing module cannot be influenced by information from the GCS or from another module. The first is that the information made available as a consequence of lexical access should remain invariant across processing contexts. The second is that the speed with which information is made available should be unaffected by processing context.

11.2.1. Lexical ambiguity

Perhaps the most striking evidence that the information made available during lexical access remains invariant across processing contexts comes from studies of the processing of ambiguous words in context. Swinney (1979) and Tanenhaus, Leiman, and Seidenberg (1979) conducted cross-modal lexical priming experiments in which subjects made lexical decisions or named visually presented targets that were related to either the contextually biased or unbiased reading of an ambiguous word in a spoken sentence (e.g., *They all rose* followed by the targets *flower* or *stood*). Responses to targets related to either reading were facilitated when the target immediately followed the ambiguous word despite the prior presentation of biasing context, either pragmatic (Swinney) or syntactic (Tanenhaus et al.). When the target followed the ambiguous word by several hundred milliseconds, however, only targets related to the contextually appropriate reading were facilitated. Thus multiple readings of ambiguous words are initially accessed regardless of context, and context is subsequently used to select a single reading. These findings have since been replicated and extended in studies by Onifer and Swinney (1981), who demonstrated that the same pattern holds regardless of whether the context biases the more or less frequent reading of an ambiguous word; by Seidenberg et al. (1982), who demonstrated that initial access of multiple readings holds across a range of different types of contexts[4]; and by Tanenhaus and Donnenwerth-Nolan (in press), who found that multiple readings of noun/verb ambiguous words are still accessed, even when a pause is inserted between a biasing syntactic context and the ambiguous word in order to give subjects ample time to have fully processed the preceding context.[5]

If these ambiguity results are combined with the results of earlier research using the phoneme monitoring paradigm and examined within the framework of recent theories of attention, a picture of ambiguity access and resolution emerges which fits nicely within a modularity framework. Phoneme monitoring research on lexical ambiguity is based on the premise that accessing or choosing from among multiple readings of ambiguous lexical items should result in increased complexity to the processing system. As a consequence, time to detect a target phoneme should be longer when the phoneme follows an ambiguous word than when it follows an unambiguous word. Cairns and Kamerman (1975) and Foss (1970) obtained just this result when the sentence did not strongly bias a particular reading of the ambiguous word. However, in strongly biasing contexts, lexical ambiguity did not reliably affect phoneme monitoring (Cairns and Hsu, 1981; Swinney and Hakes, 1976). In light of the lexical priming research, the most reasonable interpretation of these phoneme monitoring results is that multiple readings of ambiguous words are made available without any increased costs in processing resources. However, the process of selecting a contextually appropriate reading of an ambiguous word and integrating it into the preceding context does draw on processing resources. Lexical ambiguity will increase the complexity of sentence processing only when the selection and integration process is more difficult for an ambiguous word than for an unambiguous word. This situation is most likely to obtain when the context preceding the ambiguous word does not strongly bias one of its readings (see Cairns, Cowart, and Jablon, 1981).

Now let us consider these results within the framework of recent theories of attention which distinguish between processes which are automatic and processes which are controlled (Posner and Snyder, 1975; Shiffrin and Schneider, 1977). Automatic processes are extremely rapid, they are sealed off from awareness and not subject to strategic control, and they do not draw on processing resources. In contrast, controlled processes are slower, they are subject to strategic modification, they may be conscious, and they draw on processing resources. Controlled processes can be divided into two general types: veiled controlled and conscious controlled (Shiffrin and Schneider, 1977). Veiled controlled processes are opaque to consciousness, faster than conscious controlled processes, and they make fewer demands on limited processing resources. Within the framework of dual process models of attention, accessing multiple readings of an ambiguous word can be seen as an automatic process, while choosing a correct alternative can be seen as a veiled controlled process (Seidenberg et al., 1982; Tanenhaus et al., 1979; Yates, 1978). Evidence that ambiguity resolution is a controlled process comes from phoneme monitoring results demonstrating that it can lead to increased complexity. Evidence that accessing multiple readings is automatic comes from a recent study conducted in our laboratory by Collings (1982), in which subjects shadowed a list of words presented to one ear while another list was simultaneously presented to the unattended ear. The logic of the study was based on Lewis (1970), who demonstrated that an unattended word could interfere with the shadowing of a related word. On critical trials, the word being shadowed was related to either the dominant (more frequent) or subordinate reading of an ambiguous word presented to the unattended ear. The ambiguous word interfered with shadowing the related word even though the ambiguous word was not being consciously attended. The finding of greatest interest was that ambiguous words interfered equally with words related to their dominant and subordinate readings. This is just the pattern of results that is expected if accessing multiple readings is an automatic process. This study also demonstrates that clear evidence for multiple access can be obtained using a paradigm other than lexical priming.

Taking a somewhat broader perspective, it seems reasonable that operations performed by processing modules should be automatic. These operations are sealed off from the rest of the general cognitive system and they operate on a limited, highly specific vocabulary. In contrast, the operations of the GCS, which draw on a nearly unlimited domain of linguistic and extralinguistic knowledge, need to be subject to strategic control and, clearly, draw on processing resources. These points are considered again later in this paper in the context of parsing models. It will be sufficient for now to assume that the lexical processing module makes available all readings of an ambiguous word which are consistent with the phonetic input and then the GCS selects a contextually appropriate reading. We will return to a discussion of some of the methodological implications of research on ambiguity later in this section. Before doing so, however, we will evaluate a number of well-known results on context effects which have been widely interpreted as violating Forster's claims about the autonomy of lexical access. These challenges all have in common the claim that information presented in a processing context can facilitate lexical access.

11.2.2. *Loci and mechanism of priming*

Meyer and Schvaneveldt (1971) first demonstrated that recognition of a word is facilitated when the word is preceded by a semantically or associatively related word (e.g., doctor-nurse, rat-cheese). It is this lexical priming effect that was used in the ambiguity research to demonstrate initial multiple access. The mere presence of these effects, it might seem, constitutes counterevidence to the claim that lexical access is autonomous. After all, associative priming would seem to be a clear case in which knowledge of the world, in particular knowledge about the frequency with which words or concepts co-occur, influences the operation of a processing module.

Forster (1976, 1979) has argued that lexical priming effects do not violate autonomy assumptions, because they can be considered intralexical. For example, priming might occur because entries within the lexicon are semantically cross-referenced, perhaps for the purposes of speech production (Fay and Cutler, 1977; Forster, 1976; Fromkin, 1971). Another alternative is that semantically related items are stored closely together in the lexicon and the access of one entry automatically activates entries stored nearby (Collins and Loftus, 1975; Seidenberg et al., 1982). Both of these explanations assume that priming reflects the organization of the lexicon and not the influence of nonlexical knowledge on lexical access, and therefore does not violate modularity.[6]

But it is not clear that all lexical priming effects need to be attributed to the operations of the lexical processor. In order to see this, consider the task demands made by the lexical decision task, which is not only the task most widely used to study lexical access but also the task that shows the most robust priming effects.

In a lexical decision task, the subject is presented with a letter string on each trial and his or her task is to decide as quickly as possible whether or not the letter string is a word. There are at least two general models for how these decisions are made. One possibility is that once a lexical entry has been identified, the subject knows that a word has been identified and can respond "yes." This *direct knowledge* account leaves unclear why the lexical processor should be structured so that we know directly whether or not we have been presented with a word. The lexical processor was not built, after all, to make lexical decisions.

The direct knowledge account also runs into empirical problems. It cannot naturally account for why lexical decisions are relatively slow compared to other lexical tasks such as reading a word aloud. It also has difficulty explaining why lexical decisions are so easily subject to strategic influences. For example, the type of nonwords used influences the speed with which subjects make lexical decisions, the size of context effects, and even the types of information that subjects appear to be using in making decisions to words (Shulman, Hornak, and Sanders, 1977). Finally, the direct knowledge account has difficulty accounting for the range of variables that can influence lexical decisions, which include the concreteness of a word and the ease with which a context for the word can be imagined (Schwanenflugel and Shoben, 1983).

A second possible model for how lexical decisions are made is based on the assumption that once a word is recognized, various types of information about the word become available to the processing system. The cognitive system does not have direct access to knowledge that the word has been recognized, but rather to the codes made available when a word is identified, such as its pronunciation or meaning. If a lexical code is available, the cognitive system decides that a word must have been presented. In essence, this model takes the "decision" part of "lexical decision" seriously. Let us assume that the cognitive system usually makes its decision based on the availability of meanings, or – more appropriately – conceptual representations, since it is not clear that we can have conscious access to meanings. Let us further assume, following Collins and Loftus (1975), that the conceptual representation of a word is defined by pointers linking a lexical entry to a series of nodes in a conceptual memory. The intersection of these nodes defines the conceptual representation of the word, and when the word is recognized, this conceptual representation is activated. The presence or absence of an activated conceptual representation can then be used by the cognitive system in deciding whether or not a word was presented.[7]

Now let us see how priming might arise given this account. When the word *doctor* is presented, its conceptual representation is activated. Shortly thereafter, the word *nurse* is presented. Since *doctor* and *nurse* share many of the same conceptual nodes, part of the conceptual representation of *nurse* will have been partially activated by *doctor*. As a result, the cognitive system will be faster at retrieving a conceptual representation for *nurse*. This account of priming effects places the locus of priming *outside* of the lexical module. In so doing, it can nicely account for both associative and semantic priming effects, if we make the assumption that both semantic and episodic types of information (e.g., *Cats are mammals* and *Cats like to eat birds*) are integrated in conceptual memory. If this account is correct, the effects of priming are postlexical and modularity is not violated.

11.2.3. Context and visual word recognition

The decision model of the lexical decision task is useful for understanding the growing literature on the recognition of words in sentential contexts

(Fischler and Bloom, 1979; Forster, 1981; Stanovich and West, 1979; West and Stanovich, 1982). In these studies, subjects are presented with a sentence frame followed by a word (e.g., *They went to the . . . store*). The subject's task is either to make a lexical decision to the word or to read it aloud (naming). Basically these studies demonstrate two effects. First, responses to the target are facilitated when the context contains a word that is semantically related to the target. This simply appears to be a case of intralexical priming. Second, the predictability or plausibility of the target given the context has no effects on response latencies to the target *except* when (1) the resulting sentence is extremely implausible or anomalous, in which case responses to the targets are inhibited; and (2) the target is extremely predictable, in which case responses to the targets are facilitated.

The fact that context facilitates recognizing a word only when the word is extremely predictable means that using context to recognize words is not going to be useful in most processing contexts. Fishler and Bloom found robust context effects only when more than 90 percent of their subjects were able to predict correctly the target word given the context. In examining the predictability of some natural language contexts, Gough, Alford, and Holley-Wilcox (1981) found only one example of an instance of a context that was this predictable. The example they cite was an author who was presented with the first paragraph of one of his books with some words deleted and asked to fill in the missing words. The inefficiency of having context guide word recognition becomes further apparent when we consider that there are costs associated with highly unpredictable contexts: recognition of words in unpredictable contexts is inhibited.

Thus far we have been assuming that there is a unified mechanism underlying the inhibitory and facilitation effects of context. However, this assumption is probably incorrect. Consider these context effects within the framework outlined by Forster (1979) and developed most explicitly by Forster (1981) and West and Stanovich (1982). West and Stanovich (1982) argue that inhibitory effects come about because the cognitive system receives feedback that the word does not make sense in the context. There is a large set of trials in these experiments in which the target stimulus will not make sense given the context: trials on which a nonword is presented. If the cognitive system does not have direct knowledge of whether a word has been recognized, as we argued earlier, then the fact that the target fails to make sense given the context is good evidence that it might be a nonword. Thus we should expect slow decisions and high error rates when the target word is incongruous given its context. This of course is just the pattern of results that obtains.

If inhibitory effects of incongruous contexts are due to feedback from the cognitive system, what is the mechanism underlying facilitatory effects in predictable contexts? One plausible possibility is that in highly predictable contexts subjects are likely to generate a specific candidate word, an informed guess. The internal code for the predicted word is then matched against the input. If, for example, the initial letters match, then the subject may conclude that the guess was correct even though the lexical representation for the word has not yet been accessed. In other words, recognition by prediction may utilize an analysis by synthesis procedure and bypass (ignore) the normal lexical access route.

11.2.4. Monitoring for words in context

This interpretation casts a different light on a recent study by Marslen-Wilson and Tyler (1980b) which has been widely interpreted as providng strong counterevidence to the autonomy of lexical access. Marslen-Wilson and Tyler examined the effect of contextual information on rhyme and category monitoring tasks performed while subjects listened to spoken passages. In rhyme monitoring, the subject is presented with a cue word and asked to identify the occurrence of a rhyme in the passage being heard; in category monitoring, the subject is presented with the name of a category such as "toy" or "type of metal" and must identify a category exemplar occurring in the passage. The passages were either normal prose, syntactically well-formed but meaningless prose, or random word prose. The primary finding of interest is that rhyme and category monitoring latencies are shorter with normal prose than with the other types. This effect was attributed to the fact that only the normal prose passages permitted subjects to generate meaningful interpretations that were used to facilitate the processing of target words.

Interpretation of this result rests upon understanding the rhyme and category monitoring tasks. Consider the following sentence: *John jumped into the.* . . . On the basis of the information provided, a huge number of words could intelligibly complete the sequence; in the absence of other information, the probability that any single item will actually occur is quite low. Note, however, that monitoring tasks do in fact provide additional information – specifically, cues indicating that a rhyme or category exemplar will occur. These cues, in conjunction with the information provided by the context, increase the predictability of the target dramatically. Assume that you are the subject in the rhyme monitoring condition. The cue is *bar*. The sentence is: *John jumped into the.* . . . What is the target? Clearly, the cue, in conjunction with the information provided by the sentence, leads to the expectation that the target will be *car*. Thus, *car* is a highly predictable word in this context.

Although we do not have access to Marslen-Wilson and Tyler's stimuli, there is reason to believe that their effects may be due to the high pre-

Table 11.1. *Stimuli for predictability study*

Condition	Category cues		Rhyme cues
	Example		Example
Context	The men were looking for ___.		John got in the ___.
Cue and context	*metal*		*Bar*
	The men were looking for ___.		John got in the ___.
Cue, context, and first letter	*metal*		*bar*
	The men were looking for <u>g</u>__ .		John got into the
			<u>c</u>__ .

Table 11.2. *Results from predictability study*

Condition	Percentage Judged Correct[a]	
	Category	Rhyme
Context	6 (8)	8 (11)
Cue and context	48 (72)	69 (84)
Cue, context and first letter	84 (87)	89 (92)

[a] Percentage judged correct when the two most frequent responses were averaged are presented in parentheses.

dictability of targets. First, they note in their paper that they selected very common rhymes and exemplars highly typical of the categories. Thus, the manner in which they selected target stimuli would tend to ensure high predictability. Second, we have recently collected data concerning the extent to which target words in rhyme and category monitoring tasks are predictable using sentence frames such as *John jumped into the.* . . . Subjects were presented with sentence frames either alone, with a rhyme or category cue, or with the cue plus the first letter of the final word. Examples are given in Table 11.1. Their task was to complete the sentence with a word. In the no-context condition, any word sensibly completing the sentence was permissible. In the cue conditions, either a rhyme or category exemplar was required, as appropriate. When the first letter of the final word was also given, subjects had to provide a word beginning with the letter that rhymed with the cue or was an exemplar of the category. Results from 65 subjects are presented in Table 11.2. For sentences presented without additional cues, responses were heterogeneous, with no word accounting for more than a few completions. With a category cue, individual targets became highly predictable; the same target was chosen on 48 percent of the responses. With a rhyme cue, even greater uniformity in responses was observed: the same target was chosen on 69 percent of the responses. If we combine the two most frequently chosen targets, then agreement increases to 72 percent for category cues and 84 percent for rhyme cues. With a rhyme or category cue and the first letter of each target provided, subjects' responses showed nearly 90 percent agreement on both tasks. These results suggest that the context in a monitoring task – not merely the text but also the rhyme or category cue – facilitates the identification of a target word *when no target is actually present*. The process is not "interactive"; it is guessing. Given other evidence that subjects in monitoring tasks generate possible targets in an attempt to guess them (Tanenhaus and Seidenberg, 1981), it is quite plausible that Marslen-Wilson and Tyler's results reflect subjects' abilities to predict targets in advance. As such, their results may be fully consistent with the West and Stanovich (1982) claim that context has an effect only on the processing of highly predictable lexical items.

A predictability explanation is less plausible for results obtained by Morton and Long (1976). Using a phoneme monitoring task, they showed that the transitional probability of a word in context influenced recognition latency with initial phonemes in high probability words being detected more rapidly than initial phonemes in plausible but lower probability words. For example, phoneme monitor times to detect the target phoneme were faster in *plate* than *pan* when they occurred in the context *At the sink Mary washed a. . . .* This was interpreted as evidence that context facilitates the recognition of high-probability words. In a recent study, however, Foss and Gernsbacher (1983) have shown that this context effect was due to a subtle artifact in Morton and Long's materials. Foss and Gernsbacher noticed that the vowels in the high-probability words used by Morton and Long were longer than the vowels in the low-probability words. They demonstrated that phoneme monitor times to these two sets of words differed even when the words were presented out of context. In subsequent experiments they found that phoneme monitoring was extremely sensitive to the phonetic characteristics of words and extremely insensitive to contextual manipulations.

There are other cases where phoneme monitoring times are influenced by context. We have seen, for example, that phoneme monitoring times are slower following ambiguous words in neutral contexts than in strongly biasing contexts (Cairns and Hsu, 1981; Swinney and Hakes, 1976). Likewise, phoneme monitoring times are longer following words in a "bare" as opposed to a "rich" context (Cairns, Cowart, and Jablon, 1981). Cairns et al. have presented persuasive evidence that these effects are due to differences in how much effort it takes to integrate a word into its context, and not to how difficult it is to access the word (see also Swinney, 1979).

Thus, research on context effects in phoneme monitoring seems remarkably consistent with the modularity hypothesis.

11.2.5. Implications for parsing research

Research on word recognition – in particular, lexical ambiguity research – not only provides evidence that one component of the language processing system is modular; it also provides some important methodological lessons. First, this research suggests that experimental tasks based on conscious awareness of process or output may be limited in their investigative range. It is commonly accepted that, in certain domains of processing, one cannot intuit about the nature of the process itself. Rather one only has conscious awareness of the outcomes of processes. However, we may not be aware of all outcomes of processes. This is evidenced by the lexical ambiguity research, which shows that all salient meanings of an ambiguous word are obligatorily and automatically made available, in most cases without conscious awareness. In other words, we may be aware only of "final" outputs and oblivious to certain types of "temporary" outputs.

A more technical lesson is that multiple outputs of modules do not necessarily lead to significantly greater processing load. Rather, detection of multiple outputs requires measures that tap directly into the representations resulting from the operations of a module. In the case of lexical access, appropriate methodologies were already available, though the methodologies were not developed with modularity in mind. Unfortunately, however, the presence of a module does not guarantee the existence of a methodology that will be sensitive to its outputs.

The following *Gedanken* experiment on parsing illustrates some of the consequences of these methodological points. Consider a string of words S that can be assigned at least two different syntactic structures, $K1$ and $K2$. In neutral contexts, introspective judgment reveals a preference for $K1$ over $K2$. That is, subjects report the reading associated with $K1$ far more often than the reading associated with $K2$ and only rarely report being aware of any ambiguity. However, in some contexts $K2$ is judged preferable to $K1$ (while in other contexts $K1$ is even more strongly preferred over $K2$). Moreover, suppose processing load measures suggest that the processing of S is no more complex than the processing of similar but structurally unambiguous strings of words. One might reason that only one structure is initially assigned to S in any given context, and only rarely if ever are two readings considered. Therefore, any parsing model predicting that both $K1$ and $K2$ are automatically assigned to S regardless of context – as may (or may not) follow from a modular view of parsing – would simply be wrong.

This plausible line of reasoning would, of course, lead to the erroneous conclusion that only one meaning of an ambiguous word is accessed in a given context. In order to resolve the question of whether $K1$ and $K2$ are both automatically assigned to S or whether only one is assigned, methodologies must be developed which are sensitive to the presence of syntactic structure. In the absence of such methodologies, this particular issue will likely remain unresolved.

11.3. Parsing and modularity

We will now examine some of the consequences of the modularity hypothesis for a theory of parsing. We begin by making the basic assumption that the language processor makes use of the GCS, which has access to notions such as beliefs and goals in addition to the outputs of whatever processing modules there may be. Processing by the GCS is characterized by controlled processes. The modules, on the other hand, process their inputs automatically.

Examining parsing in light of our previous discussion and in light of our present knowledge, there seems to be little room for a modular parser characterized by automatic processes. It has been repeatedly demonstrated that some routines affecting the assignment of syntactic structure are subject to strategic control and that the presence of a biasing context – whether syntactic, semantic, or pragmatic – can affect structure assignment. It has also been repeatedly shown that parsing processes consume limited resource capacity, since they can interfere with performance on secondary tasks. So it would appear that the parsing routines are accomplished by the GCS, and not by an autonomous, automatic syntactic module.

However, this conclusion may be an artifact of the experimental tasks used to provide evidence for the nature of parsing routines. The models of Bresnan (1982), Frazier and Fodor (1978), Church (1980), Marcus (1977), and Kimball (1973) rely on data derived primarily from examination of the controlled processes of the GCS. Measures such as preference judgments and comprehension time studies require introspective, conscious evaluation by the subjects. Even processing load measures are by definition sensitive to controlled processes, which, unlike the automatic processes, consume limited resource capacity. If one bases a theory of parsing solely upon such data, the resulting theory will naturally give the impression that all parsing is accomplished by controlled processes.

But let us consider what a parsing model would look like which incorporates a series of one or more linguistic modules characterized by automatic processes. In what follows, we wish to present three models – two "limiting cases" and one somewhere in between. Only the rough outlines of each type of model will be presented. Our intent is not to propose and evaluate alternative models of parsing. Rather, it is to use these hypothetical models as a means of fleshing out what we might mean by a modular parser and thereby stimulate research questions about the nature of parsing.[8]

11.3.1. The linguistic system as a module

Let us first consider the hypothesis that the entire linguistic system is one unified module. It takes as its input a speech signal and computes as its output one or more semantic representations; everything in between is accomplished completely automatically. The semantic representation(s) is/are then sent to the GCS, which operates on them to create constructed representations. This simple model could be diagrammed as follows:

(12)   speech signal ⟶ LINGUISTIC SYSTEM ⟶ GCS

However, such a model does not seem to account for the participation of the GCS in the process of comprehension. If the GCS is not actively involved in building structures (since this is all done automatically), then it must be doing something else. This model allows for at least three major possibilities. One possibility is that a certain amount of attention must be given to the incoming speech signal. However, this fact alone could not account for syntactic complexity phenomena or other syntactic facts, as the incoming speech signal itself has no such structure: it is a continuous stream of uninterpreted noise. Furthermore, research on word recognition indicates that lexical access takes place with very little if any attention given the phonetic input. Attending to the speech signal would not appear a likely account of what the GCS is doing.

At the other end, the GCS has access to the output of the linguistic system, where it could be involved in two tasks. First, the GCS is operating on the output of the linguistic system to build a constructed representation. Pronouns are assigned discourse referents, inferences are made, and so forth. Second, the GCS may be involved in the resolution of semantic ambiguities. In some, perhaps many cases, a multiple output may be computed by the linguistic system, and the GCS would be responsible for selecting among these one to be mapped into a constructed representation.

Some important questions are raised in this general model for which there are at present no firm answers. One consequence of this model is that in the absence of much if not all of the GCS, semantic representations will be computed automatically given a speech signal input. So long as the GCS is able to attend to the incoming speech signal at some minimal level, the appropriate semantic representations will be automatically computed and made available to the GCS. Whether this claim is correct remains to be seen. It would require a measure sensitive to nonlexical semantic representations (should they exist), a measure we do not at present possess.

An initially suspect claim that follows from this model is that all syntactic complexity can be traced to the semantic complexity of the sentence, both in terms of number of readings made available and in terms of the number and quality of inferences and operations required to convert the reading selected into a portion of a constructed representation. There could be no "purely syntactic" effects. This would, at first sight, appear wrong in light of even a fairly cursory examination of parsing phenomena. However, to discount this possibility completely, we must first motivate the psychological connection between syntactic and semantic representations (which includes, of course, a demonstration of their existence) and examine the predictions about processing made based on that model. It could well turn out, for instance, that semantic representations would closely reflect syntactic structure, and hence preserve a considerable amount of syntactic complexity. This account would require an explanation of why some semantic representations would be harder for the GCS to "handle" than others.

11.3.2. Grammatical subsystems as modules

Let us leave this first simple model and examine a more complex modular linguistic system that allows the GCS greater access to the internal workings of the linguistic system. Let us assume, again for the sake of discussion, that the linguistic system is composed of a set of modules arranged in a partially serial fashion. Let us assume a phonetics, which converts a continuous speech signal into a discrete phonetic representation; a phonology, which maps phonetic representations to phonological representations; a morphology/lexicon, which takes phonological representations and makes available information about lexical entries with those phonological characteristics; a syntax (a parser), which takes the syntactic information about the lexical items and maps such sequences onto syntactic structures; and a semantics, which takes syntactic structures and the semantic information found in lexical entries and maps them into semantic representations. If these modules automatically make their outputs available to the next appropriate module, we have the single-module model presented earlier. As far as the GCS is concerned, so long as it has access only to representations at the ends and nowhere else, the internal complexities of the linguistic system are wholly irrelevant to its workings.

But if the linguistic system is a series of modules organized roughly in this fashion, we might question the assumption that the GCS has access only to one type of input and one type of output. It may well have access to the inputs and outputs of each of the modules. A model of this type would maintain a modular approach to language processing, yet involve the GCS much more in the comprehension process. One major task would be to resolve temporary ambiguities, rife at all levels *when each level is examined independently*. For example, a final -*s* on a word (e.g., /pæts/) could well be a plural or a possessive (or a combination of the two); a third person singular present tense ending; a contracted form of *is* or *has*; or simply the last sound of the word, as in *box* or *lapse*. In context, of course, the ambiguity is normally resolved in favor of one reading (*Pat's mother likes donuts*). Nevertheless, a modular morphology operating independently of all other systems would, presumably, present all these possibilities automatically to the GCS. If all possible outputs are computed given a certain input (as required by a modular view of processing), and if all outputs are presented to the GCS, then the GCS must at some level disambiguate outputs. One reasonable hypothesis is that the GCS intervenes in the language understanding process at the level of the output and input of each of the modules. At those points, the GCS has the opportunity to choose which of the outputs of a given module, if more than one, should be sent along to the next module for further processing. This seems to be just what is going on in lexical access, for example, and on this basis we find this model initially more plausible than the first. We assume that the process of disambiguation would proceed on the basis of strategies and heuristics, and maybe occasionally on the basis of just plain wild guessing, in the manner expected of the GCS, rather than in some completely mechanical, algorithmic way. It may even involve sending several outputs through the next module in parallel.

In this model, a second task would also be required of the GCS. It must "pair up" constituents of the syntactic representation with the meanings of the words whose syntactic properties served as input to the syntactic module. For example, in understanding the sentence *Cats chase mice*, the meaning of *cats* must be associated with the first NP position in the structure [$_S$NP[$_{VP}$V NP]], and not the second. We might think of the GCS as responsible for integrating various types of linguistic information to derive representations not constructed by any of the modules. For example, we might wish to maintain that phonological information is integrated with syntactic information to derive a representation of the following sort.

(13)   [$_S$[$_{NP}$ [$_N$ kæts]] [$_{VP}$ [$_V$ čeys] [$_{NP}$[$_N$ mays]]]]

Minimally, the GCS would have to coordinate syntactic information with information about lexical meanings. To summarize the componential model diagrammatically, it is organized along the following lines.

(14)

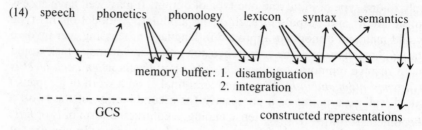

This componential model contrasts with the single module model in several ways. First, since the GCS is involved at all levels, we would not predict that semantic representations are computed with only minimal attention paid the incoming speech signal. As the GCS is actively involved in the course of comprehension, failure of the GCS to do the appropriate processing would result in a breakdown in the comprehension process somewhere along the way. In addition, since the GCS is allowed to intervene at certain specified points, we would expect to find evidence of purely syntactic (purely phonological, etc.), effects on the comprehension process derived from the effects of temporary ambiguities as well as the abilities of the GCS to "handle" certain types of structures more easily than others.

It merits some emphasis at this point that the GCS would not be involved in actually building syntactic structures. Rather, the GCS decides which information to send to which modules, and which to set aside (perhaps only temporarily). Once a decision is made to send something to the syntax, for instance, the syntactic component computes one or more structures whether the GCS wants it to or not.

Consider momentarily how "garden path" sentences might be dealt with in a system of this type. Consider Bever's famous example:

(15)   The horse raced past the barn fell.

The work on lexical access indicates that all salient information about each of the words is obligatorily and automatically computed. For instance, *raced* would (at least) be analyzed as a past tense verb, a past participle verb, and as a passive participle verb (the "real" reading). Similarly for *past*. If all this information were presented to the syntax, and its outputs subsequently to the semantics, all possible syntactic structures and meanings would be computed. At any of these levels, the GCS could make disambiguating decisions "on-line," choosing the structures that seem most plausible, or are of the type habitually chosen (because they are usually correct, statistically more frequent), or whatever. Again, lack of awareness of the presence of a given meaning or structure does not mean that it is not, in some sense yet to be made precise, "under consideration" or "available." We simply cannot intuit about these things. In this example, the GCS has the option of sending information about just one lexical entry "under consideration" to the syntax and the semantics. If it habitually and repeatedly sends to the syntax the past tense analysis of "raced" and ignores the passive participle analysis of transitive "race," a garden path will result. If the GCS intervenes at the outputs of all the modules, we would expect to find classes of garden path phenomena resulting from habitually incorrect disambiguation at different levels of structure.

One final note on the componential model. This model requires the GCS to hold in some temporary on-line memory store (the buffer in the diagram) the options presented to it until the GCS decides what to do with them. Assuming that the buffer has limited storage capacity, the GCS is under some pressure to remove stored items reasonably quickly in order to accommodate incoming information. We would thus expect to find cases where processing preferences seem to be dictated to some extent by these limitations. Of course, such limitations have been the subject of intensive research in parsing procedures; the Sausage Machine model of Frazier and Fodor (1978) is one model that springs readily to mind.

11.3.3. Grammatical rules as modules

We have considered a model in which the whole linguistic system is one single module, and one where the linguistic system is a series of modules each sending their outputs to the GCS. We have yet to consider another limiting case of such modularity – where the modules become more and more specialized and less and less complex. Eventually, we arrive at a model where each of the rules of the grammar is an independent module on its own. The rules of grammar collectively would define a linguistic system "in the head."

(16)   Rule 1   Rule 2   Rule 3   . . .   Rule *n*

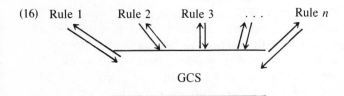

GCS

In such a model, the GCS is even more actively involved, able to intervene and make decisions at any stage of language processing. Perhaps most significantly, it is able to select one rule from a pool of candidate rules, all applicable to the input at hand. Should each of the rules have a unique output for a given input, the GCS would never have to choose among alternative outputs. Rather, the decisions in this model involve choices between rules, and not between structures. The rule-module model is quite different from the previous models presented. In the single-module model, the only choices are between meanings computed by the linguistic system. In the componential model, decisions must be made at a series of different levels; once a decision is made, though, there is no further decision required concerning which module to send the information to, as one and only one module would accept a given output as input. But in the rule-module model, the types of decisions are reversed. No longer are there multiple outputs of any modules; however, the output of a given module may serve as input to any number of other modules. Hence, choices involve which of several modules to send an output to, and not which of several outputs to send to another module.

Of the three models presented, the rule-module model is most consistent with current prevailing assumptions about the nature of the parser: that it is actively involved in rule choice (either by algorithm, which seems unlikely, or by some sort of strategic control by the GCS, for which there is considerable empirical evidence). But what in this model remains of modularity? What difference is there between this last model and one in which all parsing is a function of the GCS, with the "rules of grammar" as a part of the GCS itself?

There is a difference between regarding each rule as a module and regarding each as an element of the GCS. If each is a module, the GCS has no access whatsoever to the internal structure of the rule or its internal workings. It has access only to input and output. For all the GCS knows, each rule could be extremely elaborate and complex, though most often pressed into the service of doing simple operations. The workings of a module are not *represented* by the GCS. However, if each rule is an element of the GCS, these properties do not follow: the GCS would have access to the internal processes of each and, more important, the GCS would be where the rules are represented.

Translating these conceptual differences into decidable empirical issues is quite another matter. In the abstract, it seems a question that could be investigated empirically, but in practice we see nothing on the horizon that presents us with a means of distinguishing these two positions.

Yet another issue is raised by this model. In what sense is the set of rules in the rule-module system a "linguistic system in the head?" If there is but one large module, there is clearly such a linguistic system. If it consists of a series of smaller modules (a syntax, a phonology, etc.), with the GCS intervening between them, we have a linguistic system in the following sense: each module defines *a level of structure*, and from a given sound input, representations at each level of structure will be computed in the course of normal language comprehension. In order to derive a constructed representation from a speech signal, the GCS must send information to each module. But where "in the head" is the notion that these modules collectively define a linguistic system? It is not represented as such by any of the modules clearly. If the linguistic system is nothing but a series of modules, it cannot represent itself in any way as a linguistic system. Rather, the "linguistic system" seems to be defined operationally: that series of modules the GCS makes use of in normal language comprehension. In other words, the GCS knows where to send things – it has a representation of "the linguistic system" as a convenient fiction created to organize the flow of certain types of information. So, on the modular approach, allowing the intervention of the GCS between modules, there is in no strict sense a linguistic system; there *is* a syntax, a semantics, and so forth. The modules define levels of representation: the GCS organizes the modules into a linguistic system.

Applying this same line of reasoning to the model where each rule is thought of as a "minimal" module, what remains here? Again, each rule cannot represent the whole system as a linguistic system; each rule only works with very limited types of representations. What we would like to say, of course, is that the rules collectively define a linguistic system. But again, if this is to be a part of mental representation, the locus of the representation must be the GCS, which can "survey" all the rules and organize them in such a way as to effect language comprehension. So, in this model the linguistic system is a construct of the GCS and not of an autonomous system. Thus far the second and third models are on equal footing. But there remains a very sharp difference between them: in the componential system each module defines a *level* of representation. However, the rule-module model has no similar means of defining levels of representation. Rather, *collections* of rules define a level of representation – but the rules are not represented as a collection in any autonomous linguistic system. Instead, the GCS "collects" these modules together, representing them as defining a linguistic system. Thus, taking each rule as a module not only relegates the notion of a linguistic system to a convenient abstraction, or at best a real element of the GCS, but it also has the consequence of treating linguistic *levels* as either convenient descriptive fictions or as real elements of the GCS. The rules are real enough, but the representation of them as a system, if "in the head," is in the GCS.

So, as the proposed modules become smaller and more numerous, the greater the participation of the GCS in the comprehension process and the more opportunity for a "linguistic system" to become a function of the GCS. Insofar as our research is directed toward the task of isolating a linguistic system, the less the GCS is involved the easier it should be to separate the two systems. And as the GCS becomes more involved, the more crucial it becomes to focus research on the properties of the GCS to understand the nature of language, and the more difficult it becomes to disentangle the GCS from any linguistic system.

11.4. Levels of representation and language comprehension

In the preceding section we argued that the strongest form of the modularity hypothesis holds that the linguistic system is a single processing module. However, this view does not seem tenable given the psycholinguistic evidence reviewed earlier. The strongest form of the modularity hypothesis that appears to be satisfactory on empirical grounds is the one in which the different systems of the grammar correspond to separate processing modules. This view, which entails that listeners compute representations at each level that corresponds to a processing module, presents us with a strong methodological challenge. This challenge is to develop experimental methodologies that are sensitive to – and capable of distinguishing among – different levels of representation. We turn now to a discussion of some experiments that attempt to isolate three levels of representation during comprehension. Two of these, linguistic form and linguistic meaning (or logical form), are grammatical levels; the third, the constructed representation, is not. These experiments are preliminary in two ways. First, many of the results are merely suggestive and will need to be interpreted in the context of further experimentation. We will try to be explicit about which results we consider to be suggestive and about what further research needs to be done. Second, while our studies suggest that it is possible to experimentally isolate different levels of representation, they do not provide a definitive answer to the question of whether or not listeners compute linguistic representations.

Our experiments focus on the processing of sentences with anaphors and sentences with gaps. It is commonly assumed that anaphors and gaps have to be replaced by or at least connected to some entity in order to be understood. A basic question for the study of both structures is the nature of this entity. Different levels of representation have been proposed for different anaphors. First is the syntactic/morphological/phonological *form* of a given linguistic expression. That form has associated with it a linguistic *meaning*, which we provisionally assume to be represented by a logical form (see, for example, Sag, 1976). Finally an expression (the *form*), by virtue of its meaning, has a certain *denotation* in the world or some model of it. We take forms and meanings to be parts of a linguistic system; the denotations are extralinguistic. We make the standard assumption that assigning a representation to an anaphor involves at least two processing stages. In the first stage, possible antecedents are identified. In the second stage, the anaphor is linked to or replaced by an antecedent or a conceptual entity related to the antecedent. It is this antecedent that is used in determining the denotation of the anaphor. We will be directly concerned with the form of the representation of the antecedent. Three hypotheses are entertained, each of which corresponds to one of the levels discussed above. These hypotheses contrast with respect to the intermediate steps by which an anaphor is assigned a referent. The first, which we will refer to as the *literal replacement* hypothesis, assumes that an anaphor obtains its reference in the following way: A linguistic form is first located and identified as an antecedent. The denotation of the antecedent is then computed via its meaning and assigned as the denotation of the anaphor. It is as if the anaphor were *replaced* by its antecedent. This general hypothesis was entertained most frequently by transformational grammarians in the 1960s, where pronouns, for example, were thought to be derived from underlying fully specified noun phrases on the basis of formal identity with their antecedents. A second hypothesis is that the anaphoric element is linked to the logical form (or meaning) of the linguistic antecedent rather than its surface form. Cooper (1979) presents an analysis that can be construed as of this type. We will refer to this as the *logical replacement* hypothesis. Finally we have the *direct reference* hypothesis, which maintains that an anaphor is assigned the same denotation as its antecedent by being directly linked to some element in the constructed representation. Thus the anaphor does not first have to be replaced by a linguistic antecedent in order for it to be assigned a denotation. The analyses by Nash-Webber (1979) and by Kamp (1981) are examples falling within the general spirit of this hypothesis.

In order to investigate these hypotheses experimentally we need response measures that can distinguish between the processing of linguistic form, linguistic meaning, and the constructed representation. One plausible candidate is provided by the lexical priming paradigms that were used in the ambiguity research discussed above.

11.4.1. Rhyme priming and literal form

The first two experiments that we will discuss were conducted in collaboration with Susan Hudson. Numerous researchers have suggested that speech-based codes play an important role in maintaining linguistic information in working memory during listening and reading (for recent reviews see Levy, 1981, and Slowiacek and Clifton, 1980). Hillinger (1980) and Tanenhaus, Flanigan, and Seidenberg (1980) have demonstrated that the recognition of a visually presented target word is facilitated when it follows a phonemically related word. Let us assume that this cross-model "rhyme priming" reflects the automatic activation of phonological codes as a consequence of lexical access. If rhyme priming is only sensitive to this initial automatic activation, then it is of little value for studying post-lexical processing. Suppose, however, that phonological codes can be used to maintain the surface form of a word (literal form) and that the surface form of a word will prime phonemically related words for as long as it is available. Rhyme priming can then be used to trace the availability of surface form.

The stimuli in our first experiment were two-clause sentences constructed from pairs of rhyming words such as *cream-theme*. One member of the pair served as the target while the other member of the pair (the prime word) occurred within the sentence. For example, one pair of test sentences read as follows:

(17)   Since Jane forgot to put in all the $\left\{ \begin{array}{l} \text{milk} \\ \underline{\text{cream}} \end{array} \right\}$, the cake was dry.

At the end of the sentence, the target *theme* was presented in a lexical decision task. The facilitating effect of the presence of *cream* could be observed by contrasting it with the same sentence containing *milk* in its place.

There were two manipulations of the materials. First, the effect of syntactic structure was examined by having the priming word either in the first or the second clause. The clause manipulation was chosen because a number of studies have demonstrated that words in the first clause of a sentence are less accessible than words in the second clause (e.g., Caplan, 1972). Bever and Hurtig (1975) have suggested that this result obtains because information within a clause is maintained in verbatim form. The other manipulation controlled for the number of words intervening between prime and target. This resulted in a 2×2 design with either four or seven intervening words between prime and target, and the target in either the first or second clause.

The results are summarized in Table 11.3. Rhyme priming obtained when four words intervened between the prime and target. But with seven intervening words, the rhyme priming effect had completely disappeared. There was no effect of clause structure; whether the prime word was in the first or second clause did not affect the pattern of rhyme priming. These results suggest that the phonological code for a word becomes available as a consequence of lexical access and then decays within four to seven words. The duration for which the phonological code remains available may be an important parameter, if phonological code is important for parsing, as Slowiacek and Clifton (1980) suggest. It may, for example, set constraints on the number of words that can easily be chunked together during parsing. However, it is also possible that the

Table 11.3. *Mean lexical decision times (msec) for rhyme clause study*

Condition	Stimulus Sentences and Targets	Results Target	Rhyme	Non-rhyme	Facilitation NR-R
First clause					
4 intervening words	Since Jane forgot to put in all the $\left\{\begin{array}{l}\text{cream,}\\\text{milk,}\end{array}\right\}$ the cake was dry.	*theme*	696	730	+34
7 intervening words	If the pitch was a $\left\{\begin{array}{l}\text{ball,}\\\text{strike,}\end{array}\right\}$ the other team would win the game.	*haul*	713	717	+4
Second clause					
4 intervening	Because the murderer left no clues, the $\left\{\begin{array}{l}\text{sleuth}\\\text{cop}\end{array}\right\}$ couldn't crack the case.	*booth*	681	702	+21
7 intervening words	The thief got away but the $\left\{\begin{array}{l}\text{purse}\\\text{fur}\end{array}\right\}$ was soon found in the back alley.	*verse*	696	698	+2

rhyme priming we observed is simply a lexical effect and unrelated to postlexical comprehension processes. This interpretation seems less likely in light of results we obtained using sentences with filler-gap dependencies, sentences that plausibly require listeners to maintain a verbatim representation of part of the sentence.

In a study using sentences with relative clauses, Wanner and Maratsos (1978) found that there was an increase in working memory load between the head noun in a *wh*-phrase and its gap. Our experiment used the rhyme priming methodology to test the hypothesis that the literal form of a filler is maintained in working memory in the processing of a sentence with a filler-gap dependency. If this is the case, facilitation in making lexical decisions to a target rhyming with the filler ought to obtain, even when as many as seven words intervene between the filler and the gap. Materials were constructed from sentences with embedded *wh*-questions such as

(18)   The man was surprised at which $\left\{\begin{array}{l}\underline{\text{beer}}\\\underline{\text{wine}}\end{array}\right\}$ the judges awarded the first prize

to ___.

Each sentence was followed, after 400 msec, by a target word that rhymed with one of the two alternative prime words (e.g., *fear*). The controls in this experiment were sentences in which the prime was the last word in

Table 11.4. *Mean lexical decision times (msec) for* wh-*study*

Condition	Stimulus Sentences and Targets	Target	Rhyme	Non-rhyme	Facili-tation NR-R
wh-structure	The man was surprised at which $\begin{Bmatrix} beer \\ wine \end{Bmatrix}$ the judges awarded the first prize to ___.	*fear*	599	622	+23
Prime	The old man looked $\begin{Bmatrix} pale. \\ weak. \end{Bmatrix}$	*jail*	626	649	+23

the sentence, so that no words intervened between the prime and the target; for example,

(19)   The old man had been sick and he looked very $\begin{Bmatrix} \underline{pale} \\ \underline{weak} \end{Bmatrix}$.

Where the target was *jail*. The results of this experiment are summarized in Table 11.4. The same amount of rhyme priming obtained when seven words intervened between the prime and the target as obtained when the prime immediately preceded the target. These results contrast with the results of the previous study in which no rhyme priming obtained when seven words intervened between the prime and the target. In sentences with filler-gap dependencies, listeners appear to hold onto the verbatim form of the filler word until the gap is identified and filled.[9] Gap-filling is thus a case of literal replacement.

Before accepting this strong conclusion, however, we should emphasize that the results of the *wh*-question experiment need to be interpreted with some caution, until further studies have been conducted to replicate the results. First of all, only 18 subjects were used. Second, the decay of the phonological code in the span of seven words was not replicated as a part of this experiment, so a crucial comparison is being made to a different experiment using different materials and subjects. Finally, the results were not significant when items were taken as a random factor.

Nevertheless, the results are promising and more complete studies are indicated. One issue not addressed directly in this study was the role of the "gap" itself in maintaining the linguistic form of the *wh*-phrase. For example, the processor might simply put all *wh*-phrases into working memory until the end of the sentence, regardless of gap location. A second issue of interest concerns whether the *wh*-phrase is actively maintained in working memory (as the Wanner and Maratsos study would suggest), or whether there is some "reactivation" of the *wh*-phrase upon encountering the gap. The crucial experiment, which we are in the process of conducting, contrasts sentences with gaps appearing late to those in which gaps appear early, for instance:

(20) They asked which $\left\{ \begin{matrix} \underline{man} \\ \underline{girl} \end{matrix} \right\}$ John wanted the old lady to look at ____. (Target = $\underline{can}$)

(21) They asked which $\left\{ \begin{matrix} \underline{man} \\ \underline{girl} \end{matrix} \right\}$ ____ wanted John to look at the old lady. (Target = $\underline{can}$)

If the *wh*-phrase is maintained in working memory until the gap is located, and then removed, sentences with early gaps, like (21), should fail to show priming, while sentences with late gaps, like (20), should exhibit effects. Furthermore, if the *wh*-phrase is maintained in memory, rhyme priming should occur at every point between filler and gap. On the other hand, if the *wh*-phrase is reactivated upon encountering a gap, we would expect that if more than seven words intervened between the *wh*-phrase and gap, the priming effect should disappear until the gap is encountered.

Regardless of outcome, the rhyme priming methodology should prove valuable both in determining when the surface representation of a word is being maintained in working memory and in separating representations at this level from other levels.

While rhyme priming methodologies and other, similar sound-based tasks may be used to detect surface representations, they cannot be used to investigate other levels of representation. For example, rhyme priming could not be used to investigate whether anaphors, such as definite pronouns, are best analyzed as involving logical replacement or direct reference. But let us consider how lexical priming methodologies might be used to distinguish logical replacement from direct reference to the constructed representation. First, consider a series of studies on pronominal anaphors.

11.4.2. Lexical priming and pronouns

These studies use lexical priming to diagnose the assignment of reference to a pronoun. The logic is straightforward. When a target word related to the referent of a pronoun is presented after the pronoun, its recognition should be facilitated relative to a word that is unrelated to the referent of the pronoun. The question is whether the lexical priming results in pronoun studies can distinguish between the logical replacement hypothesis and the direct reference hypothesis. To find the denotation of a pronoun, do we need to access other meanings? We believe the results distinguish the two approaches and show that direct reference is more nearly correct, as linguistic evidence would suggest.

First, we look at a study that gives unexpected results. Marslen-Wilson and Tyler (1980a) report a study using a cross-modal lexical decision task to investigate pronominal anaphora resolution in sentences such as

(22)   The sailor tried to save the cat but it/he fell overboard.

Lexical decisions to the target words *boat* and *dog* were facilitated when they followed *sailor* and *cat*, respectively. No differential facilitation obtained, however, when these targets were presented following *he* and *it*. This result is somewhat surprising, as it would appear to be incompatible with either hypothesis. It suggests either that lexical priming is insensitive to pronominal anaphora resolution or that reference assignment does not take place immediately following the pronoun. Several recent studies rule out the first explanation.

Consider first a study we conducted in collaboration with Debra Senytka. In this study subjects were presented with sentence pairs such as

(23)   The <u>fire</u> raged through the <u>forest</u>. It was $\left\{ \begin{array}{l} \text{destroyed} \\ \text{destructive} \end{array} \right\}$.

The first sentence contains two definite noun phrases, and the second sentence contains a pronoun that could refer to either noun phrase. The last word of the sentence disambiguates the pronoun's referent. Two versions of each second sentence were constructed by changing the last word to select the first or the second noun as the appropriate antecedent of the pronoun. The sentences were presented one word at a time, each word being displayed for approximately 400 msec. The second sentence was followed by a target word presented for lexical decision. For the critical sentences the target word was one of the nouns from the first sentence (e.g., *fire*). The target word was either the appropriate antecedent of the pronoun or not, depending on the final word of the second sentence. Lexical decisions to the target word were faster when it was the appropriate antecedent of the pronoun (629 milliseconds) than when it was the inappropriate antecedent (667 msec). Thus the results demonstrate that lexical priming can be sensitive to pronominal anaphora resolution.

This study, though, differs from Marslen-Wilson and Tyler (1980a) in several potentially important ways. Marslen-Wilson and Tyler presented their sentences auditorily, while we presented ours visually. Secondly, Marslen-Wilson and Tyler used a word related to the antecedent of the pronoun as the target while we used the antecedent word itself. Finally, the target interrupted the sentence in the Marslen-Wilson and Tyler study, while it followed the sentence in our study. A recent study by Leiman (1982) suggests that neither the modality of presentation nor the use of

Table 11.5. *Examples of Leiman's stimuli*

Condition	Example	
Pronoun anaphora control	The attorney argued forcefully.	The council listened to him.
	The president argued forcefully.	The council listened to him.
Noun phrase repetition control	The attorney argued forcefully.	The council listened to the attorney.
	The president argued forcefully.	The council listened to the president.
No-anaphora control	The attorney argued forcefully.	The crowd was persuaded.
	The president argued forcefully.	The crowd was persuaded.
Target word: *lawyer*		

the referent word itself (rather than a related word) explains the different results obtained in these studies. Leiman used a cross-modal naming task in which subjects listened to pairs of sentences and then named a visually presented target word. Examples of his materials are presented in Table 11.5.

The second sentence in the set ended with: (1) a pronoun whose antecedent was the subject of the first sentence (pronoun anaphora); (2) repetition of the subject of the first sentence (noun phrase repetition); or (3) a noun phrase that did not refer back to the subject of the first sentence (no anaphora). Target words were either synonyms of, or unrelated to, the subject of the first sentence. They were presented immediately following the second sentence or at delays of 250 and 500 msec. In the no-anaphora condition, related targets were not facilitated compared to unrelated targets at any delay interval. For pronoun anaphora, facilitation obtained at both the no-delay and 250-msec delay conditions. Thus subjects appear to assign an antecedent to the pronoun extremely rapidly. Noun phrase repetition showed no facilitation until the 500 msec delay. Leiman's results indicate that cross-modal priming can be obtained to words related to the antecedent of a pronoun.

Attributing Marslen-Wilson and Tyler's results to a pronoun assignment effect is also questionable because their targets were presented in mid-sentence. In the Leiman study, though the pronouns were sentence-final, priming effects were observed for targets presented immediately after the pronoun. It is also unlikely that pronoun assignment is deferred until the end of the sentence, in light of the results of Marslen-Wilson and Tyler

(1981). Recall that in this study, priming effects were observed in mid-sentence, both for definite pronouns and for null pronouns (i.e., the subject of a gerund such as *Running toward the house . . .*).

A possible explanation for the different results obtained in the Leiman and Marslen-Wilson and Tyler studies is suggested by results obtained by Merrill, Sperber, and McCauley (1981). They had good and poor readers read such sentences as

(24)   The boy petted the cat.

(25)   The boy was scratched by the cat.

Five hundred milliseconds after reading the sentence, subjects named the color of a word related to either a contextually salient or contextually subordinate property of the word *cat* (e.g., *claws* or *fur*). Only the contextually salient word showed interference for good readers, while both related words showed interference for poor readers, just as they would in the absence of context (facilitation in naming or lexical decision corresponds to interference, not facilitation, in Stroop tasks). Merrill et al.'s results, combined with the picture of lexical access which emerges from studies of lexical ambiguity resolution, suggest that lexical access initially makes available a context-independent representation of a word and activates a field of information related to the word. Any target related to anything that is activated is capable of being primed at this point. The word is then rapidly integrated into the context as the constructed representation is formed. Once the word is integrated into the context, only targets related to elements of the constructed representation can be primed.

In the Merrill et al. study the constructed representation for the good readers highlighted the contextually salient properties of *cat*. Thus, following sentence (24), the constructed representation of the good readers emphasized the boy petting the cat's fur, while following sentence (25) the constructed representation emphasized that the boy was scratched by the cat's claws. In effect the constructed representation included inferences driven by the verb in each sentence. The fact that priming obtained only to the contextually salient property of *cat* demonstrates that not all target words semantically or associatively related to a word in a sentence will continue to be primed once the word is incorporated into the constructed representation.

Now consider again the pronoun studies discussed above. In our study with Senytka, and in Leiman's study, the target word was either the antecedent of the pronoun (Senytka) or a synonym of the antecedent of the pronoun (Leiman). In these studies the targets would be related to both the antecedent word and the representation of the referent in the con-

Table 11.6. *Results of the* steak-meat *experiment*

Condition	Delay between end of sentence and target (msec)[a]		
	0	600	900
Appropriate	858	717	855
Inappropriate	905	846	918
Control	825	742	849

[a] Scores are lexical decision times to targets.

structed representation; that is to say, the contextually salient properties of the referent. However, in the Marslen-Wilson and Tyler study it is likely (given their example sentence) that the target was not related to the representation of the referent *in the constructed representation.* If pronouns refer to representations in the constructed representation, then priming would be expected to obtain only when targets are related to the contextually salient properties of the referent.

11.4.3. Priming and the constructed representation

Now let us consider how these observations might be used to distinguish logical replacement from direct reference. First consider the results of an experiment that does not make direct use of pronouns, which might be considered an anaphoric variant of Merrill et al. (1981). In this experiment subjects listened to sentences such as (26) followed by sentence (27a), (27b), or (27c).

(26)   Mary couldn't decide whether to buy steak or hamburger.

(27)   a.   She finally decided to buy the more expensive meat.
       b.   She finally decided to buy the less expensive meat.
       c.   She finally decided to go to another nearby store.

In sentence (27a) real-world knowledge establishes that the referent of the NP *steak* is the referent of the noun phrase *the more expensive meat,* while in sentence (27b) it establishes that the referent of the NP *hamburger* is the referent of the noun phrase *the less expensive meat.* Sentence (27c) serves as the "nonreferent" control. The target word *steak* was presented for lexical decision immediately following (27a–c) or after a delay of 600 or 900 milliseconds. The results are presented in Table 11.6.

In the immediate delay condition, lexical decisions to inappropriate targets were 47 msec slower than lexical decisions to appropriate targets. The difference between appropriate and inappropriate targets indicates that listeners have already begun to make the inference necessary to assign the appropriate referent to *meat*. This result replicates and extends the work of Merrill, Sperber, and McCauley (1981) and illustrates the speed with which constructed representations develop. Lexical decision times to targets in both the appropriate and inappropriate conditions were slower than lexical decision times to targets in the control condition. This pattern of results is fully expected for the inappropriate targets. Appropriate targets were probably longer than controls because listeners had not always finished making the inference necessary to assign a referent to the noun phrase. Making an inference presumably leads to an increase in processing load that would slow decision times. It should be noted that the type of inference required in the sentences preceding appropriate and inappropriate targets is not required in the sentences that precede control targets.

At the 600 msec delay, the difference between responses to appropriate and inappropriate targets increased to 127 msec. Responses to appropriate targets were now marginally faster (35 msec) than responses to control targets. This effect replicates the results obtained in the Senytka pronoun study. The relatively small magnitude of this effect is somewhat unexpected, however.[10] One possible explanation comes from reports from subjects, who often noted that they were sometimes unable to draw the inference necessary to determine which antecedent was correct. The results at the 900 msec delay interval fall somewhere between the no delay and 600 msec delay condition. The difference between appropriate and inappropriate targets is 63 msec and the appropriate and control conditions are nearly identical.

The results of this study demonstrate that priming can be obtained to elements of the constructed representation. They also demonstrate that lexical priming techniques can be used to trace the time course of inferencing – and, by extension, anaphora resolution. Perhaps more important, these results provide us with a tool for distinguishing between the logical and direct reference accounts of how referents are computed for anaphors.

Consider, for example, the materials given in (28).

(28) Mary couldn't decide whether to buy steak or hamburger.
  She finally chose the

  a. more expensive meat when she realized that it/ was on sale.
  b. less expensive meat when she realized that it/ was on sale.
  c. more expensive meat when she realized that there/ was a sale.
  d. less expensive meat when she realized that there/ was a sale.

The question at issue is how the listener assigns a referent to the pronoun *it* in (28a). According to the logical replacement hypothesis, the listener must first link the pronoun to the logical form of its antecedent, the noun phrase *the more expensive meat*. In contrast, the direct reference account maintains that the pronoun is linked directly to the denotation of the noun phrase. The results of the study just presented provide evidence that the denotation of the noun phrase *the more (less) expensive meat* in the listener's mental model will be related to the denotation of *steak*. If we make the assumption that a detectable amount of processing time is taken when a denotation must be arrived at via a meaning (logical replacement), then the materials in (28) can be used to distinguish between the logical replacement and direct reference hypotheses. In an experiment currently in progress the target words *steak* and *meat* are being presented at the slash points in (28). The logical replacement hypothesis predicts that there should be a point in processing where the target *meat* should be facilitated following the pronoun *it* in (28a). Shortly thereafter, once the denotation is assigned, then facilitation should obtain to *steak*. This prediction stems from the assumption that the denotation of the pronoun is arrived at via the meaning of the noun phrase which contains *meat* as its head noun. In contrast, the direct reference hypothesis predicts that there is no such intervening stage. Thus the target word *steak* should be facilitated immediately following the pronoun *it* in (28a). Sentences (28c) and (28d) serve as the nonreferent controls. The predictions described are subtle; they assume that it is possible to distinguish between stages in processing which occur extremely rapidly. Nonetheless, they represent a straightforward extension of the studies that have already been successfully completed.

11.4.4. Deep and surface anaphora

The experimental logic described becomes of even greater interest when we consider how it can be used to investigate other types of anaphors. For example, Hankamer and Sag (1976) and Sag and Hankamer (1984) have linguistically identified what they call *deep* and *surface* anaphors. Deep anaphors have many of the properties that would be expected from the direct reference hypothesis. In particular, they allow nonlinguistic or pragmatic control and they have a fairly "loose" connection to surface linguistic form. Surface anaphors, on the other hand, have certain properties that would be expected from the logical replacement account. They do not allow pragmatic control and they show considerable sensitivity to surface linguistic form. It should be noted that we are assuming that the level of logical form is closely related to surface form, as for instance, logical form (LF) is related to S-structures in Chomsky's government-binding (GB) framework (Chomsky, 1981).

For example, VP-Ellipsis is a surface anaphor while definite pronouns are deep anaphors. VP-Ellipsis does not readily allow for pragmatic control and it requires a certain syntactic parallelism in its antecedent. Definite pronouns, though, do not have these constraints. The following examples are from Sag and Hankamer (1984):

(29)   (Hankamer fires a gun at stage right. A blood-curdling female scream is heard.)
      Sag: *I wonder who was (no pragmatic control, surface anaphor)
      Sag: I wonder who *she* was? (pragmatic control possible, deep anaphor)

Syntactic parallelism is demonstrated by the examples (30):

(30)   The oats had to be taken down to the bin,
                            a.   *so Sandy did. (surface)
                            b.   so Sandy did *it*. (deep)

Sag and Hankamer (1984) have recently hypothesized that surface anaphors are linked to elements in the logical form of a sentence while deep anaphors are linked to elements of the listener's discourse model. These two hypotheses correspond to our logical replacement and direct reference hypothesis. The same logic that we described using the *steak* and *meat* materials can be used to test predictions based on the hypothesis that the direct reference account holds for deep anaphors, while the logical replacement account holds for surface anaphors. Consider the following example.

(31)   John couldn't decide whether to buy steak or hamburger.

    a.   He finally *chose the more expensive meat.*
    b.   I'm glad that he did Ø.   (*meat/steak*)

Under the logical replacement hypothesis, the antecedent of the null VP in (31b) is the meaning of the VP *choose the more expensive meat.* If this hypothesis is correct, presentation of *meat* immediately following (31b) should show greater relative facilitation than presentation of *steak.*

    The crucial comparison is to then run the same study but with a deep anaphor in (31b), which involves direct reference. Replacing (b) with (b′) would do this:

      b′.   I'm glad that he did *it.*

If the direct reference hypothesis holds, the referent of *it* in this context would be the activity of choosing steak, *not* the meaning of the VP *choose the more expensive meat.* So in this case we anticipate greater relative facilitation to steak following *it* than to *meat* – precisely the opposite results even though both continuations (b) and (b′) intuitively "mean the same thing."

    An observation by Sag and Hankamer (1984), also noted in Nash-Webber (1979), suggests that deep and surface anaphors are in fact processed differently. They noticed that a great deal of material can intervene between a deep anaphor and its referent, while surface anaphors must closely follow their referents. Consider, for example, the following.

(32) Somebody has to paint the garage.

      a. Let's take a vote and see who has to do it.
      b. Let's take a vote and see who.

Sentence (32) can be followed by a sentence using either a deep anaphor, as in (32a), to bring to mind *painting the garage*, or a surface null anaphor, as in (32b), to bring to mind *should paint the garage*. With intervening material, however, the deep anaphor becomes much more preferable. Sentence (32a) is perfectly fine when it follows (33), while (32b) is terrible.

(33) Someone has to paint the garage. The paint is peeling and the wood is beginning to rot.   ??(Let's take a vote and see who.)

(We find there to be no linguistic support for the idea that (33) is *ungrammatical*, as grammaticality is a sentence-level and not a discourse-level notion.) This fact can be explained if we assume that surface anaphors are linked to a representation at either the level of literal or logical form. One of the more robust results in the psycholinguistic literature is that the availability of the surface form of a sentence decays extremely rapidly (Sachs, 1967; Wanner, 1974). While the critical experiments have yet to be done, we assume along with Hankamer and Sag that memory for logical form also decays fairly rapidly. In contrast, the constructed representation remains available in memory for much longer durations. Thus if we assume that surface anaphors need to be linked to elements in either the surface or logical form of a sentence, then we have a principled explanation for why surface anaphors become less acceptable when material intervenes between the surface anaphor and its antecedent.

We have experimentally verified the intuition that surface anaphors are more difficult to process than deep anaphors when the anaphor and the antecedent are not close together using materials similar to those in (32, 33). Subjects read paragraphs that were presented one sentence at a time on a cathode ray tube and pressed a key when they had understood each sentence. Critical paragraphs began with an "antecedent sentence" such as (32). The antecedent sentence was either immediately followed by a sentence that contained a deep (such as 32a) or a surface anaphor (such as 32b), or one sentence intervened between the anaphor and its antecedent. Comprehension times to deep and surface anaphors are presented in Table 11.7. In the immediate condition surface anaphors were comprehended 223 msec faster than deep anaphors. This difference probably reflects the fact that surface anaphors contained fewer words than corresponding deep anaphors. The intervening sentence increased compre-

Table 11.7. *Mean comprehension times to deep and surface anaphors (msec)*

Anaphor	Condition		
	Immediate	Intervening sentence	Difference
Surface	2,228	2,435	207
Deep	2,451	2,367	−84
Difference	223	−68	

hension times to surface anaphors by 207 msec. Thus we experimentally replicate the intuition that surface but not deep anaphors become more difficult to process when a sentence intervenes between the anaphor and its antecedent.

We conducted a second experiment in order to test more directly the hypothesis that deep and surface anaphors find their antecedents in different levels of representation. Subjects read an antecedent sentence followed by a sentence containing either a deep or a surface anaphor and then decided whether or not a verification sentence was true or false given the preceding sentences. Verification sentences either matched the form of the antecedent sentence or differed from it in form but not conceptual content. Mismatches between the antecedent sentence and the verification sentence were created in one of two ways. Structural changes were introduced by using antecedent sentences that contained a verb + particle construction. In the matching condition the form of the particle in the antecedent sentence (shifted or unshifted) matched the form of the particle in the verification sentence, while in the mismatching condition the form of the particle in the antecedent sentence and the verification sentence differed. Lexical changes were introduced by replacing a "general" verb such as *bid* with a more specific verb such as *buried*. The verification sentence always contained the more general verb. Sample materials are presented in Table 11.8.

We predicted that mismatching verification sentences would be responded to more slowly than matching verification sentences and that this mismatch effect would be more pronounced when the verification sentence followed a surface anaphor. This prediction was based on three assumptions. First, surface but not deep anaphors find their antecedents in a representation that preserves some of the details of the linguistic structure of the antecedent. Second, linking an anaphor to or replacing it by its antecedent should keep the linguistic representation of the antecedent active. Third, the similarity in form between a verification sentence and the antecedent of the preceding anaphor should affect verifi-

Table 11.8. *Examples of materials for deep and surface anaphora*

Sentence type	Structural change materials Sentences
Verification sentence	Jenny asked Ann's boyfriend out.
Matching antecedent sentence	Jenny asked Ann's boyfriend out yesterday.
Mismatching antecedent sentence	Jenny asked out Ann's boyfriend yesterday.
Surface anaphor	Ann was furious that she did.
Deep anaphor	Ann was furious that she did it.
	Lexical change materials
Verification sentence	My sister bought a new car.
Matching antecedent sentence	My sister decided to buy a new sports car.
Mismatching antecedent sentence	My sister decided to get a new sports car.
Surface anaphor	Because she is conservative, I was surprised she did.
Deep anaphor	Because she is conservative, I was surprised she did it.

Table 11.9. *Results of the deep and surface anaphora verification study*

Change	Anaphor	Verification condition		
		Match	Mismatch	Difference
Structural	Surface	2,190 (3.6)	2,817 (5.4)	627
	Deep	2,320 (1.8)	2,289 (3.6)	−31
Lexical	Surface	2,080 (1.8)	2,068 (3.6)	−12
	Deep	1,895 (3.6)	1,965 (1.8)	70

Note: Response times are decision latencies. Errors are in parentheses.

cation times, with similar sentences being understood faster than dissimilar sentences.

The results are presented in Table 11.9. For structural changes, verification latencies were much slower in the mismatching condition than in the matching condition for surface but not for deep anaphors. This result is completely consistent with the hypothesis that surface anaphors are understood by going back to a linguistic representation, while deep anaphors are understood by going back to a nonlinguistic representation. For lexical changes, verification latencies were similar in both the matching and mismatching conditions and there was no interaction with type of anaphor. These results are difficult to account for on a literal replacement explanation, as lexical changes should lead to a mismatch between the surface structure of the antecedent sentence and the verification sentence. One explanation, explored in some detail in Carlson and Tanenhaus (1984) is that surface anaphors find their antecedents in logical form representations in which lexical items are replaced by their corresponding conceptual representations.

11.5. Conclusion

We began this chapter by contrasting two views about the mental representation of grammar. One view, most forcefully argued for by Chomsky and his colleagues, is that grammar is a real mental entity. We labeled this view *linguistics as explanation*. The opposing view is that the grammar is not a real mental entity, but rather a convenient descriptive framework for organizing interesting facts about language. We labeled this view *linguistics as description*.

Ultimately, deciding between these two positions depends on answering the question of which theoretical constructs of linguistic theory are real mental entities and which are not. To illustrate the distinction, consider such psychological constructs as "word recognition," "attention," "intuition" and the like, each with plausible intuitive content. If there are real mental entities, it is necessary to demonstrate that productive theories can be constructed with these notions as their primitives, and then to demonstrate that these notions are not derivable from other more primitive psychological notions. In other words, a theoretical construct cannot be considered to be a mental construct in a psychological theory simply because it explains mental processes and behavior (folk psychology is rich in constructs of this sort). It is also necessary to show that the construct is a primitive mental construct and not a derivative one (folk psychology has little to say about this matter).

Returning to linguistic theory, the argument about the mental status of grammars can be approached from several different perspectives. An extreme version of the linguistics-as-description position maintains that the constructs of linguistic theory do not play a serious role in explaining how people actually learn and use language. Therefore, these constructs cannot be real mental entities. This assumption is not uncommon in the psychological community.

A less radical version of the linguistics-as-description position takes grammars to be mental entities, as their constructs appear to play a real explanatory role in describing linguistic behavior. However, this approach also denies that the constructs are mental primitives. Rather, it seeks to show that the linguistic constructs are derivative, and follow from other mental properties such as the nature of the perceptual systems, concepts, the information processing systems, or an interaction among a series of independently motivated systems.

Finally, the approach that we have explored, linguistics as explanation, claims that the constructs of linguistic theory are both mental and primitive.

We have explored in some depth the hypothesis that the grammar is a mental subsystem distinct from the general cognitive system. The grammar as explanation position does not logically require that there be an autonomous linguistic system in the mind. There remains the possibility, for example, that the mind contains a "linguistic system" as an interacting part of the general cognitive system (Crain and Fodor, this volume). Nevertheless, we have argued that linguistic autonomy, as it translates quite naturally into the modularity hypothesis, represents the strongest position from which to evaluate empirical evidence. The modularity hypothesis as applied to language comprehension assumes that the language comprehension system contains one or more processing modules that operate autonomously and correspond to different linguistic levels. These processing modules operate in conjunction with the general cognitive system that has access to the outputs of the modules as well as to extralinguistic knowledge.

We have argued that methodologies sensitive to the on-line availability of different levels of representation are central to evaluating the modularity hypothesis. The importance for methodologies sensitive to representation stems from the fact that the operations of the processing modules cannot be directly observed. However, it appears that the outputs of modules can be observed in the form of the representations that the listener assigns to a sentence or part of a sentence. These representations can then be used to make inferences about the operations and in turn the vocabulary of the modules. There is, of course, no guarantee that the output of a module will provide information about all of its vocabulary and operations. Consider, for example, the case where a module contains within it several smaller modules and the outputs of the smaller modules cannot be observed. Nonetheless, the different types of representations that can be observed should correspond to the output of different processing modules. Thus evidence that listeners compute linguistic representations at different levels provides evidence about what types of modules are contained within the language processor.

On-line measures become important because the outputs of processing modules may be available only briefly. This will happen, in particular, when a processing module makes available multiple outputs, some of which are rejected as being incompatible with the outputs of other modules. Results showing temporary ambiguity at a given level provide perhaps the strongest evidence for the processing system containing autonomous processing modules.

We explored evidence that one processing module, the lexical processor, does in fact seem to operate as an autonomous processing module. We then explored some of the implications of the modularity hypothesis for a theory of parsing. Finally, we reviewed a series of experiments on sentences with gaps and sentences with anaphors. These experiments provided preliminary evidence that methodologies could be developed which were differentially sensitive to two levels of linguistic representation – linguistic form and logical form – and representations which included extralinguistic information. These methodologies, and the research strategy that we adopted in using them, should shed light on the question posed by the title of this paper.

Notes

This research was supported by grant IST 80-12439 from the National Science Foundation, grant HD 16019-01 from the National Institute of Child Health and Development, grant NSERC 7294 from the National Science and Engineering Research Council, and a grant from the Quebec Ministry of Education. Support was also provided by the Merrill Palmer Institute of Wayne State University. We would like to thank the members of the OSU parsing conference and Aurelie Collings, Susan Hudson, James Leiman, and Debra Senytka for their collaboration on many of the studies described here. We have also benefited from discussions with Steve Lapointe and Pat Siple. Special thanks are due to Helen Smith Cairns and Janet Dean Fodor, each of whom carefully reviewed a preliminary version of this paper.

1.   By *linguistic representations* we mean mental representations that are isomorphic to the representations that the grammar assigns to a sentence or part of a sentence. Thus these representations are defined solely by the grammar. They do not, for example, make reference to real-world knowledge. A representation that combines elements of sentence structure with real-world knowledge would not be a linguistic representation according to our distinction.

2.   Tyler and Marslen-Wilson (1977) have also argued that context can guide online syntactic decisions. They found that reaction times to name the visually presented target word *are* were faster following sentences such as (i) in which the context biased the nominal reading of the ambiguous phrase *landing planes*, than following (ii), in which the context biases the gerundive reading. The word *are* is a grammatical continuation only on the nominal reading.

(i)   If you walk on the runway, landing planes. . . .
(ii) If you have been trained as a pilot, landing planes. . . .

However, Hurtig (1978) did not find evidence that context could initially disambiguate similar types of phrases. See Cairns (in press), Cowart (1978), and Townsend and Bever (1982) for criticisms and reinterpretations of Tyler and Marslen-Wilson's results.

3.   An alternative proposal is that listeners do not compute linguistic representations. Rather, the general cognitive system uses linguistic rules. This hypothesis is discussed later in this chapter, in the section *parsing and modularity*, and in greater depth in Crain and Fodor (this volume).

4. Seidenberg et al. (1982) did find one case where prior context seemed to restrict lexical access to the contextually appropriate reading of an ambiguous word. Selective access occurred when an ambiguous word whose component readings were from the same grammatical class (e.g., *pipe*) closely followed a semantically or associately related word (e.g., *The smoker lit his pipe*.). This result is most probably due to lexical priming.

5. An important by-product of the autonomy of the lexical processor is that more information than necessary is frequently made available. Since words are recognized in terms of other codes, in particular an orthographic and a phonological code, the question arises as to whether multiple code access also obtains for these other codes. Classic studies have demonstrated that reading a letter or a word results in the access of sound-based information (for a recent review see McCusker, Hillinger, and Bias, 1981). More striking perhaps is the fact that the converse also holds, namely, that auditory word recognition results in the access of information related to spelling. One source of evidence comes from a study by Seidenberg and Tanenhaus (1979) in which subjects heard a cue word followed by a spoken list of semantically unrelated words. Reaction times to decide that the cue and a word in the list rhymed were faster when the cue and target were spelled alike (e.g., *pie-tie*) than when they were spelled differently (e.g., *pie-rye*). These spelling results – in conjunction with the results of studies demonstrating phonological access in visual recognition – indicate that multiple codes for words are made available as an automatic consequence of word recognition, regardless of task demands.

6. See, however, Cairns (in press) who argues that lexical priming *does* violate modularity.

7. These "pointers" could also be thought of as the "semantic" representation of a word's meaning, in a linguistic sense. The possibility that there is a semantic system connected with language "below" the conceptual level is a natural one to entertain given the very common philosophical distinction between linguistic meaning and "pragmatics," and the arguments against a purely psychological notion of linguistic meaning (see, for instance, Partee, 1979, and Putnam, 1975). We think there is some very suggestive experimental evidence for a distinction between these two systems, but the critical work has yet to be done, and we leave it an open issue (see Godby and Fox, 1981).

8. An autonomous theory of parsing must account for the on-line nature of the parsing process, instead of claiming that a whole sentence must be completed before any parsing begins. This means that the input to the parser at a given moment will not be just a string of lexical categories, but rather a string of lexical categories and one (or more) structures, representing the structure assigned to the words in the sentence to date. The parser then specifies the ways the lexical categories can be fit into the structure at hand. In this way, earlier decisions about structure assignment can affect subsequent decisions. In order for this view to be made plausible, how this is accomplished needs to be fleshed out in considerably more detail. One straightforward hypothesis would be that the input consists of the string of unintegrated lexical categories, and the set of rightmost nodes in a given tree. The parser then assigns the incoming string a structure and specifies how it might be attached to the rightmost nodes. The outputs are then examined by the GCS, a choice is made among alternatives, and the result is "reattached" to the structure at hand. Given that the GCS can only efficiently store about six or so words at a time as an unintegrated string, the Sausage Machine model of Frazier and Fodor is virtually reproduced in such a model, though here with the entire burden of preference phenomena attributed to the GCS, and not to the autonomous parser that itself has no "preferences."

404 Tanenhaus, Carlson, and Seidenberg

9. Janet Fodor has pointed out to us that it seems implausible that listeners hold onto the verbatim form of the Filler NP when the NP is very long as in the sentence *We wondered which very tall girl with athletic ability the basketball coach would try to recruit.* Fodor suggests that listeners hold onto the logical form of the filler. One possibility suggested by Steve Lapointe is that listeners hold onto the verbatim form of only the head of the filler NP, perhaps because it serves as a good retrieval cue for the meaning. Fodor also points out that maintenance of the verbatim form of the filler NP may be due to its being the head of a relative clause and not due to its role as a filler. This hypothesis will be tested in our experiment in progress using materials such as (20) and (21) in which the same filler can occur with a late gap or an early gap, respectively. If rhyme priming obtains to the head of any relative clause, then an equivalent amount of rhyme priming should obtain to *man* in (21) as in (20) even when the rhyming target is presented late in the sentence.

10. While the magnitude of the "pronoun assignment" effect, 35 msec, is comparable in magnitude to the 39 msec effect obtained in the Senytka study, only the effect in the Senytka study was statistically reliable.

References

Bever, Thomas G., and Richard R. Hurtig. 1975. Detection of a non-linguistic stimulus is poorest at the end of a clause. *Journal of Psycholinguistic Research* 4:1–7.

Bransford, John D. 1979. *Human cognition: learning, understanding and remembering.* Belmont, Calif.: Wadsworth.

Bresnan, Joan. 1978. A realistic transformational grammar. In: Joan Bresnan, Morris Halle, and George Miller (eds.), *Linguistic theory and psychological reality.* Cambridge, Mass.: MIT Press.

1982. *The mental representation of grammatical relations.* Cambridge, Mass.: MIT Press.

Cairns, Helen S. In press. Current issues in research in language comprehension. In: Rita Naremore (ed.), *Recent advances in language sciences.* San Diego, Calif.: College Hill Press.

Cairns, Helen S., Wayne Cowart, and Ann D. Jablon. 1981. Effect of prior context upon the integration of lexical information during sentence processing. *Journal of Verbal Learning and Verbal Behavior* 20:445–53.

Cairns, Helen S., and Joan D. Kamerman. 1975. Lexical information processing during sentence comprehension. *Journal of Verbal Learning and Verbal Behavior* 14:170–79.

Cairns, Helen S., and J. R. Hsu. 1980. Effects of prior context upon lexical access during language comprehension: a replication and reinterpretation. *Journal of Psycholinguistic Research* 9:1–8.

Caplan, David. 1972. Clause boundaries and recognition latencies for words in sentences. *Perception and Psychophysics* 22:73–76.

Carlson, Greg N., and Michael K. Tanenhaus. 1982. Some preliminaries to psycholinguistics. In: Kevin Tuite, Robinson Schneider, and Robert Chametzky (eds.), *Papers from the eighteenth regional meeting of the Chicago Linguistic Society.* Chicago: Chicago Linguistic Society.

1984. Lexical meanings, structural meanings, and concepts. In: J. Drogo, V. Mishra, and D. Testen (eds.), *Papers from the parasession on lexical semantics.* Chicago: Chicago Linguistics Society.

Carroll, John M., Michael K. Tanenhaus, and Thomas G. Bever. 1978. The perception of relations: the interaction of structural, functional, and contextual factors in the segmentation of speech. In: W. J. M. Levelt and G. Flores d'Arcais (eds.), *Studies in the perception of language.* New York: John Wiley and Sons, pp. 187–218.

Chomsky, Noam. 1980. Rules and representations. *The Behavioral and Brain Sciences* 2:1–62.

 1981. *Lectures on government and binding.* Dordrecht, Holland: Foris.

Church, Kenneth W. 1980. On memory limitations in natural language processing. Bloomington: Indiana University Linguistics Club.

Collings, Alan K. 1982. Lexical processing in schizophrenics and normals. Unpublished Ph.D. dissertation, Wayne State University, Detroit, Mich.

Collins, Alan M., and Elizabeth F. Loftus. 1975. A spreading activation theory of semantic processing. *Psychological Review* 82:407–28.

Cooper, Robin. 1979. The interpretation of pronouns. In: Frank Heny and Helmut Schnelle (eds.), *Syntax and semantics. Vol. 10: Selections from the Third Gronigen Round Table.* New York: Academic Press.

Cowart, Wayne. 1978. Production, comprehension, and theories of the mental lexicon. Paper presented at the Linguistic Society of America, Boston, December 1978.

Fay, David, and Anne Cutler. 1977. Malapropisms and the structure of the mental lexicon. *Linguistic Inquiry* 8:505–20.

Fischler, Ira, and Paul A. Bloom. 1979. Automatic and attentional processes in the effects of sentence contexts on word recognition. *Journal of Verbal Learning and Verbal Behavior* 18:1–20.

Fodor, Janet D., Jerry A. Fodor, and Merrill F. Garrett. 1975. The psychological unreality of semantic representations. *Linguistic Inquiry* 6:515–31.

Fodor, Jerry A. 1983. *The modularity of mind: an essay on faculty psychology.* Cambridge, Mass.: MIT Press.

Fodor, Jerry A., Thomas G. Bever, and Merrill F. Garrett. 1974. *The psychology of language: an introduction to psycholinguistics and generative grammar.* New York: McGraw-Hill.

Forster, Kenneth I. 1976. Accessing the mental lexicon. In: Roger J. Wales and Edward Walker (eds.), *New approaches to language mechanisms.* Amsterdam: North-Holland.

 1979. Levels of processing and the structure of the language processor. In: William E. Cooper and Edward C. J. Walker (eds.), *Sentence processing: psycholinguistic studies.* Hillsdale, N.J.: Lawrence Erlbaum.

 1981. Priming and the effects of sentence and lexical contexts on naming time: evidence for autonomous lexical processing. *Quarterly Journal of Experimental Psychology* 33A:465–95.

Foss, Donald J. 1970. Some effects of ambiguity upon sentence comprehension. *Journal of Verbal Learning and Verbal Behavior* 9:457–62.

Foss, Donald J., and M. A. Gernsbacher. 1982. Lexical access during sentence processing: phonetic structure vs. semantic structure. Paper presented at the Midwestern Psychological Association Meetings, Minneapolis, Minn.

Frazier, Lyn, and Janet D. Fodor. 1978. The Sausage Machine: a new two-stage model of the parser. *Cognition* 6:291–325.

Fromkin, Victoria A. 1971. The non-anomalous nature of anomalous utterances. *Language* 41:27–52.

Godby, C. Jean, and Robert Fox. 1981. Relatedness and strength of association in semantic memory. In: Carrie S. Masek, Roberta A. Hendrick, and Mary F. Miller (eds.), *Papers from the parasession on language and behavior.* Chicago: Chicago Linguistic Society.

Gough, Philip, J. A. Alford, and Pamela Holley-Wilcox. 1981. Words and context. In: O. J. L. Treng and Harry Singer (eds.), *Perception of print: reading research in experimental psychology.* Hillsdale, N.J.: Lawrence Erlbaum.

Hankamer, Jorge, and Ivan Sag. 1976. Deep and surface anaphora. *Linguistic Inquiry* 7:391–426.

Haviland, Susan E. and Herbert H. Clark. 1974. What's new? Acquiring new information as a process in comprehension. *Journal of Verbal Learning and Verbal Behavior* 13:512, 521.

Hillinger, Michael I. 1980. Priming effects with phonemically similar words: the encoding bias hypothesis reconsidered. *Memory and Cognition* 8:115–23.

Hurtig, Richard R. 1978. The validity of clausal processing strategies at the discourse level. *Discourse Processes* 1:195–202.

Kamp, Hans. 1981. A theory of truth and semantic representation. In: Groenendijk, Janssen, and Stokhof (eds.), *Formal methods in the study of language.* Mathematical Centre Tract 136, Amsterdam.

Kimball, John. 1973. Seven principles of surface structure parsing in natural language. *Cognition* 2:15–47.

Lakoff, George. In press. Categories: an essay in cognitive linguistics. In: In-Seok Yang (ed.), *Linguistics in the morning calm.* Seoul: Hanshin.

Leiman, James M. 1982. A chronometric analysis of referent assignment to pronouns. Unpublished Ph.D. dissertation, Wayne State University, Detroit, Mich.

Levy, Betty A. 1981. Interactive process during reading. In: Alan M. Lesgold and Charles A. Perfetti (eds.), *Interactive processes in reading.* Hillsdale, N.J.: Lawrence Erlbaum.

Lewis, J. L. 1970. Semantic processing of unattended messages using dichotic listening. *Journal of Experimental Psychology* 85:225–29.

Marcus, Mitchell. 1980. *A theory of syntactic recognition for natural language.* Cambridge, Mass.: MIT Press.

Marr, David. 1982. *Vision.* San Francisco: Freeman Press.

Marslen-Wilson, William D. 1975. Sentence perception as an interactive parallel process. *Science* 189:226–28.

Marslen-Wilson, William D., and Lorraine K. Tyler. 1980a. Towards a psychological basis for a theory of anaphora. In: Jody Kreiman and Almerindo Ojeda (eds.), *Papers from the parassession on pronouns and anaphora.* Chicago: Chicago Linguistic Society Press.

1980b. The temporal structure of spoken language understanding. *Cognition* 8:1–71.

1981. Modeling human parsing strategies? Paper presented at the University of Texas conference on modeling human parsing strategies.

Marslen-Wilson, William D., Lorraine K. Tyler, and Mark S. Seidenberg. 1978. The semantic control of sentence segmentation. In: W. J. M. Levelt and G. B. Flores d'Arcais (eds.), *Studies in the perception of language.* London: Wiley.

Marslen-Wilson, William D., and Alan Welsh. 1978. Processing intersections and lexical access during word recognition in continuous speech. *Cognitive Psychology* 10:29–63.

McCusker, L. A., M. L. Hillinger, and R. G. Bias. 1981. Phonological recoding and reading. *Psychological Bulletin* 89:217–45.

Merrill, E., R. D. Sperber, and C. McCauley. 1981. Differences in semantic coding as a function of reading comprehension skill. *Memory and Cognition* 9:618–24.

Meyer, David E., and Roger W. Schvaneveldt. 1971. Facilitation in recognizing pairs of words: evidence of a dependence between retrieval operations. *Journal of Experimental Psychology* 90:227–34.

Morton, John, and John Long. 1976. Effect of word transitional probability on phoneme identification. *Journal of Verbal Learning and Verbal Behavior* 15:43–52.

Nash-Webber, Bonnie. 1979. *A formal approach to discourse anaphora.* New York: Garland Press.

Onifer, W., and David A. Swinney. 1981. Accessing lexical ambiguities during sentence comprehension: effects of frequency of meaning and contextual bias. *Memory and Cognition* 9:225–36.

Partee, Barbara. 1979. Montague grammar and issues of psychological reality. In: J. Lowenstamm (ed.), *Occasional papers in linguistics* vol. 5. Amherst: University of Massachusetts, pp. 93–110.

Posner, Michael I., and C. R. Snyder. 1975. Attention and cognitive control. In: Robert L. Solso (ed.), *Information processing and cognition: the Loyola symposium.* Hillsdale, N.J.: Lawrence Erlbaum.

Putnam, Hilary. 1975. Is semantics possible? In: Hilary Putnam, *Mind language and reality: philosophical papers, vol. 2.* Cambridge, England: Cambridge University Press, pp. 138–152.

Rayner, Keith E., Marcia Carlson, and Lyn Frazier. 1983. The interaction of syntax and semantics during sentence processing: eye movements in the analysis of semantically biased sentences. *Journal of Verbal Learning and Verbal Behavior* 22(3):358–74.

Sachs, Jacqueline S. 1967. Recognition memory for syntactic and semantic aspects of connected discourse. *Perception and Psychophysics* 2:437–42.

Sag, Ivan. 1976. Deletion and logical form. MIT Ph.D. dissertation. Bloomington: Indiana University Linguistics Club.

Sag, Ivan, and Jorge Hankamer, 1984. Toward a theory of anaphoric processing. *Linguistics and Philosophy* 1.

Schwanenflugel, P. J., and Edward J. Shoben. 1982. Differential context effects in the comprehension of abstract and concrete verbal materials. *Journal of Experimental Psychology: Learning, Memory, and Cognition* 9:82–102.

Seidenberg, Mark S., and Michael K. Tanenhaus. 1979. Orthographic effects in rhyme and monitoring. *Journal of Experimental Psychology: Human Learning and Memory* 5:546–54.

Seidenberg, Mark S., Michael K. Tanenhaus, James M. Leiman, and M. A. Bienkowski. 1982. Automatic access of the meanings of ambiguous words in context: some limitations of knowledge-based processing. *Cognitive Psychology.*

Shiffrin, Richard M., and Walter Schneider. 1977. Controlled and automatic information processing: II. Perceptual learning, automatic attending, and a general theory. *Psychological Review* 84:127–90.

Shulman, Harvey G., Rosemary Hornak, and Elizabeth Sanders. 1978. The effects of graphemic, phonetic, and semantic relationships on access to lexical structures. *Memory and Cognition* 6:115–23.

Slowiaczek, Maria A., and Charles Clifton. 1980. Sub-vocalization and reading for meaning. *Journal of Verbal Learning and Verbal Behavior* 19:573–82.

Stanovich, Keith E., and Richard F. West. 1979. Mechanisms of sentence context effects in reading: automatic activation and conscious attention. *Memory and Cognition* 7:77–85.

Swinney, David A. 1979. Lexical access during sentence comprehension. (Re) consideration of context effects. *Journal of Verbal Learning and Verbal Behavior* 18:645–60.

Swinney, David A., and David T. Hakes. 1976. Effects of prior context upon lexical access during sentence comprehension. *Journal of Verbal Learning and Verbal Behavior* 15:661–89.

Tanenhaus, Michael K. 1978. Sentence context and sentence perception. Unpublished Ph.D. dissertation, Columbia University, New York.

Tanenhaus, Michael K., and S. Donnenwerth-Nolan. 1981. Syntactic context and lexical access. Unpublished ms. Wayne State University, Detroit, Mich.

Tanenhaus, Michael K., H. Flanigan, and Mark S. Seidenberg. 1980. Orthographic and phonological code activation in auditory and visual word recognition. *Memory and Cognition* 8:513–20.

Tanenhaus, Michael K., James M. Leiman, and Mark S. Seidenberg. 1979. Evidence for multiple stages in the processing of ambiguous words in syntactic contexts. *Journal of Verbal Learning and Verbal Behavior* 18:427–41.

Tanenhaus, Michael K., and Mark S. Seidenberg. 1981. Discourse context and sentence perception. *Discourse Processes* 26:197–220.

Tyler, Lorraine K., and William D. Marslen-Wilson. 1977. The on-line effects of semantic context on syntactic processing. *Journal of Verbal Learning and Verbal Behavior* 16:683–92.

Townsend, David J., and Thomas G. Bever. 1982. Natural units interact during language comprehension. *Journal of Verbal Learning and Verbal Behavior* 28:681–703.

Wanner, Eric. 1974. *On remembering, forgetting, and understanding sentences.* The Hague: Mouton.

Wanner, Eric, and M. Maratsos. 1978. An ATN approach to comprehension. In: Morris Halle, Joan Bresnan, and George Miller (eds.), *Linguistic theory and psychological reality.* Cambridge, Mass.: MIT Press.

West, Richard F., and Keith E. Stanovich. 1982. Source of inhibition in experiments on the effect of sentence context on word recognition. *Journal of Experimental Psychology* 8:385–99.

Yates, Jack. 1978. Priming dominant and unusual senses of ambiguous words. *Memory and Cognition* 6:636–43.

Index

across-the-board convention, 187
active edge, 267
Ades, Anthony E., 327–8
Adverb Preposing, 37, 54–7
adverbial clauses, 177
agenda, 267, 268
agreement
  between filler and gap, 67–9
  gender, 68
  number, 68
ambiguity, 10
  avoidance of, 95–6
  constraints against, 137–45
  lexical, 366–8
  phrase boundary, 186
  resolution of, 320–1, 324–5, 328–38, 367–8
  in unification grammar, 257
analogous similarities of languages, 181
anaphors, 69–71
  bound, 175
  interpretation of, 385
  see also deep anaphors, direct reference hypothesis, logical replacement hypothesis, surface anaphors
antecedent, 69–71
A Priori Plausibility, Principle of, 330
artificial intelligence, parsing in, 7–9
Aspects grammars, grammar/parser relationship in, 97
asymmetry constraint on code switching, 192–6
ATN, *see* augmented transition network
attention, models of, 367–8
attribute in unification grammar, 253, 255–7, 290–1
augmented transition network (ATN)
  parser, 103–4, 307–8
  vs. parsing in unification grammar, 270–3
automatic vs. controlled processes, 367–8

autonomy, 323–5, 346, 401, *see also* modularity
auxiliaries in Finnish, 286
auxiliary tree in a TAG, 208, 209–11

Bach language, 228
bare plurals, 336–7, 340
base-generative theories of grammar, 327
basic feature in unification grammar, 259
Bever, Thomas G., 97
binary branching vs. flat structure, parsing of, 150–2
bottom context in a derivation predicate, 218–19
bottom-up parsing, 6, 308, 317–18
  undirected, 269
buffer
  PARSIFAL, 185
  three-item, 159–63, 168

Carlson, Greg N., 68
categorial grammar, 327
chart, 267
Chomsky, Noam, 87
Clifton, Charles, 104, 111
closed class, 191
closure of functional descriptions under set operations, 259–60
Closure Principle, 334
code switching, 190–4
cognitive grammar, 359
competence grammars, 255
compilation, 253–5, 267, 273–6
complement clauses vs. relative clauses, 342–5
complementizers in code switching, 196–7
complete minimal governing category, 174–6
complex noun phrases, 177
Complex NP Constraint, 83–4, 236
complexity metric in processing, 129–30

409